Massillon – Canton '05.

Discover your legacy!

Gregg Finney

GRIDIRON
LEGACY

Pro Football's Missing Origin Story

THE WEATHER.
Washington, Nov. 25—Ohio—Rain Monday; Tuesday rain or snow; colder, fresh brisk south winds.

Massillon Morning Gleaner.

PUBLICITY can be secured by advertising, if the Medium can be found.
THE GLEANER is that Medium six days in the week.

THE GLEANER RECEIVES THE PUBLISHER'S PRESS WIRE AND CABLE SERVICE OF FROM EIGHT TO TEN THOUSAND WORDS EVERY NIGHT.

VOL. V. NO. 139. MASSILLON, MOHIO, ONDAY MORNING, NOVEMBER 26, 1906. ONE CENT—SIX CENTS WEEK

THEIR HONOR INVIOLATE

THE FAMOUS MASSILLON TIGERS OF 1906 COULD NOT BE BOUGHT OFF WITH A PRICE

Details of a Plot to Disrupt and Corrupt the Tiger Team and Management Which Failed.----$5,000 In Cash and a "Sure Thing" in a $50,000 Betting Pool Offered But Never Considered.

With the conclusion of the series of games between Canton and Massillon for the world's championship foot ball honors, the time has now arrived to make clear some peculiar and unpleasant conditions which have surrounded the Tigers, coach and management, during the entire season.

Many Massillon fans were surprised at the discharge of Walter R. East, who, during the early season, played right end on the Tiger team, inasmuch as East had shown wonderful abilities in this position.

The reasons for East's discharge by the Tiger management were not made public at the time. It was suspected by a few that he had been a traitor to the team, but no public statement was offered by the management for the reason that it would have done irrepairable damage to professional foot ball in this vicinity, and the management and coach firmly believed that the Tigers could win the game at Canton notwithstanding the handicap of being unable to use old signals, plays and style of play which had been practiced all season.

For this reason the explanation was not offered. Now the time has arrived for an exposure of one of the greatest plots which has ever been attempted.

East was the man who attempted to engineer the deal, with Coach "Blondy" Wallace of the Canton team as an accomplice and thief were backed by a crowd of gamblers, who agreed to furnish $50,000 to be used for betting purposes and all expenses incured and $5,000 in cash to the Tiger's coach and management.

As is usual with crooks and crooked gamblers their operations are shrewd to a certain point, and then they overlook the fact that all men are not like themselves. East and Wallace and their accomplices figured on the old adage that "Every man has his price," but they made the mistake of their sporting lives when they figured that the Massillon team, coach and management could be bought.

Their scheme was that Canton was to win the first game, Massillon win the second game and a third game should be played in Cleveland and this game to be played on its merits. East represented that one year ago he "fixed" a deal whereby Western University of Pennsylvania lost to State College by the score of 6—0, that no suspicion was attached to him, and that it would be just as easy to "fix" the Canton-Massillon series.

He also claimed that the Akron base ball club, of which he was manager during the past season, finished in second place instead of first place because there was more money in it for him, and again no suspicion was entertained as to crookedness.

East found a ready accomplice in Wallace. Massillon was able to sign East because Wallace wanted him on the Massillon team.

East began his treacherous negotiations and made another mistake. He approached Captain Robert Shiring, Right Guard Robert Maxwell, two of the best and most loyal players on the Tiger team. They turned him down immediately. The result would have been the same had they approached any of the other players. Both of the players approached were indignant that East or any one else should make them such a proposition.

They immediately reported the affair to the coach, who commenced necessary action to trap East and learn if possible the names of his accomplices and the method by which he proposed to "fix" the games.

East then made his second great mistake. He had the nerve and audacity to approach the coach with the same identical proposition. In an effort to trap him, the coach told him that $5,000 was a great deal of money and that he would think it over. Immediately after this proposition was made to the coach, a meeting was held at which Coach S. H. Wightman, Manager E. J. Stewart and H. A. Croxton attended. A plan was devised, which worked successfully with one exception, that being that Massillon did not win the first game as she should have. With but five days intervening before the first game, Massillon was compelled to change signals, change plays and formations, and while they are unable to prove conclusively that East carried information to Canton, as to the Tiger signals, plays and formations, the fact that the Canton team expected and were prepared to anticipate each play made by the Tigers in the first game is evidence in itself that Wallace had received the Tiger signals and plays from East.

There never has been a question as to Massillon's ability to defeat Canton if Canton played fair foot ball, but under such a handicap, any one can readily see that Massillon had the superior team, as the score of 10—5 would indicate, and that Massillon played particularly strong in the positions of Shiring and Maxwell, the two men they tried to buy.

A statement was prepared, stating the facts. This statement is now in the hands of a Cleveland attorney, hired for the purpose of catching these crooks. This statement was sworn to before Ex-prosecuting Attorney R. H. Day, of Massillon, who was called from his bed at a late hour at night for this purpose.

A contract was drawn by a Cleveland attorney, $500 of their money together with a bond for $3,500 was put up in trust with a prominent Cleveland banker. Before this money was so placed and contract drawn the statement was read to the Cleveland banker and the necessary steps taken to mark the bills and they are now held in the Cleveland bank and can be easily identified. Included in the statement was an agreement to discharge East immediately and this was done.

After the coach apparently agreed to their crooked proposition money in large quantities immediately came to the surface in Canton available as bets that Canton would win the first game. Within two hours of the time that East was discharged, practically no money could be found to back the Canton team. Draw your own conclusions.

The money deposited by these crooks is now in the Cleveland bank. The coach has mailed to the Cleveland banker a receipt and if they are willing to sign said receipt, which admits that they tried to bribe the Tigers and failed in their attempt, they can recover their money. Otherwise the Cleveland bank is at liberty to hold it as long as they like.

Second Game.

On the return of the Massillon team to Massillon, after their defeat at the hands of the Canton team, or more properly speaking, Wallace and East, the loyal supporters of the team were discouraged, as they knew that something was wrong. The coach and manager and players were not discouraged. They knew that crooked work had cost them their first defeat in four years.

In the meantime the entire proposition had been opened up to half of a dozen of Massillon's most reputable business men, who agreed, with the coach and management that Wallace and East could not "turn the trick" a second time.

In the first game it was apparent to every spectator, player and official of the game that Maxwell, Shiring and Lamson completely out-played their opponents, Kerckhoff, Sweet and Lang. A plan of attack was devised in which Sweet, Kerckhoff and Lang were the targets for Massillon's plunges. East was unable to carry this information to Wallace with the result that whenever the Tigers needed a sure gain, it was made through Kerckhoff, Lang and Sweet.

Davidson was unable to play in the first game, owing to the fact that he was not familiar with the signals, and on offense the Tigers would have been crippled.

In connection with this entire affair it is the firm belief of those who have carried the weight of this unpleasantness that the Canton management, aside from "Blondy" Wallace, is in no ways to blame. Thursday night, preceding the game at Canton, the entire exposure was made to Financial Manager George Williams and John Rommel, of the Canton team. They were dumbfounded and could scarcely believe it, and it is the firm belief of all who know the details of the plot that they were not in any way connected with East, Wallace and Co., and that they have done everything in their power to have two games of foot ball played on an absolutely fair basis.

In conclusion it can be said that the Massillon Athletic Club will have nothing to do in the future with anything that Mr. East or Mr. Wallace is in any way connected with. Massillon plays fair and square and plays to win at all times, if the winning can be fair and square. When Massillon can not play fair and square she will refuse to play.

There is a moral contained in the above exposure that it would be well to think of. In all athletic sports let the best man or team win. In hiring managers for athletics and players for teams be careful that you are not complicated with East, Wallace & Co. and their kind.

The proof of the reliability of this article in the nature of the signed papers, can be found in the safe of the Massillon Iron and Steel plant, and Mr. Croxton, whose services have so materially assisted the Tiger team this fall, will be pleased to exhibit them to any and all who care to see them.

The above is given upon our authority with all the proofs in our possession.

E. J. STEWART,
H. A. CROXTON.

GOMPERS

Was Re-elected President of American Federation of Labor.

Minneapolis, Nov. 24—Samuel Gompers was re-elected president of the American Federation of Labor here this morning.

WHITE CAPS

Lafayette, La., Nov. 25.—200 white caps, masked, and armed with shot guns and pistols, created a reign of terror, last night, are Carenore near here, brutally murdering Antone Domingue, a peaceable negro, after robbing the man of his horse and buggy. They also held up a score of other negroes.

The town was at the mercy of the band throughout the night. Domingue was stopped in the road while going home, and on resisting, the white caps was beaten. He deserted his team to go home and secure a revolver. On his return he was met with a volley from the whitecaps, his body being riddled with bullets. The white caps got away before officers from this place arrived.

LANDSLIDES ENGULFS VILLAGE.

Berne, Switzerland, Nov. 25.—Great landslides caused by heavy rains have overwhelmed Teglio, an Italian village near the Swiss frontier. It is reported that six persons were killed in the slides and many injured. Rescuers are at work digging in the mass of earch to recover the bodies. In several instances farms were completely covered.

BALCONY FELL

KILLING ONE WOMAN AND INJURING MANY MORE WOMEN AND CHILDREN.

Newark, N. J., Nov. 25One woman was killed and a score or more women and children injured by the collapse of the lobby of New Century Hall here tonight. Several hundred people congregated at the hall to attend a Yiddish vaudeville benefit performance and the accident was caused by the overcrowding of the vestibule. The balcony was fifteen feet square and about 75 people packed into the small space, while more than 200 were standing on the steps. Mrs. Rebecca Schwarts was killed. The injured were taken to a hospital. Nine of them were fatally hurt.

TROLLEY FATALITL.

Pittsfield, Mass., Nov. 25.—One passenger was killed and seven others injured, one fatally, as the result of a trolley car of the Pittsfield street railway company overturning today. The accident occurred through a rock in the groove in the rails causing the wheels of the car to jump the track, the car skidding down a three foot embankment and crashing into a tree. The car was going about 20 miles an hour when the accident occurred, but no blame is attached to the motorman.

SPLENDID VICTORY FOR THE TIGERS

Opening Line-up.

The line-ups:

Massillon	Canton
Parrott, l. e.	r. e. Wood
McNulty, l. t.	r. t. Ernst
King, l. g.	r. g. Riley
Shiring, c	c. Sweet
Maxwell, r. g.	l. g. Kerchoffe
Lamson, r. t.	l. t. Lang
Nesser, r. e.	l. e. Schrontz
Davidson, q	q. Hayden
Thomas, l. h. b.	r. h. Farabaugh
Findlay, r. h. b.	l. h. Reynolds
Wightman, f. b.	f. b. Cure

TIGERS 13—BULL PUPS 6.

That score tells the tale of a victory won by the world's champion Massillon Tiger foot ball team, under ideal conditions, before a vast crowd, and on a field which was perfect.

Well Earned Victory.

It was a well earned victory for the Tigers. It was a vindication for the management, coach and players which will be the more appreciated when the big handicap under which the team, coach and management labored during the entire season becomes known.

Bull Dogs Out-Classed.

From start to finish, the Tigers outclassed the bull dogs. In departments which last Saturday seemed the strongest, Canton was out-played. While all along the line and in the entire back field the Tigers showed superiority which left no doubt in the minds of even the Canton admirers that the game of last Friday was a fluke pure and simple, and that the Tiger team was better by a good percentage than the bull dogs.

According to the opinion of the critics and officials of the game, it was one of the most scientific games ever played in this section of the country.

The Versatile Tigers.

The Tigers showed a varied plan of attack and on defense showed stronger than even their own supporters hoped. The variety of plays which the Tiger quarterback used with such telling effect proved conclusively that the local team was the better coached aggregation, while the fact that none of Canton's plays against the line or around the end, worked indicated that the Tiger defense was much stronger than last Friday. On the other hand Canton showed improved form both on defense in the line and offense with open plays.

Hayden out-Generaled.

Field General (?) "Jack" Hayden, the player who last Friday was touted as a star at manipulating a victorious team, was completely out-classed by Homer Davidson, the Cleveland Central High School player, picked up last week by the Tiger management. In fact, Davidson was the star of the game. He out-punted the famous Reynolds, out generalled Hayden and in bringing back punts and carrying the ball, showed conclusively that he is entitled to honors even among the All-American class of players into which he was thrust.

Out For Vengeance.

It was a great and glorious victory for the Tigers. Defeated by the score of 10—5 at Canton, Nov. 15, and in a measure handicapped by the loss of support of a number of the "knockers" of the team, the Tigers went upon the field Saturday to prove their superiority. They had labored hard all week in preparation, smarting under the sting of criticisms which were hurled by the fans who showed that one defeat will shatter their loyalty, and when that squad of players marched onto the field a few minutes before 2 o'clock, it was with a determination to wreak vengeance upon the Canton Bull Dogs and show the "wise ones" that they were the champion team of the country.

The Teams Welcomed.

Enroute to the grounds, the team was delayed considerably, owing to the congested condition of the street car company's tracks. They arrived at the grounds at 1:40 o'clock and in five minutes were on the field. Canton's hosts showed their red and white uniforms at the south end gate, but a minute later, and as both teams filed into their respective sections, they were greeted by wild cheering and waving of colors. It was a great demonstration. The entire east side of the field was one waving, fluttering mass of humanity with colors flowing in the wind, while a deep circle of spectators completely fringed the field. The free bleachers, the grand stand and the reserved seat section on the west side was filled, and were waiting with bated breath for the referee's whistle.

Officials of Game.

Without any trouble, A. A. Brewster, of Cornell and Akron, was chosen as head linesman. Dr. Newton, of New York, acted as umpire and Referee Whiting, of Philadelphia, held the referee's whistle. A. H. Coleman and L. W. Day, of Canton, were paired as time keepers, and there was no dispute between them.

Promptly at 2 o'clock the referee's whistle sounded and the teams lined up, Captain "Bob" Shiring having won the toss and selected to defend the south goal and receive the ball. This was the first piece of fortune which came Massillon's way as a slight breeze from the south assisted in the punting.

No further delay was experienced, after Coach Wightman and Coach Wallace had settled the argument over ball. The ball used was an official intercollegiate Victor ball, but was blown so hard that the Canton coach objected. However the officials decided in favor of the Massillon coach and the game was on.

THE GAME

Reynolds kicked off for Canton, the ball flew to the east and took a bad bound away from "Ted" Nesser. The tow head grabbed it, however, tucked it under his wing, and went up the field at a terrific clip before tackled. Then the battle waged.

Quarterback Davidson tried two plunges into the line, then an end run before making the first down. Short but consistent gains were made until the ball was well towards the center of the field, before Canton forced the locals to punt, and then "Divy" began the punting which was largely responsible for the victory over Canton. His first attempt went fifty yards, and Reynolds brought it back but five yards before being downed.

Reynold's Big Run.

Reynolds skirted the Tiger right end for thirty yards before brought to earth by Davidson. This set the Canton cohorts to cheering and almost paralyzed the Tiger fans, who had been lead to believe that the Tiger ends had been greatly strengthened. That one run was the last for the Canton team during the entire game.

Thereafter every gain made by the Canton team was on a forward pass, the Canton players showing some form at this new game play.

Spectacular Foot Ball.

For twenty minutes the ball zigzagged back and forth across the field, and the spectators watched one of the prettiest, and hardest fought battles ever played on a gridiron in the middle west, if not in the country. It was a game which spectators had a right to expect from twenty-two of such famous men as constituted the two teams. Time and again the two teams would hurl their strength against the line of the other only to be stopped short of the coveted ten yards.

Two futile tries at line bucking or end running, during this period would usually bring a punt on the third down from the two kickers, Davidson and Reynolds.

Davidson's Punting.

It was in this department of the game that Massillon's little quarterback, demonstrated that he has a right to be classed above the world's famous Reynolds. Not once, but ten times during the game did the little Clevelander out-kick the Pennsylvanian. Four times did his punts shoot over the heads of both Reynolds and Hayden, who under-estimated his punting ability and played too close to the line of scrimmage.

First Touch Down.

One of these kicks and misjudgment of Hayden and Reynolds, resulted in a touchdown for the Tigers. The ball, which was kicked from the twenty yard line of the Tigers, sailed over Hayden's head and bounded for the goal line with Hayden and Reynolds in hot pursuit.

Suddenly a flash of yellow and black shot out of the mass of players from scrimmage and fairly flew down the field after the two opposing players and the elusive ball. It was Findlay, the Wisconsin half back, and the way that westerner covered ground was thrilling. As the ball neared the goal line, Findlay gained on the two players with it, and as it crossed the side line, two yards from the goal line, "Finke" brushed aside Reynolds and dove for the ball just as Hayden grabbed for it. Findlay's speed carried him in a long slide over the ground and into the fence where he tangled with Hayden and the ball, emerging a moment later with the ball securely tucked under his arm. Referee Whiting carried the ball in fifteen yards, and when Massillon formed on the offensive and it was realised for the first time, that the Tigers had the ball within striking distance of the Bull Dog's goal line, the crowd broke loose. A fumble without gain sent the shivers down the backs of the Massillon fans, but Davidson had made a good recovery and the next moment Roseth plunged over the goal line for the touchdown which looked like the winning score then. It was off to one side of the field, and a kick out was necessary. McNulty sent a pretty spiral fairly into the arms of the waiting Maxwell, who heeled the ball and then tried for the goal. The ball went wide by a few inches and the score stood five to nothing in favor of the Tigers.

For another five minutes the teams battled in this half and the time keeper's whistle sounded.

Intermission.

With the score 5—0 in favor of the Tigers, the enthusiasm broke loose on the Massillon side of the field. The Tigers were cared for in a warm bed of straw on the west side of the field, while the Canton team was taken to its special car outside of the grounds. Hot coffee and beef broth was served to the Tigers during the intermission, and this served to stimulate the players.

SECOND HALF.

Captain Shiring kicked to Farabaugh in this half, the Pennsylvanian bringing the ball back ten yards before being downed. Canton's gains were few and far between and within a short time, Massillon had the ball. An exchange of punts followed and on a quarterback kick Canton gained twenty-five yards, carrying the ball well past the middle of the field.

Canton's Score.

Line plunges and end runs were futile for Canton and Quarterback Hayden was forced to resort to the forward pass to gain. Several times this play was worked successfully and the ball was carried to the three yard line in this manner.

Canton's stands were now in an uproar as a touchdown was in sight while Massillon's side of the field looked glum. Once Canton was held but on the second attempt the Tiger line yielded just enough to allow Reynolds to worm over the goal line for a touchdown.

Canton Ahead.

After heeling the put out, Hayden held the ball and Reynolds booted it fairly between the goal posts for the point which placed Canton in the lead and gave them an advantage.

Tigers Ferocious.

It seemed that this was the very stimulant which the Tigers needed, as they marched down the field thereafter in a style which was grand to see.

(Continued on last page.)

GRIDIRON
LEGACY
Pro Football's Missing Origin Story

By Gregg Ficery
FOREWORD BY Franco Harris

"Gridiron Legacy is pro football's Book of Genesis. The story helped me understand the roots of the passion for pro football in Pittsburgh that I experienced in my career with the Steelers. If you're as big of a football fan as I am, it's a must-read."

—**Jerome Bettis**, Pittsburgh Steelers, 1996–2005;
Super Bowl XL champion; Pro Football Hall of Fame

"As a passionate football historian, who played for the Pittsburgh Steelers and served as an ESPN NFL analyst, I am excited by the revelations in Gridiron Legacy. *The previously untold story and unpublished images are important additions to the history of our sport. Gregg Ficery's inspiration to unearth the pro game's roots in Pittsburgh and Ohio through his family history adds a special dimension."*

—**Merril Hoge**, Pittsburgh Steelers, 1987–1993;
ESPN football analyst, 1995–2017

"The pre-NFL period of pro football is practically a lost era. It lasted nearly three decades after starting in the early 1890s in Pittsburgh, where I built my career as part of the Steelers dynasty in the 1970s. The world needs to know the game's origin story, and the sport's pioneers deserve recognition for their place in its history. Their story is fascinating and somehow still shrouded in a mystery that caused the first chapter to go missing. Gregg Ficery followed the trail of his great-grandfather's career as one of the early greats to reveal a dramatic and profound tale and resolve the cold case that has kept the story in the dark for over a century. With its groundbreaking research and incredible never-before-published photos that Gregg inherited, Gridiron Legacy *is unprecedented in providing pro football with its compelling birth story."*

—**Rocky Bleier**, Pittsburgh Steelers; 1968 and 1970–1980;
4x Super Bowl champion

"About the Immaculate Reception, I will never tell. But about Gridiron Legacy, *I will tell that this story is immaculate."*

—**John "Frenchy" Fuqua**, Pittsburgh Steelers, 1970–1976;
2x Super Bowl champion

"This amazing book is a fresh new contribution to American football history. Gregg Ficery deftly weaves a story of professional football's peculiar Pennsylvania roots and its evolution in Ohio and beyond. It is at once a personal story of the search for a forgotten footballer on his own Pittsburgh family tree, but the author's detective work quickly reveals a much bigger story that sorts out professional football's origin myths and legends. The book is packed with rarely seen photos that will astound sports historians and draw readers into some wonderful storytelling."

—**Andrew E. Masich, PhD,** president and CEO, Senator John Heinz History Center

"Gregg Ficery's Gridiron Legacy *not only examines the all-too-often misunderstood pre-NFL years of pro football, but his sleuth-like research uncovers untold tales of the roots of America's game."*

—**Joe Horrigan**, senior advisor, Pro Football Hall of Fame

"Gregg has done a masterful job telling the stories of early football history. He has dug deep into the pre-NFL era and has uncovered information rarely seen, if ever. The photographs and illustrations are exceptional. Once you start reading, you will not be able to put this book down. It is a must for any football history collection or for any football fan interested in how this game was formed."

—**Ken Crippen**, former president, Pro Football Researchers Association; founder and president, Football Learning Academy

"This thorough investigation of early football preserves an almost-lost era of history and contains all the excitement and drama of which myths and legends are made. A must-read for all historians and football fans!"

—**Alexandra Nicholis Coon**, executive director, and **Bailey Yoder**, curator of football heritage, Massillon Museum

"Gridiron Legacy tells the story of the very beginnings of professional football at an unprecedented level. Seeing the impact that the pro Massillon Tigers had on professional football is enlightening and inspiring. Another generation from now, these stories may have been lost. Now I can continue to share the story with my players to help them better appreciate our tradition. Thank you for preserving the history and telling the story of the birth of this great game."

—**Nate Moore**, head football coach, Massillon Tigers

"Playing high school football for the Massillon Tigers changed my life. We were so poor when I was growing up in the 1950s that my mother sometimes didn't eat so that my sister and I could. My father was in road construction and we lived in several rural areas in Ohio. The schools at which I started playing in high school were small and poorly coached. Scouts recognized my talent, and my father was offered a job in Massillon if I would come to play there for my senior year. Massillon's coaches had vision, energy, and taught me how to be a technician of the game. I was then recruited by Ohio State, where I became an All-American and was drafted by the Baltimore Colts, coached by Don Shula. I was the smallest offensive tackle in the NFL and protected MVP John Unitas's blindside, playing in two Super Bowls and winning Super Bowl V. Being a Massillon Tiger helped me become the best I could be in football and in my career afterward. Reading Gridiron Legacy *helped me understand the dominion of Massillon football and the history of what became a tremendous experience for me."*

—**Bob Vogel**, Baltimore Colts, 1963–1972; Super Bowl V champion; Massillon Tigers, 1958

Published by The Ringer, LLC
Watersound, Florida

ISBN: 978-1-61188-370-1

Designed by Tom Carling, Carling Design Inc
www.carlingdesign.com

Cataloging-in-Publication Data is on file with the Library of Congress.

Printed in South Korea

First edition: August 2022

10 9 8 7 6 5 4 3 2

✦

To my daughters, Meredith and Charlotte.

As my grandmother told me in sharing her father's story,

"This is the stock from which you came....

I pass this on to you of the same character."

With love, Dad

CANTON

MASSILLON TIGERS

Champion
Foot Ball Team,
of Ohio.

THE NEW RULES

Vol. XXIII. No. 275   AUGUST, 1906   Price 10 cents

SPALDING'S
ATHLETIC LIBRARY

Official
FOOT
BALL
GUIDE
for 1906

Edited by WALTER CAMP
American Sports Publishing Co.
21 Warren Street, New York.

TABLE OF CONTENTS

During my enshrinement weekend at the Pro Football Hall of Fame in Canton, Ohio, in 1990, when I put on my HOF gold jacket for the first time, I was overtaken by the collective history of football. It was a powerful feeling, as if I was absorbing all of its energy from the beginning, of all who played before me. We were now connected in pro football's history: those who played before me, with me, and after me.

History is a force. It speaks to us. It has much to teach us, if we listen. If we do not learn from it, we may be doomed to repeat it.

Events also happen for a reason. As a Pittsburgh native, Gregg Ficery crossed my path several times during my career and life there afterward. When Gregg was a boy in the '70s, I signed an autograph for him at a charity event. We played in a tennis fundraiser together in the '90s. In 2012, we reconnected while serving on the Champions Committee,

a board of advisors at the Senator John Heinz History Center, in sight of Heinz Field and the nearby site on which pro football was born in 1892. Later in 2012, at the celebration of the 40th anniversary of my "Immaculate Reception" at the History Center, Gregg and I walked the HOF's traveling exhibit titled Gridiron Glory together. He showed me a large image on display of his great-grandfather's Massillon Tigers team on a checkerboard field in a 1906 championship

Franco Harris with the author

game against the Canton Bulldogs, while proudly pointing out his ancestor. I was fascinated.

Gregg explained that he was working on related book and film projects that would reveal essential pieces of the story of pro football's beginnings before the National Football League's founding in 1920. He asked for my support and I agreed, but he said he would need some time. I encouraged him to persevere, as I recognized the significance of the projects, since so little is known about the game's origins.

Now that *Gridiron Legacy* is complete, it strikes me that no other book on the history of pro football has been crafted in such detail and color. Given his family connection to one of the most prominent players of the era, Gregg is able to share a unique collection of images from his great-grandfather's pre-NFL career. Further, he has an unmatched passion to dig deeper than ever before to discover and reconcile the truth of the unresolved accusations that stunted the game's early growth.

History provides us with valuable lessons. *Gridiron Legacy* honors Gregg's great-grandfather's legacy of integrity and the legacy of the game I love. You may not be able to put on a HOF gold jacket, but you can open *Gridiron Legacy* and experience what I did in Canton: absorb all of pro football history's energy from the beginning.

—**Franco Harris**
Pro Football Hall of Fame

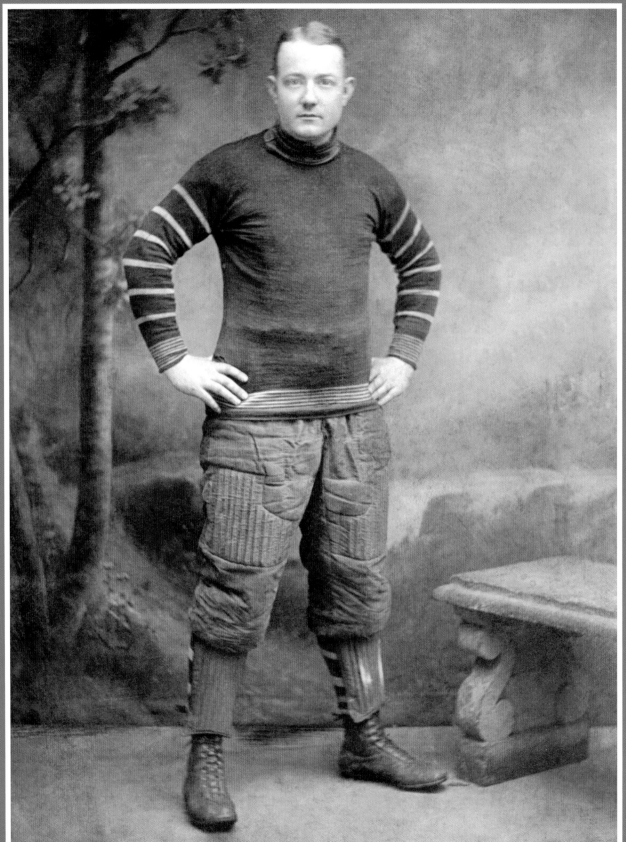

Bob Shiring—1901 Homestead Library & Athletic Club

Every good origin story includes a period of chaos. The genesis of professional football is no exception, and the chaos was spectacular.

Pro football's actual birth predates the National Football League's 1920 founding by 28 years. Until now, certain crucial parts of the game's backstory have been missing. The key to unlocking the story involved a quest to solve the mystery surrounding a 1906 game-fixing scandal involving the two greatest pre-NFL teams: the Canton Bulldogs and the Massillon Tigers, rivals from neighboring Ohio towns. The scandal's fallout killed the group of renowned teams that only later became known as the Ohio League. It also halted pro football's advancement for years, until the Bulldogs were resurrected in 1912, leading to the formation of the NFL.

My great-grandfather, Bob Shiring, was a central figure in the 1906 drama. He was the Tigers' center from 1903 to 1906 and captain in the pivotal final year in which he was initially victimized by accusations of collaborating in the scheme. A century later, in my grandmother's basement, I discovered Shiring's personal collection of football photographs from his career. This moment led to a journey of discovery that expanded on family lore and unearthed historic finds on the untold story of the men who laid the foundation for pro football in America. Like Ray Kinsella in *Field of Dreams*, I was called to answer questions that remained outstanding from a prior generation. This book is a tribute to the men, like my great-grandfather and others, who overcame many tribulations, including scandal, to shape the game of professional football. They inspired me to discover the truth about the game's fall from grace, its rebirth, and the legacy of these pioneers.

THE KICKOFF OF A NEW SPORT

Despite the massive popularity of the NFL, pro football's origin is a mystery to most fans. For starters, consider a few questions:

✦ When and where did professional football start?

✦ Who was the first professional football player?

✦ What was the first professional football team?

✦ Why is the Pro Football Hall of Fame located in Canton, Ohio?

Many guess that pro football started in Ohio and that Jim Thorpe was the first professional player. Both are incorrect, although Ohio and Thorpe did play essential parts in the story. In truth, there's much more to the origin story and a compelling narrative to be shared about pro football's "missing link."

Super Bowl 50 in 2016 marked a half-century since the first championship game between the NFL and AFL in 1967, and the NFL celebrated its 100th anniversary in the fall of 2020. These are significant milestones, but what happened on the rocky road to the NFL's founding after the first player documented to accept money to play a football game in 1892? More importantly, why has the story of the pre-NFL era been lost?

Diving into my family history provided me with the honor of tracing the roots of professional football through the career of my great-grandfather, Bob Shiring, described in a 1909 article by the *Coshocton Daily Age* (Ohio) as "the world's greatest center." Following his

Canton and Massillon face off in a game circa 1920.

1901 Homestead Library & Athletic Club

Front row: Joe Steen, Frank Maxson, Willis Richardson, Frank Woodley, Artie Miller, Alexander "Sandy" Shields. Middle row: Howard Nieman, Fred Crolius, Bemus Pierce, David Fultz (captain), Pete Overfield, Bob Shiring. Back row: John Gammons, Arthur Poe, John Winstein, Carlton Randolph, Hawley Pierce, Arthur St. Ledger Mosse, Perry Hale, Irving Hunt, Max McNulty, Rody McCutcheon.

VIEW OF STEELWORKS PARK.

career with most of the "world championship" teams of his era in Western Pennsylvania and Eastern Ohio at the turn of the twentieth century revealed answers about the game's roots. Previously unconnected dots became connected, and missing pieces to the puzzle fell into place.

Three of Shiring's original team photographs were my inspiration. These were displayed in my grandmother's home, in the industrial Pittsburgh suburb of Wilmerding, when I was a young boy in the 1970s. One of the photos was identifiable only by an "H" on a few of the players' sweaters, and the other two were labeled as "Tigers '05" and "Tigers 1906." However, it wasn't until 2007 that I embarked on a quest to understand the images' significance after discovering a larger group of photos in my grandmother's basement. Images tucked away for more than a century, before the NFL's founding fathers' established the league, were the first clues to discovering pro football's earlier revolutionary period.

Published here for the first time are many of the original images from Shiring's collection. Before he retired, Pro Football Hall of Fame executive director Joe Horrigan told me, "To us, this is like finding an original Constitution."

As the Hall of Fame did not have or know of these images, I realized that it was not only an opportunity but also a responsibility to make them available to the public. The images enrich the narrative, put faces to names, and provide a stronger emotional connection to these pioneers.

Pieces of Shiring's playing days were known and shared in our family through the years. His teams were said to be professional and at the championship level. He played the center position, opposed the center on defense when all players lined up on both sides of the ball, and never wore shoulder pads since he felt that they slowed him down. Shiring was also a kicker and was once lauded for bending a game-winning field goal through the posts on a windy day, but he admitted to the family that it was all luck. The most interesting tale, though, was about a scandal. He was praised for refusing a bribe to throw a championship.

What seemed to be family lore was national news at the start of the twentieth century, and the key to understanding the rise and fall of the pre-NFL era of pro football.

The full narrative is rich with fascinating characters and icons of the era: Canton captain Charles Edgar "Blondy" Wallace, accused by Massillon backers of participating in the bribery scheme; Bob "Tiny" Maxwell, for whom the modern-day Maxwell College Player of the Year Award is named; Hall of Fame baseball pitcher and little-known pro football player Christy Mathewson; Charles Follis, the first African American pro football player;

Icons: Christy Mathewson, one of the greatest pitchers of all time, was Bob Shiring's teammate on the 1902 Pittsburg Stars. Charles Follis broke pro football's color barrier with Shelby (Ohio) shortly before playing against Shiring's Massillon Tigers in 1904. This image of Follis from Shiring's collection is published here for the first time.

Shiring collection

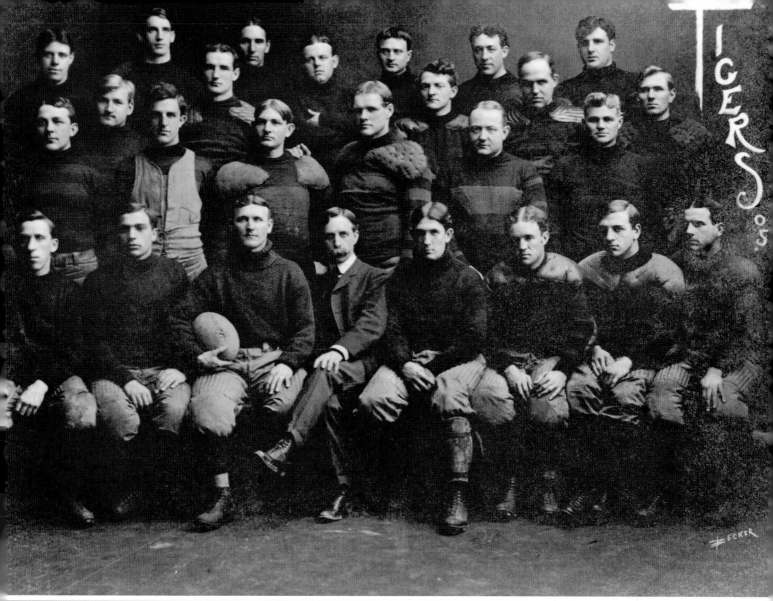

Shiring collection

1905 Massillon Tigers

Front row: Charles "Mully" Miller, Frank Bast, Julius "Baldy" Wittman (captain), Jacob J. Wise (manager), Edward J. Stewart, Jack Hayden, Dan "Bullet" Riley, Charley Moran. **Middle row:** Leroy Scholl, Mike Bennett, Max McNulty, Herman Kerkhoff, Bob Shiring, Frank Botoner. **Back row:** Bob Featheringham, Ted Nesser, Clark Schrontz, "Doc" McChesney, J.T. "Teck" Mathews, William "Budget" Seaman (trainer), William "Doc" Merriam, Louis "Red" Salmon, Jack Lang, Arthur "Tige" McFarland, Fred Haag, John Nesser.

the Nesser brothers, ferocious mercenaries who farmed themselves out to multiple teams; and Shiring, who rose from a blue-collar background to lead the country's best players, most with elite college pedigrees.

After a generation stoking the passions of amateur football at the collegiate level, and a decade in the Pittsburgh area trying to avoid the initial shame of professionalism, the pro game came of age in Ohio shortly after the turn of the twentieth century via the initiative of an ambitious group in the town of Massillon. A rivalry for the ages ensued with its neighbor Canton. Massillon's Tigers and Canton's Bulldogs went toe to toe on and off the field in the buildup to their inevitable 1906 championship battle. They fought intensely over players, schedules, and, of course, money. The chance to tap into a newfound money pot did not stop with the teams but also overflowed to players. Some chose loyalty to their team and community, while others opted to make a better living by exchanging colors. One dared to try to make a killing by initiating a scam.

Infamy loomed over the outcome of the tumultuous in-state rivalry, and the entire future of the sport, rivaling what later befell baseball's 1919 Chicago Black Sox. But multiple claims and counterclaims of fraud and double-dealing were never substantiated or resolved for the historical record.

As only rumors and accusations have survived, the full truth of pro football's early scandal has never been told. In a shroud of mystery, the legacy of a group of bold and accomplished men, who are deserving of honor, has largely been lost. Maybe the story was hidden because the people who lived through it preferred to forget. History does not always want to be disturbed.

According to Pro Football Hall of Fame vice president of exhibits/museum services Saleem Choudhry, though, "The story of the pre-NFL era can't be told without the 1906 scandal."

Massillon Tigers fans sported pin-ribbons like this one in 1906. The city eventually replaced its original official colors with the Tigers' black and orange.

The Canton Bulldogs adopted their nickname during the 1906 season amid the heat of controversy in their rivalry with the Tigers.

Prominent Figures in Canton-Massillon Football Upheaval.

CAPTAIN SHIRING,
Of the Massillon Tigers, who is alleged to have been approached by football bribers.

RIGHT GUARD MAXWELL,
Of the Massillon Tigers, who is another player said to have been approached by bribers.

"BLONDY" WALLACE,
Coach of the Canton Bulldogs, who is accused of being mixed up in the alleged football "sell-out."

Initial rumors implicated Shiring and Maxwell of the Tigers and Wallace of the Bulldogs as being complicit in the 1906 game-fixing scheme.

Origin stories, including those of football, baseball, and life itself, have proven difficult, if not impossible, to document. Thus, they make for interesting debate and controversy. The gospels of the Bible are compelling because they capture firsthand testimonies of those who witnessed historical events key to the understanding of Christianity's roots. So, too, would be the legal case file of Blondy Wallace's libel suit against the Massillon newspaper and team backers, if it existed.

Detective work in Ohio led me to discover that file.

Depositions from several key figures in the case weave a captivating and nuanced morality play with an unexpected outcome that definitively solves pro football's historical mystery.

Yet, this quest was incomplete without contextually understanding how prior events led up to this crisis period that rocked the foundation of pro football. There was further excavation required to connect with and complete the game's creation story.

The result was a revelation beyond imagination.

1906 Massillon Tigers

Front row: Patrick "Butch" McAllister, Charley Moran, Edward J. Stewart (manager), George "Peggy" Parratt, Bob Shiring (captain), Laurence "Cooney" Rice, William Robison, Dan "Bullet" Riley, Julius "Baldy" Wittman. **Middle row:** Max McNulty, Leonard Roseth, Otis Lamson,

1906,

Edward Vanderboom, Harley Kirby, Ted Nesser, Homer Davidson. Back row: Frank Bast, Albion Findlay, Homer "Sandy" Thomas, Bob "Tiny" Maxwell, Sherburn Wightman, Fred Haag, E. Pratt King, Frank Botoner, J.I. "Doc" McChesney.

THE GAME: A CALL TO ACTION

We live for moments as athletes when, in a flash of glory, we become more than we thought we could be. Some of these experiences last for mere seconds and are experienced alone. Others accumulate over a career, may be carried with us for the rest of our lives, and thrill the world.

The shape of the ball or object of the game is irrelevant. A score is undeniable, permanent, and objectively satisfying. What matters is our skill and courage, summoned from within, in pursuit of our athletic dreams. Frequently, right or wrong, the extent of our athletic accomplishments enhances our self-esteem and how others regard us. Competition in the form of sport irresistibly blends art and science, tactics and strategy. It is part of our nature and inspires us to thrive and progress, on and off the playing field. Iron sharpens iron. At once, both brutal and ethereal, competition captures life's duality.

What is often less understood in the heat of battle are the lasting consequences to our legacies of our actions while playing or organizing the sports about which we are passionate. Spectacular plays and tremendous victories may be overshadowed by perceived transgressions, even if momentary, unintended, impulsive, or worse, untrue. We are left to reflect on history to consider lessons learned from those remembered as heroes, as villains, or as daring victims of fate.

Champions who survive the crucible of sport and other fields deserve to be honored and memorialized as models for future generations. Integrity matters. But it is often only with hindsight that the contributions of innovators vilified for having been disruptive are revealed. They play by the rules, while making transformative contributions, and also deserve respect. The champions and challengers of the status quo are connected. We need them both, and they need each other.

History is dynamic. To make history is to dare to challenge the status quo, to break barriers, to take another step forward in evolution. Conflict is a cruel byproduct of the struggle between those who challenge the norm to achieve progress and those who cling to it fearfully or profit from it. The only constant is change. With such a lens, we are better able to understand the history and future of the game of professional football, its outcomes, and ourselves.

⪦ Initial Sparks ⪧

Ball games have evolved since the early Greek and Roman eras. The basic idea has not varied much from kicking or carrying a ball of some shape and size across an arbitrary goal. One of the earliest literary references to a ball game of any kind appeared in the ninth century in Wales. The forms and boundaries of these madcap first games in the Middle Ages went virtually as far as the imagination and physical stamina could take them. Opposing goals would even stretch from the streets of town to neighboring town, with players advancing an inflated pig's bladder by any means necessary in a game called mob football, including at annual festivals such as Shrovetide in Derbyshire, England, as early as the twelfth century. Field sizes typically followed whatever was available, even if bordered by stone walls in the case of a game called "wall ball" in England. Both are still played today.

A sport called football began to appear often in twelfth-century literature and was said to have been played enthusiastically by lower classes. Later in the sixteenth century, Shakespeare associated the term "football" with "a low form of amusement."

Americans are often accused of misappropriating the word "football" by the rest of the world, which is also confused about our use of "soccer." It turns out that neither side has claim to the original term. Football may originally have referred to games played by peasants on foot in medieval Europe instead of those by aristocrats on horseback, and had nothing to do with kicking. King James I of Scotland attempted to prohibit such games in the Football Act of 1424, which stated, "The King forbiddes that na man play at the fut ball under the payne of iiiid." The "payne of iiiid"

**Circa 1890s Spalding
die-cut image**

Early Games

Medieval ball games were played on the streets, with property and those nearby at risk. Early footballs took different shapes, including this 1887 Shrovetide football. Wall ball was invented at Eton College in Berkshire, England, in 1766, and is still played today.

referred to a fine of four pence. It was the monarchy's futile attempt to squash peasants' joy in such raw and rugged games and may have served to fuel their fire. Interestingly, it was not until 1906 that the law was officially repealed.

The first known image of football (the kicking type) played on U.S. soil, residing at Yale University, is a rare 1807 engraving of Yale students casually playing with a ball on the lawn. It may also be the first known reference to the sport in America other than some early mentions of Native Americans playing similar games.

1807 image of students appearing to play football on Yale's lawn

⤸ Rugby and Soccer: A Fork in the Road ⤹

As intramural school soccer became popular in both English and American schools, a monumental evolutionary event occurred in 1823 at the

William Webb Ellis's seminal feat is duly marked at the Rugby School in England.

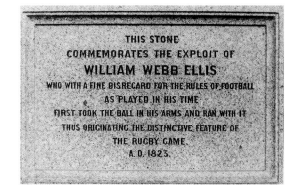

THIS STONE
COMMEMORATES THE EXPLOIT OF
WILLIAM WEBB ELLIS
WHO WITH A FINE DISREGARD FOR THE RULES OF FOOTBALL
AS PLAYED IN HIS TIME
FIRST TOOK THE BALL IN HIS ARMS AND RAN WITH IT
THUS ORIGINATING THE DISTINCTIVE FEATURE OF
THE RUGBY GAME.
A.D. 1823.

A circa 1890s postcard touting football's growing popularity

Rugby School in England. Legend has it that 16-year-old student William Webb Ellis took the bold and rebellious initiative to catch the ball as time was running out in a scoreless game that he found boring. He ran toward the opponents' goal, all while dodging those who were greatly offended. The proverbial light bulb switched on, and the sport of rugby was born.

Both the kicking and carrying forms of the sport then continued to muddle forward for decades at home and abroad. A new type of American football first started branching off at an intramural level at northeastern high schools as early as the 1840s. When interscholastic sport burst in growth in England from 1850 to 1860, it became necessary to standardize the rules, permanently ensuring that the carrying game would survive.

The word "soccer" was actually derived in England from a short form of the term "association football," which referred to the traditional kicking form of the game. During the 1860s, a uniform set of rules was developed to create order for organized play, primarily in schools, from the chaos of the many versions of the evolving game. At the time, it was a common English colloquialism to add "-er" to make words like "rugger" for rugby. "Assoc." was thus morphed into "soccer."

JUST FEETBALL. THATS ALL.

⪦ American Football: The Next Step ⪧

Organized American football first started being played at the amateur club level in Boston by the Oneida Athletic Club in 1862. Various prep schools in the area played versions of the game at the intramural level with their own rules. One young player, Gerrit "Gat" Miller, a graduate of the Latin School of Epes Sargent Dixwell, grew frustrated with the chaos and organized some other local grads to play on the country's first official amateur club team. The game's rules were known as "the Boston game," and the team was identified with red handkerchiefs instead of standardized uniforms. The team's games were played on the Boston Common through 1865, and the team never gave up a point, let alone lost a game.

The ongoing flow of British immigrants to the northeastern U.S. continued to bring interest in all forms of the game to America, and the carrying and kicking contingents continued here on their separate evolutionary paths. National magazines depicted sketches of soldiers playing some variation of football in Civil War camps. No standardized rules existed, and contact was substantial and virtually uncontrolled.

1896 Spalding die-cut image

Holiday in Camp—Soldiers Playing "Foot-Ball," **sketched by Winslow Homer, published in** *Harper's Weekly***, July 15, 1865.**

Courtesy of *Princeton Magazine*

⪦ Collegiate Foundations ⪧

When American life turned toward peacetime rhythms after the Civil War, young men began focusing on new recreational activities as an outlet for their physical energies and aggressions. Before amateur adult club teams developed, universities started forming teams in the late 1860s, each school creating its own set of rules. While the game still essentially looked and felt like rugby for decades, it slowly but surely began to distinguish itself as a different form of the traditional game. The first colleges to form teams were in the Northeast, and they initially applied the hybrid label of "rugby football."

November 6, 1869, marked what is considered the first college football game ever played, in front of approximately 100 spectators between a pair of New Jersey intrastate rivals, Rutgers and Princeton. Rutgers players wore scarlet-colored scarves on their heads to distinguish them from their opponents, thus leading to their current nickname of the Scarlet Knights. Rutgers won 6–4, though the rules would not be recognizable relative to those of today's football. The round ball could be moved only by kicking

The Scarlet Knights of Rutgers took the color part of their nickname from the scarves on their players' heads in the first college football game on November 6, 1869. The game was played in New Brunswick, New Jersey, against the College of New Jersey, later known as Princeton.

HARVARD vs. YALE.

Y. U. F. B. C.

H & S

FOOT BALL MATCH.

HAMILTON PARK,

Saturday, Nov. 8th, 1879.

PRESS OF T., M. & T.

or hitting it with the feet, hands, head, or sides, but throwing or carrying the ball was not allowed.

Teams of 25 players attempted to score by kicking the ball into the opposing team's goal. The contest consisted of 10 "games," and when a team scored one goal, it counted as the end of one game. The team with the most goals after 10 games was the winner.

The Rutgers-Princeton game inspired other nearby universities to join in, with the other two of the Big Three, Harvard and Yale, quickly establishing their teams as the strongest. It is no coincidence, then, that these schools' leaders also took positions on committees to develop and document rules, bringing standardization, order, and direction to the suddenly popular and rapidly evolving game. In 1873, leaders from Princeton, Rutgers, Yale, and Columbia gathered for the inaugural meeting of the Interscholastic Football Association (IFA) at the Fifth Avenue Hotel in New York City. At the group's second meeting in 1878, at the Massasoit House in Springfield, Massachusetts, Yale's captain, Walter Camp, took an active interest, and his initial innovations and commitment to the sport for the next half-century led him to become known as "the Father of American Football."

Walter Chauncey Camp was born in New Britain, Connecticut, and played halfback for nearby Yale from 1876 to 1882, graduating in 1880 and continuing to play while in medical school. He started his playing career at a slight 156 pounds and is remembered more as one of the era's best all-around athletes than a great football player.

He played on several varsity teams at Yale, including

Walter Camp circa 1898

Camp, seated third from left in the middle row, pictured with the 1876 Yale Rugby Football team

the track team, where he initiated the modern technique for jumping hurdles.

Camp attended the 1878 IFA meeting in the first of his three years as captain of the football team. He boldly proposed that the rugby scrummage rule, in which all players formed a scrum at the spot of the ball after each tackle, be replaced by a line of scrimmage from which the offensive team begins each play. The motion was denied, and he raised it for vote again at the following year's convention, at which he also proposed that safeties count as two-point scoring plays for the defensive team. Both changes were again denied. They were finally approved at the next meeting in 1880, along with his motion previously brought forward by Yale in the initial 1873 meeting, to standardize the number of players on the field to 11 for each team. Until then, many colleges were still insisting on playing 15 per side when playing on their home fields.

The adoption of the line of scrimmage was perhaps the most impactful rule change in the history of football, or any sport. It was also the American game's final point of divergence from rugby. Simultaneously, a logical extension of the line of scrimmage rule was the creation of the snap-back to start each play, initially by the center's foot, to a player in a new position that Camp named the "quarter-back." Positions on the line and backfield were all given new names, and coaches across the land enthusiastically engaged in developing new formations and strategies.

An unintended consequence of the 1880 rule changes was that teams would intentionally maintain possession of the ball as long as possible to run out the clock or to prevent stronger teams from having an opportunity to score. Critics called for a return to the old rugby rules. Camp again solved the problem by successfully proposing another major rule change in 1882: "If on three consecutive fairs and downs a team shall not have advanced the ball five yards, nor lost ten, they must give up the ball to opponents at the spot of the fourth down." A change of possession was now required to open up the game. To measure if necessary progress was achieved for a first down, Camp also invented the horizontal lining of the field with white limestone chalk. The term "gridiron" was coined at the meeting for the look of the new field with the following exchange, according to John Stuart Martin's "Walter Camp and His Gridiron Game":

> **Cabot of Harvard:** *How, Walter, do you propose to tell when five yards have been made?*
> **Camp:** *We shall have to rule off the field with horizontal chalked lines every five yards.*
> **Peace of Princeton:** *Gracious! The field will look like a gridiron!*
> **Camp:** *Precisely.*

Early football helmets were made of soft leather and took many forms in their evolution. This classic dog-ear style was popular circa 1915–1924.

NAMING THE GRIDIRON

The word "gridiron" originated in late thirteenth-century England and referred to a metal grate for cooking over a fire. According to *Merriam-Webster*, "In Middle English, such a grating was called a *gredil*, a root that gave modern English both *gridiron* and *griddle*."

As it applies to football, contrary to popular belief, the origin of the term "gridiron" stems only from the horizontal lining of the field, starting with the new rule in 1882 to assist the referee in measuring if 5 yards were gained in three plays to earn a first down. The checkerboard pattern on the field was implemented in 1903 to help in officiating another new rule in which quarterbacks were allowed to run the ball for the first time, but only allowed to cross the line of scrimmage with the ball 5 yards or more from the spot of the center snap. Mass plays were also barred in the checkerboard area between the 25-yard lines in an effort to minimize injuries by creating a more open style of play.

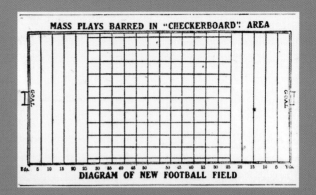

DIAGRAM OF NEW FOOTBALL FIELD

When the forward pass was legalized in 1906, the checkerboard was extended to cover the entire field to assist officials in managing the constraint on the rule that, according to *Spalding's Official Foot Ball Guide*, "a forward pass might be made provided the ball passed over the line of scrimmage at least 5 yards from the point at which the ball was put in play." In 1910, the 5-yard restriction was removed from both plays, and the longitudinal lines were removed from the field.

Camp went on to coach at Yale from 1888 to 1892, with three of those teams recognized as national champions. Through various collegiate committees, he continued to contribute meaningfully to the evolution of the game's rules until his death in 1925.

The genie was out of the bottle. The magic of college football spread across the land in the late 1800s in its early and evolving form, until it resembled the foundation for today's version of American football. Innovative coaches such as the Carlisle Indian Industrial School's Glenn "Pop" Warner, the University of Chicago's Amos Alonzo Stagg, and the University of Michigan's Fielding Yost were among those whose passion and intellect contributed greatly to the early development and popularity of the game. While their names are generally part of American football fans' consciousness, their specific contributions are not. This is likely because the public takes more interest in the games than the technical aspects of coaching.

Amos Alonzo Stagg, 1906

THE VICTORS

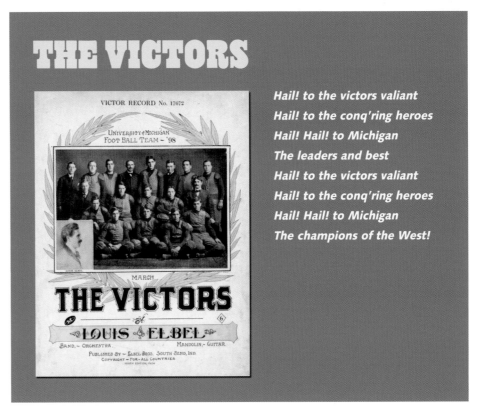

Hail! to the victors valiant
Hail! to the conq'ring heroes
Hail! Hail! to Michigan
The leaders and best
Hail! to the victors valiant
Hail! to the conq'ring heroes
Hail! Hail! to Michigan
The champions of the West!

Fielding Yost built the University of Michigan into the first college football power outside of the traditional northeastern programs. His "point-a-minute" teams had a record of 55–1–1 from 1901 to 1905 and won the first bowl game over Stanford in the 1902 Rose Bowl.

The "western" teams of Michigan and Chicago were the first from their region to rise up and compete at the highest level. They struggled mightily, however, to earn the respect of the schools and the press in the East. Before Yost took over at Michigan in 1901, Warner captained the 1894 Cornell squad that lost to the Wolverines and was the first of the traditional northeastern powers to lose to a western team. This event confirmed for all, other than those schools whose status was threatened, that the game's power structure was shifting. Passions were inflamed, and pageantry blossomed on campuses and local communities far and wide.

Michigan's belief in its regional supremacy was further bolstered after its 1898 one-point league championship win on Thanksgiving Day at Chicago. This triumph provided the inspiration for Michigan student Louis Eibel to write the school's fight song, "The Victors," in which the Maize and Blue faithful proclaim themselves to be "champions of the West."

It is just one of many iconic fight songs from the era that endure today. Marching bands continue to perform on fields at halftime and in stands throughout games, inspiring cheers and warming the hearts of students, alumni, and fans for the foreseeable future.

Rivalry games such as these then became huge social outings. Commercial efforts were also initiated to capitalize on the growing popularity of the game and crowds flocking to stadiums. Interestingly, this enthusiasm also created outlets for other new and fantastic expressions of the imagination. People donned Victorian fashion to games and created programs and advertisements with colorful sketches that are still highly collectible and nostalgic today.

The inevitable intersectional comparisons and debates made for popular conversation and fodder for the press, including the beginning of the selection of All-America teams in 1889. As a national leader, Camp became synonymous with the annual naming of these all-star teams. Eastern names from established programs initially dominated the lists, right or wrong, either due to superior coaching, bias in the eastern press, or both.

Such individual recognition bred the first national football heroes, including names attached to some of today's annual collegiate awards. The Heisman Trophy for the year's "outstanding player whose performance best exhibits the pursuit of excellence with integrity" is named for legendary John Heisman, who had an unremarkable playing career

Michigan gained respect for western football despite losing at highly ranked Penn 11–10 in 1899. This game ball pictured in the team photo was presented to Michigan captain Allen Steckle.

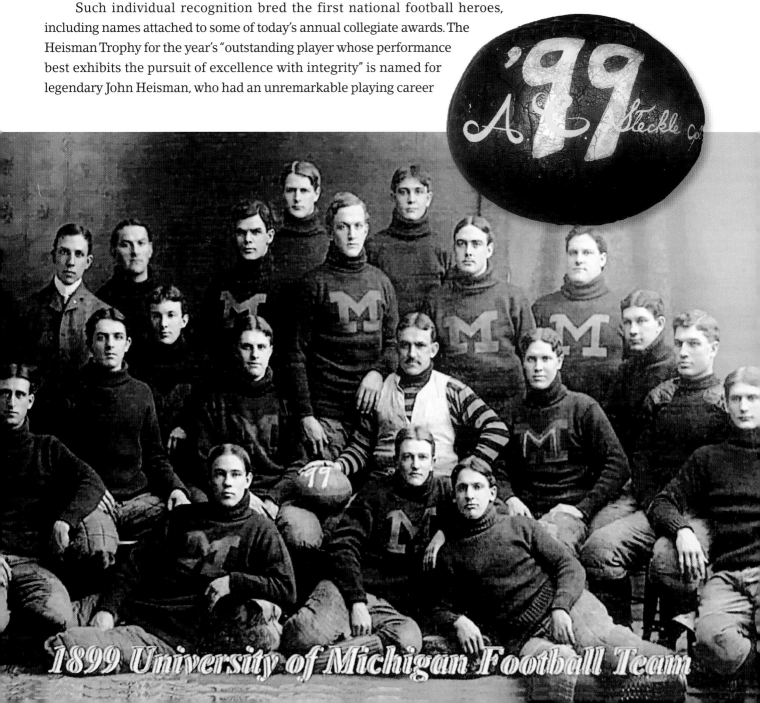

1899 University of Michigan Football Team

Try "SATURDAY NIGHT"

Hoo-rah! Hoo-rah! Hoo-rah!
PENN—SYL—VA—NI—AH!

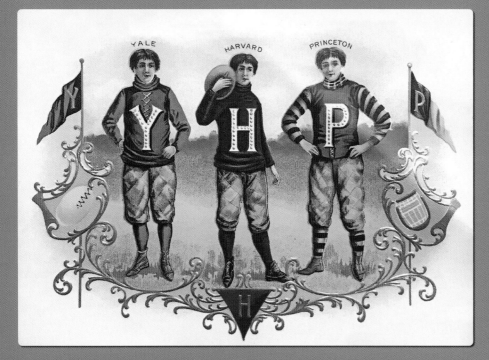

YALE   HARVARD   PRINCETON

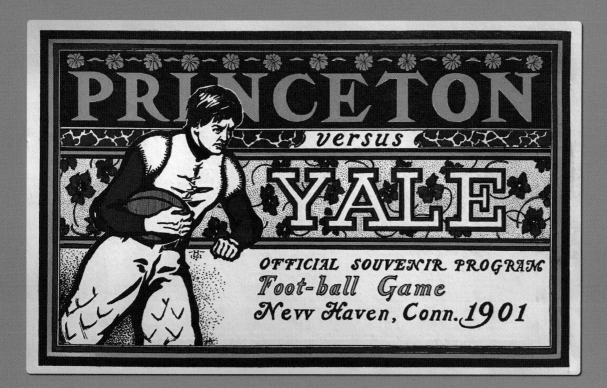

PRINCETON *versus* YALE

OFFICIAL SOUVENIR PROGRAM
Foot-ball Game
New Haven, Conn. 1901

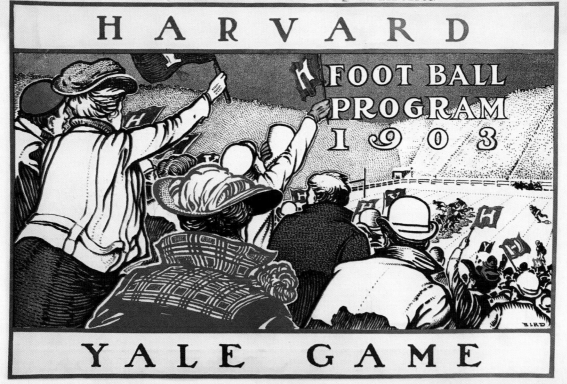

HARVARD

FOOT BALL PROGRAM 1903

YALE GAME

as a center and tackle at Brown for two years before graduating from Penn with a law degree. He made his mark as the "pioneer of southern football," coaching at nine colleges from 1892 through 1927, winning a national championship in 1917 at Georgia Tech. The Outland Trophy for the best collegiate interior lineman is named for John H. Outland, Penn's gridiron standout, who led the Quakers to a 15–0 record as a tackle in 1897. Also, the Maxwell Award, named for Robert "Tiny" Maxwell, is presented annually "to the college football player judged by a panel of sportscasters, sportswriters, National Collegiate Athletic Association head coaches, and the membership of the Maxwell Football Club to be the best football player in the United States."

Maxwell was a behemoth lineman in his era, playing at 240 pounds at a time when average linemen weighed in at less than 200 pounds. He refined his skills under the tutelage of Stagg at Chicago, where he was referred to as "Fatty" and "Tubby" during his first two years of college ball, starting in 1902. For reasons never made public, Maxwell then transferred to Swarthmore College in Philadelphia for his final two years, where he became known more affectionately as "Tiny."

Of these early heroes of the game, Camp, Heisman, and Outland joined the coaching fraternity immediately after their collegiate playing days.

John Heisman   **John Outland**   **Bob Maxwell**

Jim Thorpe received
third-team All-America
honors at Carlisle in 1908
and, after a hiatus, first-
team in 1911 and 1912.

Only Maxwell went on to play professionally among the early great teams, loyally wearing his Swarthmore sweater during games before uniforms were standardized. His dominant play on the field set him apart, and resulting rivalries soon led to his involvement in a key storyline in the sport's history that overlapped with his collegiate and professional careers.

Warner's time at Carlisle distinguished his coaching career. Not only did he tone down his aggressive coaching style, but he also developed a number of the first top professional players, helping usher in the early pro game. In addition to having the Indians (the school's chosen nickname) frequently ranked in the top 10 while playing against the top schools, players such as the Pierce brothers, Bemus and Hawley, and Artie Miller were fixtures among the best pro teams in Pennsylvania in the first decade of the 1900s.

After leaving Carlisle to coach at his alma mater from 1904 to 1906, Warner began his second stint with the Indians in 1907, which coincided with the enrollment of a member of the Sac and Fox Nation named Jim Thorpe. That fall, Thorpe convinced Warner, who was also the school's athletic director, to let him try out for the football team despite Warner's concern that injury would prevent Thorpe's participation on the track team. When Thorpe unexpectedly ran both over and around the defense in inconceivable ways at the tryout, he famously flipped Warner the ball and said, "Nobody is going to tackle Jim." Another college football hero was born, and in certain ways, history would conspire to make him pro football's savior, as the game's hard-earned education from its collegiate past was only prelude to its complicated professional proposition.

John Brallier—Latrobe Athletic Club

PROFESSIONAL FOOTBALL IS BORN: THE PITTSBURGH ERA

Football is one of the greatest games in the world for a young man. It teaches him self-reliance, quickness of thought, calmness under the most discouraging circumstances and fits him better than any sport with which I have ever been familiar, to be in condition to grasp the stern realities of life when he leaves the field of play and enters into that broader struggle for existence in which we must all sooner or later take part. —William Chase Temple, 1901

Many young men in the late 1870s enjoyed their collegiate football careers so much that they decided to continue playing afterward. The concept of club-sponsored amateur teams spread, first to large cities in New York and New Jersey, and then to Pennsylvania. With newfound money and leisure time on their hands, the nouveau riche sought outlets for athletic competition and soon also found them useful for social climbing. Civic leaders in Western Pennsylvania, for some combination of prestige and charitable intent, were pleased to provide capital for a few such venues. Success in sports—including track and field, wrestling, and boxing— enhanced clubs' statuses and increased membership. While the spirit of club sports was to offer members participation in athletics, membership was often made possible, or at least more attractive, to those with strong athletic skills, especially football players.

During the Industrial Revolution, Western Pennsylvania's largest city formed its cultural identity around the growing awareness of the potential of its natural resources. One of its challenges in the city's formative years was sorting out the spelling of its own name. In 1891, the newly created U.S. Board on Geographic Names eliminated the *h* in the word "Pittsburgh" to "maintain uniform geographic name usage throughout the Federal Government." Confusion ensued for three decades, and to a small extent into perpetuity, as names of the city's nonfederal organizations, such as newspapers, athletic clubs, and professional sports teams, were not required to adopt the official spelling. Local political pressure ultimately led to a special meeting of the board in 1911 to reverse the decision and include the long-preferred Scottish suffix of *-burgh* instead of the German suffix of *-burg*. Thus, references to publications and other groups that adhered to the status quo without including the *h* in their names explain any such apparent misspellings herein.

⊱ John Brallier: The First Pro Player Myth ⊰

Several athletic clubs in the Pittsburgh area were interested in fielding amateur football teams but found themselves without many experienced adult football players to take the field. The best local talent matriculated at elite northeastern colleges (before the Ivy League) to play on the top national teams. Thus, competition demanded that clubs recruit some athletes who had yet to enter college. It is impossible to know for certain when a team first slipped a player a few dollars under the table to suit up for a game. For decades, it was commonly believed, though, when the Pro Football Hall of Fame opened in Canton, Ohio, in 1963, that John Brallier was the first person to openly accept cash to play football. Born on December 27, 1876, in Cherry Tree, Pennsylvania, Brallier was only 18 years old, stood just 5-foot-6, and weighed but 125 pounds in 1895 when he agreed to take cash to play for the Latrobe YMCA team, approximately 40 miles southeast of Pittsburgh.

Expense reimbursement, job placement, and various noncash maneuvers were offered to athletic club members in the amateur football world for years. These were simply a means to preserve the Victorian notion of the propriety of amateurism. More important, they kept the Amateur Athletic Union (AAU) from disbarring member clubs, precluding participation in its national championship events across other sports that clubs supported. At some point, it was inevitable that a cash transaction would take place between a club and a player, and that a player would fess up to having been on the receiving end.

John Brallier began his football career at the age of 16 at Indiana Normal School in 1893 (above, far back, left). At 18, in 1895, he suited up for Washington & Jefferson College (right, front), as well as the Latrobe YMCA (below, front row, second from right).

(Courtesy of Latrobe Area Historical Society)

In 1893, Brallier played quarterback for his West Indiana public high school and then the following year for the precollegiate Indiana Normal School (now Indiana University of Pennsylvania), graduating in 1895. Latrobe established its amateur team in the fall of 1895. But on the day of its opening game, team manager David J. Berry, who would play a significant role in managing several pro teams over the next decade, had a problem: Latrobe's quarterback had a scheduling conflict due to a previously scheduled baseball game. In a 1951 publication, *The History of the Brallier Family*, Brallier tells of his resulting first dalliance with professionalism in his own words:

> In 1895 the Latrobe Y.M.C.A. gathered together a team composed of ex-college men who were working here (Latrobe, Pa.). The first game was with Jeannette (Pa.) at Latrobe, on Tuesday, Aug. 31, 1895. They needed a quarter-back, and as I had played the year before at Indiana Normal—quite near Latrobe—I was secured for their game. It was a red-letter day in my life. I wore my first long trousers to Latrobe, and I played my first game for money—ten dollars and expenses! The next week I went to Washington and Jefferson College and played quarterback until the end of the season, and returned to Latrobe and played in another game, receiving another "ten and cakes."

Other accounts by Brallier add that he had already accepted a scholarship offer from nearby Washington & Jefferson (W&J) for the year ahead. He then initially declined Berry's proposal, thinking that the risk of injury was not worth jeopardizing his academic award. In its Summer 2012 issue, the *Latrobe Historical Gazette* reported that, in a confession of sorts, Brallier wrote a letter to Father Regis McCoy at St. Vincent Archabbey on September 4, 1936, explaining his decision to accept money to play the game:

> D.J. Berry, the manager of the Latrobe team, got in touch with me by 'phone in Indiana, Pa., and wanted me to fill in Blair's position for expenses. I was not anxious to do so on account of entering W&J in a few weeks from that date. After a lengthy conversation over the 'phone, D.J. Berry offered me ten dollars and expenses and a promise of several other games at the same figure. Well! When a kid is still in short trousers and going to college in a few weeks, ten bucks looks big, and I fell.

Brallier arrived in Latrobe the night before the game in time for practice under a streetlight and kicked two field goals in the next day's contest to help the team beat the Jeanette Athletic Club 12–0 when field goals were worth six points.

Courtesy of Latrobe Area Historical Society

Latrobe's teams of 1897 and 1898, with Brallier and coached by the bearded David J. Berry, provided strong competition among the small group of professional teams in the Pittsburgh area.

(Courtesy of Latrobe Area Historical Society)

Brallier's services continued to be in demand across the region. He enjoyed a successful playing and coaching career with many stops at the collegiate and pro levels, next jumping briefly to West Virginia University for part of his sophomore year. He explained his motivation for this move in his family history:

> The following year I went to the Univ. of West Virginia and played quarterback, with Fielding Yost as tackle and "Doggie" Trenchard as coach. About in the middle of the season the management got into financial difficulties and could not pay the players, so three of us, Eddie Wood (later end at Penn State), Dick Ely (halfback at W & J in 1895) and I went to Latrobe and played the remainder of the year for the grand sum of $150 and expenses.

Let the implications of a college paying football players in 1896 sink in. Brallier continued:

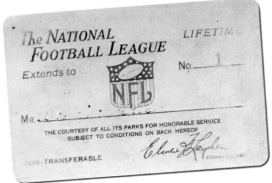

> The next year—'97—Latrobe went into pro football stronger and secured some outstanding college stars…. That year we defeated the great team at Greensburg, Pa., which had the famous Lafayette backfield.
>
> After returning from the Spanish-American War in '98, I played with Pittsburg Athletic Club, composed of college stars; then went to Medico-Chi in Philadelphia and played and captained the team three years. Then back to Latrobe to practice my profession and coached, played, captained and managed the team for six years. In all that six years we lost only one game, to the Canton "Bull Dogs." This game was my last in any capacity after playing for seventeen years.

In 1944, the NFL honored Brallier with its "No. 1" lifetime pass in recognition of his status at the time as the first professional football player.

(Courtesy of Latrobe Area Historical Society)

The University of Pennsylvania offered Brallier a scholarship in 1899 to stay on top of the college ranks after relinquishing its 1897 national championship. It reconsidered, however, fearing that Brallier's professional experience may threaten his eligibility and the school's reputation.

Brallier enjoyed the notoriety that the claim of being the first pro player brought for the rest of his life. In recognition of the honor, on October 25, 1944, the NFL awarded him with a lifetime pass labeled "No. 1." He died on September 17, 1960, at the age of 83, as a beloved member of the Latrobe community with a long career as a dentist, possibly still believing that he was the "first pro football player." In hindsight, it seems likely that he learned otherwise at some point.

⇋ The Birth Certificate of Pro Football and the Mystery of Nelson Ross ⇌

The Brallier myth still prevailed when the Pro Football Hall of Fame opened in September 1963, but the lore lacked the official record that the Hall preferred for posterity. The Hall's executives prioritized research to find related documentation, given Brallier's importance to the game's history. It was generally known that a group of professional teams had grown out of athletic clubs in the Pittsburgh area in the early 1890s, so the answer would logically come from their stories and records to the extent that they existed.

The owners of the Pittsburgh Steelers, the Rooney family, had an important hand in providing two key pieces of documentation to help the Hall's cause. Sometime before the Hall opened, the Rooneys sent boxes of documents from the Steelers' archives for HOF president Dick McCann to investigate. Included in one of the boxes was an accounting ledger, prepared by Allegheny Athletic Association (AAA) founder and manager Oliver D. "Ollie" Thompson, that dispelled the Brallier myth.

The accounting ledger memorialized the first known cash transaction for playing football. Under the heading "Game of Nov. 12, 1892—AAA vs. Pittsburg A.C.," the club paid a "game performance bonus to W. Heffelfinger for playing (cash) $500.00" (approximately $13,000 today). McCann privately displayed the register in his Hall office, pinned on the bulletin board, for some time. He and his staff were likely unsure when and how to position a document that would debunk the longstanding Brallier legend, especially given that, near the Hall's entrance, there was a prominent exhibit honoring Brallier's place in history.

Later, sometime in the early '60s, though the date is undocumented, an unknown guest walked into the Steelers' office, without an appointment, bearing a history-changing gift: a 49-page manuscript full of research on the earliest days of pro football culled from old Pittsburgh newspapers. Steelers owner Dan Rooney, then team president, described his recollection of the occasion to Pro Football Researchers Association president Ken Crippen in an interview in Rooney's office on May 13, 2007:

> **Rooney:** *I was there.... This fella came in to see me. He stopped at the secretary. The receptionist said that there is a fella here who wants to see you. I usually talk to people. He came in. I don't even think that he sat down. He had this book. He says, "I'd like to present this book to you." I said, "What is it?" He said, "It's good. You are going to enjoy it. It is the history of professional football." I expressed my appreciation. So he leaves. He was only with me*

Bob Carroll of Pittsburgh founded the Pro Football Researchers Association in 1979. He assisted the author in his initial research in 2007, identifying players in Shiring's photos.

Expense Accounting Allegheny Athletic Assoc.
Football Club
Game of Oct. 29, 1892 — AAA vs. Washington, D.C.
    balance carried over (account) $432.20
    guarantees gross profit (check) $258.00
    team traveling expenses (cash) $221.85
    net profit $ 36.15
    total balance $468.35

Game of Nov. 12, 1892 — AAA vs. Pittsburg A.C.
    balance carried over (account) $468.35
    game receipts gross profit (cash) $1,683.50
    visitors guarantee expense (check) $428.00
    park rental expense (check) $ 50.00
    Donnelly, Malley, Heffelfinger expenses (cash) $ 75.00
    Schlosser hotel bill for above (check) $ 9.00
    game performance bonus to
    W. Heffelfinger for playing (cash) $500.00
    total expenses $1,062.00
    net profit $621.00
    total balance $1,089.85

Game of Nov. 19, 1892 — AAA vs. W.J. College
    balance carried over (account) $1,089.85
    game receipts gross profit (cash) $ 746.00
    visitors guarantee expense (check) $ 238.00
    park rental expense (check) $ 50.00
    payment B. Donnelly for playing (cash) $ 250.00
    total expenses $ 538.00
    net profit $ 208.00
    total balance $1,297.00
This above accounting is hereby certified as
correct by the below signed team manager:
                  O.D. Thompson.

"Birth certificate": 1892 Allegheny Athletic Association accounting ledger documenting William
"Pudge" Heffelfinger as the first football player to be paid as a professional

(Courtesy of the Pro Football Hall of Fame)

fifteen minutes at most. He leaves. So I start looking. This is tremendous. So I turned it over to the Hall of Fame and they said that this is really great. They said, "How can we get this guy?" "I don't know. He walked into my office and gave it to me. I don't know." So we actually put it in the paper, but he never came forward. I am sure you saw it.

Crippen: *Yes. I have read through it.*

Rooney: *It was amazing to get it that way.*

Crippen: *He just drops it off and leaves.* (Chuckles)

Rooney: (Chuckles) *Exactly.*

Crippen: *It was truly groundbreaking, that manuscript.*

Rooney: (Laughs) *Yeah, it was. They still have it over there.*

Apparently, the man never told Rooney his name. Rooney's receptionist said that she thought she recalled his name as Nelson Ross. It has been known as the "Ross Manuscript" ever since. Researchers have theorized who "Ross" may have been but have never confirmed the mystery man's identity.

Ross's work, which often quotes the *Pittsburg Press*, established the narrative behind Thompson's accounting ledger, in which pay-for-play in football started at least three years earlier than Brallier's experience. Ross began by describing that there were still only four amateur club teams in the United States in 1884: Boston's Oneida AA, the New York Crescents (organized in 1878 in Brooklyn), the Baltimore Athletic Club (formed in 1882), and the Chicago University Club (1884). The AAU, formed in 1888, then created a major obstacle, setting out on a mission to serve as the guardian of amateurism.

Most every athletic club in the country joined the organization, since they would have the ability to compete in prestigious national championships for multiple sports. As such, they were highly motivated to avoid being suspended or disbarred for violations related to professionalism. In short order, though, club football teams tested the AAU's limits by obtaining jobs for players. This practice was not prevented, but led to the creation of the term "semi-pro." Then, clubs awarded pricey trophies to star players that they could pawn for cash, but the AAU banned this practice in 1892.

⋛ Pudge Heffelfinger: The First Pro Player ⋚

The AAA of Pittsburgh's Northside was part of a large group of new amateur independent clubs formed around the country in 1890, given the AAU's attraction. The Alleghenys, with blue and white uniforms, played their football games at nearby Recreation Park, home of the city's National League baseball club then also called the Alleghenys. With no teams for the AAA to play, the Western University of Pennsylvania (WUP), which became the University

1897 pin-ribbon celebrating the 110th anniversary of the Western University of Pennsylvania, renamed as the University of Pittsburgh in 1908

of Pittsburgh in 1908, formed its first team on short notice and lost to the Three A's 38–0. The Alleghenys' first season concluded with a 2–2–1 record after they won against a pickup team of Pittsburgh all-stars, lost to Princeton University and the Cleveland Athletic Club, and tied the Detroit Athletic Club.

The attention and increase in membership that the startup AAA club received locally spurred the city's old-line East End Gymnasium club to join the football mix in 1891. The East Enders came out of the gate as a semi-pro organization, given the participation of its salaried physical education instructor William Kirschner. While not an offense by AAU standards, local newspapers noted that Kirschner's teaching salary increased considerably during football season, while the number of his gym classes diminished greatly.

The Alleghenys refused to play East End in 1891 but agreed to a game with its renamed Pittsburgh Athletic Club (PAC), under a red and white

1892 Allegheny Athletic Association team before Heffelfinger joined

SUTTON, R. H.   ROWAND, C.   KOUNTZ R. G.
McCLINTOCK, F. B.   FLOY, R. E.   BLUNT CAPTAIN and R. T.   COATES L. G.   VALENTINE L. H.   EMERY, L. T.
ALBREE, R. T.   RODEN, R. H.   EWING, Q. B.   DONNELLY, L. E.

THE ALLEGHENY ATHLETIC ASSOCIATION FOOT-BALL TEAM.

THE PITTSBURG ATHLETIC CLUB FOOT-BALL TEAM.

The 1892 Pittsburg Athletic Club team lost the recruiting battle for Heffelfinger to the AAA and faced him on the field instead. Jim Lalus (back row, second from right) later coached his own club team to multiple amateur championships.

banner, on October 21, 1892. Enthusiasm reached new heights in the media for the birth of the rivalry, as the *Pittsburg Post* reported the day of the game:

> Oh, but won't there be wrenching, pulling, bucking, tackling and, perhaps, slugging, fists coming in contact with heated faces, heels crunching into dust-covered and sweaty heads of implacable opponents. Fierce assaults of main body against main body, dashing breaks by daring and resource- fully fleet runners, with the whole pack of panting and furious enemies at their heels. Such is the scene to be viewed this afternoon at the East End grounds before thousands lining the field and in the grandstands.

Tensions ran high between the clubs and among their supporters at PAC Park after Kirschner suffered an injury that PAC alleged resulted from dirty play. The Three A's hurled countercharges, accusing him of professionalism. During one fracas, an AAA player yelled, "Don't kick the life out of me!" A late Alleghenys touchdown and the subsequent two-point kick resulted in a 6–6 tie, and a rematch was hastily scheduled a few weeks later for November 12.

Meanwhile, stories of valuable trophies and job opportunities had spread across the Midwest to star players on the Chicago University Club (CUC). The club held firm to the letter of the AAU's principles, though, which led the entire team to quit the club and form its own independent team under the name of the Chicago Athletic Association (CAA). Spite drove CUC to inform nearby Northwestern University and other colleges about CAA's practice of paying excessive travel expense money to its players. Some teams then canceled games with CAA, and it needed to travel farther for games against like-minded clubs beyond the reach of local rumors.

1896 Chicago Athletic Association membership card. The CAA embraced and advanced pro football in the face of pressure from the AAU.

The new Chicago squad scheduled an eastern tour with six games in 12 days, and significant "expense money," to play a hefty schedule, including losses to Penn, Princeton, and Harvard, and a tie with the New York Crescents. Controversy over their professional tendencies dogged the players at every stop, including a story that they were soliciting other independent clubs to form a professional league. The stir was enough to discourage many of the Chicago players and drive them to leave the team before it returned home. One of these was a former three-time All-American from Yale named William Walter "Pudge" Heffelfinger.

The CAA's first stop on its eastern swing had been for a match with the Cleveland AA. In the stands that day were two Pittsburghers. One was an old friend of Heffelfinger's from Yale, and the other was George Barbour, manager of the PAC team. Both were in awe as Pudge slammed a Cleveland runner so hard that he forced a fumble, picked it up, and sped across the Cleveland goal for a touchdown. Barbour needed a replacement for Kirschner, and he now had an in with the best guard in the country. Princeton's Knowlton "Snake" Ames also impressed in Chicago's backfield to the point that Barbour was ready and willing to go all-in with cash offers to bring both of them on board with PAC.

Three-time All-America guard William "Pudge" Heffelfinger at Yale

However, word of an offer leaked to the *Press*, which ran the following on October 30, 1892:

> A very improbable sort of a story is being circulated at present about the P.A.C. offering Heffelfinger and Ames of the Chicago football team $250 to play with the East End team on Saturday, November 12 against the A.A.A.

It was still early in Chicago's season, though, so Heffelfinger and Ames deferred their decision until the eastern games were over to avoid further controversy.

Heffelfinger had reportedly headed to Yale to help coach the Elis after Chicago's last game against the Crescents, while in Pittsburgh, PAC and AAA were in stealth mode about their lineups for their rematch. When the teams took the field for warmups that fateful day, all hell broke loose. Heffelfinger and two of his Chicago teammates, Ben "Sport" Donnelly and Ed Malley, were on the field, but with AAA, not PAC.

Barbour initially refused to let his team play on the ironic grounds that it would hurt amateur contests in the future. But AAA manager Thompson, who had played halfback alongside Walter Camp at Yale, responded that he had only accomplished what PAC had failed to do. Perhaps it was Thompson's and Heffelfinger's Yale connection that brought Pudge into the fold.

To save face, and an estimated $10,000 from the bankrolls of PAC's constituents, Barbour offered to play a scrimmage and declared "all bets off." Thompson initially rejected the offer and accepted the referee's decision to award the Alleghenys a 6–0 forfeit. Thompson also had the goods on Barbour with a letter in his possession from Barbour to a former Princeton player who had spurned his cash offer. He had Barbour on the hook but let him off due to pressure from managements of both clubs and the crowd. After a delay of over an hour, Thompson agreed to Barbour's terms, and the game began. Heffelfinger then duplicated his feat in Cleveland by crushing a PAC runner, forcing a fumble, and racing 25 yards for a touchdown and the only score in a 4–0 win.

Barbour spent days afterward digging to find out how he got snookered. He learned through his sources that he was outbid for Heffelfinger's services by twice the amount of his offer, though Donnelly and Malley settled for only twice the amount of their train fares. Only Pudge was bold enough to throw caution to the wind with his amateur status. He was fed up with the hypocrisy and satisfied to live with the consequences, whatever they may be.

AAA backers countered with inside information that Kirschner's spot had been filled by a star lineman named Simon Martin from the prominent

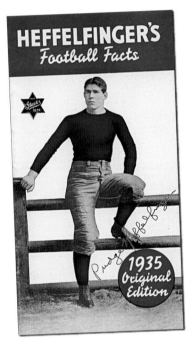

Heffelfinger's popularity endured for decades. From 1935 to 1950, he edited this annual publication named in his honor.

W. W. Heffelfinger

Steelton Athletic Club team. PAC members admitted to this but stood on the semi-pro grounds of the AAU by offering Martin a job (for the rest of his life) in Pittsburgh, where he played for PAC for many years.

Thrashing continued among the two clubs and in the *Press* for weeks. In the meantime, Heffelfinger and Malley returned to Chicago, but Donnelly was motivated by $250 in cash to stay and play for another week with AAA against W&J. PAC threatened to report the Three A's to the AAU but thought better of it, given its role in the situation.

Thompson soon faced the music for his actions, though, as two AAA track and field athletes also ran afoul of AAU professionalism rules earlier that summer. As a successful lawyer, he was able to escape the heat in Pittsburgh by negotiating a trip to AAU headquarters in New York, on November 20, to win a reconsideration of the club's six-month suspension from the AAU's Atlantic Association. He was also wise enough to stay there a few weeks longer until the club's football season ended, along with the controversy for the time being.

Though Ross's manuscript provided thorough, compelling detail of Heffelfinger's early role in pay-to-play football, it still took several years, until the early '70s, for the Hall to roll out the news. The Latrobe community also resisted the process, clinging to its long-standing pride as "the Birthplace of Pro Football." Eventually, the facts were too strong to ignore, and the Hall's opening exhibit in its rotunda was changed, featuring Thompson's 1892 AAA accounting ledger as a permanent fixture. It is fondly known as "the Birth Certificate of Professional Football."

Yale's 1891 national championship team under coach Walter Camp was undefeated at 13–0, outscoring opponents 488–0 during a 37-game winning streak. Heffelfinger is seated middle row, center.

≒ The Allegheny Athletic Association Dynasty ⇒

From the time AAA opened Pandora's box in 1892 to covertly pay Heffelfinger and establish local football supremacy, there was no going back to the romantic era of amateurism. With each passing season, the volume of professionals increased, and the veil of amateurism lifted further.

The following year, in 1893, former Swarthmore College player Grant Dibert signed the first known professional football contract to play with PAC for $50 per game. Notably, while his contract stated that he would not play for any other team that season, Dibert ended up leaving PAC for the Three A's, just before the teams' rematch, over a lack of playing time. His teams won both games, as AAA avenged its initial loss to keep the local championship in front of a rowdy crowd, unprecedented at an estimate of 8,500 fans.

On the field, the feisty Sport Donnelly marked the contest by nailing an opponent with a jarring tackle and commencing a jig around the inert body. Despite Sport's badly damaged knee, PAC's Heppenstall, enraged by such outrageous conduct, stormed over and kicked Donnelly directly on his injured joint. Sport responded by smashing Heppenstall into brief unconsciousness before calling for AAA's coaches to help him hobble to the bench.

The *Pittsburg Post* reported that fans of the Blue & White celebrated onfield by swarming over the fence despite police efforts, and off the field until the wee hours of the morning at a victory party at the Duquesne Hotel. According to the story:

PAC's Simon Martin "warding off a tackle" of an AAA opponent, according to the *Pittsburg Bulletin* caption

The Three A's were drinking deeply of the mead of victory as their heroes waged a stubborn battle to down the tough P.A.C. eleven, 8–4. Fair women were at the contest en masse to smile on the winners and cry for the losers. It was hard to tell if this was a society soiree or a rough football game. The gay toilets of the beautiful ladies, the swell drags and conveyances of the gentlemen, the waving of the red or blue flags by the ladies, the shouting of the club yells and the fluttering of streamers in the bright sunlight made the scene one to be long remembered.

Football is finally entrenched in the affections of the people. What matter if all the fine points were not understood? What matter if thousands of colds were caught? What if the favorite was defeated? What if players were bloodied or disabled? These were small matters compared with the mighty rushing, courageous tackling, fleet running, strategies of generals, and all the other features of the splendid game.

An AAA running back
makes a "bold buck"
through the PAC line, per
the *Bulletin*'s description.

Dangerous and monotonous mass plays, in which all team members moved as a group, were eliminated in 1894, increasing fan interest, season attendance, and profits. Over 5,000 turned out to see the Three A's claim their third consecutive title, and a trophy cup awarded by the *Pittsburgh Chronicle Telegraph*, in a decisive victory over PAC in their third matchup of the season. Greensburg also became the third team in the area to employ pro players in 1894, its first being Lawson Fiscus, "the Samson of Princeton."

Despite mounting rumors of professionalism in football circles and the press, nothing was yet proven, and the AAU was kept at bay. In September 1895, though, the AAU got off the sidelines and launched an investigation of the Three A's as the instigators of the pro movement. To avoid an expulsion that would include all of its sports, the club proactively shut down its football team, at least for the season.

The formation of the Duquesne Country & Athletic Club (DC&AC) at the beginning of the season provided timely competition for PAC in the city limits. In the Pittsburgh area countryside of Westmoreland County, the Latrobe YMCA, with Brallier, also formed as a rival to Greensburg. Under manager William Chase Temple, the former Pirates owner who sold his stake in the team after the 1894 season, the Red & Black Duquesnes strengthened quickly. In a retrospective piece in the *Press* on November 24, 1901, Temple wrote of his entry into football:

William Chase Temple

P.A.C. deplored the fact that there were no teams in this vicinity that were worthy to compete with them on the gridiron, so … purely for the good of the sport, J.B Vandergrift, Henry Thornton and the writer organized the Duquesne Country and Athletic Club, the sole intention at the outset being to get together a football team composed of local talent, which would again do battle with the P.A.C.'s for the athletic club championship of Western Pennsylvania. Instead of being welcomed by P.A.C., as we confidently expected, for some reason the new team was ridiculed and every obstacle imaginable thrown in the way of its organization and success. Money was freely offered by some of the enthusiastic P.A.C. supporters that Duquesne would never put a football team in the field.

The 1895 DC&AC team won the Western Pennsylvania title, though AAA would not relinquish the championship cup to them.

DC&AC then took great pleasure in edging PAC 10–6 in the season's final game on Thanksgiving Day of 1895. However, uncertainty over the Three A's status, and the club's pride, led AAA to controversially decide to withhold possession of the Chronicle Telegraph Cup from DC&AC.

Not satisfied with AAA's self-imposed sanctions, the AAU followed in 1896 by permanently banning the Alleghenys for having paid cash to their

athletes. Meanwhile, other clubs in the city were typically paying players a going rate of $50 per game, with those in the surrounding smaller towns at $20. While the club itself did not close, bitterness from the Alleghenys' other sports teams marginalized the football squad. Having long since adopted a spirit of rebellion over compliance, the boldest members of the group offered to pool their own money and bring the band back together. Heffelfinger and Donnelly were the first to agree to join a renegade unit, previously unmatched in talent, to keep the cup under the AAA flag. Pudge thought that the idea was so "dandy" that he reached out and brought in a bunch of other former All-Americans, forming the greatest team ever assembled to date for a quick two games against DC&AC and PAC, with an unheard-of schedule of back-to-back days in mid-November.

They did not give up a point. The city teams were already weakened and hesitant to play the galaxy of AAA stars since some of their regulars had retreated to the rural clubs to avoid being classified as professional and losing their collegiate eligibility. In deference to the situation, the Alleghenys made an unusual agreement with the Duquesnes to play "no dirty football" to get the first game played. Fewer than 2,000 fans turned out at Exposition Park to see the Blue & White march to a clean but unspectacular 12–0 win, which included a blocked punt by Heffelfinger recovered for a touchdown.

This modest score did not sit well with the Three A's, as the *Pittsburg Dispatch* reported on November 12, the day after their game with PAC:

> The all-star aggregation of football players, composed of Heffelfinger, Brooke, Lee, Donnelly, Trenchard and others, won the silver cup emblem at the Western Pennsylvania championship, for their employers, the Allegheny Athletic Association yesterday by a score of 18–0, defeating the Pittsburg Athletic Club, but not until the police were called on the field to quell one of the most bitter games ever seen in Pittsburg. The all-stars evidently sore at the small score made against Duquesne on Tuesday, started in with a rush, "Short" [sic] Donnelly was at left guard against Bovard. In the first mix up Donnelly and Bovard got into a fight. Bovard came out of it with a badly bruised face, and in the next mix up they got in an awful struggle. Donnelly was knocked down cleanly, and while he lay Bovard kicked him twice. The whole team of stars then piled on Bovard who was badly bruised before his fellow players could raise a hand. The police rushed on the field and arrested Bovard, and the game went on. Near the close of the second half Donnelly broke through the line, and in full view of three thousand spectators rushed at Stuart who had called a fair catch on a punt, and struck him full in the face, knocking him almost senseless, and sent two teeth down his throat. The feeling in Pittsburg is bitter.

Nonconformists that they were, this rowdy lot of new pros likely did not care how others felt about them as they celebrated their exploits. The club's enthusiastic backers blew their bankroll at reports of $100–$300 per player for each game, and the squad was officially done for the season.

According to Nelson Ross, the Three A's continued an unpaid barnstorming tour playing amateur clubs around Pittsburgh, West Virginia, and Ohio. Although documentation of such games has not been found, this story contributes to their legend. They were said to revel in their carefree camaraderie, downing beers together well into the night both before and after game days, free of the AAU.

"It was a happy, carefree bunch," said Ross in his manuscript, "that sadly parted in December after freezing cold and deep snow ended that 'just one more game before we break up' plea."

Including the possible extra games, Ross also stated that the 1896 AAA "incidentally compiled the first unbeaten, untied, and unscored on record in pro football history.... In many ways, it was perhaps Pittsburgh's most famous pro team."

Two days later, the CUC suspended six players who intended to skip out only temporarily for the Three A's. They all denied having received money for playing in Pittsburgh and were technically not proven guilty. The decision was upheld, though, not based on professionalism but on "insubordination and conduct prejudicial to the reputation of the association in allowing themselves to be open to the suspicion of professionalism."

It was worth the price, though, for those who sought the freedom to be paid professionally for playing a sport they loved. As a team, the Three A's made their point and moved the philosophical ball forward. When the CUC recruited Heffelfinger, who had not been a member of the club, to reload its roster, it was the final act of the amateur charade. It was too late, though, for AAA, which could not recover from being the AAU's sacrificial lamb.

Latrobe's Dave Berry was undeterred. He had pushed the envelope before, initially paying Brallier in 1895 and then strengthening his team the following year by paying players under the AAU's radar outside the city. In 1897, he went whole hog and openly declared in the *Pittsburg Dispatch*, "Dissidents are to be removed and the team will be a completely professional paid organization." The *Dispatch* found Berry's frankness refreshing while recognizing that it might cause other players and teams also to make the leap and cause problems for college programs.

PAC and DC&AC were still content to position themselves as amateur for the moment, but results in 1897 forced them to embrace the future. Latrobe embarrassed PAC 47–0, despite Berry signing an affidavit

that every player on his team that day was a Latrobe native. The next day Greensburg shut out the Duquesnes 24–0. PAC also did not score a point against Greensburg, DC&AC, or W&J later in the season. A crowd of only 1,850 for Latrobe's home game against Greensburg on Thanksgiving was its smallest ever for a holiday game.

After these debacles, Pittsburgh sportswriters declared that joining the professional movement was the only way to be competitive going forward. When 14,000 fans poured in at W&J to see the home team blank DC&AC 14–0 to close out its season, the Red & Black's manager Temple concurred in saying, "The W&J crowd proves Pittsburg will only support a winning team. So DC&AC will be a bona fide professional team next season.... We will seek out the best talent in the country for Pittsburg fans and hope that Latrobe, Greensburg, and PAC strengthen up also so as to be competitive with us!" Temple was a man of his word.

With the city teams weakened, the 1897 title was up for grabs. Greensburg and Latrobe split their two games, but the Greenies' season-ending win over their natural rival in their second game gave them the only pro title of the era not won by a team within Pittsburgh's city limits.

1897 PAC team picture from the estate of AAA team founder and manager Oliver Thompson

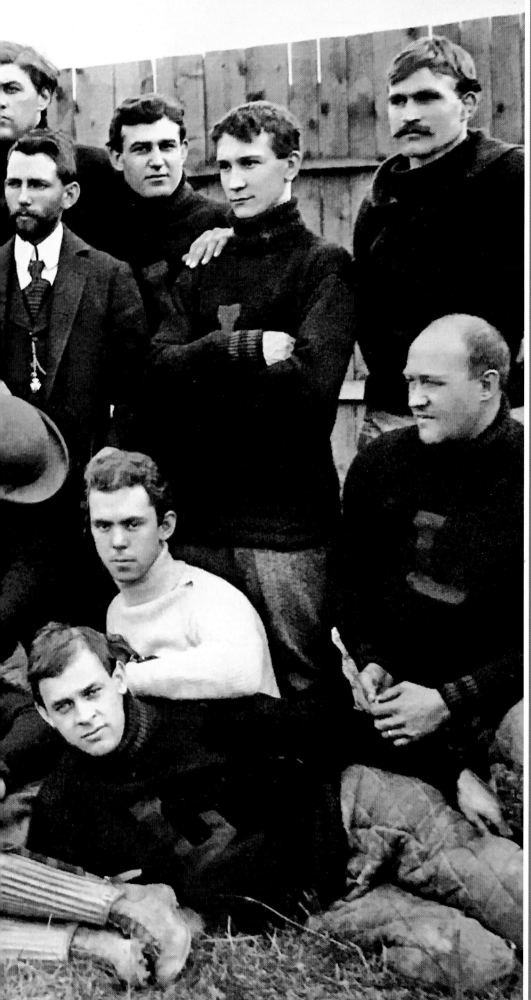

The 1897 Latrobe Athletic Club was the first openly professional team on which all of the players were paid.

⪦ Duquesne Country & Athletic Club: The Rise of a New Champion ⪧

By definition, for better or worse, pro football was now a business. In the game's new order, the sponsoring clubs either covered their expenses or subsidized them to compete for civic pride. Ticket sales, miscellaneous advertising, and sponsorships ramped up to cover the salaries of additional professional players. Berry also creatively raised money for Latrobe by raffling game-used footballs and coordinating picnics, dances, and performances.

It was murky at best for the clubs' leadership to forecast a return on their investments. Weaker local clubs and colleges filled out an already short schedule and typically drew only a few hundred attendees. Then, with a limited number of competitive games against the powerhouse clubs, weather alone could wreak havoc on attendance, swaying a club's net income for a season from a projected profit to an actual loss. For

William C. Temple (top left) shifted allegiances in 1898 to head up the new DC&AC championship team.

Temple · Wagenhurst · Eagye · Becker · Gammons · Lawler · Kiefer · McNeil · Greenwoo
Young · Randolph · Brown · Smith · Winstein · Keyes · Okeson
Mason · Church · Jennings · Jackson · Williams · Farrar · Gelbert

those passionate about being involved in the developing game, these were mere obstacles.

The pro game reached another plateau in 1898, as DC&AC's football committee elevated William Chase Temple from team manager to chairman. Temple was a principled man. In 1894, he divested his ownership in baseball's Pirates in disgust after the reputation of the Temple Cup he had commissioned to the winner of a National League playoff was tainted by misappropriation of the related prize money. Temple had a vision for pro football, and an ownership role earlier in the game's development than baseball afforded him more control. He wanted the best or nothing, and the public wanted a winner.

Thus provoked, the AAU came at DC&AC with a vengeance. On October 19, AAU secretary James Sullivan said in the New York City–based newspaper the *Sun*, "The AAU has got a chance now to put the screws on. By disqualifying the Duquesne eleven, it will force other athletic club elevens to either apply for registration or be suspended, too. If clubs do not apply for registration it can be taken for granted that they are violating the amateur rule."

In the same article, Temple was unfazed, his response definitive:

> The Duquesne Club is furnishing professional football. We admit it and have not denied it. In fact, at the close of last season we announced that for the next season we would put up the best article of football that could be procured for money; we would get the best men and pay the best prices. All last season we were strictly amateur, and we went against clubs that were largely or fully professional and which claimed to be amateur. They got better men for their money than we could get for love of the sport. Besides, we can control the habits of professionals. Previously our amateurs would do as they pleased, practice only when they wanted to and go into the games only when it suited them. Men who work for a living can't go out every afternoon and practice. Without practice there can be no teamwork, and without teamwork no football. We also found that the public only cared for the best football, and this we could not give without having professionals.

The Rubicon had been crossed, and the Red & Black moved forward signing new star players, including Brown's flashy running back John Gammons. The Duquesnes stormed to an undefeated 9–0–1 championship season in which their goal line was never broken, outscoring opponents 265–5. Only a scoreless tie with Greensburg and a State College field goal (then worth five points) tarnished an otherwise perfect record.

Fans were initially reluctant to embrace these unfamiliar, imported players. But sensational play, particularly Gammons's exciting runs, gave

John Gammons of Brown brought a new level of excitement to Pittsburgh pro fields with his speed and breakaway runs.

the people what they wanted and brought them out in increasing numbers. Passionate fans flocked across counties for rivalry games. Some unfortunate Latrobe rooters were even charged with trespassing in the Pennsylvania railyards for attempting to ride freight trains home, their pockets empty from betting on their team against DC&AC in Pittsburgh.

However, team salaries, rumored to range from $2,500 for some and up to $18,000 for DC&AC, were impossible to recoup despite teams' novel efforts. Once the Duquesnes captured their crowds' hearts, Temple raised ticket prices to $1 and charged $15 for the privilege of parking carriages on the sidelines. Latrobe manager Berry also convinced Temple to have his DC&AC team play against the first group of pro all-stars from the other big three pro teams in the last game of the season. It still was not enough. All four teams lost money, but the public concluded that the season was a success in every other way. According to the *Pittsburg Daily Post* on November 28, 1898:

> This [professionalism] took the public by surprise. It came too suddenly, and it took a little time before the people could be reconciled to the new idea—new in football. But the enthusiasm demonstrated by the public in the last two games played by the stars showed beyond a doubt that the people approved of the new idea, as they had long ago done in the matter of baseball. Professional football has caught on here and will likely be a permanent institution.

True enough, but the pro game in Pittsburgh did not continue to evolve in a straight line. The AAU also suspended PAC in midseason of 1898. In the October 2, 1898, issue of the *Pittsburg Dispatch*, a PAC management committee member blasted the AAU's action in saying:

> We do not give a rap for the AAU and its eastern seaboard nabobs. If DC&AC had not walloped the Knickerbockers nothing would have been done to us. We stand by DC&AC and other western clubs. To heck with them.

Despite its philosophical support for the pro model, however, PAC chose not to spend to try to keep up with DC&AC and surprisingly folded its team for the 1899 season. While rainy weather dampened attendance more than anything else, red ink also led Greensburg to withdraw from pro football in 1899. Without a nearby rival, Latrobe saved its cash and reverted to the amateur level, even though it had initially secured Heffelfinger to coach. Players scattered. Some moved to DC&AC for more money. Others went farther to the eastern part of the state, following available employment opportunities with new teams.

⇝ The James F. Lalus Athletic Club: Connecting the Dots ⇜

Many amateur teams also entered the epicenter of football in Pittsburgh during this period. It had been seven years since Heffelfinger's debut as the first pro with the AAA, and a younger group of players was coming onto the scene. One of PAC's first players who had played in that pivotal game against Heffelfinger in 1892, Jim Lalus, formed his own football club in Pittsburgh's East End in 1895 to train the second generation of aspiring pros. While strictly amateur, by 1899, the James F. Lalus Athletic Club (LAC) took over not only PAC's red and white colors but also PAC Park as its home field.

Identifiable by a bushy mustache, the popular Lalus made his living as a lieutenant for Pittsburgh's East End police force. He continued to play guard for PAC into the 1897 season while managing his new club. In what he had said beforehand would be his last game as a player, in a game against DC&AC on November 2, Lalus was kicked in the face above his right eye. He paid little attention to the wound and erysipelas, a blood poisoning condition, soon set in.

After Lalus had been bedridden for a month and refused hospital admittance, authorities feared that he had gone mad from his illness. They even thought he had attempted suicide when witnesses heard two shots fired from inside his home. Denying this claim to a reporter, his wife stated that she thought Lalus would have succeeded if he had tried to end his life. She clarified the incident by saying that several drunk Italians broke into the shed behind their house, at which time two shots were fired and the men scattered. She did not say who fired the shots, but Lieutenant Lalus was the logical conclusion.

As a result of the severe injury, Pittsburg Police Bureau superintendent A.H. Leslie said that a policeman has enough opportunities to lose his life without playing football. He then issued the following policy statement:

> Hereafter no man connected with the police force of this city will be permitted to play foot ball [*sic*]. I am not one of the people who think the game should not be allowed, but I will not permit any man under me to engage in such a dangerous sport.

Given his playing experience and local connections, Lalus had the right skill set to develop up-and-coming players and secure games against top competition. In so doing, he coached his team to an undefeated, unscored-upon season and the Western Pennsylvania amateur championship in 1899, including a win over the best WUP team to date. He also prepared some of his trainees to take their games to the top level. One in particular was a young man from the club's North Side neighborhood named Shiring.

LALUS,

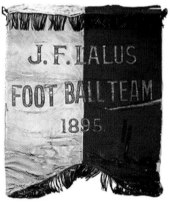

From playing against Heffelfinger in his first pro game to coaching Bob Shiring as an amateur, Jim Lalus played a key role in pro football's early development.

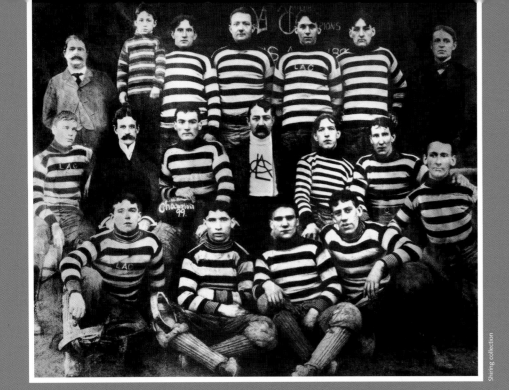

James F. Lalus Athletic Club

Lalus's undefeated teams of 1899 and 1900 both won Western Pennsylvania's amateur championship without conceding a point. Lalus recruited Shiring early in the '99 season and astutely converted him to the center position.

Bob Shiring: The Protégé

Charles Robert ("Bob") Shiring was born on April 13, 1876, in the nation's centennial year. Like many of his era in Pittsburgh and elsewhere, he completed his formal education after the eighth grade to begin working to help his family. Shiring's grandfather was a first-generation American from Germany, and his father established himself as a capable executive in the Westinghouse Corporation. Bob's heritage, as well as his father's career and connections, were considered to be assets in the community.

Charles Robert Shiring, Pittsburgh, Pennsylvania

(Shiring collection)

At age 21, on November 13, 1897, Shiring made his first documented appearance on an amateur football team for the Marquette Athletic Club (aka the Turtle Creek Indians) from the Monongahela Valley, 10 miles east of Pittsburgh, against the Pittsburg College Athletic Association in a 38–0 loss. The *Pittsburg Daily Post* commented on his play the following day: "Shiring, the fullback, also played a fine game, his tackling and interference being particularly noticeable." The *Pittsburg Press* also noted, "Shiring played a star game all the way through."

Shiring continued to hone his play for the Swissvale Athletic Club in 1898 and the East Pittsburg Athletic Club in 1899, where his strong play in an 18–0 loss against Lalus's squad early in the season led Lalus to bring Shiring over to his team for the remainder of LAC's amateur championship campaign. Lalus then made a seminal strategic decision before LAC's next game by moving Shiring to the center position. Before the forward pass, centering the offensive line, while also occupying the opposing spot on defense when all players played on both sides of the ball, was most key to a team's establishing control of a game. Shiring would go on to dominate the position for the rest of illustrious his career.

⤞ Homestead's Reign ⤝

As LAC rose to the peak of the amateur level, another pro team entered the picture. Andrew Carnegie leveraged his success in the steel industry to generously donate the capital for the construction of one of the first of four magnificent library facilities in the Pittsburgh area in the eastern suburb of Homestead. Located approximately seven miles east of downtown Pittsburgh, the Homestead Library & Athletic Club (HL&AC) opened to the public in 1898. It offered residents an unusually luxe set of civic facilities, including a concert hall, a swimming pool, a basketball court, and duck pin bowling, in addition to the library. The red brick mansion covered a full city block and stood aloft among the homes of executives of the Homestead Works for the Carnegie Steel Company, overlooking its mills on the Monongahela River a few blocks below.

HL&AC joined the football fray with respectable amateur teams in 1898 and 1899, despite its 53–0 loss to DC&AC in the latter year. In 1900, though, a dissenting group within DC&AC pushed for a return to amateurism, causing Temple to resign his post. The team was dominant in 1899, but its finances were stressed by taking on extra players returning from the Spanish-American

War, partly to prevent them from joining other teams. The club's members preferred profit to total domination. However, conceding a competitive advantage for the sake of a few dollars was not an option to Temple. His account in the previously mentioned *Press* article provided clarity to some historical notions:

Before accepting the management of the team of '98, I told the football committee of the DC&AC that if I ran the team that year there were only two things I would promise to do; first that our team would beat W&J and secondly that the club would not lose any money, no matter how much the football team cost, as a few of us would band together and stand all the losses without allowing the club to be out a dollar. Both of these promises were kept, but some of the people interested, in spite of the agreement that had been made before the season opened, seemed to feel that the football team should have shown a big profit on the season and put money in the treasury of the club, in spite of the heavy expenses we had been under.

This led to my retirement from football entirely in the year 1899, but in 1899 the Duquesne football team played two games of football with Homestead, winning both of them. Several of my warm personal friends were supporters of the Homestead football team and in the spring of 1900,

Members of the 1900 Western Pennsylvania professional champion Homestead Library & Athletic Club take their positions: Arthur Poe, John Winstein, P.J. "Dats" Lawler, John Gammons, George Young, Fred Crolius, Pete Overfield, Bemus Pierce, Willis Richardson, Otto Wagenhurst, John Hall.

I was requested by one of these friends to unite myself with Homestead in getting together a team for the season of 1900. I agreed to do this under the same conditions that I took the Duquesne team in '98; that was that I would agree not to show any profit for the Homestead Library & Athletic Club, but to show no loss and to beat Duquesne. This was done.

With his statement that the terms of his deal with HL&AC were identical to those with DC&AC, Temple dispelled the belief that has lingered ever since that his one-year stint with Homestead made him the first owner of a pro football team. In both situations, he indicated that he controlled the operation while sharing the financial responsibilities with partners, while the clubs maintained governance.

Temple's separation with DC&AC was not amicable. Matters turned sour from the outset when Duquesne initially reneged on its offer to play Homestead, while telling Temple to get his team a reputation first. They followed by convincing W&J to spurn Homestead, as well, with a mutual $1,000 guarantee on the commitment. Without other strong competition available, Temple enticed Berry with the offer of recruiting support to rally teams back together in Latrobe and in Greensburg. It was then a matter of course that Temple signed many of Duquesne's best players, including Gammons and his former Brown backfield mate, David Fultz, who was named captain. This upset the Duquesnes even further, who somehow expected that their stars would stay to play without compensation, or at least not as much as Homestead later offered when DC&AC decided to remain professional.

Temple countered that Duquesne was afraid of losing the game and its prestige to a stronger newcomer, which was probably true. To facilitate the resolution of the argument, the *Pittsburgh Commercial Gazette* intervened by sponsoring a handsome silver trophy cup, shaped like a football, as an incentive to schedule the games and provide honors for winning the

Arthur Poe, as pictured in a 1901 Homestead Library & Athletic Club program

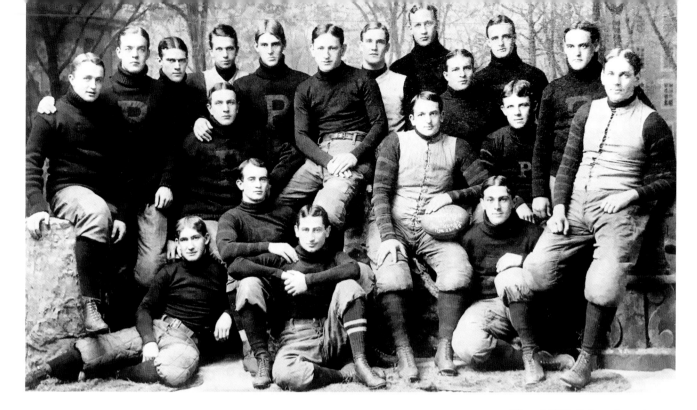

championship of the big four pro teams. DC&AC management relented but still offered Homestead only a typically untenable share of one-third of the gate, which Temple accepted for the satisfaction of handing his former club its just deserts.

With revenge in mind, Temple stopped at nothing to create a group of talent that surpassed anything DC&AC had put on the field. He successfully recruited five All-Americans, including player/manager Bill Church of Princeton, who coached at Georgetown the previous year, center Pete Overfield and fullback George Brooke of Penn, and ends John Hall of Yale and Arthur Poe of Princeton. At 5-foot-7, 146 pounds, Poe was named first-team All-American by virtually every major publication in 1899 and retroactively

The 1898 Princeton team finished with an 11–0–1 record and included Poe and captain "Big Bill" Edwards (with ball), who later refereed one of the games in the controversial 1906 championship series.

Poe running around the Carlisle end for Princeton in 1899

In this 1900 letter and telegram, Greensburg coach Ralph Hutchinson (pictured) reached out to Syracuse star Lewis Carr with a cash offer to join the team.

M. L. PAINTER,
President.

E. M. GROSS,
Vice President.

FRANK B. MILLER,
Secretary.

LUCIEN CLAWSON,
Treasurer.

GREENSBURG FOOT BALL ASSOCIATION.

EXECUTIVE COMMITTEE:

DENNA C. OGDEN.   WILLIAM G. THEURER.
EUGENE E. HUGHES.   EDWARD A. CREMER.

GREENSBURG, PA., 11-7-_____ 1900.

Mr. Lewis Carr,

Union Springs, N. Y.

Dear sir:--

Your letter was received as well as telegram. This is
a good town and I know you will like it here. We have a nice
crowd of fellows--Seneca, of the Indians; Steckle, University
of Michigan, and other western players are here. We are in a
league with Homestead, D. C. & A. C., of Pittsburg, and Latrobe,
and are fighting it out for the championship of Western Pennsylvania. We need an end and half back and think you can fill the
bill. We telegraphed you to Syracuse yesterday, offering you
$50 each and expenses for less than three weeks' playing. Next
season we will again be in the field and if you will care to
play with us again you will be able to get a good thing out of
it. Forgot to tell you that Jack Davall, of Cornell, is with us.
You had better come out and have a good time for the balance of
the season. If you determine to come wire us and start at once
as we have an important game on Saturday.

Very truly yours,

P. F. Hutchinson

THE WESTERN UNION TELEGRAPH COMPANY.

INCORPORATED
21,000 OFFICES IN AMERICA.   CABLE SERVICE TO ALL THE WORLD.

This Company TRANSMITS and DELIVERS messages only on conditions limiting its liability, which have been assented to by the sender of the following message.
Errors can be guarded against only by repeating a message back to the sending station for comparison, and the Company will not hold itself liable for errors or delays
in transmission or delivery of Unrepeated Messages, beyond the amount of tolls paid thereon, nor in any case where the claim is not presented in writing within sixty days
after the message is filed with the Company for transmission.
This is an UNREPEATED MESSAGE, and is delivered by request of the sender, under the conditions named above.
THOS. T. ECKERT, President and General Manager.

RECEIVED at 133 South Salina St. (Cor. R. R. St.), SYRACUSE, N. Y.

BU 127 F CR   17 PAID)   2:20 P

Greensburg, Pa. Nov. 6, 1900

Louis S. Carr,

Care Syracuse Athletic Assn,

Syracuse, N. Y.

Have important game Saturday, come at once give fifty each

and expenses need half back   quick wire.

Ralph F. Hutchinson.

This Telegram has just been received at the office, 133 South Salina Street,
where any reply should be sent.

CABLE OFFICE.   **ALWAYS OPEN.**

as college football player of the year by the Helms Foundation decades later. He was also one of six famous brothers who played at Princeton, all second cousins twice removed of poet Edgar Allan Poe.

Tension built in the press for Homestead's clash with DC&AC at Exposition Park on Election Day, November 6. The *Pittsburg Dispatch* billed it as the game for the national pro football championship. The odds were published at even money. It was publicly known, and not discouraged, that players were in on the action. According to the *Dispatch*, Duquesne players pooled $600 to bet on themselves, and Homestead players raised $900 to wager on their side. Homestead's Overfield put up an additional $500 of his own money. New Pirates owner Barney Dreyfuss laid $1,000 on Duquesne against former owner Temple's side.

A controversial ruling on a first-half punt, recovered by Overfield for a Homestead touchdown, infuriated Duquesne's captain, Roy Jackson, captain of Penn's 1896 and 1897 teams. Jackson stopped the game to the point that he threatened to pull his team from the field unless the referee changed his ruling. Play continued, however, except for three other official timeouts to allow Poe to pop his dislocated "trick knee" back into place. A second-half 10-yard TD run by Gammons, after a fake handoff to another back, resulted in a 10–0 Homestead win (two five-point touchdowns and two failed extra points).

The HL&AC juggernaut could not be stopped. The team enjoyed a new home facility at Homestead Steel Works Park and an undefeated record of 10–0 in 1900. Its goal line was uncrossed, with the lone score against the Blue & White being a Greensburg field goal, on the way to securing the *Commercial Gazette*'s trophy cup as the champion of Western Pennsylvania. Temple nearly did not live to claim the trophy for his club. During the season, he accidentally shot himself in the chest at his home while pursuing noises that he thought were caused by burglars.

Meanwhile, the following weekend, DC&AC proceeded to drop its next game to Latrobe, at home, by a score of 5–0 in front of over 8,000 fans. In an indication of local sentiment, the *Dispatch* reveled in the outcome: "Duquesne, the bullies of Western Pennsylvania football, like all bullies, fall to small pieces when finally dominated." Berry borrowed Shiring from Lalus to bolster his "Coke Eaters" at center against Duquesne, as he did for their two wins over Greensburg. Shiring and his Lalus teammates also went on to win another local amateur championship in a season in which they were again undefeated and held their opponents scoreless.

The dogged persistence of Temple and Berry to support the pro game kept it on life support through the 1900 season. Large crowds turned out when the weather was fair, but DC&AC's fans lost enthusiasm after its

THE COMMERCIAL GAZETTE TROPHY CUP.

1900 Western Pennsylvania championship football trophy sponsored by the *Pittsburgh Commercial Gazette* and won by Homestead

losses to Homestead and Latrobe. Torrential rains flooded Exposition Park, which bordered the Allegheny River, causing the Duquesnes' Thanksgiving Day game with W&J to be rescheduled for the following weekend when far fewer were able to attend. The resulting financial damages caused a deficit at the end of the season and pushed DC&AC to sue the Pittsburg Athletic Club (owner of the Pirates), which had rented them the park, to no avail.

Ironically, Homestead benefited the most from the flooding, as more fans attended its holiday game with Latrobe on the higher ground of Steel Works Park. Despite the team's massive payroll, the champions effectively broke even. Many Greensburg players sued their team for back pay, however, including for games from the prior season. The team's management countered that the players had violated their contracts because they did not keep themselves in top condition. While the case's resolution is unclear, the Greenies did not return the following season. Berry vowed to keep pro football in Latrobe, but it was not about money to him. While he was resourceful, and likely had skin in the game, it was not all his money that was being lost.

Financial pressures continued to shape the competitive landscape moving into the 1901 season. As it became clear that it was going to require an even more significant financial commitment to stand up to Homestead, HL&AC's other traditional local rivals. DC&AC and Latrobe, faced a seemingly impossible challenge to take the title from HL&AC on the field. Thus, both of them threw in their cards and folded.

Undeterred, Homestead moved forward and filled an 11-game schedule, mostly with collegiate teams, including Brown, Lafayette, Penn State, and a few smaller schools. W&J was anxious to finally have a game with

Homestead's football team and baseball's National League champion Pittsburg Pirates played in Exposition Park in 1901 along the banks of the Allegheny River.

the Homestead champions after being coerced by DC&AC to freeze them out the previous year, even though Duquesne ended up breaking the agreement for a better financial proposition. Despite his best efforts, Temple had no luck scheduling the top northeastern schools because of their reluctance to be associated with professionalism, as well as the risk of taking a hit to their playing reputations if they were to lose. Two games were also scheduled with LAC, which assumed the old East End name, as well as two with a new pro challenger from across the state—the Philadelphia Athletic Club.

As most of the Homestead pros were then from other states, team members were requested to report on September 27 to the team's Monongahela House headquarters. Accommodations during the season were provided for the whole team, including rooms and a training table with restrictions on diet, stimulants, and curfew.

⇌ Captain David Fultz ⇌

Bill Church returned to coach at Georgetown, and David Fultz replaced him as team manager while remaining field captain. Fultz was a star on and off the field. According to the Society for American Baseball Research (SABR), he was captain and All-American on both the baseball and football teams at Brown in 1896 and 1897 before completing a law degree from Columbia in 1904. No one surpassed Fultz's scoring records at Brown for a century.

Of his toughness, a teammate said, "I think Dave Fultz played under more difficulties than any man that ever played the game. I have seen him play with a heavy knee brace. He had his shoulder dislocated several times, and I have seen him going into the game with his arm strapped down to his side, so he could just use his forearm. He played a number of games that way. That happened when he was a captain. He was absolutely conscientious, fearless, and a good leader."

Sportswriter Grantland Rice thought highly enough of Fultz to place him in the lofty company of some all-time greats. Per SABR, of the athletes who had played both baseball and football, Rice considered Jim Thorpe, Christy Mathewson, and Eddie Collins in the mix as the best of this lot, while saying, "Fultz would come close to winning the bet."

Fultz's character was exemplary. He was recognized as a heady, selfless player, focused on executing nuanced strategies to help his teams win. He also did not swear, drink, or smoke, exceptionally rare for ballplayers of that era, and included in his contracts that he would not play on Sundays. Fortunately for the football world, pro games were not scheduled on Sundays at that time.

Fultz, Fielder, New York.

Fultz played for four teams over a seven-year major league career, including the Philadelphia Athletics and the New York Highlanders.

By the time he reached Homestead, Fultz had already served as head coach at the University of Missouri in 1898 and 1899. He also played center field for the Philadelphia Phillies and the Baltimore Orioles in the National League in those same years. In 1901, he joined the Philadelphia Athletics, led by Hall of Fame manager Cornelius McGillicuddy (aka Connie Mack, an unofficial name that he initially adopted to accommodate a scorekeeper) in the first year of the American League.

"Dave was one of the greatest outfielders that ever lived," Mack said in SABR's bio on Fultz. "Fultz played inside ball. His arms and legs were mere factors in the game. His brain dominated his work. He impressed me so that I have since looked to the colleges for players, and have seven of them on this team."

Among the new players Fultz added to Homestead's roster were two Native Americans: end Artie Miller and fullback Hawley Pierce, captain of the Carlisle Indians the previous year. Pierce's brother Bemus also played guard for Homestead in 1900. Established in 1879 as an act of compassion by Lt. Richard Pratt under U.S. government authority, Carlisle was the first federally funded off-reservation Native American boarding school. The Indians started competing at the intercollegiate level in 1894 and consistently produced one of the top collegiate teams in the country, until

The 1895 Carlisle Indians featured future Homestead players Artie Miller (back row, third from left) and the Pierce brothers, Bemus (captain, middle row, center) and Hawley (back row, right).

Cover of Homestead's October 26,1901, souvenir program from its game versus Baltimore Medical College

the school closed in 1918 to serve as a hospital to treat soldiers wounded in World War I.

To fill the backup center position, Fultz relied on Pete Overfield's knowledge of the position and experience with available talent. Given his dual responsibilities, Fultz also relied on Overfield to help him coach the team, particularly the line. Overfield was vested in the decision, and he recommended Shiring, who had faced off against him with the pesky LAC team in 1900. It may have seemed surprising to promote a local man from an amateur team to the most crucial position on the line for the finest team in the land. With his modest middle school education, Shiring was also thrust into a crucial role among a group of former collegiate stars with degrees from many of the most elite universities in America.

Undaunted, Shiring assumed the responsibility, and HL&AC continued its unbeaten streak. With three games remaining, two with Philadelphia and W&J in between, the team's record stood at 8–0. The Blue & White averaged 35 points per game and had given up a total of only seven, all in its two games with the Lalus club. The fact that any team crossed the Homestead goal was enough to cause a stir, as noted by the *Press* on October 19: "A new controversy has started. If you want an argument at the Monongahela House or in the East End, just ask 'Was the Lalus score a fluke?'"

Fultz was known to be a humble sort, but the *Press* reported on November 4, 1901, that he admitted, when prompted, that he believed Homestead's 1901 team was stronger than the previous year. He said that "the team work is better than it was last year; also the men have a better system than was in vogue last season."

Shiring relieved Overfield in the second half of some games and played full games against weaker teams. The only games in which he did not play were against LAC, likely due to the risk of repercussions playing against his former team. With the benefit of this experience, he was prepared for greater challenges that he would soon face.

Blondy Wallace (inset) won the New Jersey high school state championship with the Peddie Institute in 1896 and 1897. (Wallace back row, third from left, with 1896 team below)

⇆ "Blondy" Wallace: The Enigma ⇄

Charles Edgar "Blondy" Wallace was still supposed to be playing football for Penn in the fall of 1901. In fact, he was elected captain for his senior season. His road to Penn and afterward is a case of truth being stranger than fiction.

Born in 1880, Wallace grew up in the small rural town of Chesterfield in northern New Jersey. Chesterfield was originally named Recklesstown, foretelling of Wallace's life. Wallace's secondary education began as a first-year student in the fall of 1895 at the Peddie Institute, a top prep school in nearby Hightstown, where he helped the school win state football championships in 1896 and 1897. School records clearly show, however, that he neither attended nor graduated from Peddie with its class of 1899 in what would have been his senior year.

Nonetheless, Wallace managed to enroll at Penn as a dental student in the fall of 1898. He cleverly gamed the system at a time when the university

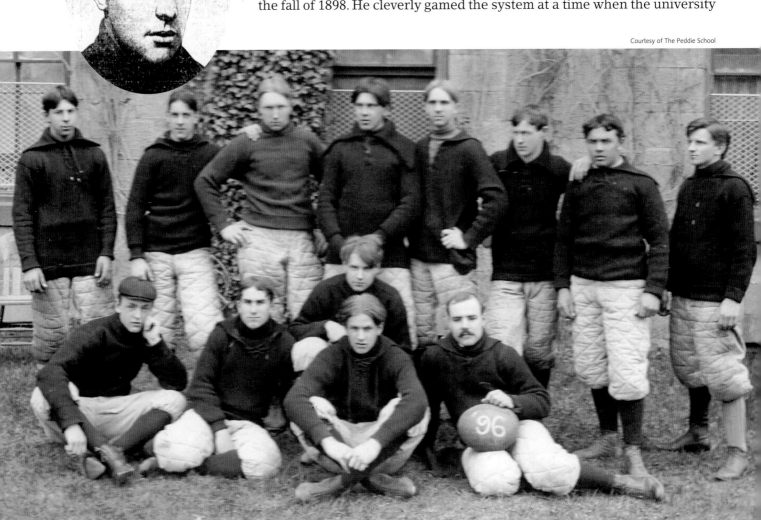

was desperately trying to improve its status relative to the Big Three of Harvard, Yale, and Princeton. By increasing the size of its student body through new programs, including dentistry, without any admissions requirements, Penn could enhance its endowment while stockpiling athletes. Though he did not make the varsity roster in his freshman year, it was still no small feat for Wallace in his sophomore year, in the fall of 1899, to hold down a starting position on a team at this level. Most impressive was that his linemates included All-Americans Overfield and John Outland, for whom the Outland Trophy is named. The trophy continues to be awarded annually to the best interior lineman in college football.

After a subpar record, by Penn's standards, of 8–3–2 in Wallace's sophomore season, the Quakers rebounded in his junior year of 1900 with an outstanding 12–1 mark. Their 17–5 loss to Harvard at Cambridge left them out of contention for top honors behind only undefeated national champion Yale and Harvard, which was beaten soundly at New Haven for its only loss. Four Penn players were recognized on the 1900 College Football All-America Team, with Wallace receiving second-team honors at the tackle position.

Wallace's strong performance on the field and winning personality led the team to elect him as captain at the end of the season for his following senior year. The *Philadelphia Inquirer* congratulated him for the honor on November 30, 1900:

Penn's 1899 team featured Wallace (middle row, left) on the offensive line with All-Americans John Outland (back row, second), Pete Overfield (back row, third), and captain Truxtun Hare (middle row, center).

C. Edgar Wallace will be Penn's leader in football next season.... Wallace is a whole-souled, genial fellow, born full of life and very popular.... All through the past season he has put up a star game, being strong on the defense and making strong and consistent gains running with the ball.... We congratulate him on his success and wish him every success the coming season.

Continuing the trend that he started at Peddie of not finishing the drill, however, graduation once again eluded Wallace. Before the close of that academic year, the *Inquirer* reported on May 15, 1901, "Prospects for a championship football team at Penn next season seem at present to be very poor. Several of the old men will not return.... Wallace, the captain, is not likely to get through his college work, in which case he will be ineligible."

Blondy Wallace at Penn in 1900

Three days later, the *Inquirer* announced Wallace's official resignation, calling it embarrassing to Penn. The following day, the *New York Times* brought further attention to Wallace's plight:

Charles Edgar Wallace, Captain of the University of Pennsylvania football team, threw a bomb into the Quakers camp yesterday by announcing his resignation from the team and his severance from the institution, giving as his reason that he purposed joining his brother in business on the Pacific Coast. It has been known for a long time—in fact almost since the day that Wallace succeeded Hare as captain—that the giant tackle was hopelessly behind in his studies in the dental department at the university. Further than that, he has exhibited a laxity in squaring his tuition fees. There has been no secret as to the pressure against Wallace in these particulars, and the general belief is that he realized the inevitable and tendered his resignation, which will no doubt be promptly accepted.

Wallace may have been the proverbial rat leaving a sinking ship. The 1901 Quaker roster was further decimated with the departure of multiple other underclassmen, in addition to the graduation of many stars. This left legendary coach George Washington Woodruff, an 1889 Yale alum with three national championships under his belt while coaching Penn in the 1890s, with an unenviable task.

Midseason losses to Navy and Columbia had Penn students calling for Woodruff's head. They hastily considered a movement to amend the constitution of the university's athletic association to add sufficient student representatives to create a majority for such a vote. After a 10–5 record and losses in four of the Red & Blue's final five games, including a decisive season-ending home loss to Cornell, Woodruff resigned.

≒ Cross-State Challenge: Philadelphia Professionals ⇌

Whatever Wallace's business aspirations may have been in California, if any, he soon turned to the subject that he knew best: football. On October 7, 1901, the *Inquirer* reported his role in a new startup venture called the Philadelphia Football Club, backed and managed by former Penn student Wilson Wright. Given that Wallace's focus in school was more on the gridiron than the classroom, the opportunity to be among the first generation to be paid to play pro ball was too good to be true.

The professional organization named Wallace captain and former Quakers quarterback Albert Kennedy coach. Seven other former Penn players also enlisted, as well as some from DC&AC, Latrobe, and State College from across the state. The enterprise had been in the works for some time, as Philadelphia's National League baseball park was already secured for the team's home games as of the article's date, and practice was to start that day. The squad's tentative schedule included Lafayette College, Bucknell, Orange AC of New Jersey, and at least one but possibly two games with Homestead.

HL&AC welcomed the challenge to its title, but the logistics were challenging given an already full schedule and its commitment to play all of its games at Exposition Park. In the bigger picture, the *Press* expressed excitement about the prospects of expanding the pro game the very next day: "Now that Philadelphia has a professional team perhaps New York, Boston and some of the other cities that are large enough to support the luxury will get out of their trance and that by next fall an interesting series can be arranged."

Prophetically, whether due to travel expense, home-field advantage, or both, Wallace flexed his negotiating muscle and would not budge on the location of the game. Fultz had sufficient financial backing and confidence in his team's credentials, so he willingly agreed, and the game was on for November 23 in Philadelphia. With terms set, the *Press* announced on October 31 that the Philadelphia pros had gladly accepted an offer by an anonymous Pittsburgh admirer of both teams, who commissioned a spectacular silver trophy cup to award for the athletic club football championship of the United States.

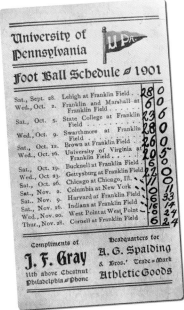

Penn's 1901 team suffered through a disappointing season after Wallace's premature departure.

Silver Trophy Cup.

Beautiful article offered by Homestead backers to winner of the game at Philadelphia.

Without any other serious professional competition, the rest of Homestead's and Philadelphia's games that season were literally played by men against boys—college boys. The only points that either team conceded before their clash were a legitimate touchdown that Homestead yielded to LAC in their first battle and a safety in their second. These scores upset the gamblers, who believed that their champions could not be scored upon, more than anyone. Homestead played eight games before traveling to Philadelphia, and Wallace's team played only four.

⊱ Gambling Rules the Day ⊰

As sports gambling was pervasive, among friends and with bookmakers, games between prominent professional teams drew much attention from the betting crowd. Homestead loyalists expected gambling profits, as well as onfield victories, from their champions, whom they perceived to be invincible. After cruising on November 5 to an amicable 34–0 win over Brown, from which Homestead had four alums, Fultz was indignant over rumors that his players did not pile up a larger score to assist bettors wagering that Homestead would not score more than 40 points. Further, one person who lingered at the park after the game claimed that he gave Fultz

The COLLEGE MAN'S NUMBER

THE SATURDAY EVENING POST

An Illustrated Weekly Magazine
Founded Aº Dˢ 1728 by Benj. Franklin

Volume 173, No. 17   Philadelphia, October 27, 1900   Five Cents the Copy

Copyright, 1900, by THE CURTIS PUBLISHING COMPANY   PUBLISHED WEEKLY AT 425 ARCH STREET   Entered at the Philadelphia Post-Office as Second-Class Matter

The Curtis Publishing Company Philadelphia

$10 to have the team score its last touchdown, which would have covered his bet of a point spread of 34 points or more.

In response, Fultz said in the *Homestead Messenger* on November 7:

> We are not running the team in the interest of speculators. The rumors of betting have reached my ears, but I can't see where there is any necessity for an explanation from me. We played a strong game against Brown, scoring 22 points in the first half. In the second half, we were not particular whether we scored or not.

The 1901 Homestead Library & Athletic Club national professional champions, seated on the front steps of the club

Naturally, bigger contests such as the Philadelphia game brought about heavier than usual betting action. According to the *Dispatch*, the speed with which Homestead loyalists used business agents to match an initial $5,000 of Philadelphia coin gave Philly supporters reason for pause. Odds listed in

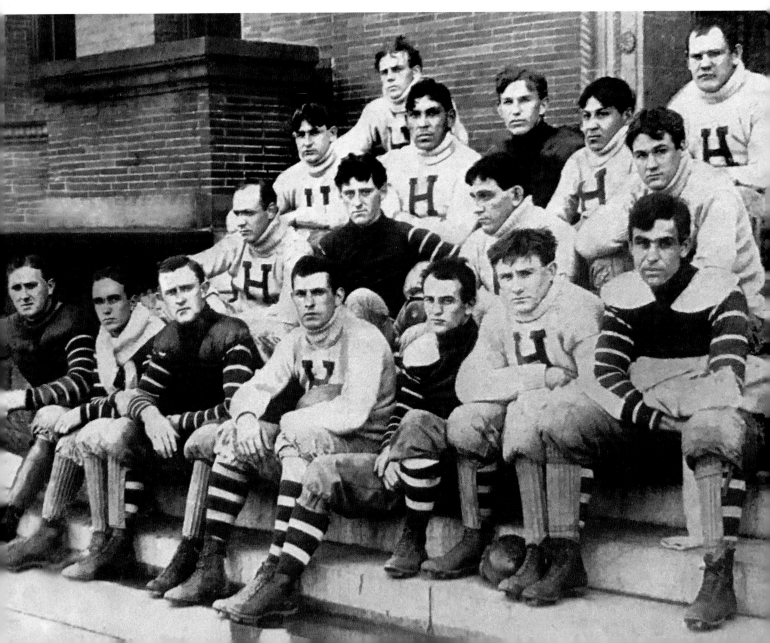

The tackles-back formation was commonly used before rule changes required all linemen to start plays on the line of scrimmage.

the papers shifted to up to 2–1 in favor of the Blue & White. Homesteaders, including players, were still willing and able to put up large sums of money but had difficulty finding takers. Despite his otherwise ethical moorings, the *Dispatch* reported in the week leading up to the game that Fultz was "tearful" when unable to find anyone who would bet with him. Fultz said:

> When I heard of a lot of people with Philadelphia money being in town I put up my lightning rod hoping to get a chance to bet a little, but I can't find the people with the money. The *Dispatch* can say that if there is anyone in Pittsburg who wants to bet against Homestead on Saturday's game let them come to me. We are going to beat Philadelphia and beat them good.

This fact is not to cast a shadow on Fultz's reputation, as he was clearly known for his strong character. But it emphasizes the extent to which sports gambling was accepted, even at the end of the Victorian era.

A hard-fought 17–2 win over LAC in their rematch on November 9 put another hole in the locals' wallets when HL&AC scored less than the minimum 40 points expected. With little on their own team's resume, this modest result provided the Philadelphia crowd with hope. When asked about the teams' relative strengths, Philadelphia coach Kennedy said in the *Messenger* that the Homestead 11 had a backfield that was probably the finest ever gathered. But he added with a sideways glance, "You know a backfield is not all, and we feel confident that our line is considerably stronger than theirs."

Yet, the Blue & White topped Lafayette 48–0 on November 16, which more than doubled the 23–0 margin that Philadelphia managed against the teams' only common opponent earlier in the month. Philly believers also put stock in the fact that many of Wallace's squad had trained together at Penn in Coach Woodruff's guards-back offensive line formation that Homestead was not accustomed to facing.

⇋ 1901: The First Pro Football Championship of the United States ⇌

Strong arguments by both sides created the highest level of public interest and anticipation in a pro game in several years, and possibly ever, up to that point. The burgeoning intersectional rivalry also led to broader and more detailed press coverage with opposing perspectives. Writers from both cities agreed, though, that the pending contest represented the professional football championship of the United States.

The Homestead team and hundreds of supporters boarded their train with fanfare, brimming with confidence as they rolled out of the steel town an hour late two nights before the game. Before the train passed through the Pittsburgh suburbs, though, fate seemed to conspire against the contest taking place—and possibly the advancement of pro football itself—as the locomotive derailed. The following morning, readers of the *Homestead Messenger* were shocked by the news of the train accident.

The full article laid out the alarming details that threatened not only the big game but also the Homestead heroes' lives:

Irwin, Nov. 22—The second section of fast line East scheduled to leave Pittsburgh at 9 p.m. running an hour late and at about 40 miles per hour ran into an open switch at Shafton at about 10:30 last night.

Engine 1962 was hauling the train with John McCabe at the throttle and fireman Ed Long on the other side. They had no time to jump. Fortunately, the engine did not topple over but tore up the ties and road bed for some distance. Behind the engine were three express and three baggage cars. They left the track and ran over ties for fully 100 yards and then overturned and piled up with the express matter piled about the scene.

The only one injured was Charles Cole who was cut in the hand in getting out of his car. The three day coaches and three Pullmans did not leave the rails. The passengers were shaken up but not injured.

The Homestead team was aboard enroute [*sic*] to Philadelphia. The passenger cars were taken back to Larimer and sent east. Three tracks were blocked for several hours by the wreck. Engineer McCabe says that the cause of the accident was an open switch and no lights.

It is both remarkable and paradoxical that amid the perceived romance associated with the prim and proper styles, manners, and music of the Victorian era that events in daily life were frequently more than brutal and often fatal. Due to industry's early stage of development, accidents in the mills and on railways claimed lives seemingly on a near-daily basis in various shocking and horrific ways. Newspapers were riddled with stories of unfathomable tragedies resulting from spontaneous explosions and accidents that cost countless lives, often in groups. As dangerous as it was to play football at that time, it may have been statistically safer than working in a mill or for a railway company.

The Homestead corps took an early train out of Pittsburgh the following morning, per the *Dispatch*, but another railway accident threw a wrench into the team's already compressed preparation schedule. This time, a separate train, following the team's locomotive and carrying all of its equipment, crashed in the Allegheny mountains. Players were disconsolate when they learned the news upon their arrival at the ornate Hotel Walton in downtown Philadelphia. Fultz went into problem-solving mode and prepared to order two dozen silk stockings from a local theater for the team to be able to dress for an evening practice. Shouts of joy rose from the ranks when the uniforms arrived in time to prevent an embarrassing scene.

As the town janitor went about lighting the streetlights to help with visibility for the team's drills on the Huntingdon and Broad Street grounds, the squad was further delayed by a uniform mix-up. Trainer Davy Sheahan and a group of hotel porters hurriedly distributed the togs to the players' rooms, but they mistakenly switched Shiring's and Poe's uniforms. As Poe was five inches shorter and 95 pounds lighter than Shiring, he was heard pleading for help, and Shiring "registered a roar that was heard to the tenth floor," according to the *Dispatch*.

The clanking of the players' spikes on the Walton's auditorium floor set fashionable onlookers gasping as the athletes marched through the hotel lobby heading to practice in the dark of night. Their procession was interrupted by a prosperous-looking chap who was known to have bet $1,000 on Philly. He jovially patted Gammons on the ribs to test his girth and slapped quarterback "Little" Willis Richardson on the back. Richardson

Halfback "Little" Willis Richardson stood at 5-foot-6 and 165 pounds but had no problem sacking a Philly gambler in a hotel lobby.

then threw the fellow back against a radiator "for a loss of two yards," per the *Dispatch*, and had a few words for him that his colossal teammate, lineman John Winstein, said provided grounds for libel and slander.

Richardson also brought wads of $20 bills to capitalize on a Homestead victory against the highly touted but unseasoned Quaker City gang. However, at that point in the fracas, his efforts to convince the sporting admirer of HL&AC's weakness lost credibility, and his proposition to the instigator to wager more of his fortune against Homestead fell on deaf ears. The gentleman buttoned his coat and walked out, perhaps looking for someone else to take money on the other side of his original bet.

When the Blue & White finally reached the park, the streetlights were not of much service. The *Dispatch* reported that the team managed to practice for an hour with a white-painted ball and no light but a friendly star. Locals, not accustomed to such zeal in their athletic idols, stood by in amazement.

Afterward, Captain Fultz settled into his hotel room to take stock and make some decisions. He nearly did not make the trip to Philadelphia due to a severely swollen eye that a Pittsburgh doctor diagnosed as neuralgia. He spent hours in a dark room, calming his brain at the team's home clubhouse at the Monongahela House, before the first train ride east gave him clarity on his mission.

"I'll be in that game, never fear," Fultz said to a *Messenger* reporter on the Pullman rail car, with his eye bandaged. "Tell the people I'll be in the game if I must go blindfolded. I'm going to have a bit of this Philadelphia glory." Subsequently, he announced to the reporter in his room at the Walton after practice that he would start the first half and stay in the game as long as possible.

Fultz was also in it for the financial glory. The *Messenger* journalist noted that Fultz had a roll of bills big enough to choke an elephant on his bedspread, and they all looked to be of good size.

"I brought that over to say that we could whip Philadelphia tomorrow, but I can't find anyone who disagrees with me," said Captain Fultz. "It is a shame."

Of the 22 men on Homestead's roster that traveled to Philadelphia, the only other one with an injury concern was its most recent addition. Perry Hale, known as "the Human Battering Ram," had been a first-team All-American at Yale the previous year and was said to be the best collegiate fullback in the country. He signed on before the season with the stipulation that he report on November 10, after he completed his high school coaching duties at Exeter in New Hampshire. His arrival gave Wallace additional cause for concern:

"We are not afraid of Homestead, but we expect a close game," said Wallace in the *Messenger* on November 18. "Homestead had a fine team

Captain David Fultz demonstrated impressive leadership playing through illness and injury in the 1901 championship game.

Perry Hale's Legacy

I am privileged to be the daughter of Perry Titus Wells Hale. After graduating with an engineering degree from Yale and coaching one season at Phillips Exeter, Perry played with Bob Shiring on the world championship Homestead team in 1901. He then became head coach at Ohio State in 1902 and 1903. He continued various athletic pursuits after leaving Ohio to return to Connecticut to marry Alice Pease Austin, work at various engineering jobs, and start an engineering business.

In October 1913, one day after his 35th birthday, Perry was blinded in a chemical explosion. He spent several years as a semi-invalid, trying to figure out how he could make a living. In 1919, he applied for a patent for the Perry Hale Kite, which he marketed for many years. Alice died in 1920, after which Perry attended a school for the blind in Baltimore. The day he left the school, he married staff member Anne Howarth Geary. He and Anne ran insurance and real estate businesses in Perry's hometown of Portland, Connecticut. Perry became the town's tax collector, worked on various municipal positions, and lectured on history and sports. Wishing to be a credit to the blind community, he was also a motivational speaker. Perry and Anne divorced in 1935.

My father married my mother, Wilhelmina Piekarz, in 1936. To this May/December marriage, my brother Perry was born in 1938; I was born in 1942. My father died when I was five years old. My recollections of this amazing man are vague, but I have spent years getting to know him by recalling my mother's stories about his intellect, initiative, and athleticism. I have been able to flesh out his legacy through personal letters and Yale publications and by researching his athletic, professional, and personal accomplishments via online newspaper articles. I particularly cherish the team photos and my father's scrapbook. Regarding his affinity for football, my father is quoted in a 1925 *Baltimore Sun* article as saying, "Football was meat and drink to me."

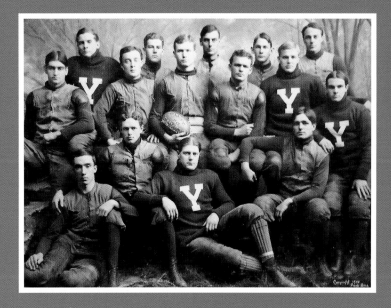

1900 Yale team (Hale middle row, fourth from left)

I was introduced to Gregg Ficery because of our common interest in the Homestead team. It has been special to connect with Gregg to share the journey of learning about our forefathers' rich experiences in the early days of pro football. To me, his historical discoveries in the NFL's centennial year are serendipitous. It is wonderful for the public to be able to appreciate them.

— Marilyn Hale Brooks, Albuquerque, NM

before Perry Hale was put at fullback, but now she is 25 per cent [*sic*] stronger. However, we have a few good men ourselves, and we will show them something before two halves are over." Hale, though, suffered a small broken bone in his shoulder during the Lafayette game the previous Saturday. His status for the Philly game was uncertain.

Game day started with the Homestead band quietly marching in step along Broad Street toward the Walton at around 8:00 a.m. Band leader H.F. Blaney continued to lead them stealthily into the Walton auditorium and, on cue, waved his baton for the band to rouse every hotel patron, letting them know that the Homestead contingent was in high spirits. Chambermaids from as high as the seventh floor screamed down the elevator shafts wondering if there was an alarm.

Ten thousand people turned out for the big event at Philadelphia's National League baseball grounds under a light rain that likely kept thousands more away. Neither team was able to sustain long drives given the conditions, but Philadelphia's lack of teamwork on punt plays made the difference. Philly punter Ben "Doc" Roller, one of the great overall athletes and strongmen of the era, fumbled a snap deep in the team's territory early in the first half. Four plays later, Dartmouth's Fred Crolius touched the ball down in the end zone after running it in from 8 yards out for Homestead's first touchdown. Arthur "Texas" Mosse kicked the goal for an early 6–0 Homestead lead.

Later in the half, Poe shoved a Philly player aside to cover a halfback punt by Crolius for a touchdown and a 12–0 lead. Prospects for Wallace's gang were bleak. Unable to move the ball against the stalwart Homestead line, they became frustrated and, despite a slight weight disadvantage, resorted to slugging tactics. The Philly boys quickly learned that the veteran HL&AC warriors could beat them at that game, too, and settled down to face the task at hand.

A 30-yard sprint around the right end by Fultz, who wore a sling-like apparatus on his face, put Homestead in position near the Philly goal for a decisive score just before the half. But a brilliant goal-line stand gave heart to Wallace's team and its supporters. Cushions and hats rained on the field in approval.

Wallace's defense continued to battle in the second half and forced Homestead substitutions due to fatigue. Crolius's strong runs kept him in the game at fullback, so Fultz inserted the versatile Hale in the game to replace Winstein, who had become vulnerable across the line from Wallace on both sides of the ball. Homestead's defense was nearly impenetrable. Five first downs on the day were not enough for Philly to threaten the HL&AC goal. Roller's 30-yard field goal attempt that fell 5 yards short was the closest the team would come to scoring.

Al Bull at Penn in 1895

To add injury to insult, the aptly named Philadelphia center, Dr. Al Bull, became disoriented and began to line up on the Homestead side. Unlike Wallace, Bull was a Quakers player who graduated from Penn's dental school with the intention to pursue the profession. Overfield, his old college pal, led him to the sideline, but the wild Bull broke away and returned to the field, insisting on finishing the game. Two policemen were required to forcibly escort Bull to a safe pen in the clubhouse.

Another Poe touchdown, on a fumbled punt snap by Roller with seconds left in the game, resulted in a final score of 18–0. Mosse's last kick, after the score, was most meaningful for the Homestead bettors who, unable to get money down on Homestead with odds, were able to secure action only by betting that they would win by 18 or more. The *Dispatch* said that it sent many Philadelphians to patronize the free lunch counters into the evening.

After the game, in the *Press*, Wallace provided a sober and respectful assessment, which was not all that common at a time when rancor tended to prevail:

> We have no excuse to offer for today's defeat. We were beaten honestly and the best team won. We were somewhat handicapped by lack of condition owing to our not playing much this season, while our opponents showed the advantage of continuous training and team work. Notwithstanding the strength of the team, we really expected to win today's game, but one team must lose and we happened to be that team.
>
> Overfield, Gammons and Poe did conspicuous work for Homestead and contributed materially to our defeat. Not only were we at a discount regarding our training, but Homestead outweighed us, averaging fully 10 pounds a man more than our players. This does not detract from the credit due our opponents, they played a fair and open game.
>
> I imagine that by this time they have fully realized they have been in a football game.

On their way out of town, the Homestead rooters could not resist delivering a song with a parting shot:

> Goodby, Phillie, we must leave you,
> And it's hard luck we all know;
> Something tells us you're not in it,
> Like your town you are too slow,
> But there's something in your city
> We like it more and more
> 'Tis the boat that leaves for Camden,
> When we go down to the shore.

Wallace gave Homestead its due and owned up to his Philadelphia team's shortcomings in defeat.

The undefeated 1901 Homestead champions accepted every challenge and continued to take professional football to a higher level. Front row: Mosse, Hale, Maxson, Richardson, Hunt, Woodley. Second row: Steen, Gammons, B. Pierce, Fultz, Randolph, Shiring. Third row: Shields, McCutcheon, H. Pierce, McNulty, Poe, Crolius, Miller. Back row: Overfield, Winstein, Nieman.

HOMESTEAD DEFEATED QUAKER CITY'S GREAT ELEVEN CHAMPION

22

Terms such as "world champion" were not yet discussed, but fans understood the implications of Homestead's victory. By definition, the Blue & White was the best there was. They set a higher bar for playing excellence than ever before. Homestead's heroes boarded the team's train as the greatest pro team in the country for the second straight year.

The *Inquirer* credited Homestead for outmatching Philly in terms of its impressive coordinated team play, whereas Wallace's squad played a more individualistic style. Notably, while it was early in both Shiring's and Wallace's careers—and Shiring did not line up in the game—it was the first of many times that their teams would go head-to-head in the biggest game of the year, with similar results and conclusions.

⇋ The Rematch ⇌

The ink had hardly dried on the game's stories in the papers before it was announced, two days later, that Wallace was interested in bringing his team to Pittsburgh for an exhibition rematch the following Saturday. Philadelphia manager Wright claimed that since his lineup was missing two of its key players and Homestead had scored all of its touchdowns on flukes, his team was entitled to a return game.

Homestead, however, still had another game to play against W&J that Thursday, on Thanksgiving Day. Fultz said that his players were up for the challenge and understood that they were under contract until the end of the month, but he doubted that HL&AC management would require them to play with only one day of rest. Further, he said in the *Messenger*, "W and J always plays her strongest game in Pittsburg, and I guess next Thursday's contest will be about the stiffest proposition of the season. The Philadelphians played hard football, but they were not in the best of condition." The team's backers decided to hold off on the decision until after the W&J game.

The combination of a short week before the game and a possible emotional letdown following the hoopla in Philadelphia brought the Homestead troops off to a slow start against the "college boys," who had waited two years for their crack at the pros after the prior year's politics. The *Press* suspected that there were actually few amateurs on the field. Overfield, who had been vital at center in the Philadelphia win, also missed practice during the week due to illness and was replaced by Shiring in the heart of the line.

PRESS

E TIMES
1ILLIE'S LINE
WAS CROSSED

SUNDAY MORNING, NOVEMBER 24, 1901

OF THE

SILVER CUP
WILL COME TO
SMOKY CITY

COUNTRY

After a scoreless first half, Fultz delivered a calm but firm reminder at halftime for his men to deliver a better effort. The champions answered the bell for a 12–0 victory. The outcome was as expected, while the *Dispatch* felt obligated to note that the margin fell short of the gambler's 24-point spread

Never unwilling to face a challenge and surviving W&J without major injuries, HL&AC management fired a wire to Wright after the game: "Bring your team for Saturday and we will give it another beating." Wright replied, "We will be there."

Philadelphia brought a fresh bull in from the pen with Penn's captain, Herbert "Bull" Davidson, joining the team at halfback, as well as All-America guard John Teas, after the Quakers' Thanksgiving Day loss to lowly Cornell. Homestead's Overfield still had not recovered from his illness, though the team expressed full confidence in Shiring, saying that he had everything but experience. Oddsmakers posted initial odds of 10–7 in Homestead's favor. But the *Dispatch* countered by pointing out HL&AC's crippled condition, also noting that citizens who had to make good on rent day were inclined to bet at even odds, if at all.

From the outset, it seemed that the Homesteaders might have been overambitious. The *Messenger* painted a woeful picture of the first half:

> The Philadelphians, like the town they came from, were slow and deliberate on all of their movements. They took their time and hit the line with tremendous force.... They began to hammer Homestead's line mercilessly early. It was just like a man wielding a big sledgehammer. They spit in their hands slowly, gave the signal and then, oh, what a crash there was. It was distressing to see the Stars, who had failed all season to find their masters, hammered back, back and back, with slow terrific sledgehammer blows. Back they were smashed and hurled until the visitors tumbled over their goal line.

To make matters worse for Homestead, after stopping Davidson on the 1-yard line, Fultz remained lying on the ground. Poe and Richardson carried him off the field. His mates were noticeably demoralized, and Roller plowed in for a Philadelphia score on the next play. However, he missed the subsequent kick, as well as two field goals, one which was blocked by the enormous Bemus Pierce from Carlisle, and the score stood at 5–0 in favor of Philly at the half.

After defeating Philadelphia for the national title, it was a huge ask for Homestead to take on W&J and Philadelphia again for three tough games in eight days.

"Indian" Artie Miller replaced Fultz in the backfield and Hale, with an oversized shoulder pad protecting his injured wing, once again relieved Winstein on the line in the second half. Miller powered Homestead on a drive inside Philadelphia territory late in the game but came up limping badly after a run to the Philly 10. With time running out and their heroes' undefeated season in jeopardy, the crowd broke through the ropes and surrounded the end of the field. In the original field design with the goalposts planted on the goal lines, the crowd encroached upon the dirt where Wallace's charges tried to make their stand.

The crowd screamed for Howard Nieman to replace Miller, and Nieman removed his white turtleneck sweater to enter the game. But the Indian stood strong and blocked for Gammons on a blast of 5 yards, then another one for four more, to the brink of a score on Philadelphia's 1. Shouts from the sublime to the profane rang out for Gammons, exhorting him to cross the goal, according to the *Messenger*.

When Crolius bowled over the line on the next play, the *Messenger* reported that such cheering had never been heard before. "The spectators danced all around the players upon the gridiron, waving their hats and other foolish things," wrote the *Messenger*. "It was a proud moment for the Stars," who had somehow acquired a nickname amid the glory.

There was still the matter of the kick to decide the game. Tension filled the air as the crowd cleared the field, and Mosse prepared for the decisive stationary kick. Gammons grabbed a towel and carefully wiped Mosse's foot, covered in mud from the melted dusting of snow. He also cleaned the hands of Richardson, who was lying flat on his stomach holding the ball, as was standard at the time. Not yet satisfied, Gammons gently wiped the ball and the ground underneath it.

A hush fell over the crowd as Mosse stepped back for the kick. He lined it up and drove it through the crossbars. The crowd again stormed the field like maniacs but was quickly silenced when the referee ordered a rekick. In an unprecedented ruling, according to the *Messenger*'s game description, it was called that Gammons had not removed the index finger of his other hand from under the ball, thus providing a better kicking surface for the attempt. Mosse had already escaped the crowd but was called back for a redo.

Both teams objected, causing an extended delay. Fultz claimed that no such rule existed, and the kick should count. Wallace argued that if the boot was illegal, then the score should stand at 5–5. The mob also participated in the debate before departing the turf with shouts of displeasure and re-assuming its collective position behind the ropes as the referee stood firm.

Mosse gave the people what they wanted and again struck the ball true for the glory of Homestead. The grit and heart of the champions prevailed. Fultz received an ovation reflective of his body of work throughout

As the holder for Mosse's game-winning kick attempt, Gammons lay flat on the ground, as was customary in this era.

the season. The *Press* also praised him in saying, "The public saw only half of Davy Fultz's skill. Preserving harmony in a team of 22 members was as great a feat as was winning the athletic championship." His players honored their popular coach privately with the gift of a handsome briar pipe, for what the *Messenger* termed "his manly policy in conducting the team during the season," before scattering to their homes around the country. For their part, the players received a bonus of 20 percent of ticket sales from the extra game, amounting to nearly $50 each, according to the *Post*.

Fultz penned his reflections on the season next to Temple's in the *Press*. While the media enjoyed portraying the drama, as the engineer of the operation, he provided unique insight into the mechanics and challenges of building an effective team at the early stage of the game's development. Though appreciating the group's excellence, Fultz recognized its limitations and the possibilities for the game's progress.

> In the development of the Homestead team of the present season ... the possibilities of this strong aggregation, composed as it is of many of the best players the game has produced, have never been shown. The short season and the little time allowed for preliminary work precluded the possibility of devoting much time to the rudiments of the game.... Many of the players had been pursuing sedentary vocations since the previous season, and in consequence were over-weight and soft. To these defects and the lack of time to eradicate them may be attributed most of the injuries received in the early part of the season. The form displayed in this [the Lalus] game was miserable ... for from that date their work showed wonderful improvement.
>
> The team work, however, has not reached that degree of perfection that would have been attained were it possible to have a good second eleven to work against. Nothing of this kind could be obtained in or near Pittsburg so the team has had no line-up except in the regular games.... It is safe to say that could a strong opponent have been secured every afternoon the playing strength of the team would today be 30 per cent greater.... The men have proved a hard working tractable set, and ... it is difficult to see why they should not be ranked as members of one of the best teams Pittsburg has ever produced.

Collier's **magazine frequently provided excellent football coverage and art.**

Ironically, despite his resignation from the university before the 1901 season, Wallace pulled his pro team together to end its schedule with a charity game at Penn with the Quakers—the week after Penn coach Woodruff resigned following a disastrous campaign. After Penn's provost was given the honor of starting the game with the kickoff, doing his best to push it 10 yards, the pros manhandled the varsity like many other teams did that season.

1701-1901

Yale Alumni
versus
YALE

YALE UNIVERSITY *Bicentennial*
Souvenir ~ Football ~ Program

Jo 1807

After the 1901 season, Yale's legends turned out to play its varsity in an alumni game during its bicentennial year. Returning stars included Walter Camp (with ball), Oliver Thompson (to Camp's right), Perry Hale (behind Camp to the right), and Pudge Heffelfinger (two to Hale's right).

While the *Inquirer* called pro football in Philadelphia an innovation, it did so while recognizing its potential, given strong public support. Before year-end, reports out of New York in the *Messenger* indicated that a larger professional league was being considered for 1902. Pirates owner Barney Dreyfuss was interested in the plan, having observed Homestead's games on the Pirates' field at Exposition Park. Chicago, New York, and Boston were mentioned as possible additions.

As a passionate investor and believer in the virtues of the game, Temple concluded his assessment of the season in the *Press* more convinced than ever that its future was in professionalism:

> In order to get the best of anything—in sport, science or art—you must secure people who are peculiarly adapted to the thing in which they take part, and you must secure people who have at their disposal absolutely the time necessary to perfect themselves for their positions … this is impossible unless they can obtain their means of livelihood while participating in their chosen calling, and I firmly believe that as every year goes by this hue and cry from certain minority sources as to the wrong of professionalism will become less and less until it ceases entirely.

The Quaker Oats Company

CEREALS, FLOUR AND FEED

CEDAR RAPIDS, IOWA   December 13, 1935

Mr. Perry Hale,
Middletown, Conn.

Dear Perry:

It is many years since I have seen you and I regret very much to hear of the unfortunate accident though I know nothing of the details. I saw an article in the papers which refers to this so thought I would write and offer you my deepest sympathy.

I am in receipt of a letter from Fred Crolius whom I have also not seen for twenty-five or thirty years. He is connected in some way with the Department of Public Works in the city of Pittsburgh.

Why not start a controversy and write articles for the newspaper claiming that the old Homestead team could lick anything that was playing today. Nobody could prove we couldn't. I often think of the old crowd and get out the pictures of the team which I have saved with the newspaper accounts of the old games.

I have, of course, seen Bill Church and once or twice saw Johnny Hall, George Young, also Dave Fultz and Caff Gammons. Saw Richardson a year or two before he died and saw Peter Overfield once which is about the extent of my knowledge of the old crowd. Being so far away I do not get back to the eastern games and have my difficulties in upholding the honor of the east in this hotbed of the Big Ten.

Yours truly,

Arthur Poe

AP:PE

Thirty-four years after playing together for Homestead, Arthur Poe wrote to Perry Hale to reconnect and relive their glory.

⇌ 1902: Pittsburg's Last Stand ⇌

Homestead's two-year reign atop the sport was short-lived, however. Enthusiasm for football's pro model had grown exponentially in the region, with Temple claiming in his 1901 season-ending *Press* writeup that pro teams in Western Pennsylvania numbered in the hundreds. But as the fall 1902 season approached, little appeared in the media about HL&AC's plans. According to the *Press*, in 1901, Temple and his associates lost $8,000, which was a manageable total to them. His cronies, though, were not as eager to reorganize as he was, and HL&AC initially announced plans to field an amateur team. Instead, Temple set his sights on bigger things and became chairman of the executive committee of the first National Football League.

The initial impetus for the league was the new baseball rivalry in Philadelphia generated by the start of the American League in 1901. Competition for fans and a court battle over the startup A.L. Athletics' signing of Phillies players made for constant dissension between Phillies owner John Rogers and Athletics majority owner Ben Shibe. When Rogers decided to start a pro football team, Shibe did not want him to have a leg up on that front. Albert Kennedy, the Penn alum who had quarterbacked Wallace's team the prior year, was named the football Phillies coach and captain. Wallace seized the opportunity to marry a richer spouse than his previous sponsor and convinced Shibe to stoke the local rivalry on the gridiron with himself at the helm. Shibe bought in, contingent upon his trusted minority owner and manager, Connie Mack, handling the finances.

A local championship would be nice, but a world championship sounded much more impressive and lucrative. So, Rogers and Shibe buried the hatchet long enough to realize that they needed a team in Pittsburgh to lend prestige and marketability to their operation. With every other major pro team in Western Pennsylvania out of business in 1902, they called Dave Berry to put together a team in Greensburg that would uphold Western Pennsylvania's honor. Since neither Rogers nor Shibe could trust the other to administer the league, they named Berry president.

The *Pittsburg Post* reported on September 14, 1902, that the Pirates' Dreyfuss backed the team and that it was "handled" by club president Harry Pulliam, who would become the sixth president of the National League the following year. While initially referred to as the Greensburg Pros in the local press, this name did nothing to secure a following in the Pittsburgh area. Soon they became known locally as the Pittsburg Stars. The baseball Pirates' backing was not publicized in Western Pennsylvania, but in Philadelphia, the *Inquirer* often referred to the Stars as the Pirates.

Still smarting from his exit at Penn, Coach Woodruff announced interest in leading a team in Chicago, and backers assembled to put up another

Shiring collection

**Bob Shiring,
1902 Pittsburg Stars**

squad in New York. Finally, with plans falling into place, Temple's pal, A.C. Dinkey, general superintendent of the Homestead Steel Works, who had brought Temple into HL&AC, considered reviving the Homestead operation to bring the league to six potential teams.

Shiring and other stars from the Homestead squad, including running backs Harry "Pud" McChesney, "Indian" Artie Miller from Carlisle, and quarterback "Little" Willis Richardson from Brown, who was named captain, already committed to join Berry in the countryside to chase the game. As some players retired, including Fultz and Overfield, they were replaced by other top players who would play prominent roles in the ensuing era. These included massive tackle John "Jack" Lang of W&J, who came home after playing for Wallace in Philadelphia, and giant 6-foot-5 guard Herman Kerkhoff of Purdue via a pro team in Denver.

Up-and-coming New York Giants baseball star pitcher Christy Mathewson was also recruited to lure fans in a push to reach a critical mass in attendance. "Big Six," Mathewson's nickname from New York's most famous fire engine of the time, had also starred as a college football player at fullback for Bucknell in Central Pennsylvania. He had just finished his second year in pro baseball, with a 14–17 record for the eighth-place Giants, when he was brought into Berry's fold. A condition of the multisport professional's interest, as told to the author by Shiring's daughter, Irene, was that Shiring anchor the line as the team's center to preserve Mathewson's well-being for his baseball career.

Shiring also received kudos in a September 30, 1902, *Press* article for his development the previous year:

> Shiring, who was Pete Overfield's substitute last year with the Homestead All-Stars, has improved 50 per cent over last season's form. Shiring is a Pittsburg boy, and the members of the team are congratulating him on the way in which he handles himself. Shiring was taken in hand last year on numerous occasions by Pete Overfield, who was acknowledged to be the best center rush in the business, and the schooling given the big fellow by the old Penn center will be of great benefit to him if he makes the center position this year on the Pittsburg team.

Berry initially considered Lafayette's All-American Walter Bachman for the starting center job, but Shiring won out, and Bachman landed with Kennedy's Phillies. Wallace and Kennedy went about filling their rosters mostly by splitting their team from the previous year and adding more alums from Penn. Wallace thought that he had an in with Fultz, who had played second base for Mack's 1901 Athletics baseball team, but Fultz chose to start his coaching career at Lafayette instead. Wallace landed other key talent in Hawley Pierce from Homestead and filled his last spot with center Lynn

Shiring collection

Christy Mathewson, 1902 Pittsburg Stars

Mathewson was an American icon and is still considered one of the top five pitchers of all time. He was revered for his character as much as his skill.

"Pop" Sweet, who had split his college years between Bucknell and State College. Sweet's unenviable task was to replace the expired Bull and duel Shiring in the middle of the line. Sweet was undersized for a center at 172 pounds, 60 less than Shiring, but played the position with unusual agility and an aggressive edge. They would face off for years to come.

The support and rivalry of the Philadelphia baseball backers assured the establishment of those teams. Dinkey had the desire to resuscitate the Homestead team but not the experience or available talent to make it happen on short notice. Without a competitive team, he said that he would instead provide a team the following year. A field was secured in Chicago, and White Sox owner Charles Comiskey joined the league's executive committee. Still, enough capable players could not be signed there to satisfy backers of either of the Windy City's baseball clubs. Nothing more was heard from the New York group. So, the first NFL proceeded with only three Pennsylvania teams.

The rest of the trio's schedules of between 11 and 13 games was filled with the usual college and lesser pro teams with which the game results were not in doubt. For the Stars, highlights included Mathewson playing against his Bucknell alma mater and two bloodbaths with the East End Athletic Club. One East Ender still held a grudge against Shiring for leaving the team the previous year and instigated two slugging matches with him, the second of which lasted for 10 minutes and resulted in their ejection.

"Matty," as he was also known, was outperformed in the backfield by the heavier Shirley Ellis of Harvard, but he contributed to the team as the greatest punter in the sport. When low attendance became the norm, Mathewson's salary was prohibitive for a punter on a team that rarely needed to punt. He was released with two others after the club's seventh game, a solid 18–0 win over the Phillies at the Colosseum on Pittsburgh's North Side, before the club relinquished a point on the season.

Fortunately, Mathewson was not affected by injury, as he went on to win 30 or more games for the Giants for the next three years and become the face of baseball for nearly a generation. He cemented his legendary Hall of Fame baseball career and status as a national icon by tossing three shutouts in New York's 1905 World Series win over Mack's Philadelphia Athletics. As the ace of the Giants' staff over 17 years, he finished with a record of 373–188, still tied for the most wins in National League history with Grover Cleveland Alexander.

In baseball, a sport known at the time for a culture dominated by rural roughnecks, Matty brought a new level of class and honor to America's pastime and became known as "the Christian Gentleman." One myth holds that his sportsmanship was so admired that an umpire—blinded by dust after Mathewson's slide into home plate—asked him if he was out. "He got me," said Matty. The opposing catcher asked him, "Why would you do that?"

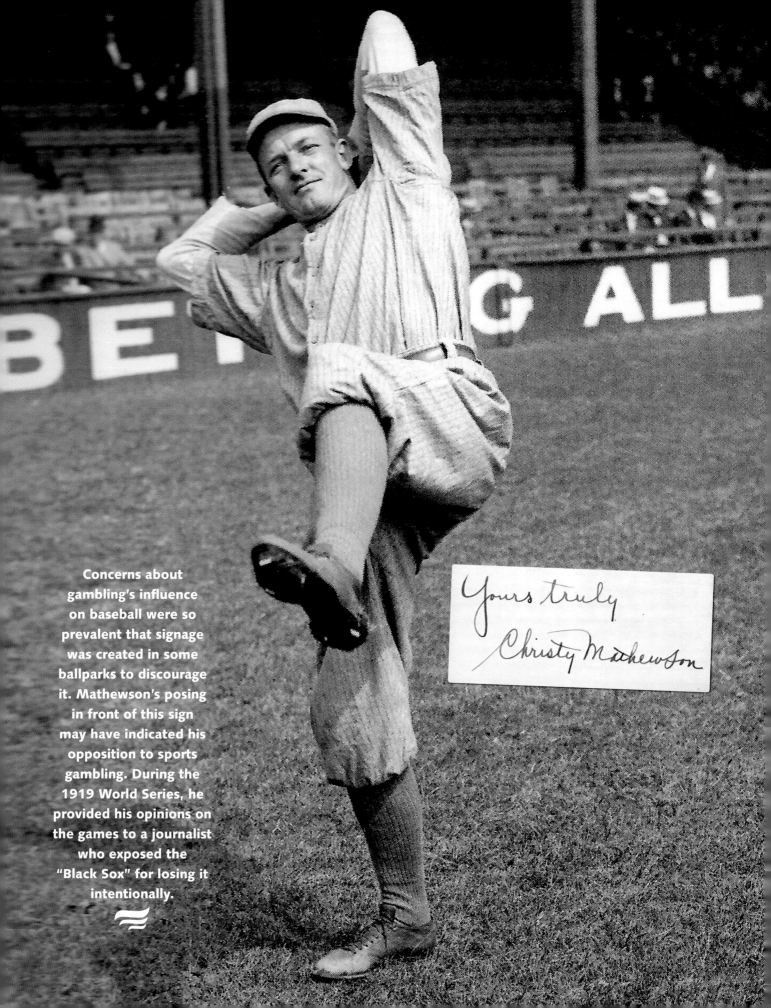

Concerns about gambling's influence on baseball were so prevalent that signage was created in some ballparks to discourage it. Mathewson's posing in front of this sign may have indicated his opposition to sports gambling. During the 1919 World Series, he provided his opinions on the games to a journalist who exposed the "Black Sox" for losing it intentionally.

1902 Pittsburg Stars

Images from Bob Shiring's team photo album

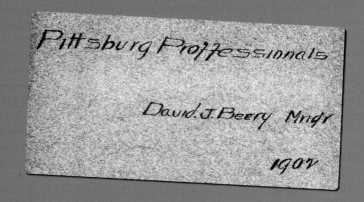

Pittsburg Proffessionals

David. J. Beery Mngr

1902

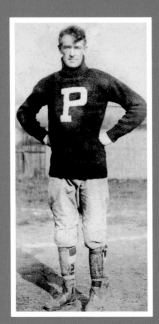

Fred Crolius–HB

Harry McChesney–HB

Artie Miller–HB

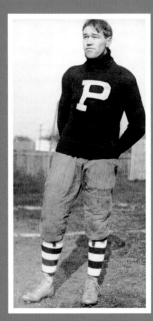

Shirley Ellis–FB

Nelson Hare–E

Max McNulty–T

P.J. Lawler–G

**Captain Willis
Richardson–QB**

Bob Shiring snapping the ball from center at a Stars practice in Greensburg, Pennsylvania

The Stars taking a break from practice

Rody
McCutcheon–T, G

Jack Lang–T

William Feightner–T

Joe Donohoe–E

Matty responded, "Because I'm a church elder." Tragically, while co-owner of the Boston Braves, Mathewson died at age 45 in 1925 after an extended battle with tuberculosis resulting from a chemical weapons testing accident during his time with the Army in Europe in World War I.

Financial pressure led Berry to try to strike a balance by minimizing expenses with player salaries and less costly facilities in Greensburg, while maximizing revenue by playing the big games in the city. But the timing of Mathewson's dismissal may have cost the team a win when punting was at a premium in the Stars' next game against Wallace's Athletics at Columbia Ball Park in Philadelphia.

A punt return by Pud McChesney for a touchdown gave the Stars an early lead. The attempt for the extra point was an adventure: an odd rule, first requiring a punt straight out from behind the goal line from the point at which the line was crossed, before a kick for one point could be attempted from the spot at which the punt was fielded by the punter's team. The Stars failed to field the punt and the score remained 5–0. The Athletics tied the score at five on a field goal by Lafayette's fullback Dave Cure. The Stars' giant Kerkhoff then scored just before the half on one of his many long plows. The *Inquirer* said he "tore through the Athletics' line like so much

1902 Pittsburg Stars. Christy Mathewson and Bob Shiring are seated next to each other at the far right of the middle row.

paper." Richardson missed the kicking part of this extra point attempt, and the Stars led 10–5 at the break.

Early in the second half, Syracuse's Paul "Twister" Steinberg carried several defenders on a 22-yard run to the Stars' 4-yard line, putting the Athletics in scoring position. As linemen were eligible to line up behind the line of scrimmage and carry the ball, Wallace did the honors himself and drove in for what turned out to be the winning touchdown on a tackle back play. Cure's successful conversion gave the Athletics an 11–10 victory. The punting duel was essential in determining field position for the remainder of the game when both teams' defenses stiffened. As fullbacks also handled punting duties, Cure outkicked Ellis to keep the Athletics in control. It was a major victory for Wallace, whose team had been underdogs by odds of up to 3–1, as he had yet to defeat a Pittsburgh team in his three years as a pro.

The championship had not yet been decided, though, because the Athletics and Phillies had split two games earlier in the season. The Stars also lost to the Phillies 11–0 in Philadelphia the week before Thanksgiving. Kennedy was given credit in the Philly papers for savvy coaching adjustments. Richardson said that both of the Stars' losses in Philly were due to the effects of the drinking water from the Schuylkill River. In either case, a win by the Stars in Pittsburgh on Thanksgiving Day would create a three-way tie.

As the season wound down, financial considerations seemed to become more pressing than the world championship to the teams' managers. Connie Mack refused to let his team take the field in Pittsburgh until he received his team's $2,000 guarantee due from Dave Berry. There was a reason he was also nicknamed "Foxy Mac." After an hour's delay, it took the head of Carnegie Steel, William Corey, to come out of the stands to appease the screaming fans and resolve matters. According to an article in the *Press* the following day, on November 28, titled "Professionals Stir Up Scandal":

> The gate receipts amounted to fully $2,000, but this money was attached by W.C. Temple, who with W.E. Corey advanced the money to pay the rent of the Colosseum. The money loaned by them had not been paid and as they had every reason to believe that the season would close yesterday W.C. Temple took legal steps to protect himself.
>
> Connie Mack is not in the game for his health, and he refused to take any chances, especially since he learned from members of the Bucknell team and from the Windsor hotel of Philadelphia, something of the method or of the lack of method in the handling of the financial affairs of the Greensburg team. He would not allow his team to go on the field yesterday until the money due him was guaranteed, but when he learned that W.E. Corey was willing to run the play he ordered his men out of the dressing room and the game went on.

Shiring's reputation continued to grow in the Pittsburgh media, per this 1902 *Pittsburg Press* illustration.

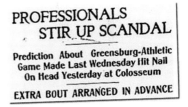

Rumors of game-fixing surfaced when a tie forced an extra game, though such allegations were common when outcomes did not favor gamblers.

Though Mack did not even know who Corey was, some more informed peers assured him that his check would not bounce. That only covered the Athletics' side of the equation, however. The *Press* further reported on why Mack may have had his guard up:

> The *Press* received information on Wednesday afternoon that the result of the Thanksgiving Day game at the Colosseum would furnish the two professional clubs with a good excuse for playing an extra game tomorrow. It was reported then that someone connected with the badly managed Greensburg team had authorized negotiations with the Western University team for possession of the Colosseum tomorrow, a date given to the WUPs in the schedule prepared last September. The guess proved to be correct. Greensburg and the Athletics played to a no score game yesterday after three thousand persons had been shivering in the stands for nearly an hour after the time fixed for the kick-off.

The fact that the Athletics missed four field goal attempts and ran an unsuccessful play from the Stars' 5-yard line, instead of trying another kick as time expired, did nothing to alter this perception. The same *Press* story then confirmed that the teams would meet again the next day. The Stars' press agent denied premeditation by saying, "The Philadelphians intended going back to Philadelphia after yesterday's game, but [the] captains … were anxious to have a more decisive battle and the managers of the teams agreed upon the game tomorrow afternoon."

The *Press* strongly asserted otherwise, in stating, "This is a mistake. Connie Mack told friends early yesterday morning that his team would play another game here and would not leave the city until Saturday night."

If true, the players likely had to be complicit in a tie outcome to justify the rematch, though a Stars win also offered cause for a tiebreaking game. It became clear immediately after the next game, when many of the players sued the team for wages due, that the Stars players knew they were in jeopardy of not being paid the balance of their contracts. So, creating another opportunity for fans to fork over money at the gates made some sense.

For the Athletics' part, after resolving the financial issue, the question of holding the world title was next on their minds. They claimed before the rematch that it would be an exhibition and preemptively claimed the championship based on the current records of the three teams against each other.

Disenchanted fans voted with their feet. Fewer than 1,500 returned for the encore, a well-played 11–0 Stars win decided only by two punts fumbled by the Athletics deep in their end late in the game. "Had the affairs of the Professional League been conducted in a manner to gain

Cornelius McGillicuddy (aka Connie Mack)

the confidence of the public, a game between two teams that had played a tie game two days before would have attracted a crowd of fully 10,000 people," the *Press* complained, "but the squabbles over the financial end of it disgusted the football enthusiasts, and only a comparatively meager number were in attendance."

Despite the Athletics' claims, publications from both cities recognized the Stars as the champions. Given identical league records of 2–2–1, as with boxing, the Stars claimed the title with the last victory. They also won based on cumulative point differential in league games. Finally, and most definitively, the Stars' David J. Berry was also president of the league, and he reaffirmed that his team was the NFL champions, in case there was any doubt.

To throw another variable into the equation, the Athletics and Phillies decided to play another game the following Saturday to decide Philadelphia's city championship. The Athletics won 17–6, with players occasionally diving from the icy turf into fieldside snowbanks after the ball. Mack's group could now claim that it had the league's best winning percentage, but even the hometown *Inquirer* would only credit them with the local professional football championship.

Regardless, many years later, Mack and at least one of his players stuck to their version of the truth. In a December 23, 1936, interview in the *Sandusky Star-Journal* (Ohio), Mack said:

The 1902 Philadelphia Athletics anointed themselves as champions despite their record and public opinion.

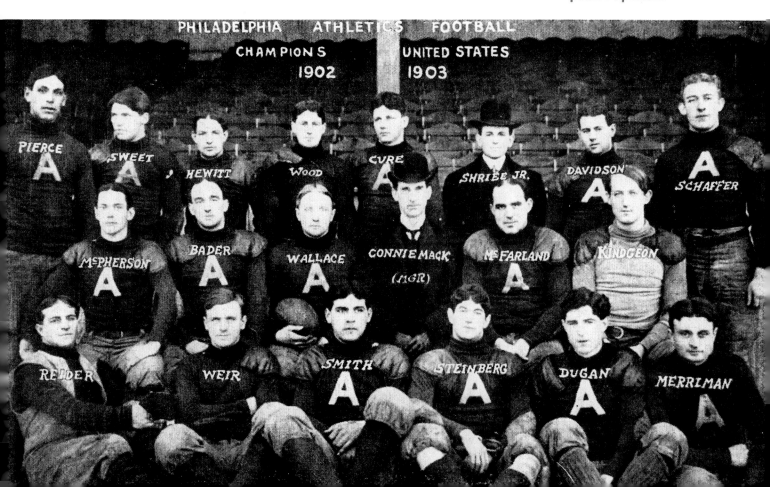

But I had another team back in 1902 that went through a season undefeated and untied. That was the year Blondy Wallace, who played some pretty good football at the University of Pennsylvania, asked me to start a professional football team.... We won every game that year. But that was the last time I tried professional football. John [Shibe, Ben's son and Athletics business manager] and I lost our shirts.

"Foxy Mac," indeed. Even if the Athletics' last game with the Stars was considered an exhibition, they lost another game to the Phillies and tied their second game with the Stars, although under questionable circumstances. The Athletics' $4,000 team loss reported by the *Inquirer* equates to approximately $104,000 in today's dollars, which is a lot of shirts to lose. Perhaps talking himself and others into believing they won it all filled the hole in Mack's wallet.

Twister Steinberg further twisted the truth in a February 14, 1953, article in the *Syracuse Herald-Journal*:

> Scoring the only touchdown in the deciding victory that brought Connie Mack's Philadelphia Athletics the world professional football championship of 1902 was my biggest thrill. We were playing Pittsburgh in the crucial game in Philadelphia. The boys from the Smoky City were leading, 5–0, with three minutes to go. Coach "Blondy" Wallace sent me around the end position played by Art Poe, former Princeton All-America, and I went 40 yards to score, shaking off several tacklers along the way.... We triumphed 6–5!

Based on multiple newspaper sources, there are five errors in those three sentences. Steinberg can be forgiven on the minor points, such as the score of the game, the length of his glorious run, or the amount of time remaining when he made it—he was 72 years old at the time of the interview. But Wallace scoring the winning TD and Pittsburgh being declared champion should have been more memorable. Maybe he and Mack thought nobody would ever bother to do a fact check on such things.

One thing that the teams and players of the first NFL could agree on was that this would be the last year of pro football in these cities ... for the foreseeable future. It would be the last pro football championship for the city of Pittsburgh until the Steelers of the 1970s. It was the end of an era.

Shiring collection

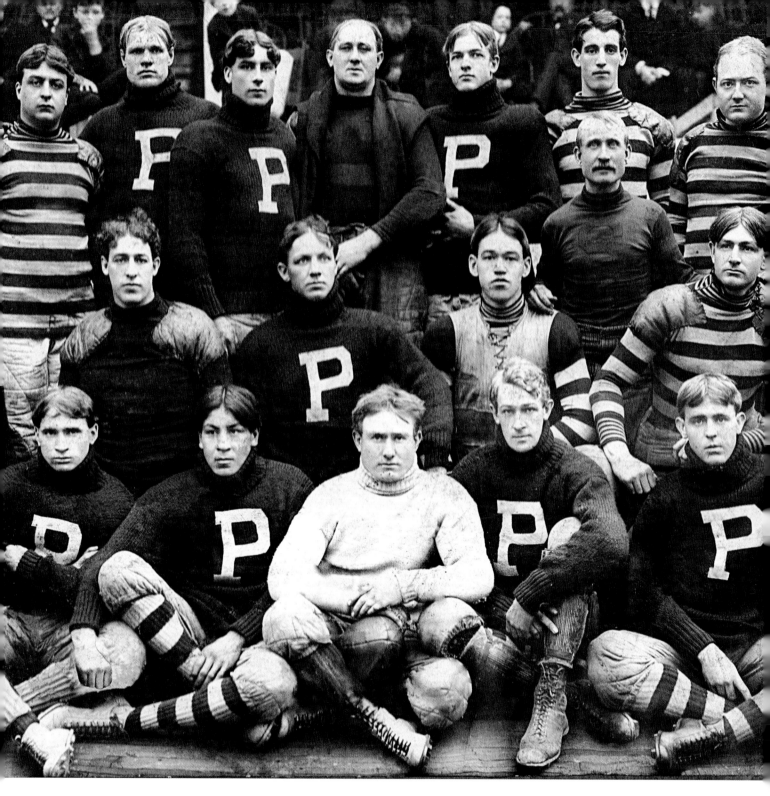

The Pittsburg Stars were the true 1902 national professional champions. Front row: Ed Sherlock, Harry McChesney, Artie Miller, Willis Richardson (captain), Fred Crolius, Charles Weller. Middle row: Willie Hensinger (assistant trainer), Nelson Hare, Jack Lang, Michael Dushane, Shirley Ellis, David Sheehan (trainer), Max McNulty. Back row: Charles Barney, Rody McCutcheon, Herman Kerkhoff, William Feightner, P.J. Lawler, Christy Mathewson, Clark Schrontz, Bob Shiring.

1902 Madison Square Garden Indoor Championship Tournament

Those passionate about the pro game, whether players or financiers, continued to experiment with its business model. Within weeks of the end of the 1902 season, Madison Square Garden manager and promoter Tom O'Rourke hastily coordinated the first indoor pro football games at the famous venue to try to fill seats during a slow time of year in sports and for his business. As the top pro teams disbanded after the recent season, the Garden planned to host the best eight teams available for the "indoor pro championship of the world." They proceeded with five: Syracuse Athletic Association, Knickerbocker Athletic Club, Warlow Athletic Club from Long Island, Orange Athletic Club, and a loosely organized team called New York. Games were scheduled from December 29 through New Year's Eve. The size of the field fitting the Garden's confines was closer to that of the modern-day Arena League. "The goal lines were seventy yards apart and the width of the playing space was scarcely more than thirty-five yards," according to the *New York Times*.

Blondy Wallace was game for anything to make a buck and recruited 11 of his buddies from both Philadelphia squads to fill out a team. So, O'Rourke branded Wallace's group as New York, intending to provide the home town crowd with the thrill of victory. As usual, things did not work out as planned. Cornell grad Pop Warner rallied some of his fellow alums—and also leveraged his influence as Carlisle's coach—to recruit the Pierce brothers to form the Syracuse AC team, which was unusually motivated for its opening game with Wallace's New York squad. As the *Jersey City News* reported on December 24, "In honor of their Indian players, the members of the Syracuse Club have adopted an Indian war cry, suggested by [Hawley] Pierce, which will be used by the 600 rooters from Syracuse when their team meets the New York palefaces in the first game of the tournament next Monday evening."

Syracuse defeated New York 5–0 in a fight-filled game that gave the fans what they wanted. However, Warner incurred a minor head injury in the game, and Wallace volunteered to replace him for the remaining games. Syracuse went on to defeat the Orange AC 36–0 for the tournament crown, which was also Wallace's first championship as a professional.

Interestingly, years later, this entrepreneurial indoor event became retroactively known as the World Series of Football. Coincidentally, or not, baseball's first World Series took place the following year, in the fall of 1903, between Barney Dreyfuss's National League champion Pittsburg Pirates and the American League champion Boston Americans (soon to play as the Red Sox in 1908). After the 1919 World Series debacle, in which most of the Chicago White Sox starters were influenced by gamblers to intentionally lose the Series to the Cincinnati Reds, Boston's all-time great pitcher Denton "Cy" Young, who won two games in the 1903 Series and lost one, revealed that he was approached with an offer of a $20,000 bribe if he wouldn't "bear down" in his outings. At that time, there were no safeguards against sports corruption, and there were no laws against bribery. Nonetheless, Young rebuffed the gambler by saying, "If you put any value at all on your money, you'd better bet it on me to win." He added, "The fellow who tried to tempt me was a man known as [John] 'Sport' Sullivan. He offered to hand over more than my salary if I would 'throw' a ball game. My salary was only $1,500 a year, but I promptly handed Sullivan a punch in the jaw and kicked him out of my room." Sullivan was a nationally known sports prognosticator who was arrested for charges related to gambling and bookmaking several times. He was also a primary figure in the Black Sox scandal.

It was a sign of the times.

The 1902 Syracuse Athletic Association team included experienced pros Hawley and Bemus Pierce and Glenn "Pop" Warner (back row, third to fifth from left). Warner previously coached Hawley at the Carlisle Indian Industrial School.

TESTING THE LIMITS OF PROFESSIONALISM: THE OHIO ERA

Stewart deserves a pretty big share of the credit due the whole team.... He's a great coach and everyone knows it. Who got the Tigers together and organized them? Stewart. Who worked with them early and late, faced tremendous discouragement and saw them through eleven big games, of which the Tigers lost one? Stewart. Who conceived and carried out the plan of winning the state championship? Stewart. —Massillon mayor Jacob J. Wise, 1903

While Pittsburgh is the birthplace of professional football, Eastern Ohio calls itself the cradle of the pro game. This is an important nuance that even the Pro Football Hall of Fame clarifies in its museum exhibits. Ohio is the cradle because the pro game moved west across the state line after its birth in Western Pennsylvania, when the first pro teams in the Keystone State failed after a decade. Figuratively, Pennsylvania handed the ball off to Ohio.

The pro game ventured west when the proud and passionate people in the small town of Massillon, Ohio, with a population of nearly 12,000 in 1900, were hungry for a winner. Their neighboring rivals from the larger cities of Canton (8 miles to its east) and Akron (22 miles to its north) and other strong amateur teams in Ohio had trounced them for years. Named after French Catholic bishop Jean Baptiste Massillon, the locality was

FOOT BALL!

AT

BUCHTEL COLLEGE GROUNDS

SATURDAY AFTERNOON AT 3:30

MASSILLON ATHLETIC CLUB,

VS

AKRON ATHLETIC CLUB.

Come and see an up-to-date game

ADMISSION, - 25 CENTS.

EDWIN MYERS PRINT, 104 MILL STREET, AKRON, OHIO.

Akron was the reigning state champion of Ohio before Massillon rose to the challenge.

Ohio Canal, Massillon, Ohio, circa 1900

Russell & Co. drove Massillon's economy through generations of industrial and community development since 1842.

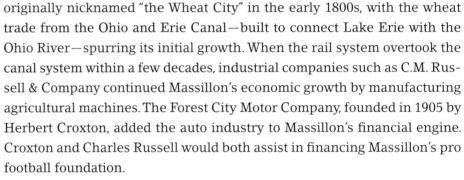
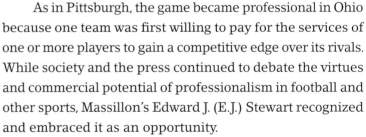

originally nicknamed "the Wheat City" in the early 1800s, with the wheat trade from the Ohio and Erie Canal—built to connect Lake Erie with the Ohio River—spurring its initial growth. When the rail system overtook the canal system within a few decades, industrial companies such as C.M. Russell & Company continued Massillon's economic growth by manufacturing agricultural machines. The Forest City Motor Company, founded in 1905 by Herbert Croxton, added the auto industry to Massillon's financial engine. Croxton and Charles Russell would both assist in financing Massillon's pro football foundation.

As in Pittsburgh, the game became professional in Ohio because one team was first willing to pay for the services of one or more players to gain a competitive edge over its rivals. While society and the press continued to debate the virtues and commercial potential of professionalism in football and other sports, Massillon's Edward J. (E.J.) Stewart recognized and embraced it as an opportunity.

Stewart, the son of a Methodist minister, was the most proactive among those wanting to bring the state championship home to Massillon. At age 26, in 1903, he graduated from medical school at Western Reserve University in Cleveland, where he played on the football team as a quarterback, and on the basketball, baseball, and track teams. He also played football and basketball at Mt. Union College in Alliance, Ohio, at the undergraduate level.

"Doc" Stewart came roaring out of the gate in his professional career full of ambition, quickly taking on multiple roles in Massillon. He held the office of city clerk and, like David Berry in Latrobe, he also entered the newspaper business as the city editor of the *Evening Independent*. The combination of these roles had the potential to create both great opportunities and conflicts of interest for him. He surely recognized that improving Massillon's football fortunes could provide a better lot in life for Massillonians and himself. Writing about his own team enabled him to market another operation in which he had a personal stake. He believed that he was the man to engineer both efforts. Bias be damned.

Jacob J. (J.J.) Wise, highly esteemed for his integrity and decency, had been mayor of Massillon from 1898 to 1902. Stewart wisely sought to enlist Wise's support in rallying community leaders to test the waters and fund one well-organized amateur team to bring home the state's football laurels. On September 3, 1903, a group of 35 Massillon civic leaders met in the town's Sailor Hotel and approved Stewart's proposal to slay the rivals that had tormented them. Beyond just wanting to win, they recognized that the Massillon community could benefit both tangibly and intangibly from a new sense of civic pride that football victories and championships had brought to other cities nearby. The people of Massillon were eager to stake their claim to some of the glory and profits.

The leadership group elected Wise to head the fundraising committee, halfback Jack Goodrich to manage the team, and Stewart to coach it. One of Stewart's first moves was to purchase new uniforms. Massillon's sporting goods store carried jerseys matching the Princeton Tigers' color scheme of black with orange stripes on the sleeves. Thus, the Massillon Tigers were born.

Stewart then recruited many of the town's burliest men to fill out his roster. Some were farmers, such as William "Farmer" Boerngen, and others were veteran police officers, such as Julius "Baldy" Wittman and Frank Botoner. Some had played the prior year for various local teams,

Shiring collection

Edward J. Stewart was the multitalented mastermind of the Massillon Tigers dynasty, on the field and in the media.

Jacob J. Wise, former mayor and the Tigers' first manager, was one of Massillon's most beloved citizens.

such as the three Miller brothers, who played for the Massillon Rolling Mill team, also known as the Stand Pats. Others, such as 32-year-old Wittman, who rarely allowed cameras to capture his bald head without a lid of some type, had never played the game at all. As one of the team's elder statesmen, he was named captain. When Stewart spotted talent during the season, including fullback Walt Roepke of the Akron Imperials, he reeled him in.

The Tigers lost their inaugural game at Wooster College 6–0 on September 26 amid typical comments that officials favored the home team. They quickly improved, though, and went on to win their next seven games without relinquishing a point, including a 16–0 win over Canton as 2-to-1 underdogs and a 34–0 win over Wooster in a Thanksgiving Day rematch initially intended to end their season.

The Tigers recruited some of their first players from the Massillon police force, including Julius "Baldy" Wittman (back left) and Frank Botoner (next to Wittman).

⇃ Akron's Airs ⇂

The Akron East Ends were undefeated over the two prior years, winning both state championships. They sounded content to claim their third without playing Massillon, gloating that the Tigers were unworthy of being on their schedule. But it eventually became clear to the Akronites that they could not avoid the Tigers without appearing to bear a yellow streak and having their title tainted.

The *Akron Beacon Journal* took offense to Massillon's initial proposition for a season-ending championship game and assumed a mocking tone in its response. In a November 27 article titled "A Ridiculous Challenge," the *Beacon Journal* wrote:

> Massillon's foot ball team manager challenged the East Akron foot ball team through the columns of a Cleveland paper Wednesday, to a game for the state championship, and had the effrontery to demand that the game be played in Massillon. After a few years' experience, it will dawn on the Massillon man that as the challenger he has no rights whatever, as regards time, place or any other conditions other than the financial one, and has no recourse but to give up all hope of ever playing for the state championship unless East Akron concedes it to him. His demand that the game be played in Massillon brought smiles to the faces of many a sporting man, and it is a cinch that the Massillon manager is either very unused to the ethics of a championship negotiation, or else he has the most colossal nerve of any man in the game. He further dictates the time for the game as December 5, at Massillon. Now, aside from the fact that all championship games are played on the grounds designated by the champions, the challenged party, Massillon has no enclosed grounds, and offers a guarantee of $100 or 60 and 40 per cent. While the Massillon manager no doubt considers this a most magnanimous offer, the management of the East Akron team would not consider it for a minute. It would hardly be sufficient to buy [Akron halfback] "Billy" Stephens' chewing gum, to say nothing of paying the other necessary expense. The East Akron team, so far from refusing Massillon's challenge flatly, has even conceded a day for a game with Massillon. But it must be played in Akron; it must be played next Saturday, a week earlier than the Massillon man suggests; the winner takes all and the loser pays his own expense.

The following day, Akron manager Kasch took it a step further, saying to a delegation of Massillon representatives during negotiations on terms, "Why you're only a green team. You couldn't possibly hope to defeat our seasoned aggregation of experienced salaried players with your one year team." The Tigers acceded to all of Akron's terms, including accepting only a 75/25 split. But Akron's condescending tone in the process may have played a part in provoking Massillon's next move. Many of the Tigers' forces suffered from injuries that would prevent them from playing, including Boerngen, who had a finger amputated during the week, when it became entangled in equipment during a shift at the Russell Engine Company shops. Egos were on the line, and circumstances forced Stewart's hand.

⤜ The Four Ringers ⤛

How the arrangement transpired is unclear, but on December 6, 1903, Bob Shiring and three of his teammates from Pittsburgh's East End Athletic Club, coached by Jim Lalus, joined the Massillon Tigers for the state championship game of Ohio on the home field of the Akron East Ends. Without a pro team playing in Pittsburgh in 1903, many of Western Pennsylvania's former pros were initially content to rejoin local amateur squads. Some rejoined Lalus's club, including those recruited by the Tigers: Bob Shiring, Harry McChesney, and "Doc" McChesney, who had both played with Shiring for Homestead but were not brothers, and a fellow whose full name has remained a mystery.

The main obstacle in identifying many pro football players from the turn of the twentieth century is that newspapers of that era most often did not list first names in game stories or box scores. Star players' first names appeared more often, but last names frequently showed with different spellings across various publications, even in the same publications over time. Shiring's name, for example, appeared in various sources as Sherring, Sharing, Scheuring, and so on. A misspelling may lead a search engine to miss a significant story. Some players also played under assumed names to avoid the taint of professionalism.

The Pro Football Researchers Association did yeoman's work, starting in 1979, to produce the research that it did before the Internet. Still, its founder, Bob Carroll, was not able to solve the mystery of the fourth pro Tiger's name in his article, "Ohio Tiger Trap," on the 1903 season. In his usual style, Carroll joked about "Pfeifer," "F. Piper," or "Peiper's" sterling reputation as one of Massillon's four ringers. On October 25, 1903, the *Pittsburg Press* listed a tackle for Lalus's East End AA as Peifer. However, further research for this project documented the American legal name of the Tigers' fourth pro recruit as Frank John Piefer.

According to Baltimore passenger lists on Ancestry.com, Franz Piefer was born in Germany in 1879 and arrived at age two in the U.S. with his immigrant parents and three siblings in 1881. Piefer's amateur football career may have started when he suited up with Doc McChesney on a United States Army team that played on the arsenal grounds in the Lawrenceville section of Pittsburgh in 1900. Army registration and burial records show

Rivals

The 1903 Tigers (top) and Akron Athletic Club faced off in a hotly contested and controversial championship that brought Ohio football into the professional era.

Doc McChesney—
Massillon Tigers. Along
with being two of the
four ringers, McChesney
and Bob Shiring were
close football comrades,
playing together on three
teams for at least part
of every season from
1903 to 1908.

that they were both veterans of the 1898 Spanish-American War. On October 21, 1900, the *Pittsburg Post* remarked about Uncle Sam's team's 28–0 victory over the Empire State AC of Allegheny: "The Army team is surprising its followers by putting up a fine game. The feature of yesterday's game was an 85-yard run by Pieper for a touchdown."

It is uncertain whether the star tackle named Peffer, who played for a good Beloit College team (aside from its 89–0 loss to Michigan) in Wisconsin in 1901, or the 1902 Cleveland AA tackle Piper, is the same person. However, shortly after Cleveland's season ended in mid-November 1902, the *Post* reported on November 22 that "Piper" showed up to play for Oil City, north of Pittsburgh, alongside many of the imported Lalus East End team, including one of the McChesneys. They proceeded to beat wealthy rooters of their close-by rival, Franklin, out of a wad of money, 6–5, in their first of three consecutive contests within a week. The *Post* then reported on November 28 that "Pieper" was in the lineup for the second game against Franklin the following weekend, a scoreless tie, in which the East End boys did not play. They returned en masse, though, as well as "Pieper," for the following day's rematch that Oil City won 11–0 to solidify Venango County bragging rights.

Clearly, Piefer's connection to both McChesneys and Lalus's team brought him to play for Lalus in 1903. "Frank Peiffer" appears in a *Pittsburg Post* article on August 30, 1903, "East End A.A. to Be Made Up of Many Stars," which mentions that he also played for the team in 1902, though this remains undocumented elsewhere. His name also appears as Frank Piper in the *Pittsburg Press*, on November 4, 1903, in a game against WUP a few weeks before the Massillon vs. Akron East Ends game: "Frank Piper and Doc McChesney, the tackles, were strong at their positions and were good ground gainers."

J.I. "Doc" McChesney's first name is more elusive than Piefer's last name. Searches of newspaper databases rarely reveal even his first initial. It turns out that his family and legal documents referred to him by his middle name. Unlike Doc Stewart, who had a medical degree, J. Irwin McChesney of Verona, Pennsylvania, was not a doctor. He was employed as a railroad detective in Pittsburgh. Most likely, his nickname came about because he was not fond of the name Irwin, as the 1900 census and his marriage and death certificates listed him.

Harry Vincent "Pud" McChesney was born in Pittsburgh, according to his death certificate, and his father's name differs from Doc's. He bore no resemblance to Doc, as Doc was a tall, 6-foot-1, 190-pound, dark-haired lineman, and Harry was a short, 5-foot-9, 165-pound, fair-haired versatile running back, who also performed well as a placekicker and punter. Harry also had a long career in professional baseball, spending 22 games with the Chicago Cubs in 1904 and the rest of his 12-year career across four minor league associations.

Shiring collection

Frank Piefer: the previously unidentified fourth Massillon ringer

⊱ Akron's Angst ⊰

Rumors circulated in Eastern Ohio during the week leading up to the title clash with Akron that Massillon would put pros from outside of Massillon on the field. Akron management stated in the papers that its team would not play the game under these circumstances. But financial interests likely won out, and plans for the game went forward.

The ringers did their part in a victory that a *Beacon Journal* writer called "hollow" on December 7. "Shirring" and "Peiper" helped dominate the line of scrimmage, and Doc picked up a fumble of a punt by his fellow McChesney for the Tigers' first touchdown. Stewart recounted in the *Independent* the following day that after the touchdown, "A carrier pigeon shot out from the crowd, circled once or twice, then darted home with the first message from the field.... The message, scribbled on a piece of faded yellow ribbon, of 'Tigers 6, Akron 0, first half,' was sent to the *Independent* office. The *Independent* posted the bulletin and the crowd cheered in Massillon."

One more touchdown in the second half provided the Tigers' final 12–0 margin of victory. The *Independent* described it beautifully:

> Once inside of the twenty-five yard line and it looked all off for Akron. "Right tackle back," sang out the quarterback, and "Doc" McChesney sprang back of the line; "20-28-34" came the signal, and "Doc" launched himself at the line. It gave way, and the runner burst through, though a dozen hands reached for him, only to lose their grip. "Doc" set sail for the line. Akron's quarterback was in the road, but with a plunge "Doc" met him and the man rolled to one side. The collision had been a hard one, however, and the ball shot out of Doc's hand into the air and on towards the goal line. Vogt, Peiper, Haag and Stewart were after it like lightning. Stewart was deliberately tackled in the open and thrown, but Vogt and Peiper dove for the ball at the same time and it was "Herm's" [Vogt] and the second touchdown had been recorded. Again did the Tiger fans simply go mad. Dignified business men danced about like children, hats, canes and ribbons fluttered in the air.

A bitter *Beacon Journal* writer declared, "It is hard to determine just where Massillon finds any glory in winning out with a team imported from another state to fight out a game for the championship of Ohio." In fairness, the *Beacon Journal* also reported the account of several Canton spectators who commented that Massillon's new stars outperformed two Akron newcomers from Yale and Princeton, while at the same time denying that the claim was true.

Decades later, on December 12, 1933, the *Beacon Journal*'s article, titled "Burns, After 30 Years," continued to complain about the officiating of the game and Massillon's use of ringers:

> When they raised hades with football officials in the good old days they did it right … so well that the criticism modern day handlers receive for their shortcomings is mere peanut stuff.
>
> Yes Sir! In the jolly days of 1903 when Massillon and Akron clashed upon the gridiron that striped terrain was in truth a battlefield. And when one essayed to officiate in such a contest he indicated that he was either extra brave or plenty dumb.
>
> George Hise of Salem was brave…. I'm wondering if you know just how lucky you are that you did escape with your life.

Hise, who called only the second half of the game after Akron's manager refused to allow the first-half official to continue, let the Tigers' second touchdown stand by ruling that it occurred due to a fumble instead of a forward lateral.

Frank Botoner, at age 95 on February 26, 1965, was the oldest known living original Tiger when he shared some of his fond and humorous memories of the game with the *Independent*. "The frozen field was like marble," said Botoner. "Like some of the other players, I never wore a helmet or padding of any kind," he added. Botoner also related that the Tigers forgot to bring footballs and had their pregame warmups with a basketball. "You'd have died laughing at the halftime show," Botoner continued. "Chief Ertle was leading the band, wearing the high helmet that we policemen had in those days, when an Akron fan threw a frozen piece of mud and cinders that knocked the chief's hat flying," he said with a smile.

Massillon rejoiced in its accomplishment. As the *Independent* described in its 1965 article, "Some 3,000 jubilant fans greeted the special train when it returned to Massillon, skyrockets soared, bands played and old black and gold ribbons decorated the streets in a football victory celebration that became familiar in these parts." Stewart also could not resist admiring his own work in his *Independent* article. "It was the equal of any demonstration of a similar nature in the country," he said.

Notably, Massillon's fervor for its Tigers eventually led the city to change its official colors from black and gold to black and orange. However, the city's historians are uncertain when this occurred.

Before the four ringers headed back home to Pittsburgh, they expressed in the *Independent* that they were so elated with their treatment in Massillon that they planned to return for the 1904 season. However, financial accounting of the season, announced by Manager Goodrich on December

1903		
T	SEPT. 26 0=6	Wooster
I	OCT. 17 16=0	Mt. Union
G	OCT. 24 6=0	Akron Imp'ls
E	OCT. 31 38=0	Akron Blues
R	NOV. 7 34=0	Panhandles
S	NOV. 14 16=0	Canton
	NOV. 21 29=0	All Clevelands
	NOV. 26 34=0	Wooster
	DEC. 5 12=0	Akron

Page from a 1905 Tigers game program showing that the team rolled to the state title without conceding a point after stumbling in their inaugural game

The Vogt Family Legacy

My parents moved to Massillon in 1948, when football fervor was flying high. My father, Bob McFadden, instantly an avid Tigers fan, somehow garnered midfield season seats two rows in front of the press box, directly behind the Vogt family. I joined him until I could sit in the student section.

Stronger than his love of the game was my father's passion for Tigers tradition and the town's unique history. A compelling storyteller, he intrigued me with stories of Coxey's Army, the canal, downtown, and football. At the Massillon Museum, I later discovered his stories barely delved into Massillon's diverse history. Smitten forever, I have authored three Massillon history books and shared local legends on walking tours.

When I married into the Vogt family, I learned about Elmer (my husband's grandfather) and Herman (Elmer's brother, older by eight years). Both played alongside Bob Shiring for the professional Tigers. Team photographs came out frequently at family gatherings. Elmer's daughter, Ruth Lash—now 100 years old—remembers the broad-shouldered brothers as "bulky."

During their football years, Elmer and Herman worked for their father's paving company and lived in their childhood home on Wellman Avenue—a neighborhood later home to Yankees standout Tommy Henrich and football innovator and coach Paul Brown. Herman starred on the football field; Elmer, the business-minded brother, carried on the construction company with Herman as foreman.

What serendipity it was when Gregg Ficery stopped at the Massillon Museum asking about the Vogts and I was near enough to hear his question! Destined to collaborate, we shared an adventurous day seeking the location of Sunnyside Field, where the Tigers played on the grounds of the old state hospital. We quickly learned we were not welcome—the security officer punctuated his displeasure with lights and sirens. Then we sleuthed through Brookside Country Club, hoping to discover a photograph of Lakeside Field, where the Tigers and Bulldogs competed. Again unsuccessful, this time we were not given the bum's rush; the manager even allowed us to investigate a storage area.

It has been exciting to hover at the margin of this project. Gregg's perseverance and enthusiasm inspire me. The results of his passionate research create an accurate, entertaining record of a colorful chapter in Stark County's heritage and professional football's history.

—*Margy Vogt, Massillon, OH*

1906 "All-Massillon" amateur team. Front row: Jack Miller, Frank Bast, Louis Brown. Middle row: Bob Featheringham, Joe Bordner, Albert Bonk, John Fisher, Fred "Flax" Miller, Harry "Nutter" Getz, Charles "Mully" Miller. Back row: Elmer Vogt, Harry Anderson, Emery Powell, Orrie Ames, Mel Trotter, Tim Nolan, Leavitt Shertzer, Herman Vogt (coach).

15, revealed that the team's profit of approximately $200 on $1,300 in revenue was only enough for each player to receive less than $10 for their season's work. When the team was not able to cover medical bills for the injured players, citizens generously donated funds to cover them. Nonetheless, the *Independent* stated that all of the players were satisfied since they won the state title.

For a patchwork startup group to begin with a loss to a college team and come together in just over two months to claim the Ohio state title was a remarkable feat. It was only the beginning for the Tigers.

⇂ Franklin's Powerhouse ⇃

Meanwhile, back in Pennsylvania, Blondy Wallace searched for another rivalry from which to profit through his football skills in 1903. He found one brewing nearly 80 miles north of Pittsburgh between Franklin and Oil City, towns 9 miles apart. Franklin organized its first football team in 1890, as did Oil City in 1893. Oil City held the upper hand after stacking its lineup in 1902, and Franklin had sufficient resources and motivation to change the balance of power.

On October 13, 1903, the nearby *Titusville Herald* lamented the state of sporting affairs between the two neighbors:

> Franklin is loading for the annual foot ball war with Oil City. While this is one of the matters best decided by the interested parties, it seems deplorable that industry should be paralyzed, interest in things laudable be forgotten and even the dead left unburied during this cruel annual warfare. A civilized and educated citizenship should resort to arbitration for the settlement of such issues and not permit the whole world to weep bitter tears as the struggle goes on relentlessly. When will the white winged dove of peace unite these ancient enemies?

Venango County, in which both cities are located, was blessed with vast wealth from the oil industry and flourished after the first successful use of an oil well in its town of Titusville in 1859. Within a few years, it became host to the headquarters of Pennzoil, Quaker State, and Wolf's Head, three motor oil companies.

Similar to Pittsburgh and Eastern Ohio, simultaneous growth in industry and football into the 1890s and early 1900s naturally led to financial support for amateur and then professional football organizations in other parts of these states and the Midwest region. This connection explains why pro football continues to be supported most viscerally in what became known as the Rust Belt.

On November 23, 1903, an article in Franklin's *News-Herald* claimed that its football team had lost only five games in its history: three to Oil City and two to Lalus. But who is counting? None stung Franklin's pride or pocketbooks more, though, than its loss to Oil City on Thanksgiving Day of 1902, when the entire Lalus team, several of the pros from Philadelphia, and other outsiders took the field in Oil City uniforms to ensure victory. Venango County's population did not justify paying full rosters of players from a business standpoint. But fans from both parts of the county were feverish about putting their plentiful cash down on their team's colors. The Franklin side took a big hit. Its leadership would ensure to recoup its supporters' losses the following year.

Although Franklin claimed a moral victory that day in 1902 by holding a vastly superior team down to an 11–0 score, albeit on a muddy field, its moral ground was not indeed very high. Two days earlier, on November 25, the *Pittsburg Daily Post* reported that Franklin manager Dave Printz was in Greensburg, offering big money to several Pittsburg Stars players to finish the season with Franklin after the Stars' 18–0 loss to the Philadelphia Phillies the day before. The *Daily Post* was also pleased to report that "neither his money or his tongue availed him anything and the men stood by Captain Richardson to a man."

It was another story, though, for the Stars players when the team dissolved after the season, and most of them retained legal counsel in efforts to recover alleged balances for services rendered. They must have kept Printz's contact information, as many of them committed to Franklin for 1903 within days after the season, including Kerkhoff, Schrontz, Lang, and lineman Max McNulty of Notre Dame. Then, when Printz enlisted Wallace and named him captain, Wallace pulled in his comrades from Philadelphia, including Sweet, Steinberg, Davidson, and Arthur "Tige" McFarland, to join Franklin's festivities.

Unfortunately for Franklin, all of this successful recruiting effectively became overkill. The 74–0 beating it put on Youngstown in its first game, on October 21, only served to cause Oil City to wave the white flag and fold before its season started. Despite this group's tremendous prowess and results, Franklin's historical excellence may not be fully appreciated given that it had little credible competition against which to measure itself. Franklin's 12–0 win over a good Syracuse University team was the most impressive in its perfect 10-0 season, with an aggregate score of 438–0.

Most satisfying for Franklin's followers, though, was the revenge achieved with the team's 23–0 result over Lalus's East End team, which masked itself as Oil City the year before. Shiring was not part of the East End team that pulled that trick, as he was with the Stars in Greensburg. But he bore the brunt of the mismatch in 1903, only a few days before he and three of his teammates headed to Massillon to change the course of professional football.

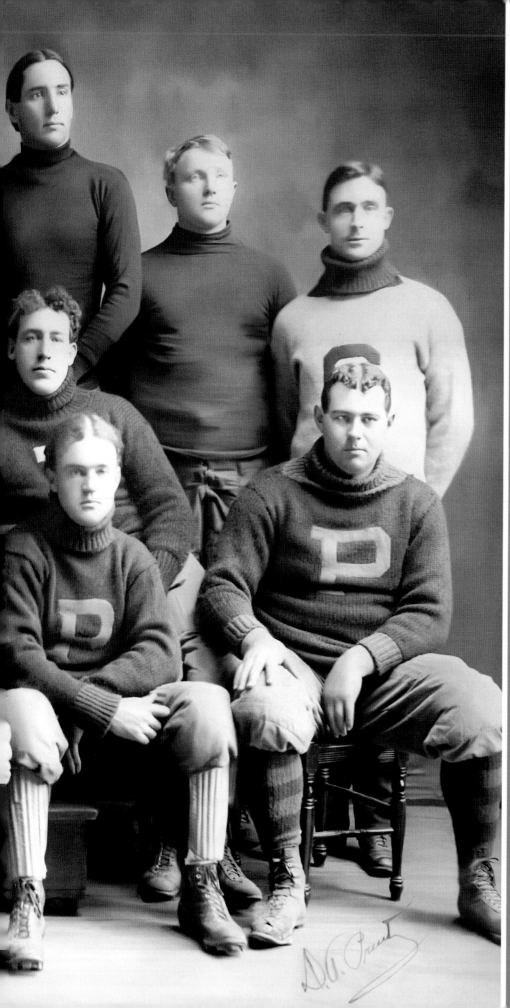

1903 Franklin Athletic Club

Front row: Bert Sutter, Paul "Twister" Steinberg, Lynn "Pop" Sweet, Jack Hayden, Herbert "Bull" Davidson. Middle row: Clark Schrontz, Max McNulty, Bill McConnell, Dave Printz (manager), Jack Lang. Back row: Arthur "Tige" McFarland, Herman Kerkhoff, John "Teck" Mathews, Charles "Blondy" Wallace, Charles "Chal" Brennan.

COMMERCIAL BREAK:
1903 Indoor Championship Series

Franklin's opportunity for validation came via Madison Square Garden's second attempt at an indoor year-end event. The Watertown (New York) Athletic Association Red & Blacks provided the strongest competition, also sporting an undefeated record. Against all logic, media in its area boasted about Watertown being national professional champions for the prior three years. The Red & Blacks suspiciously avoided the indoor event the previous year, instead lending its backfield to the Syracuse team that ushered Wallace's New York squad out of the tournament in the event's first game. The second time around, Watertown manager and ex-mayor James B. Wise not only signed up but also leased the Garden for the event.

The winning team would receive $1,250 with the second-place team earning $750. The four-team field included the Oreas AA of Asbury Park, New Jersey, and the Orange AC, in addition to Franklin and Watertown. The weeklong football festival held from December 14 to 19 also included a tournament for local teams, Gaelic football, and a high school all-star game.

Franklin and Watertown survived their first games by margins of 12–0 and 5–0, respectively, to set up the climactic title game. Betting was heavy, but the crowd was not. Both offenses performed well, though Franklin's defense made the difference in a 12–0 win to claim the national independent title. The *Pittsburg*

Bulletin later reported that the event lost $10,000, twice as much as it did the previous year.

Franklin's Clark Schrontz described the challenges of playing indoors to the *News-Herald* after the event. "The naked electric light bulbs cast heavy shadows on the gridiron," said Schrontz. "I remember in one of the games I dived for what I thought was the ball and found myself catching at a shadow. The roof of the Garden was not high enough and occasionally a high punt would strike the bulbs and scatter broken glass on the field and delay the contest until new lights could be placed."

Upon returning to Franklin with its coffers overflowing, satisfied that it had proved itself as the best, and with nothing more to accomplish, Printz announced that Franklin would not field a professional team the following year. After Franklin completed its perfect season, its local *News-Herald* published an article on December 21, 1903, "The Elements of Victory," capturing the essence of the reward that drives cities to invest so much, financially and emotionally, in producing championship football teams:

1903 Watertown Athletic Association team pin

It is not by accident that Franklin takes the lead in many lines of endeavor; that our industrial plants are famous all over the world; that our business men are possessed of wide reputations and are trading in every civilized land against the most astute commercial interests on the globe, and that in the field of sports we excel are legitimate results of the events which shaped the city's life and of the character developed by the enterprise and thrift of the Oil Country. Franklin holds the championship of the United States in foot ball because it has developed in that game the elements of success ever characteristic of this neighborhood. The people who settled by French Creek and the Allegheny River were strong in muscle and brain and the discovery of oil brought here the most enterprising, plucky, hardy, and fearless men of the whole earth. They came from every land and mingled here in a community of hardship and a brotherhood of courage. The weak and the easily discouraged, the men not fitted to endure a life that taxed every resource, were sifted out by the struggle for fortune in the early days and soon went elsewhere, and the spirit that has

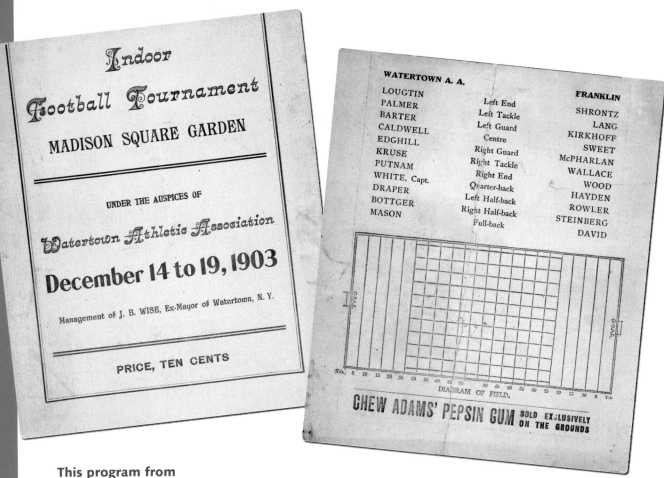

This program from the 1903 Indoor Football Tournament at Madison Square Garden, from the author's collection, is the only known one of its kind.

dominated this town has been one of optimism and enterprise, little marred by defeats. Hence, when we go into athletics, we have a goodly heritage of blood and brawn and we send out men that do not know how to be whipped on the gridiron. Our victories have been sneered at by the jealous, while the games were fought here and in neighboring small cities, but there is no longer any chance to belittle the athletic power of Franklin.

When our men went into the light of the arc of lamps of Madison Square Garden and whipped the best that could be produced by the Nation they demonstrated that the Nursery of Great Men is entitled to its name. Not only can we produce strong leaders of finance, able industrial managers and brilliant and great soldiers, but we send out men physically and mentally able to take the championship in the most strenuous game we have from the best that the Nation can send against them. New York State, with its thousands of physical giants and the great cities with their traditions of many victories, could find none among their millions who could break the Franklin line. Amid the cheers of great multitudes and in spite of prize ring methods, our boys wrung from the strangers the admiration they did not expect to give and brought back to the land of derricks and furnaces the right to fly its colors above that of any team on this continent. Franklin is proud of them and of the enterprises that have enabled the city to become as famous in the athletic world as in the industrial realm. Good men, all of them, they took up the task of representing this city and worthily discharged it and as long as they live they will be remembered by our citizens as those who went out to defend our right to leadership and did not leave us cause for shame.

On the same page, the *News-Herald* ran a much shorter story about "a couple of Ohio men" in Kitty Hawk, North Carolina, who had perfected a flying machine. People and pro football were taking flight.

But great innovation is not achieved without similar risk. In early December, newspapers around the country published the annual accounting of football deaths, totaling at least 19, and accompanying calls for reform or abolishment. As none of the deaths were on "first class elevens," some articles said that the tragedies occurred due to lack of proper training and conditioning. "There are a good many deaths from trolley cars every year, but nobody is proposing to abolish trolley cars," said the *Topeka Capital-Journal*.

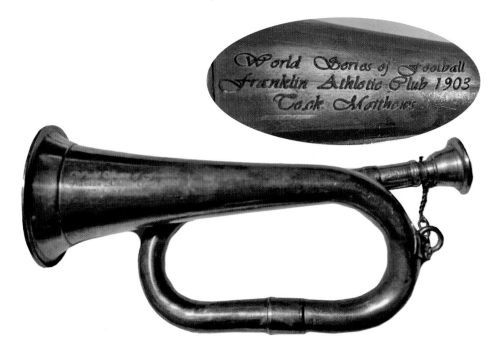

The inscription on this 1903 World Series of Football horn, presented to John "Teck" Mathews, suggests that the belief that the term "World Series" was not associated with either of Madison Square Garden's pro football events may be inaccurate. Recently discovered by the author, it is the only known item to document the connection.

Collier's

NOVEMBER 19TH 1904

VOLUME XXXIV   NUMBER 8   PRICE 10 CENTS

In the game within the game, this was likely the one instance, occasionally referenced in the following years, in which Pop Sweet got the better of Shiring in the matchup of the sport's top centers. It was the only point that detractors used to needle Shiring as he and Sweet continued to battle against each other within major championship contests, and one that Shiring used as motivation.

⇌ 1904—Onward in Ohio ⇌

The horse was out of the barn, and attempts at public shaming were not going to deter Massillon from continuing to employ a few professionals to defend its championship heading into the 1904 season. Any teams serious about competing for the state championship of Ohio were going to need to improve their levels of talent and play. While recognizing the need, for the time being, to maintain fan support by fielding mostly locals, free market forces increasingly populated the fields of Ohio with some of the best players in the land in the 1904 season.

Disappointed by a lack of available postseason profit sharing, some wise players started to negotiate better terms. On August 12, the *Pittsburg Post* indicated that Massillon manager Wise had visited Pittsburgh to offer the four ringers spots for the season ahead. Only Doc McChesney bit right away, with the *Post* saying that "he would just as soon play football as eat."

With a family to consider, Shiring sought more security. His second child, named Susan after his deceased first wife, was born on March 13, 1903. According to the *Independent* on August 29, Shiring made a proposition to Wise to come to Massillon for the season in exchange for "cash consideration which will exclude him from any division in the gate receipts." Effectively, he asked for a fixed salary, a novel concept in football at the time. Wise responded that he would put the matter to a team vote.

A follow-up story in the *Independent* on September 6 indicated that Shiring had signed and would report for the team's third game. However, he could not leave his team in the lurch. The paper informed inquiring fans that Shiring wrote to McChesney on the Tuesday before the Tigers' first game against Canal Dover on Saturday, September 24, that he had been practicing with his local team in Wilmerding and would arrive in Massillon the night before the game.

On game day, the *Independent* reported in its piece "Massillon Is Football Mad" that a "happy throng" of the Tigers' new Knockers fan club and others filled the Massillon train station the night before, rushing to meet Shiring and welcome him back for the upcoming season. One startled onlooker remarked, "What the h___'s the matter here, is Roosevelt on this train?" Another responded, "Naw, it's football, haven't you heard?"

Weaker club and college teams thought better of playing the enhanced Tigers, so Massillon entered the season with a seven-game schedule that was short but challenging, or so it seemed. Initial results were lopsided, to say the least. Opening wins of 57–0 over Canal Dover and 56–6 over the Franklin Athletic Club of Cleveland were eye-opening, especially to prognosticators who wagered at much lower spreads. Then, on October 15, the Tigers exploded, setting a record for points by a pro team that still stands in a 148–0 win over Marion.

Before the game, Marion players pooled their cash, with the winner being the one guessing closest to the final score. After losing to Shelby 29–0, and with the roster in better condition, the guess with the highest margin was 20–0. The Tigers led 63–0 at the end of the 25-minute first half, and then they set their sights on 100 points. Eight minutes into the second half, they had put up 103. Word spread through the crowd that the "world's record" was within reach. The *Evening Independent* reported that it would seem nothing less than a slaughter to try for the record at that point, but "the fever was aroused":

> During it all the eight hundred spectators remained to a man. The news scattered throughout the crowd that the Tigers were out after national honors, and when the twenty-sixth touchdown was recorded and goal kicked, making the score two points above the previous record, hats were thrown into the air and a demonstration made which would have been expected if that final touchdown was the only one recorded in a grueling contest and brought victory for the Tigers.

Mercifully, if it can be called that, the game was ended with six minutes remaining. The *Independent* praised Marion's players for their "pluck, determination, gentlemanly play, and not seeming to know the meaning of the word fear." The *Marion Star* had no hard feelings in writing: "Every man on the Marion team played hard and time and time again was cheered by the audience for his excellent playing."

It is important to note that such high scores at the time were facilitated by a rule that, before 1903, required that the team that scored then received the kickoff. Then, until 1910, the rule changed such that the team that gave up the points had an option to kick or receive. Some teams preferred to continue kicking off since they felt it would help them keep the total down because the other side would have farther to go to score again. As the kickoff was from midfield, and the alternative was to either turn the ball over or punt from deep in their own territory, many teams preferred to try sparing themselves from worse defeats, and maybe win some wagers, by keeping losing margins as narrow as possible.

Shiring collection

Next up was the Pittsburg Lyceum, which came to Massillon not having lost a game in three seasons. The Tigers went to battle with only eight of their regulars due to injuries, but the "giant rancher" Herman Kerkhoff made his timely Massillon debut. The Lyceums confidently predicted, "We can defeat a whole team of Kerkhoffs," and oddsmakers offered lines of 0 up to 12 points.

In its postgame summary, the *Independent* raved: "'Kerky' simply tore the visitors' line to pieces. On defense he was like a steam engine. He could not be denied and with the ball he never failed to make the required distance." The story also recognized Shiring's performance. "Shiring against the vaunted Bloom made his hard task look easy by the manner in which he sifted through the line and blocked interference and helped his own men," said the *Independent*. The Tigers' win by a surprising 44–0 margin was another indication that this team was exceptional.

Shelby was next in line and eager to reclaim its state championship glory from prior years. With many players still injured, the Tigers welcomed a weekend off before Shelby came to town. Shiring made the most of his time off, making a trip home to Pittsburgh to bring Frank Piefer, who was expected at the start of the season, back with him.

Imported Tigers players were embraced by their teammates and the Massillon community. Here, Bob Shiring (center) enjoys a light moment during the 1904 season with Teck Mathews (far left) and local players Frank Botoner, Baldy Wittman, and Herman Vogt.

CHARLES FOLLIS—
"THE BLACK CYCLONE"

The greatest of the Shelby Athletic Club stars was also the most significant from a historical perspective: Charles Follis (aka "the Black Cyclone"). Follis started his football career by organizing and captaining Wooster High School's first teams in 1898 and 1899. He attended Wooster College but played for the Wooster Athletic Association (WAA). According to the *Cleveland Plain Dealer* on November 28, 1901, Shelby manager Arthur Rice was so impressed by Follis's running and overall play in the team's win over WAA that weekend that he "signed" the "negro marvel" for the next season. As Shelby was, at least officially, a semi-pro team in the 1902 season when it was called the Giants, Follis's compensation for "signing" seems to have been his employment at the local Seltzer & Sons hardware store.

Nonetheless, the *Shelby Globe* reported that the club's trustees were "pleased to no end" when Follis reported to play the following fall and hoped that his job would enable him to remain in Shelby "during the season and hopefully all the time." They were likely even more pleased when he erupted, scoring three touchdowns in the first half of his first game with Shelby in a 27–0 win over the Akron Planets. Follis's popularity with Shelby fans grew weekly as he continued on a streak of games with multiple touchdowns and exciting long runs and kickoff returns.

Follis was inevitably on the short end of brutal tactics for competitive and racial reasons. But his teammates had his back. In a 1903 game with Marion, Follis received a spike in the head that the *Globe* said was resolved by his fellow halfback delivering "a dazzling jab to the same place that the chicken got the axe!"

In a beautiful twist of fate, one of his Shelby teammates from 1902–03 was future Brooklyn Dodgers general manager, president, and partial owner Branch Rickey, who signed Jackie Robinson to his Major League Baseball contract in 1947. In 2003, an ESPN panel voted Rickey "the Most Influential Figure in Sports of the 20th Century." Though Rickey never discussed it, one theory is that his appreciation for Follis's character and endurance of racial abuse encouraged him, in part, to support Robinson.

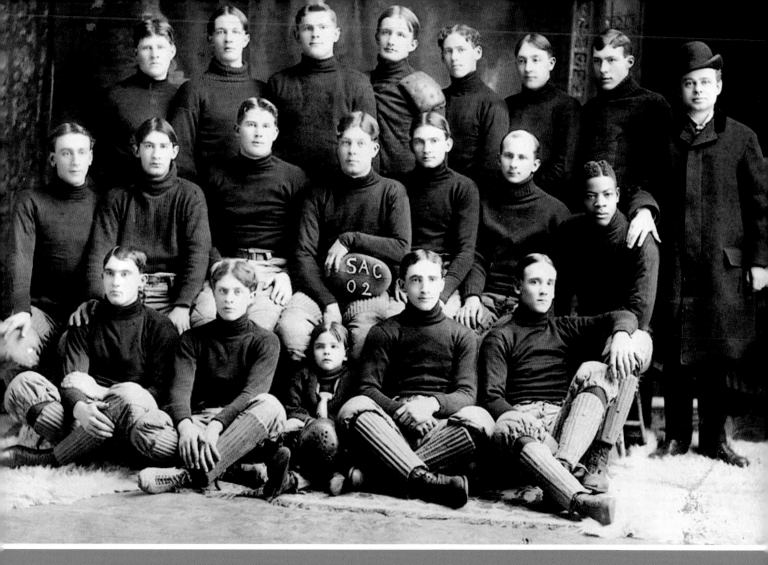

On September 16, 1904, a *Globe* headline read, "Charles Follis has signed for the season" with the team then called the Shelby Blues. This is commonly believed to be the date on which Follis signed his first professional contract. It is a matter of semantics whether the *Plain Dealer*'s account of Shelby's signing Follis in 1901 involved a physical contract, whether Shelby was technically a professional team at either time (and by what definition), or whether either contract was professional due to including cash compensation. Shelby clearly paid cash to at least some players in both years, including Rickey, in 1902, while he was playing for Ohio Wesleyan. In any case, as the first African American to sign a football contract with a team that paid players, thus making it professional, Follis is effectively football's Jackie Robinson, only more than 40 years earlier.

Injuries ended Follis's football days after the 1906 season, though he went on to a successful baseball career as a catcher with the prominent Negro League Cuban Giants of Long Island. His life was cut short when he died of pneumonia after a Giants game in 1910 at age 31.

Follis played on this 1902 Shelby Athletic Club team with future Brooklyn Dodgers executive Branch Rickey (back row, second from left), who signed Jackie Robinson to the Dodgers. The Shelby manager's protective gesture of his hand on Follis's shoulder is a touching tribute.

Shelby came loaded for Tiger hunting with "probably the greatest number of bright college stars ever gathered together in Ohio for a foot ball game," according to the *Independent*, including an unusually large (for the time) 296-pound guard named Dyer. The article went on to say, "The Tigers contain no such bunch of individual stars as these but will probably have the advantage of team work over Shelby. Whether or not this quality will offset the brilliant playing of these college stars is a question which remains to be settled."

Shelby's strength placed doubt in the minds of some Tigers players and, thus, over the entire future of the team. "If we don't win I'll see Sunday morning's sun rise in Lafayette, Ind.," said Kerkhoff. "Me back to Pittsburg," said Piefer, according to the *Independent* on November 5, the day before the game.

They did not need to worry. The Tigers "showed unexpected form," according to the *Independent*, two days later. It was a resounding 28–0 victory attended by 3,000 fans, including 500 from Shelby, shortened 10 minutes by mutual agreement when the outcome was clear. The relentless hammering of Massillon's heavy formations drove the ball straight down the field for a Kerkhoff touchdown eight minutes into the game. They never looked back, as Follis and Shelby's other star halfback, Ted Nesser of the famous seven football-playing Nesser brothers, were stifled by Massillon's defense.

After the game, Shelby fullback "Heifer" Resch said, "Massillon has the best team I ever played against. I will not except Michigan, for I believe that Massillon could beat Michigan." As Resch played twice against Michigan in his years at Case, he knew whereof he spoke. Despite intercollegiate rules prohibiting such a contest, the *Independent* reported on October 26 that Tigers manager Wise still extended an audacious invitation to Michigan for a Thanksgiving Day game in Massillon. The Wolverines politely declined.

Predictably, the *Beacon Journal* had nothing but criticism for the Tigers, stating that Kerkhoff made them a one-man team that was ordinary caliber without him, and that Akron was faster and would defeat the Tigers on Thanksgiving Day. The *Independent*, though, praised the Tigers' depth, including Shiring: "There is just one more member of the Tigers who is deserving of the plaudits of the fans, 'Bob' Shiring at center. Thus far his work against visiting teams has been so easy that he never had a chance to star, but the way he put it over Tucker and the giant Dyer in Saturday's contest stamps him as the premier center in this part of the country."

It was not all good news for Massillon, as Doc McChesney would miss the rest of the season with an injured shoulder. Nesser, though, was eager to join the Tigers as a high-quality replacement, starting with their 63–0 reprieve the following week against the previously unscored-upon Sharon Buhl Club that was in contention for the Western Pennsylvania title.

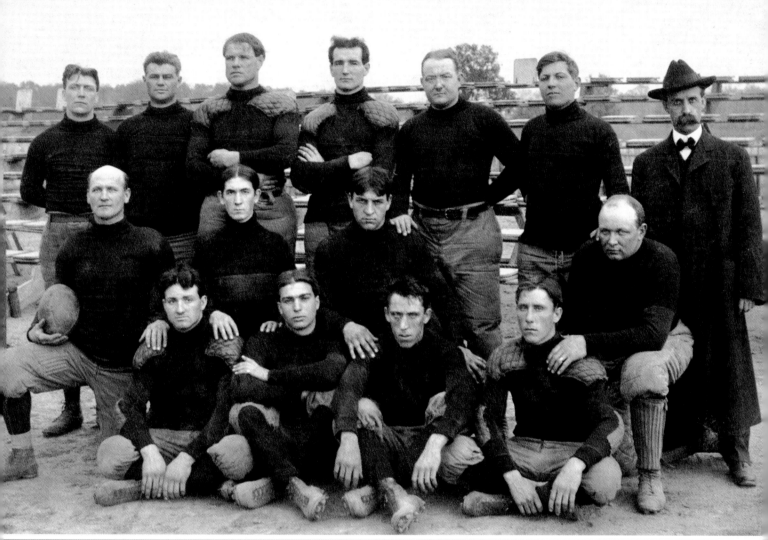

Shiring collection

1904 Massillon Tigers

Front row: Emery Powell, Frank Bast, Mully Miller, Jack Miller. Middle row: Baldy Wittman (captain), E.J. Stewart, Dan Riley, Harry Anderson. Back row: Frank Piefer, Frank Botoner, Herman Kerkhoff, Doc McChesney, Bob Shiring, Herman Vogt, J.J. Wise (manager).

With another weekend off before Massillon's final Thanksgiving Day championship bout with Akron, there was plenty of time for media buildup. "On to Massillon!" was the cry in Akron, though it had to settle for the challenger's road game and a more generous 40/60 split than it provided to Massillon the previous year. The Akron side did none of the spouting off before the game that it had done the year before. With Arthur Poe as its coach, who had won many wars with some of the Tigers' stars at Homestead in 1901, Akron's players knew better than to poke a resting Tiger.

Instead, rumors abounded that Akron was romancing the country's best college player, Michigan's superstar running back Willie Heston, to sign on. On November 15, the *Independent* reported that Akron's manager had confirmed to the Tigers that Heston had signed for the game. But the handsome Heston overplayed his hand by attempting to negotiate a counteroffer from Massillon. The *Plain Dealer* reported at various times that the bidding ranged between $500 and $1,000 before both teams called off their bids. Massillon, though, did seal the deal with Jack Lang to bring him over from his latest team in Latrobe and fill McChesney's spot on the line for the big game, while moving Nesser back to his natural halfback position. Lang was then part of each of the most significant season-ending contests with four different teams since 1901.

Despite Akron's scoreless tie with Shelby, wagers could be made on the game at even-money odds, given that Akron's roster included 10 ex-college stars gathered from around the country. The Tigers' roster of 15 players still included only 3 ex-collegians (all from Ohio, including Stewart), 8 of their original locals, and 4 others (Shiring, McChesney, Piefer, and Nesser) from the school of hard knocks.

The paid crowd of 5,288, estimated at a total of 7,000 with freeloaders climbing fences, got its money's worth. Hundreds of doctors, nurses, and mental health patients also gathered on the hillside of the State Hospital property to watch the festivities on the lower grounds that became known informally as Asylum Field.

The *Canton Repository* set the stage. Orange and black bunting and streamers covered the town. Men, women, children, and dogs also donned the colors. Four lovely ladies paraded a goose decked in the team colors around the field to grand applause. Orange chrysanthemums were held in the hands of "flushed and excited ladies" and pinned to the lapels of their escorts, making a beautiful scene in the numerous carriages parked on the north part of the grounds.

Twelve tightly packed rail cars, carrying 1,500 fans from Akron on the B&O railroad, arrived 30 minutes late, delaying the game's start until after 3:00 and subjecting its end to darkness. Adding to the intrigue, previously unannounced players showed up on both sidelines before the game. Speedy end

Clark Schrontz made the trip from Pittsburgh for Massillon. Guard "Doc" Rayl, a practicing physician out of the University of Cincinnati, turned up for Akron.

Massillon dominated the first half, though its two fumbles deep in Akron's territory kept the game scoreless until Emory Powell plunged across the goal line for the Tigers five minutes before the half. The Tigers' band and fans "tore loose with a cacophony of sound and raced onto the field in their excitement," according to the *Morning News*. After order was restored, Stewart converted the extra point from a difficult angle to make the halftime score 6–0.

With Piefer's collarbone broken late in the first half, the teams fought evenly in the second half until Akron scored a controversial touchdown with time running out. The Tigers asked the officials several times to stop the game due to darkness before Stewart fumbled a punt in the dusk, giving Akron the ball on Massillon's 30-yard line. After the Tigers stopped an Akron ball carrier near Massillon's 10-yard line with seconds remaining, Rayl dragged two opposing players clinging onto the ball toward the goal line. Onlookers claimed that the ball did not cross the line, but the officials signaled a touchdown.

With anxious fans gathered behind the goalposts and on the sidelines, making the Akron kicker's job harder, the result came down to the extra point attempt that the *Independent* described with flare:

> In the gathering gloom seven thousand people held their breath as the Akron quarterback, Fogg, of the University of Wisconsin, prepared the ball for the goal which would either tie the score or mean defeat for Akron and a second state championship for the Tigers. With the utmost care the ball was adjusted. The angle was difficult and a cross field wind was blowing. If the goal was kicked it would be a wonderful piece of work. As Fogg stepped back for the kick, waved his hand to the referee that he was ready and the ball was touched to the ground the hearts of four thousand Massillonians almost stopped beating. Fogg stepped forward and the thump of his toe into the ball was followed by a thousand cheers as the ball bounded away to one side and Massillon had won.

Regardless of Massillon's narrow escape against Akron, the team had achieved a new level of performance and excellence in the sport throughout the season. By retaining the championship, the Tigers' reputation grew. During a time when most cities hosted a team at some level, the Tigers became known as the top team in the country. More importantly, winning kept the team together. According to the *Independent*, at a team celebration the evening of the game, each team member was cheered as he promised to return. Powell received a $5 gold piece for scoring the winning touchdown against Akron. Stewart was duly flattered when he was awarded a $200 diamond ring in appreciation of his services, prompting him to predict even greater success for 1905.

Champions OF Ohio. TIGERS

1904
SEPTEMBER 24
Tigers 57
vs.
Canal Dover 0

OCTOBER 8
Tigers 56
vs.
Franklin A. C. 6

OCTOBER 15
Tigers 148
vs.
Marion 0

OCTOBER 22
Tigers 44
vs.
Pittsburg 0

NOVEMBER 5
Tigers 28
vs.
Shelby 0

NOVEMBER 12
Tigers 63
vs.
Sharon 0

NOVEMBER 24
Tigers 6
vs.
Akron 5

⋛ 1905: Canton Covets the Crown ⋛

In 1904, Canton fielded a local team, the Imperials, without aspirations of competing for state laurels. Its city leaders were initially less eager to admit to its slightly more highbrow community that it was acceptable to field a professional team. But literally watching from the sidelines while its smaller neighbor amassed glory was a matter that its envious dignitaries could no longer tolerate. The die had been cast. Before the calendar turned to 1905, on December 14, Stark County clerk William L. Day, a Michigan football alum and son of associate Supreme Court justice William R. Day, confirmed earlier reports that the Canton Athletic Club had been formed. Its mission, according to the *Independent*, was "to build up a strong professional foot ball team with the object in view of wrestling from Massillon the state championship bunting." The Giants, as they were first known, would instantly add fuel to the towns' natural rivalry.

Massillon's off-season presented multiple opportunities for events at which to celebrate its victors. On January 2, 1905, the *Independent* held its

10th Annual Newsboys' Dinner at the town's popular Sailor Hotel. Amid occasional flying food, city leaders attempted to entertain and inspire 140 young guests with stories of their football heroes. Mayor Bell quickly deferred to a Reverend Darsie, who knew which subject would hold his audience's attention. According to the *Independent* on January 5, the exchange went as follows:

> "Boys," he said, "who do you think of most when you talk about foot ball?"
> "Stewart," yelled the company as with one voice.
>
> "Yes, Stewart," said Mr. Darsie, "but there is another man I am thinking of just at this moment and that man is Shiring." The speaker then drew a word picture of the magnificent proportions of the popular football player. "I want you to be big, strong men like Shiring," he said. "Not only strong physically but strong morally. New Year's day is a good day to make resolutions. I wish you would resolve before you leave this place that you will never smoke, never drink alcoholic drinks, never swear, and never take anything that does not belong to you."

A rare on-field image from this era shows Massillon Tigers teammates gathering during a break in the action. Bob Shiring (the only player facing forward) seems to have the team's attention.

Image detail courtesy of the Massillon Museum

1905 Canton Giants

The Giants were initially led by player-coach "King" Bill Laub (front row, third from left) and University of Michigan alum Harry "Cotton Top" James (middle row, second from right) at quarterback.

For Shiring to be recognized as such as a nonresident, and among a group of the game's greats, was indicative of how he had endeared himself to the people of his home away from home. By the end of March, rumor had it that Stewart would be following Wise's former path to the mayor's office, which he initially denied before the season. Wise was nominated for mayor while serving as manager of the Massillon baseball club, elected to two terms, and held the office of clerk of courts while managing the Tigers.

The Ohio and Pennsylvania minor league baseball circuit then took over regional sports headlines for a few months. Reports had surfaced of Massillon's attempts to secure some of its out-of-town gridiron greats for jobs on the city's baseball team to maintain their interest in staying in town for the fall. However, the plan did not pan out, and the *Independent* announced on July 24 that Piefer and Harry McChesney would not be returning to the Tigers.

The Akron-Massillon rivalry overflowed onto the baseball field, though, in Massillon on August 22, when Akron manager Walter East pulled his team off the diamond, quitting in midgame after a disputed call at home plate in the fifth inning when trailing 2–1. East would become a well-known figure in Massillon and Canton football circles before long.

In response to a telegram from Manager Wise, Shiring arrived in Massillon on September 7. For the second consecutive year, he began the season with another mouth to feed in his family, as his third child, Louis James Shiring, was born on January 14, 1905. Shiring's return to the Tigers' practice that afternoon "injected accuracy and ginger into every play and each one was run off smoothly," according to the *Independent*.

Wise continued to go about his business of reassembling the Tigers roster while competing with Canton for the first time in the process. With Canton in the mix, it was tougher to bring back halfback and Canton native Dan Policowski (aka Dan "Bullet" Riley, when he played for the Tigers in 1904). However, the move became easier for Riley after the unfriendly treatment he received on Canton's baseball team for being a traitor during football season. Other changes to the Tigers' initial 1905 roster included the addition of Ted Nesser's brother John and Tige McFarland, veteran of the Pittsburgh gridirons, last seen as a star on the 1903 Franklin squad.

Canton laid the cornerstone of its first pro roster by outbidding Akron for player-coach "King" Bill Laub. Laub, who would become Akron's mayor in 1916, then built the foundation of the team by imperiously poaching six other Akron players, leading Akron to revert to a local level of play. While the *Independent* reported, on July 28, that Canton and Massillon managements cordially agreed to prevent a bidding war for each other's players, a lesson they learned from the Heston experience the year before, the publication itself had no mercy in critiquing Canton's other new players. "Ozersky seems fat compared to his condition when he played here with the Sharon, Pa.

After Ted and John Nesser played for the Tigers, the six Nesser brothers all joined the professional Columbus Panhandles in 1907. One of the 14 original NFL teams in 1920, the Panhandles were named after the Panhandle Division of the Pennsylvania Railroad in Columbus, Ohio, where the brothers worked.

- NESSER BROTHERS -

team last season. Pearson is as gray headed as Frank Botoner, of the Tiger team. Cure looks good but has been out of the game for several years," said the unnamed *Independent* writer, who was likely Stewart, on September 25.

From the outset of the new gridiron rivalry, Stewart took extra steps to stoke the conflict beyond the bounds of neutral reporting. From player moves to negotiations on terms for the Thanksgiving game still months ahead, it was open season for the *Independent* on the Canton Giants. This provocation was not surprising given Stewart's leadership role on the Tigers but was questionable from a journalistic standpoint. From a commercial perspective, though, passion and controversy would probably sell more tickets and papers. Canton sportswriters played along and shot barbs back in Massillon's direction, including when they predicted a Tigers' loss to Ohio Medical University in its first game. Still, their tone was rarely as aggressive as that of the *Independent*. It was not clear whether Stewart could or cared to separate his personal interest in the Tigers from his coverage.

Through mid-November, both teams ran up high scores without granting a point to opponents who dared to take the field with them. In attempts to break Massillon's scoring record, Canton surpassed 100 points twice, including 121 against a team from the USS *Michigan*, with an exceedingly light schedule for its first four games. The Giants likely would have broken the Tigers' 148-point record against Dayton on October 21, after scoring 85 points in the first half, but the game was called due to darkness

10 minutes into the second half at 107–0, after all of the scoring slowed the pace of the game.

Massillon took on stronger teams early on, which had pros and cons. Stewart's playing career ended in the Tigers' 22–0 win over the always eager Shelby Blues on October 21, when he suffered torn knee ligaments. Injury may have been the only way that Stewart would have replaced himself at quarterback, but it likely became clear to him at some point that his back-ups were more capable. Jack Hayden was an experienced field general and kicker, having been a bit of a tramp athlete for multiple eastern colleges, and playing for Blondy Wallace in Philadelphia in 1902 and Franklin in 1903. He and speedy Charley Moran, also of numerous colleges in Tennessee, would probably serve the team better when it mattered most in the games ahead.

In late October, Canton beat the depleted Akron team 52–0 and then took out Shelby 25–0, with pundits emphasizing that this was three points more than Massillon's victory over the Blues. Until the final few games of the season, though, the teams' most intriguing questions related to which players they would add to prepare for their first major battles in mid-November that would change the course of pro football's future.

In an effort to secure a marquee matchup to bolster Canton's reputation, provide a better return on investment than its earlier games, and prepare for Massillon, Giants manager George Williams secured an exciting matchup with the prominent collegiate Carlisle Indians on November 22 at Canton. Their contract also precluded the Indians from playing in Stark County that year against any other teams (i.e., Massillon). Not to be outdone, Massillon manager Wise called an end-around and scheduled Carlisle in Cleveland a week earlier to steal Canton's thunder.

Most experts outside Ohio did not give the Tigers much of a chance, with odds against them up to 2–1. Massillon was heavier, especially after bringing back Jack Lang from Latrobe for the occasion, but Carlisle was faster and thought to have better teamwork. The Indians were ranked as a top-10 eastern independent college team and had lost only to Harvard by 23–11 on November 4.

Circa 1900 Carlisle
Indians pennant

They were led by quarterback Frank Hudson, the first Carlisle Indian named to an All-America team, which he accomplished in 1898 and 1899. He was also recognized as the top kicker of the era, able to dropkick field goals from up to 55 yards. Although he and Bemus Pierce were both coaches at Carlisle in 1905, neither could resist getting into the action against Massillon.

Hudson's day did not last long. Early in the game, he tried to stop Bullet Riley as Riley was flying around an end. As Riley saw Hudson, he lowered his head, striking Hudson in the face. "Hudson went down and out," according to the *Independent*. The Indians coach, Ralph Kinney, blamed a wet and snowy field for his younger athletes' inability to leverage their speed. More accurately, Stewart outcoached him. The Indians gave up their speed advantage on the outside to bolster the middle on defense, but Riley and Moran were surprisingly able to work end runs more effectively than their counterparts. Moran also hauled down an Indians runner for a safety and, ironically, halfback John "Teck" Mathews, a part–Native American veteran of the Pittsburgh trenches, scored the winning touchdown for the Tigers in the second half of their 8–4 win. The *Independent* quoted Kinney as saying, "On a dry field we would have won in a walk." But he likely underestimated the Tigers' prowess.

Two days later, before facing Carlisle, Canton took on its first real challenge in a clash of titans at Latrobe, with John Brallier still at quarterback and Lang, who had hustled back from Massillon, at tackle for the Miners. Latrobe had not lost a game in three years starting in 1903, though its primary competition in Western Pennsylvania since then had been only

Bemus Pierce and Frank Hudson were two of the all-time great Carlisle Indians players.

THE INDIAN CENTRE.
Lone Wolf, Centre; B. Pierce, Right Guard; Wheelock, Left Guard; Hudson, Quarter-back.

Steelton. With its final three games against Latrobe, Carlisle, and Massillon, fans would soon find out what Canton was truly made of.

Jack Ernst, a midseason addition to Canton who had captained Lafayette College in Easton, Pennsylvania, and played for Steelton against Latrobe the year before, praised his team while also identifying its weak spot in a letter to the *Latrobe Bulletin* on November 16:

> Canton expects the hardest game of the season when it tackles the La-trobe aggregation. There is no question in our minds as to the outcome of the Canton-Massillon or Canton-Carlisle games, but the game with the Latrobe eleven is the one that seems to be hardest to the Canton sports. The Canton team, without doubt, is the finest and best collection of football teams in the country. The team is the best that could be gotten together, regardless of cost, with the sole aim of taking the championship from Massillon. The team, as it will line up, is not the same as the one that will line up against Massillon, as several new players are to join our team, among them being one or two of Latrobe's players.

The day before the game, Coach Laub would neither make a prediction nor plant an excuse for his team, per the *Bulletin*:

> I do not know the strength of the Latrobe team so I could hardly make a prediction.... I have implicit confidence in my team and I consider it very strong. It is the strongest aggregation I could get together. When the team was organized, I was told to go ahead and get the best, without considering the cost, and with this carte blanche I proceeded. If the same order should be given to me today, I don't see where I could get a team

The collegiate 1905 Carlisle Indians dared to take on both the professional Massillon Tigers and Canton Giants. After suffering significant injuries in these games, and losses, Carlisle would no longer play against professional teams.

together better than the one I have now. We don't really know our own strength as yet, the team not having been up against any other eleven which has forced it to exert its full strength. The game with Shelby was the only close contest we have had all season.

Two fine teams played an even game that was decided, like many during its time, by a special teams misplay. After a scoreless first half, Canton's Dave Cure, another former Lafayette star, fielded a high second-half kickoff just under his goalpost near the goal line. Cure's best play would have been to let the ball cross the goal line, given the rule at the time in which a kick that went untouched over the goal line would be rekicked from its original spot at the midfield mark on the 55-yard line. Instead, with Miners charging at him, he lost his focus and touched the ball, which slipped by him 20 feet past the goal line. Cure won the chase to the ball and, to avoid a safety, tried to legally punt it out into the open field. However, Latrobe blocked and recovered the pigskin for the game's only score in a 5–0 Miners win.

As devastating as Canton's first loss was to its dreams of glory, matters worsened when coach, captain, and King Laub was lost for the season with a gruesome leg injury. According to the *Bulletin*, "He was tackled fiercely by three or four of Latrobe's players, and in being thrown one leg was pushed forward while the other was dragged behind forcing him to do the split."

The 1905 Canton Giants line up in their offensive formation with captain Bill Laub calling the signals behind center before his season-ending injury.

Courtesy of the Pro Football Hall of Fame

Necessity bred invention for Canton Athletic Club's management to salvage its investment—and its season—with battles against Carlisle and, most important, Massillon still ahead. With the available greats from Western Pennsylvania already enlisted by Massillon, and Ohio talent picked over, Canton had to broaden its search for a new leader. The logical solution for someone with that level of professional experience and presence was to target the Pittsburghers' earlier rivals from Philadelphia. Their choice was clear: Blondy Wallace.

Without a team for which to ply his trade since the great 1903 Franklin team folded, Wallace coached the line at Penn during the Quakers' national championship season in 1904. He stayed on for 1905, and the team had another undefeated season in the works, albeit with one tie, and two games remaining. So, when Canton approached Wallace at that point, he had leverage. Ahead of his time, like some highly sought-after coaches a century later, Wallace agreed to take on the role only if he could take over as captain. Laub technically remained as coach, at least for the time being, though that dynamic would be left to sort itself out.

Canton gained a measure of redemption against Carlisle with a solid, if not spectacular, 8–0 triumph. Wallace filled in more than admirably for Laub on the field and helped lead the Giants' line on a first-half scoring drive. Canton guard John "Buck" Hall, a preseason addition from Yale

New 1905 Canton Giants captain Blondy Wallace, as pictured in the *Canton Morning News* upon his hiring

and Michigan, was equally as insightful in his postgame remarks in the *Independent* as Ernst had been before the Latrobe game:

> Our defense was simply great, and the game was the best ever played by the team. The improvement in the playing on our part showed the good effects of our defeat last Saturday. Another hard game on Saturday would put us in the best possible shape. The team work could have been better. We took no chances in the second half but punted several times on the second down, preferring to be on the defensive.

Regardless of how the Giants' team concept was progressing, Laub's plan all along was to put an early twentieth-century version of a fantasy football team on the gridiron for the Massillon game. It did not make sense to blow out the bank against creampuffs early on, and many national-level stars would not have been interested in playing unless the stakes were high. If it were an 11-card-draw poker game, and players were cards, Laub traded in six. Massillon manager Wise drew only one.

Canton's six hitmen included a trio of new running backs. Wallace may have had a hand in recruiting Penn's Marshall Reynolds and Andy "Bull" Smith of Penn, but the Giants' "ace in the hole" was everybody's All-American, Michigan's Willie Heston. Willie's slickness in playing both sides against the middle cost him good money during his previous year's financial negotiations. He seemed to be going down the same road, though, while also leveraging his coaching role at Drake University in Iowa. But a larger Michigan contingent on Canton in 1905, including Hall and quarterback Harry "Cotton Top" James, likely swayed him the Giants' way. A sum of $500, twice Wallace's rate, sealed the deal.

Canton had put together a dream team. The question was whether they could put a real team together in eight days.

If Stewart was fazed, he had a good poker face. He expressed confidence that his team would win, "owing to teamwork and the fact that his men had played together all season." Manager Wise said that he "has plenty of good men on the Tiger team to defeat Canton and does not like to have the impression abroad that he is continually beseeching every player he meets to join the Massillon team," according to the *Independent*.

With the Giants' roster locked and loaded, the crowing began from Canton's officials, at least according to the *Independent*. "Why how can the Tigers expect to win? We've got the best players in the United States. We have the stars of the football world. Whoever heard of the players on the Tiger team?" Despite the Giants' star power, the oddsmakers called it an even-money proposition. Canton was also still trying to position itself for a rematch with Latrobe for an undisputed claim to a national

Willie Heston

University of Michigan coach Fielding Yost claimed that Heston was the greatest player of all time. In Heston's four years at Michigan, he rushed for over 100 touchdowns and several 500-yard games, leading the Wolverines to a 43–0–1 record. He was a four-time All-American and voted by the Football Writers Association of America as the halfback for college football's all-time team for football's first half-century.

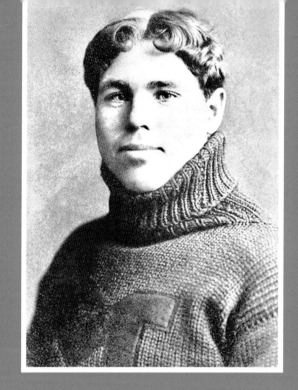

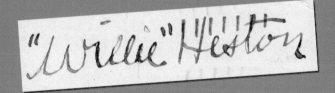

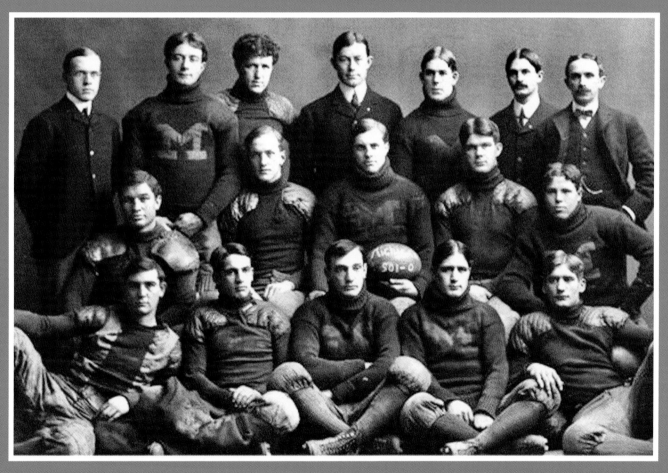

As noted on the ball in the image, Michigan's 1901 team outscored its opponent's 501–0 in 10 regular-season games. The Wolverines went on to defeat Stanford 49–0 in the first Rose Bowl game on January 1, 1902. Heston (middle row, far right) had 170 yards on 18 carries in the game.

Jackson

CURE

HESTON

REYNOLD

SMITH

Giants on the Field

College football legend Willie Heston
calls out the signals at practice for the
1905 Canton Giants.

Courtesy of the Pro Football Hall of Fame

championship, which the Miners said they would consider only if the Giants beat the Tigers.

Paranoia abounded among both teams. The Tigers ate and drank nothing but inspected food and water. The Giants secluded themselves, living in cottages at nearby Congress Lake, to prevent onlookers from catching a glimpse of their roster, while practicing twice a day.

Game day. November 30, 1905. An estimated 6,000 to 10,000 fans and $50,000 in wagers flooded the city of Massillon. Some people who claimed to have spotted Heston during the week claimed that he looked pudgy, and bettors wagered whether he would finish the game.

Fortune seemed to be on Canton's side from the toss of the coin. Tigers coach Stewart and captain Wittman noticed a strong wind toward the north goal during pregame punting drills. Wittman won the toss and chose the south goal for Massillon. At that exact moment, the wind changed direction. Wittman pleaded to change goals, but the referee would not allow it. As a result, Canton enjoyed a substantial advantage in the kicking game for the first half.

Massillon started shakily, fumbling on the first play from scrimmage, but recovered. Canton grabbed the momentum, stopping the Tigers on their first two possessions and holding good field position at the 55-yard line. Heston sprung for 15 yards around end, with the Tigers' massive Kerkhoff flattened by lead blockers. But the Tigers' defense stopped the Giants' surge. A fake punt enabled Canton to keep the pressure on, but the Giants subsequently fumbled the ball away as they approached kicking range.

The Tigers' lone new star, Louis "Red" Salmon from Notre Dame—who received two recruiting visits from Manager Wise when Salmon was busy helping to build the Lincoln Tunnel in New York—received most of their early carries but was sidelined twice by big hits. He continued to answer the bell. Play circulated around midfield for much of the half as both sides struggled for an edge. Massillon's defense anticipated and attacked Heston's end runs. On one early play, Heston slipped and fell on an ice patch covered by hay while a group of Tigers defenders piled on, bloodying his face. The Tigers clawed their way to Canton's 25-yard line, where McChesney's placekick was blocked. Canton fumbled on the next play. One play later, McChesney tried a dropkick from straight away on the 17-yard line that missed badly, rolling across the goal line.

While Massillon began to gain ground, Canton could not get in sync on offense. Quarterback Harry James continually paused at the line to explain signals to new teammates unfamiliar with them. James then fumbled a long Salmon punt, putting the Tigers in position for another dropkick attempt from 35 yards. This time, quarterback Jack Hayden successfully converted it for a 4–0 lead.

The *Beacon Journal* pointed out that too little preliminary work together was costly to the Giants in failing to support James on punt returns. "Time

MASSILLON TIGERS

Champion
Foot Ball Team,
of Ohio.

SOUVENIR PROGRAM

Program cover from the Tigers' November 30, 1905, "world championship" game with the Canton Giants

and time again," the *Beacon Journal* said, "Quarterback James received the ball on a punt only to be downed instantly by the active Tigers. He was not given any kind of support in his efforts to return the ball. On the other hand, the Tigers were ever present to assist the player in returning the punt."

However, the Giants gave themselves a scoring chance by blocking a Salmon punt deep in Massillon's end. Canton stalled once again, and Marshall Reynolds nailed a 23-yard placekick for Canton to salvage a 4–4 tie going into the half.

A crucial turning point occurred early in the second half, when Canton's guard, Doc Rayl, slugged a Massillon player, resulting in Rayl's ejection. His substitute, Max Ozersky, whose conditioning Stewart mocked in the *Independent* early in the season, became the target on the defensive line for the Tigers' onslaught. Massillon pressed into Canton territory, but a 15-yard holding penalty ended a Tigers drive. The Giants started to respond with a drive of their own, as Heston broke away for a 10-yard end run, his second and final substantial gain of the day, to cross midfield. Canton's fourth fumble killed the drive, but its defense held once again, forcing a booming 54-yard Salmon punt that pinned the Giants inside their 20. Canton's QB James was shaken up when the Tigers again smothered him without blocking help on the return, which may have led to the Giants' coughing up their fifth fumble on the next play.

Sensing the kill, and with an unreliable kicking game, the Tigers went for a first down on third down and 4 yards to go from Canton's 16, but failed. Massillon's defense stuffed the Giants on their next two plays, and Reynolds' short punt from his goal line gave the Tigers the ball on the Canton 29. On consecutive third-and-5 plays, the Tigers again chose to forgo field goal attempts, and both times Salmon came up with the goods, once outside and once inside, for first downs. Another Salmon blast for 8 yards, through Ozersky, on Canton's left side, put the ball within 2 yards of pay dirt, where he tore through the right side for the score on the next play. McChesney's extra point attempt failed, and the Tigers led 9–4 with 20:38 remaining in the game.

Without confidence in their offense, the Giants chose to kick to the Tigers in hopes of a turnover or defensive stop to net them better field position for a chance at a tying score. Reynolds punted the kickoff from midfield to Salmon at Massillon's 5-yard line, and the Tigers coordinated another strong return to their 32. From there, the Tigers started what the *Independent* declared "a triumphant procession of Tiger colors." The mighty Salmon pounded the rock all but twice through a Canton defense that the *Independent* described as "straining and terrified" in a touchdown march of over 10 plays, consuming more than nine minutes. Hayden missed another extra point attempt, giving Massillon a 14–4 lead.

Louis "Red" Salmon was Notre Dame's first All-American and outperformed Willie Heston in the 1905 professional championship game.

Kickoff at the November 30, 1905, "world championship" game between the Massillon Tigers and Canton Bulldogs at Sunnyside Field on the grounds of the Massillon State Hospital

Massillon – Canton '05.

Panoramic images such as this one of the 1905 Tigers were in vogue in the early 1900s.

With 10 minutes left and its troops decimated, Canton surrendered. Coach and King Laub gave up his crown and threw up the sponge from the water bucket as a sign that the Giants conceded the game.

Salmon's dominance was a revelation, especially given that his reputation —and Notre Dame's program from which he came—did not rival Heston's and his Michigan powerhouse. Canton's Bull Smith, who was said to be the best defensive fullback ever produced at Penn, heaped praise upon Salmon to the *Independent* two days after the game. "Well, I'll tell you, if I could forget that red head in my sleep, I might feel fine, but the minute I drop asleep all I can see is his red head bearing down on me like a dozen locomotives, and then I wake up. Talk about your battering rams, that fellow's got them all beaten."

The aftermath of the battle of titans was not kind to the Giants organization. The *Columbus Citizen* called it as it saw it:

> Massillon played like a team, Canton like the bunch of individual stars that they were. Willie Heston, Murphy, Smith, Graver, Cure, Wallace and all of the rest of the stars played great foot ball—that is by themselves and individually. As a team, Canton was a failure, a rank one. They got mixed signals, did not play together and the result of the game proved the prediction of Coach Stewart of the Tigers, who said that he was satisfied that his team would win owing to team work and the fact that they had played together all season.

The *Cleveland Plain Dealer* echoed these sentiments in saying, "This game has proven conclusively that no matter how many star players a team

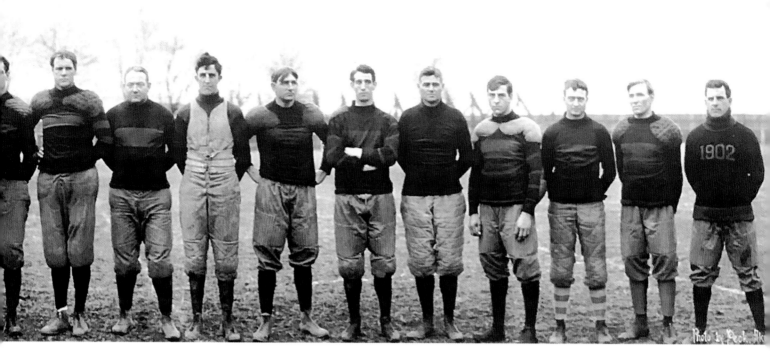

may bring together at the eleventh hour, the brawn, with fewer stars, but who have been drilled together and have the team work, which is the sole secret of success in foot ball, is the one to win."

The *Canton Morning News* was humble and respectful in defeat:

Canton in acknowledging defeat and waiving all rights to the state championship, does so with full respect for the eleven which wrested victory from us and blasted our fondest hopes. That Massillon has the best foot ball team and Canton second best seems to be the net result of yesterday's figures. Massillon deserves credit for the impregnable fortress in the shape of moleskin which it has been able to build up and now that our sister city has won we take off our hats, not with malice but good will and the hope that she may derive all the benefits of the fruits of victory. That the contest was pulled off in a sportsmanlike manner is also a credit for Massillon and that the Giants took their medicine gamely is no small feather for Canton.

Stewart initially tried to maintain decorum in the *Independent*'s column, "Team Work Won for the Tigers," the day following the game. Salmon received his due, though the story also spread the praise in saying, "Salmon did great work, but the strength and science of the men in front of him should not be forgotten."

But Stewart could not stop there. "Heston was a disappointment," the *Independent* said, though it was obviously Stewart hiding his authorship behind a thin veil. The *Independent*, or Stewart, continued, "Now that the game is lost, it is the opinion of the Canton backers that it was a case of

1905

OCT. 7 34=0	O..M. U.
OCT. 14 42=0	Norwalk
OCT. 21 22=0	Shelby
OCT. 28 51=0	Lorain
NOV. 4 88=0	Cleveland
NOV 9 40=0	Toledo
NOV. 15 8=4	Indians
NOV. 18 27=0	Reserves
NOV. 25 39=0	Canal Dover
NOV. 30 14=4	Canton

T I G E R S

For the second consecutive year, the Tigers completed an undefeated season and did not relinquish a point until their final game.

organization against a mob. Massillon had a highly organized team that worked together as an almost perfect unit. Canton had better players but they had not been trained together, and as a result organization won."

In a separate story on the same day titled "Canton Whistles Were Not Blown," the *Independent* seemed to dedicate itself to gloating:

> Whistles were not blown in Canton on Thursday evening from 7 to 8 o'clock as intended. Fires had been kept under the boilers in manufacturing plants. Wagon loads of fireworks had been secured and a jubilee was to be started when the victorious hosts reached the city. Disappointment and the blackest gloom took the place of joy and intended festivities and the disappointment was a rude one. It was a serious disappointment. Whether false hopes had been built up in Canton or not the people had been led to believe that the Canton team could not be defeated. The utter defeat was a sad blow. The inability of the Giants to hold the Tigers during the last part of the game was a circumstance that had not been thought of. Those at the head of the team could not express their sorrow and disappointment. Some were too downcast to express their feelings, while others wept in their sad plight. The blow fell hardest upon those who had boomed the Canton players for weeks. It was their share to tell why they had done so, and why false hopes had been raised so high. Canton is now in a sad way from many standpoints in the athletic world.

One of those standpoints was the business end. The Giants roster reportedly cost the Canton Athletic Club approximately $7,000, while yielding only $5,000 in revenue. Those who wagered on the team, some of whom were trying to gain a return on their investment, lost another $7,000 at Latrobe and estimates of up to $50,000 on the Massillon game. Only two days after the game, the *Independent* reported that the club would likely not support a team again for the 1906 season:

> With the Canton sports there is a feeling of soreness that cannot be disguised. Canton was confident that they would win the contest and when the loss came it found them entirely unprepared. It is very doubtful if another effort will be made to wrest the leadership from the Massillon bunch. The game is too expensive, and the local people have not made a study of the preparatory points of the game, and after the experience of Thanksgiving day they are not inclined to take many lessons at the price that must be paid.

On Massillon's side, everything was rosy. Always honest and transparent, Wise published the Tigers' balance sheet in the *Independent*. As with Canton, the players' salaries also came in at nearly $7,000. The team's net profit at season's end, on $16,038 in revenue, was $22.25, which was the extent of Wise's compensation as manager. The balance sheet may not have balanced precisely, and the paper said that a few small bills arrived after its publication. Effectively, Wise and the team broke even, other than the city's gambling windfall.

Tigers management did not immediately announce plans for a team the following season. First, there were the celebrations. The Tigers and Giants gathered together for entertainment at Canton's Courtland Hotel on the afternoon of the day following the game, where good fellowship prevailed. In the evening, the Tigers partied at Massillon's Conrad Hotel. The Giants declined their invitation, as many had already left town for their homes. Colors of both teams hung in decoration, and the Tigers gave three cheers for the Giants at the banquet's end.

Later in the month, on Thursday, December 21, Manager Wise was called to the Conrad under the premise of an outstanding bill. He was taken to the doors of the dining room, which signaled a chorus of cheers from 60 of his friends at a banquet table as he entered. Massillon mayor Bell was the toastmaster and, after toasting Wise for his hard work and success, he gifted him with a $300 diamond ring. Wise was overcome with emotion and briefly deferred to Coach Stewart, who recalled how Captain Wittman held the team together in its infancy after its discouraging loss to Wooster College in the team's first-ever game in 1903. Wittman stood up and said he was willing to do everything in his power for another year for the "bunch of Irish and Dutch," as quarterback Jack Hayden had come to call his comrades.

When he gathered himself, Wise's statement to those who donated the gift in his honor was from the heart:

> This present is worth more to me than any amount of money and this meeting here of friends, whom I have known for many years, reaches to the bottom of my heart. It brings a feeling upon me that cannot be expressed in word. I never was in just such a position before and I want to say here that I shall never forget the history connected with this gift, which I shall cherish as long as I live. I simply want to say that I hope Massillon will have a championship team next year and I am willing to do my little part in making the annual foot ball season a success.

To the victor go the spoils.

The Tigers became so popular in 1905 that team postcards were produced and sent around the country.

Camaraderie with Canton

It speaks to the camaraderie and sportsmanship among many of the pre-NFL era's players that several photos in Shiring's collection are of teams and players that he played against. Among the prominent players in this unique image of the 1905 Canton Giants from Shiring's collection are Blondy Wallace (second row from back, third from left) and Willie Heston (second row, second from right).

1905 World Champion
Massillon Tigers

The image to the right was provided as a
souvenir premium in the *Evening Independent*
newspaper during the 1905 season.

Top Row—Sch
Second Row—Moran, Wittm

THE EVENING INDEPENDENT

MASSILLON TIGERS—1905

McNulty, McFarland, Shiring, Kerchoffe, McChesney, Haag, Clapper.
ot.), T. Nesser, Wise (Mgr.), Stewart (Coach). Hayden. Riley, J. Nesser, Mathews.
ird Row—Featheringham, Miller, Bast, Merriam.
Fourth Row—Master Wittmann (Mascott).

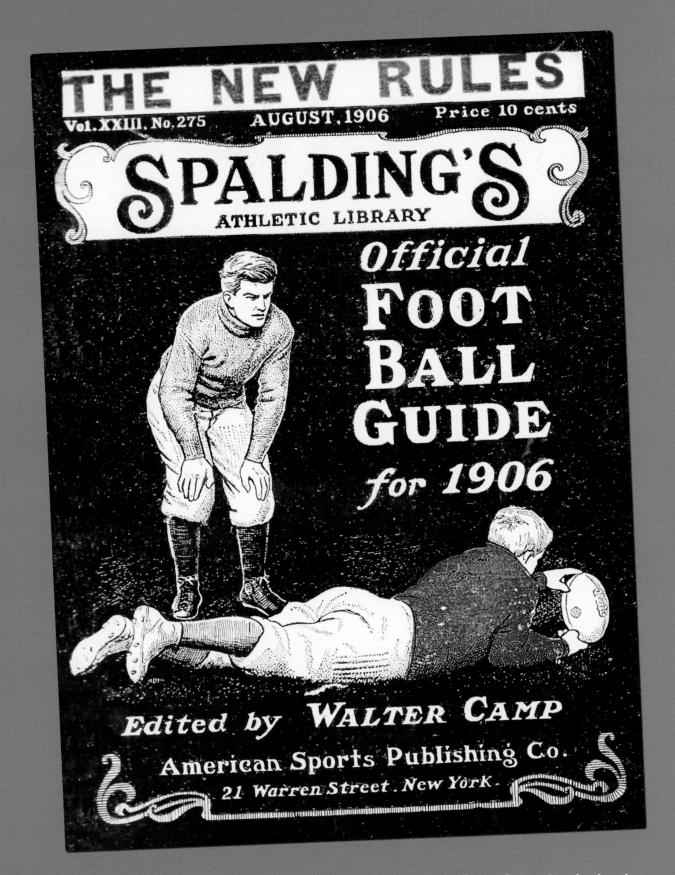

With an assist from the Oval Office, the 1906 season introduced a set of transformational rules that made the game safer and more exciting, including the forward pass.

VIOLENCE AND DEATHS LEAD TO RULE CHANGES

"Football is on trial!" —Theodore Roosevelt

For far too many young people whose passion for football led them to take up the sport at the turn of the twentieth century, it turned out to be a lethal adventure. According to the *Washington Post*, at least 45 people died from football-related injuries from 1900 through October 1905. Estimates of up to 25 football fatalities in 1905 alone caused the *Chicago Tribune* to label that season a "death harvest." Head, neck, and spinal trauma were the usual culprits, as well as various internal injuries. As in the days of the Wild West, there were few rules and plenty of leeway for untried aggressive tactics. Many unprepared and unfortunate players fell victim as a result.

These deaths and hundreds of serious injuries were mostly attributable to playing schemes and formations that bordered on savagery. The foremost of these was the flying wedge, an offensive formation in which linemen created a V-formation with locked arms with the ball carrier tucked behind them. Linemen were not required to set up on a line of scrimmage. They were also allowed to interlock their legs before the snap to prevent defensive linemen from penetrating the wedge. Thus, the offense effectively created a plow in which defenders were virtually unable to engage an opponent one-on-one and were frequently trampled.

1910 Georgetown
University silk premium
produced by Murad
Cigarettes

1905 Swarthmore
College postcard. "Tiny"
Maxwell is second from
left in the middle row.

While only three of the casualties occurred in college games, with the rest at the prep school level, awareness about the sport's hazards had been building for several years in the collegiate ranks. After Georgetown University running back George "Shorty" Bahan was seriously injured in an 1894 Thanksgiving Day game against the amateur Columbia Athletic Club, *Washington Post* sports editor John F. Wilkins expressed concern in a letter to his former Princeton schoolmate, All-America tackle Bill Church (later Homestead Library & Athletic Club coach in 1900), that there would never be another college football game played in Washington, D.C., if Bahan died. After a short period of paralysis, he did die. Georgetown then abolished football, and its administration took the initiative to encourage other colleges to do the same before the Hoyas returned to play in 1898.

When a prominent college player suffered a grotesque (though not fatal) injury in 1905, the president of the United States stepped in, bringing national attention to player safety. Robert Maxwell, playfully nicknamed "Tiny" at 240 pounds, was a giant of a man for that time, with credentials to match. He started his college career in 1902 at the University of Chicago's powerhouse program under the tutelage of legendary coach Amos Alonzo Stagg. Despite great success, he transferred to small Swarthmore College in Philadelphia for his final two years, along with teammate Sherburn Wightman, for reasons that have never been confirmed. One theory is that Maxwell's nickname of "Fatty" at Chicago irritated the oversized young man, who also suffered the stigma of a

stutter. Perhaps the modification to "Tiny" while at Swarthmore made him feel more welcome.

Despite its student body's size, Swarthmore was a highly rated team with aspirations of competing for top football honors. The opening game of its 1905 season at the Quakers' Franklin Field, scheduled against the national champion, Penn, represented a huge opportunity for Swarthmore and a far greater challenge than a friendly local warmup game for Penn.

The Quakers were a perennial contender for the national title, given their model of leveraging their Ivy League status to attract top players who may not have qualified academically for admission to their rival institutions. News stories regularly called out Penn for irregularities in its gridiron program, including a series of years in which its captains failed to graduate, including Blondy Wallace after the 1900 season. Chaos seemed to be the rule with Penn football, but it still generally thrived over the prior decade with a full complement of All-Americans and attitude.

By all media accounts, Penn's roughnecks eventually had their way with Swarthmore's squad on October 7, 1905, but not with Maxwell. In the game's waning moments, with the contest firmly in Penn's hand with an 11–4 lead, Quakers quarterback Vince "Demon" Stevenson paused after a meaningless play to compliment Maxwell on his outstanding performance. "Tiny, you've played the greatest game we've ever seen," said Stevenson. "You can lighten up now. We've got the game, so we're going to take it easy on you." On the next play, Stevenson called a QB plunge through the line straight at Maxwell. With Tiny's guard down, Stevenson laid a forearm shiver squarely in Maxwell's face, shattering his nose and covering him with enough blood to cause a grisly sight. In his follow-up column, renowned sportswriter Grantland Rice suggested that Maxwell's face looked like steak tartare. Wallace was on Penn's sideline as the offensive line coach before Canton recruited him later that season.

Legend holds that a newspaper photo of Maxwell's on-field condition caught President Theodore Roosevelt's attention. It was said to be the final straw in leading Roosevelt to declare that the game must be reformed. However, the meeting had been planned well before the Maxwell incident. Roosevelt's son, Ted, was on Harvard's freshman team, and some felt that the president's paternal instincts were influencing his outlook on the game. In any case, two days later, Roosevelt held a football summit at the White House with the coaches and other administrators from Harvard, Yale, and Princeton, including Walter Camp. While no transcript of the meeting exists, Roosevelt reportedly opened the conference by saying, "Football is on trial!"

Although Roosevelt did not play football due to his nearsightedness and lack of size, he was a firm believer in the "strenuous life," the cultural trend of "Muscular Christianity," and the character-building qualities the sport instilled. As head of the First U.S. Volunteer Cavalry Regiment, nicknamed the Rough

Quarterback Vince Stevenson at the University of Pennsylvania in 1905

Riders, during the Spanish-American War in 1898, he intentionally selected men with college football experience. While some feared that Roosevelt would push to abolish the sport, following the effort of Charles Eliot, president of Harvard, Roosevelt's alma mater, he continued the gathering by proclaiming, "Because I believe in the game, I want to do all I can to save it. And so I have called you all down here to see whether you won't all agree to abide by both the letter and spirit of the rules, for that will help." In fewer words, fix it.

The immediate result of the two-hour meeting was a vague statement by Camp acknowledging the group's obligation to "carry out … the rules of the game of football relating to roughness, holding, and foul play." Under the name of the International Football Rules Committee, these leaders began meeting to discuss potential reforms. The following month, though, on November 25, 20-year-old Union College star Harold Moore died of a cerebral hemorrhage shortly after a game against New York University. The knee of an NYU lineman struck his jaw while Moore attempted to make a tackle during a mass play. NYU chancellor Henry MacCracken stated that this tragedy motivated him to take the lead from the heads of the elite football powers to rally delegates from 13 colleges, separate from Camp's group, to join an exploratory December 6 meeting in New York City to consider other options.

Many believed that MacCracken's inner circle was intent on abolishing the sport, and the group came within one vote of passing a resolution to do so under the rules at the time. Instead, their debate led them to reconvene in New York for the National Football Conference of Universities and Colleges on December 28, attended by a much larger group of representatives from over 60 universities.

Without support for abolition from the group at large, a consensus formed to select an Executive Committee responsible for drafting a constitution and bylaws for a new organization to be called the Intercollegiate Athletic Association of the United States (IAAUS). Given broader concerns raised over various forms of admission and compensation commonly known to be provided to student-athletes across many sports, the entity's mission statement became "the reform not only of football but intercollegiate athletics as a whole." Arrangements were made within weeks for the Intercollegiate Football Rules Committee to merge with the IAAUS to promote joint action. The IAAUS was then formally constituted on March 31, 1906. It was renamed the National Collegiate Athletic Association (NCAA) in 1910.

The IAAUS's rule changes were radical, and they further and permanently distanced American football from its rugby roots, while creating the foundation for today's style of play. Most prominent among the modifications was the implementation of the forward pass. Backward laterals were previously passed on from rugby, and pitchouts for end runs were the only alternative to interior line mass plays in the running game. Adding a

President Theodore Roosevelt's belief in football's benefits led him to push the game's leaders to institute reforms to improve the game's safety.

THE PRESIDENT GOES TO THE FOOTBALL GAME

line of scrimmage with a neutral zone, requiring all linemen to start on the scrimmage line, and allowing other players to split wide from the line to break downfield to receive passes, added entirely new dimensions to the game. Also, the distance required to gain a first down was increased to 10 from 5 yards, and the game was shortened from 70 to 60 minutes.

With offensive linemen now assuming designated spots on the line, mass formations like the flying wedge were eliminated. The committee's thinking was that this would lead to more open field play and fewer injuries, along with a more exciting and fan-friendly product. Rule makers hoped that these changes would end the game's dark ages, allowing the uniquely American sport that had spread across the country to be preserved and grow in a more streamlined and palatable form heading into the 1906 season. Since the professional game followed collegiate rules, the pros would also need to adjust to a very different style of play in the season ahead.

President Roosevelt crossing the field at halftime of the Army-Navy football game with members of his cabinet in Philadelphia on November 30, 1901

> In life as in a football game the principle to follow is: Hit the line hard; don't foul and don't shirk, but hit the line hard.
> Theodore Roosevelt.

**A forward pass thrown in the first year of its implementation
in a 1906 game at Exposition Park in Pittsburgh**

THE CANTON-MASSILLON RIVALRY EXPLODES

In days of old, when knights were bold,
and barons held their sway—
The atmosphere was rife, I hear,
with war cries, day-by-day.
From morn to night, they'd scrap and fight,
with battle-ax and mace,
while seas of blood poured like a flood,
about the market place.
But no fight ever fought before beneath the
shining sun,
Will be like that when Canton's team lines
up with Mass-i-llon.
—Grantland Rice, 1906

Blondy Wallace had a bite of the apple in 1905. It left a bad taste in his mouth. He was late to the game after taking over at Canton in midseason, and the formidable Massillon Tigers machine was too much for him to overcome on short notice. He watched from close by, but from the outside looking in, as Canton's neighbors reveled in their glory and flaunted their laurels. Surely, he believed, he could tame the Tigers and conquer the pro football world, given a full season at the helm.

In 1906, Wallace decided to take pro football by storm, but opposing forces carried greater resistance than he expected. With months to brood over the hit to his ego from his failed championship guarantee and no rules from an overseeing league organization to constrain him, it seemed nothing could stop him from building the most preeminent pro football powerhouse to ever take the field. It was a land grab, like the land rush into the Unassigned Lands of Oklahoma only 17 years earlier.

It was also a power grab. But right from the start, Wallace faced headwinds, even from within his own camp. One of the consequences of not backing up his title vow the year before was that he lost the confidence of the Canton Athletic Club's backers. Initially, CAC manager George Williams did not even want to put another team on the field. Wallace had enjoyed full access to the club's wallet in '05, but his reckless spending to fortify the team with depth players only guaranteed red ink on the accounting ledger.

Pressure from fans, though, led Williams to cut Wallace a deal. CAC would take a 10 percent cut off the top of ticket sales for the use of the club's name and facilities, with Wallace assuming all of the financial risk and the rest of the reward. Taking this on was no small risk, as no organization had yet proven pro football to be a profitable venture. The entire Pittsburgh era of pro football had failed for this reason. But Captain Wallace boldly agreed, thereby also becoming Manager Wallace. Now it was Wallace, instead of CAC, who was on the financial hook. The considerable responsibilities of the manager's role also effectively precluded Wallace from focusing on his role as a position player, but he readily accepted for full control. According to the *Latrobe Daily Advance*, as reported by the *Canton Morning News* on November 24, 1906, the scope of these duties and benefits was more than one might think:

**Canton Athletic Club
business manager
George Williams**

It is his duty to make dates, act as press agent and lie to the sporting editors, get up display paper … make contracts with hotels, hire policemen and do numerous other things which keep him in the limelight except when the eleven is in the game.

It is as much his duty to break as make dates. If the coach thinks the eleven is not in the class with another eleven with which a game has been booked it is the manager's duty to break the agreement, and do it so the weakness of the team will not be disclosed. He must under no circumstances hesitate to lie if his team can't avoid defeat by any other device.

The manager must possess business qualifications of a high order. Sufficiently high to get a rakeoff from the gate receipts. If there is any graft to be distributed he should be in on it. If he isn't he is a failure as a manager.

How highly do students esteem
The man who lies so for his team!

It is notable that lying and graft were then considered an acceptable, or at least an acknowledged, part of administering a professional sport. The culture around the business dealings of pro football was becoming a constant game of one-upmanship. It certainly was not about making money; it was more about the glory and bragging rights that came to the community and the backers with a victory over rivals, while keeping the backers from losing too much money.

Losses could also be recouped by hitting up friends and foes for gambling winnings, which was neither a small nor a private matter, as newspapers constantly referenced odds on games and amounts changing hands. The Victorian values of character and sportsmanship were being marginalized, though some called them hypocritical. The Amateur Athletic Union tried to preserve the traditional culture, but the horse was out of the barn. Now the world would watch professionalism continue to play out in the football arena.

The first task at hand for every team was to put a tentative schedule together. The pro squads built their early season schedules with a mix of college, amateur, and semi-pro teams, intending to build up to big games with championship implications at the season's end. Plans often changed during the season. Managers angled to draw bigger crowds with better opponents and sometimes saved face by canceling when a massacre was the expected result. Securing a guarantee was one way to prevent a costly cancellation.

The most significant variable driving teams' financial outcomes, other than weather, was attendance. A typical crowd at the early season games was 500 to 1,000 people. Admission was usually 50 cents and another 50 for reserved seats. Big games yielded twice the fee. More competitive games drew at least a few thousand people, but there was hope that better players and stronger rivalries would drive that number higher. A home game on Thanksgiving Day against a rival and with a title on the line was the best opportunity for financial success.

Blondy Wallace boldly took on financial responsibility for Canton's football team to keep it running in 1906.

As the titleholder, Massillon was in the driver's seat heading into scheduling talks with Canton for the 1906 season. A September 7 preseason story in the *Massillon Morning Gleaner*, where E.J. Stewart had taken over as sports editor, indicated that Wallace seemed amenable to the traditional pecking order, saying his "every statement indicated that he wished to negotiate only in the friendliest sort of a spirit with fairness to both parties to the contract and in a true sportsmanlike manner." However, the article also referenced a rumor circulating in Massillon that Wallace had signed several Tigers from the previous year. Wallace bristled at the assertion, saying, "I have kept my word, and any such talk is absolutely untrue, and is probably circulated with the object of injuring my reputation." Either his guard or his poker face was up early.

To confirm the gentlemen's agreement between Canton's Wallace and Massillon's Stewart, the teams' leadership groups met at Canton's Lakeside Country Club a few days later. The *Massillon Evening Independent* reported on September 11, "It was also agreed by Managers Stewart and Wallace not to tamper with the members of the other's team."

Any cordial feelings between the two sides, if they ever existed, did not last long. Stewart made it clear from the start that he thought Massillon was entitled to the lion's share of their games' revenue because of the Tigers' status as defending world champions, for which he had plenty of his community's support. During the protracted negotiations, on October 2, the

As both sides angled for an edge in 1906, the *Massillon Morning Gleaner* and Tigers management seemed to enjoy causing Wallace pain at every turn.

TIGER DENTIST—This will materially reduce the Cranial swelling.

George "Peggy" Parratt (back row, second from right), at Case in 1905, became a legend in early Ohio pro football.

Canton Morning News quoted one rooter saying, "Why the idea of the Canton management wanting an equal share of the gate receipts, when with a second rate team like Canton has they ought to be glad to have even a chance to witness a game that the Tigers participate in. You bet they will come to our milk as they can't play with Massillon."

Meanwhile, both teams went about signing players for the season ahead. Massillon fired a shot across the bow when the *Gleaner* (i.e., Stewart) taunted Canton's management (i.e., Wallace) for missing out when the Tigers signed Cleveland lad George "Peggy" Parratt, considered by many to be the best end in the state. Parratt signed with Massillon, but his talent came with quite a bit of controversy.

Toward the end of the previous season, when Parratt was playing college football for Case, he succumbed to the temptation to play professionally for a "neat sum" from the Shelby Blues. Hoping to conceal his identity with the alias "Jimmy Murphy" and a nose guard covering his face, he suited up for the Blues against Toledo. The disguise failed when Parratt sprinted for 60 yards for the game-winning touchdown run, and the media outed him.

Case then banned Parratt from further participation on its football team, as well as its basketball and baseball teams. Other college athletes had done the same thing and stayed eligible by denying the claims. Parratt, however, brazenly admitted his moonlighting when questioned by the chairman of the school's athletic board and added that he planned to do it again. Thus, he became the first college football player to be "barred" for going pro. He remained a student and graduated from Case in 1906, going on to an illustrious career in professional sports. Parratt's first move was to commit to playing for Massillon that fall, though he required a salary advance to deter him from accepting a handsome offer to coach the Marietta College football team.

⪦ Walter East: "The Boy Wonder" ⪧

Blondy Wallace then pulled one over on E.J. Stewart when the *Gleaner* announced, on September 7, that Canton signed "boy wonder" Walter East, manager of the Akron Rubbernecks minor league baseball team in the Ohio and Pennsylvania League. Massillon was also bidding for his services.

Born in 1883 in Coulterville, Illinois, East got the most out of his college football career. He first starred for four seasons at Geneva College, outside of Pittsburgh, from 1900 to 1903. After graduating from Geneva, he then helped the Western University of Pennsylvania, while in law school there, to an undefeated 10–0 season under former Homestead gridiron hero Arthur St. Leger Mosse in 1904.

Besides football, East also excelled in baseball and basketball in college, and his many talents created multiple opportunities for him. Between his stays at Geneva and WUP, he joined the Akron baseball team, then known as the Blues, playing second base in the summer of 1904. His performance, popularity, and insight for the game led the club to consider him for more. East began law school at WUP after the 1904 season ended and returned to the renamed Akron Buckeyes in the summer of 1905. Midway through the season, Akron hired him as the O&P's youngest manager, at age 22, while he

The 1904 Western University of Pennsylvania (later Pitt) team, coached by former Homestead star Arthur St. Leger Mosse (back row, center), was undefeated with Walter East (middle row, left) playing end.

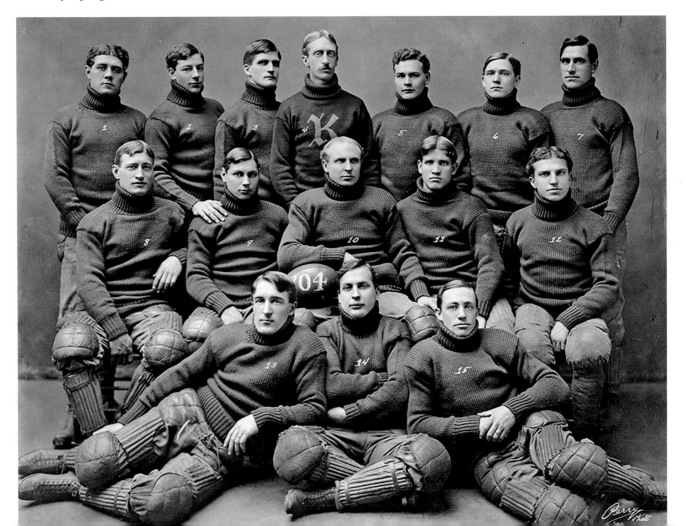

still played second base. In its announcement of the hiring, the *News-Journal* (Mansfield, OH) stated that he was 25 at the time, possibly an exaggeration on East's part to qualify for the job. East also drew interest from the American League's Cleveland Naps but did not get called up to the big leagues.

The Akron signing drew a cynical headline from the *Pittsburg Press* on May 17, 1905, questioning East's future status at the institution by stating, "WUP Student (?) Is to Have Charge of Professional Team." Despite being recognized by the *Akron Beacon Journal* for being "modest and cool-headed," and leading the team to the best season in its history (a second-place finish), the "anvil chorus" of the fans' discontent led East to resign at season's end.

Before the season ended, the *Beacon Journal* announced that East decided to leave WUP, signing to play pro football with Canton for the upcoming season. The *Press* was even less kind in its assessment of East's move, directly attacking his character. "East has come out in the role of an undisguised professional. While there is no denying his ability on the gridiron, diamond and basketball floor, he is not a fit man for a college team, for he has been receiving pay for his work for years. [Geneva and WUP teammate] Joe Thompson could probably tell something about East's career at Geneva College, and that concessions were made him at WUP last year there is little doubt. It is said that he actually demanded a large bonus to return to WUP this fall, and was curtly turned down," said the *Press*.

East planned to finish his law degree at Western Reserve in Ohio while playing for Canton, but WUP lured him back, by one means or another. On September 21, the *Press* grudgingly announced, "It is said that Walter East, end on last year's Western University eleven, has decided to re-enter the university, and try for his old position. East's demands have certainly shown that all the interest he has in the matter is from a financial standpoint, and, if eligibility rules count for anything, it is not likely that East will play football at WUP."

On the same day, though, the *Pittsburg Weekly Gazette* was more forgiving in assessing the "star end's" qualifications. "The charge of professionalism was brought against East some time ago, but not in an official way. However, the fact that he played professional baseball this summer is not expected to hurt his chances of taking his place on the WUP team," wrote the *Gazette*.

Of course, East did play for WUP in 1905. He was credited by the *Beacon Journal* for being the team's best player, though he missed a game due to a knee injury that would affect his baseball career down the road. He also lost his reputation for being "cool-headed," slugging a Washington & Jefferson player and thus getting ejected from the game. Despite a 10–2 season, with losses only to Cornell and State College, dissension reportedly ripped through the team. Days after the season-ending loss to the Nittany Lions, as they became known in 1904, East claimed that Coach Mosse played favorites on the team, and a few others said that they would not return if the school did not relieve Mosse of his duties. An unidentified player was said to want Mosse's job. East did not have the option to return to play since his six years of college football eligibility had expired, and he would soon have his law degree in hand. His football coaching aspirations were unclear, but based on his baseball managerial experience, it would have been a logical assumption that East considered dethroning Mosse.

On December 14, relieved that East had "passed through another football season and is still alive and kicking," the *Elyria Reporter* of Lorain, Ohio, wrote:

> East should give up the football game, for he is too valuable a man on the diamond to be taking a chance at the strenuous game of football. East is in much demand for 1906, but he has assured the Akron management that he will be with that team in the gentle spring. East is reported to have ye lady fair in Akron, which is also a strong inducement.

The same month, the *Beacon Journal* reported that Barney Dreyfuss had some interest in bringing East onto his Pittsburg Pirates. Either love of "ye lady fair" won out or East did not get the big-league offer, and he took over the helm again at Akron in the spring of 1906.

One word repeatedly used to describe East in multiple publications was "clever." A few years after the fact, on February 1, 1909, the *Beacon Journal* described an incident in which East's antics drew the ire of an umpire during his days managing and playing for Akron circa 1906:

> Walter East, who managed Akron then … pulled off one of the tricks on [umpire Sam] Wise which turn an umpire's head grey. East got away with it all right, and as usual the umpire was blamed for the whole proceeding.
>
> Mansfield was playing in Akron one day and Akron hadn't hit the ball hard enough to damage any of the fences. "Hezzy" Breymaier, Mansfield's catcher, was throwing well to the bases, so stealing was out of the question. Toward the latter part of the game Walter East was due to bat when two were out. Dick Nallin followed East.
>
> "If I get on," said East, "you watch me. When I'm going down I'll yell: 'Sam! Sam!' in a loud voice. Then you shove Breymaier just as he catches the ball and we'll get away with it."
>
> Well, East went to the plate and stopped a pitched ball with his ribs. Nallin then came up … East had a big lead and was well on his way to second. Just as the pitcher started to deliver the ball, East shouted "Sam! Sam!" and Sam looked around to see who was addressing him and why.

Just as Breymaier caught the ball Nallin reached far over the plate and shoved him so hard he almost sat down. Sam Wise discovered about that time that East had no business with him and turned around in time to see Breymaier standing on his feet and holding the ball. Of course, East made second base in safety.

Immediately there was a big howl. Breymaier rushed out to Wise and yelled:

"He shoved me, Sam, he shoved!"

"What if he did," responded the umpire, "I didn't see him do it," and no end of argument could persuade Wise to change his decision. Wise, however, stopped the game long enough to bawl out East and wound up by telling him he'd call him out every time he came to bat if he tried anything like that again.

At various times with Akron, East was also fined for being caught with doctored balls, admitted to stealing catchers' signs, and was ejected for baiting umpires. After a second straight second-place finish in the O&P League in 1906, it remained to be seen whether he was too clever for his own good.

⇌ The War for Talent ⇌

Along with signing Walter East to Canton for 1906, Blondy Wallace moved to firm up his team's line by securing the only center known to hold his own against Bob Shiring on both sides of the line. Lynn "Pop" Sweet had been battling Shiring alongside Wallace since their 1901 games with Philadelphia against Homestead. Wallace said in the *Gleaner* on September 7, "Sweet is the only center who ever put it over on Bob Shiring, but as Shiring was not at his best at the time, I look for a great battle when the two players clash." It was high praise from Wallace to acknowledge the Tigers' superiority in any regard. Yet Massillon's followers responded that they must be shown that Sweet "ever had, has or will have anything on our invulnerable Bob."

The last time Sweet and Shiring squared off in 1903, Sweet benefited from Franklin's overall superiority to Shiring's amateur East End team. Shiring had the upper hand in their other matchup in 1902 between Pittsburg and Philadelphia. While Shiring did not play in Pittsburg's loss to Sweet's Philadelphia team that year, he did control the rematch in which the Stars won the 1902 championship.

Wallace was under the gun in 1906 to redeem himself from his 1905 failure without going bankrupt in the process. Meanwhile, pro football was rapidly evolving, including seismic rule changes requiring entirely new skills and strategies. Team managers made many moves to fortify their rosters, which would presage the game's future. This metamorphosis from

Lynn "Pop" Sweet (pictured in a Latrobe uniform in 1905) rivaled Bob Shiring on both sides of the line at the center position in many world championship games in the first decade of the 1900s.

The undefeated 1904 University of Pennsylvania Quakers football team was named national champions by most voting organizations.
It featured four members of the College Football Hall of Fame and 10 who achieved All-American status in their careers. Three played for Canton in 1906 (Vince Stevenson—front row, second from right, Marshall Reynolds—second row, second from right, and Andy "Bull" Smith—third row, left) and one for Massillon (Otis Lamson—third row, right).

PENNSYLVANIA
OFFICIAL FOOT-BALL SCHEDULE
1904

Penn

SEPTEMBER

6 Saturday, 24, State at Franklin Field. 0
6 Wednesday, 28, Swarthmore at Franklin 4
Field.

OCTOBER

24 Saturday, 1, Virginia at Franklin Field. 0
34 Wednesday, 5, Franklin & Marshall at 0
Franklin Field.
24 Saturday, 8, Lehigh at Franklin Field. 0
21 Wednesday, 12, Gettysburg at Franklin 0
Field
6 Saturday, 15, Brown at Franklin Field. 0
16 Saturday, 22, Columbia at Franklin Field. 1
11 Saturday, 29, Harvard at Cambridge, Mass. 0

NOVEMBER

22 Saturday, 5, Lafayette at Franklin Field. 0
18 Saturday, 12, Indians at Franklin Field. 0
34 Thursday, 24, Cornell at Franklin Field. 0

(OVER)

UNIVERSITY OF PENNSYLVANIA SEASON 1904

amateurism into professionalism took place very publicly, just as the great teams and rivalries of Ohio began catching media attention nationwide.

With a limited pool of talent, Wallace preferred the devils he knew to those he did not, tapping back into his pipeline of Penn stars to bring in quarterback Vince Stevenson and halfback Bull Davidson. With injuries prevalent, and no constraints on roster size, there was no harm in stockpiling talent, especially at quarterback, as long as the money was available. Blondy Wallace was all in.

Within a week of joining Canton in mid-September, though, Stevenson's demons followed him. Police arrested him in Akron for assaulting passersby and resisting an officer. A judge fined Stevenson $25 plus court costs after Wallace defended his quarterback at the hearing, arguing that Stevenson's reputation for being rowdy had been exaggerated by Massillon reporters.

Meanwhile, in Massillon, Stewart had another epiphany that would take his team to the next level. Swarthmore's star captain, Sherburn Wightman, had grown up in the Cleveland area and started his college career at the University of Chicago under the tutelage of coaching legend Amos Alonzo Stagg. As he was familiar with Wallace's tactics, having been a part of the infamous Swarthmore-Penn game the previous year, Wightman was an ideal candidate for his successor as the team's coach. With a more prominent role for himself in mind, Stewart received assistance from Massillon's administration in suggesting to Tigers manager J.J. Wise that his role as clerk of Massillon City Council would be too time-consuming in addition to running the Tigers. While public service was not an obstacle for Wise the prior year, the humble servant took the hint and stepped aside for Stewart to fill the role. It changed everything.

The pants worn by the ball carrier in this 1904 Penn game used wooden strips for thigh protection

PRICE, TEN CENTS

THANKSGIVING 1905

Quarterbacks Vince Stevenson of Canton and Cooney Rice of Massillon faced off in this 1905 Thanksgiving game between Penn and Cornell, with Penn winning 6–5.

The 1906 Massillon
Tigers recruited
Swarthmore captain
Sherburn Wightman
(back row, center) and
Robert "Tiny"
Maxwell (front, right).

Even better for the Tigers, though, would be if Wightman could convince his dominant Swarthmore teammate, Tiny Maxwell, to join him in Massillon. With the lure of exacting justice on Stevenson, who rearranged Maxwell's face in their 1905 encounter, and his band of thugs from Penn, Tiny gratefully obliged.

Both teams continued adding to their rosters and haggling over the agreement's details for their presumptive "world championship" end-of-season games. In the meantime, with enough players in the fold on both sides, it was time to get down to the business of training. The talent already assembled on both rosters was unlike anything ever seen before in football. Canton and Massillon amassed an embarrassment of riches relative to other teams, even the ones calling themselves professional. No other team could reasonably hope to compete with either of these compilations of superstars. The 1906 season would merely be a buildup to the clash of these titans, but only if the parties could reach an agreement on terms for a dream matchup.

Heading into its opener with the Pittsburg Lyceum on September 29, Massillon had 29 players under contract. Unlike previous years, when stars might appear for just one big game, most of its top players signed on for the whole season. Thus, Stewart felt that his "clean-cut" Tigers were likely 50 percent stronger to start the 1906 campaign than his 1905 world champions. Coach Wightman, also a substitute fullback, shared Stewart's optimism, telling the *Gleaner* on September 26, "Don't believe I ever saw such a promising bunch on a foot ball field." With knowledge of the Lyceum's strength from his hometown, Bob Shiring added a dose of humility: "They'll give us a great game…. The Pittsburg gang will play their heads off to defeat the world's champions. They have a much better team than ever before."

On that rainy Saturday in Massillon, Tigers fans broke out their colors on downtown streets to support their city and heroes. The question was which colors to break out. While Massillon historians are uncertain about the exact timing of the change, it was around this time that the Tiger-like black and orange began replacing what the *Gleaner* called the "old gold and black" as representative of the city's spirit and inspiration.

At Massillon's Asylum Field, on the grounds of the state mental hospital, the Tigers methodically plodded their way to a modest 19–0 victory over the Lyceum. It could have been a notable date in pro football history, as it presented each team the opportunity to attempt the game's first forward pass. However, the slippery conditions discouraged either team from trying the new technique, especially given the punitive nature of the new rule, making an incomplete pass a turnover.

Even before the season opener, Canton's management group approached Massillon's, proposing a pair of games between the rivals. But by Tuesday, October 2, after the Tigers' first game, talks broke down. Not only did the hostility between the sides put their contests at risk, but it also began a feud between the two teams and towns that has never healed to this day.

The Tigers believed that their championship status entitled them to dictate contract terms. They provided Canton with multiple offers for a two-game series, with the second game on Thanksgiving Day at Massillon, and each scenario included a financial incentive for the winner. Confident that its Tigers would prevail, Massillon started by suggesting "winner-takes-all" revenue for each game. When Canton rejected that as a nonstarter, Massillon reduced the winner's take to 60 percent and then 55 percent. Finally, Massillon offered an even split on the condition that there would be only one game at Massillon on Thanksgiving Day. Canton management collectively stated in the *Gleaner*, "We will stand for nothing but an equal division of money, and two games."

Neither side showed signs of budging any further. According to a typically partisan *Gleaner* account on October 3:

> The meeting was not particularly warm, although Canton managers showed a slight inclination to get warm beneath the collar at times. It was the same old proposition. Canton has an exalted opinion of her value as an attraction, and believes she is entitled to as much of the gate receipts as are the Tigers. Of course, to the Massillon fans who have built up such a team after four years of hard work and the expenditure of thousands and thousands of dollars the claim is preposterous. The idea of a team springing up in a year to a position where it is entitled to an equal division of receipts with the world's champion team, is to say the least, ridiculous, and their claims were refused.

Stewart left the meeting facing a crisis. A season without at least one game with Canton was a recipe for financial failure. So, he bypassed Wallace and reached out to George Williams, financial manager of the Canton Athletic Club, to salvage a deal. Massillon Athletic Club president Herbert Croxton also had friends reach out to Wallace on a late-night call. Asked what the discussion was about, Wallace said to the *Gleaner*, "Cantonians know what the local management's stand is, and there'll never be a change."

Even while reporting the collapse in talks, the *Gleaner* gave Stewart a chance to save face by suggesting anonymously, in another story on the page, that Stewart could concede to Canton's demands and make it look like he and the Tigers were taking the high road. "Massillon's athletic teams are put into the field to fight and not to fiddle away the season bickering for slight financial advantage," the *Gleaner* wrote. "Hence Canton will be gratified for once." While Stewart, as sports editor, either supplied or approved the quote, without bylines on newspaper articles at that time, he did not have to eat crow.

It was too late, though. Wallace took a 2:00 a.m. train toward Pennsylvania to schedule a Thanksgiving Day game with Latrobe. The sentiment in Canton was, "Let Massillon go its way. Canton is big enough to support its team," according to the *Gleaner*. Perhaps at the root of the matter was a culture clash. Wallace was not from the Midwest. He subscribed to a tougher and more direct northeastern ethos. Stewart misread Wallace's resolve and was stubborn enough to believe that Wallace's trip was a bluff to force a better deal.

Any hopes for reconciliation were dashed when Wallace dropped the hammer the following day. He still had a few slots to fill on his roster before Canton's Saturday opener with Fredericksburg. Perhaps he was inspired by the *College Widow,* a popular 1904 Broadway comedy. The plot was that

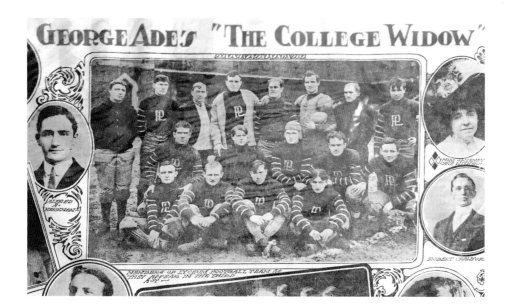

Members of the Pittsburg Lyceum, including Frank Piefer (back row, left) and Doc McChesney (back row third from right), joined the cast of the popular play *The College Widow* for a stint in the Steel City in 1908.

the daughter of a college president lures the star of a rival college football team to transfer schools. It also occurred to Wallace that his most likely path to a championship was to entice some of the Tigers to swap colors. As multiyear contracts had not yet been conceived, it was a logical solution to offer more money to a few of his friends who were now on the team on the other side of Stark County.

A series of headlines started appearing across Stark County, on October 4, about one Tigers star after another defecting to Canton. Lineman Jack Lang, Wallace's teammate on the 1903 Franklin championship team, was first. Massillon had provided Lang with a lucrative summer job at a local auto manufacturer and picked up his hotel bill, but when Wallace returned to Canton later in the summer, Lang left town "without so much as paying his board bill or bidding the team adieu," according to the *Gleaner*. Lang then went on to act as Wallace's "cat's paw," reeling in another former Franklin AC teammate, end Clark Schrontz, and making overtures to others not scheduled to rejoin the Tigers until later in the season, such as Herman Kerkhoff and Jack Hayden.

Stewart was livid, though he consoled himself by thinking that disloyal men were not the kind that he ultimately wanted on his team. While shocking to the Massillon fanbase, which prided itself on its players' character and team play, these changes of allegiance were testament to these men's trust and faith in Wallace based on their experience. Still, in violating his gentlemen's agreement with Stewart not to poach each other's players, Wallace apparently did not care whether he was considered a gentleman, which the *Gleaner* made clear:

1906 Massillon Tigers pin-ribbon

> Manager Wallace gave his hand to Manager Stewart and Assistant Manager Wittman, while the three were in conference at Meyer's Lake two months ago, that he would not at any cost touch a player on the Tiger squad, and the local management took the same obligation.
>
> That Wallace had deliberately broken his word as a gentleman was known two weeks ago concerning the signing of Lang, and now he endeavors to cover up the piece of treachery by claiming that he signed the men after the disagreement Monday.

Wallace claimed in his defense that Massillon could not afford his new recruits and that he did not decide to sign them until negotiations for an even revenue share fell through. Accusations aside, it was open season on top players, and money frequently spoke louder than words. Free agency had been born.

Further damaging Wallace's credibility were earlier reports by the *Gleaner* that he had also tried to pry Shiring away from Massillon with an offer of $500 for the season, more than Massillon offered. For Shiring, though, loyalty to his team outweighed a higher offer. The *Gleaner* sang his praises in its article headlined "'Smiling' Bob Shiring Here":

> The big good natured center, loyal as he can be, reached the city Wednesday evening. Bob Shiring is here. That is all that is necessary to cause the heart of the Tiger fan to flutter with pleasure, as it means that the keystone position on the Tiger team this fall will be taken care of as no other center in the country can care for it.
>
> Bob's arrival put a quietus to the rumors circulated by some "knockers" that the popular center would not return this season, and that Canton had bought him off. "I turned down a good offer from Canton, though" said Bob when this report was repeated to him. It might be remarked that this loyalty to Tigertown is what has made the big center one of the most popular foot ball players who ever donned the orange and black, and will insure a warm spot in the hearts of the fans and management.

In Canton, Lang voiced a more pragmatic, free-market perspective regarding his choice of teams in his interview with the *Morning News* on October 5. "I would rather play in Canton than Massillon and am sure that Schrontz would also, and seeing that Canton offered us more than the Tigers were able to produce, we signed up with Wallace," said Lang.

In Massillon's second game, on Saturday, October 6, Muskingum College literally, as well as figuratively, provided no obstacle for the Tigers, who scored 16 five-point touchdowns in a 96–0 rout. The *Gleaner* remarked that "the splendid human machine which Coach Wightman is perfecting worked Saturday with a large reserve of power, yet they worked with beautiful precision." The most notable occurrence of the game was Shiring's feat of setting a record that likely still stands by kicking 16 consecutive extra points in one game. The *Gleaner* recognized the accomplishment the following day:

> Although few of the fans realized it, and it was probable that the big center himself was unaware of it, Bob Shiring made a world's record Saturday in kicking sixteen goals after touchdown in sixteen attempts. This, too, when it was not known to the coach, management or players that the big fellow had such a great ability in this line. Many of the goals were from different angles and some against a strong wind. In looking over the records Monday it was found that Shiring had established a record in this respect and if proper application is filed and notice served it is probable that the big fellow's feat will go down in the official Spaulding's [*sic*] record book.

Jack Lang (above), pictured earlier with Latrobe, and Clark Schrontz played with the Massillon Tigers in 1905 and were the team's first to sign with Canton in 1906.

'SMILING" BOB SHIRING HERE

BIG GOOD NATURED CENTER, LOYAL AS HE CAN BE, REACHED THE CITY WEDNESDAY EVENING.

Wallace returned to Canton from his trip to Pennsylvania, with Schrontz in tow, for their first game scheduled the same day, against a team from nearby Fredericksburg, Ohio, coached by former Massillon Tiger William "Doc" Merriam. Despite its short distance from Canton, Merriam's team showed up too late to start the game, so the parties agreed to play the next day, Sunday, instead. That Wallace scheduled a game on a Sunday was another snub to traditionalists.

Most of Wallace's new platoon finally took the field on the Lord's Day, but Lang and Schrontz, who had moral objections to Sunday football, watched from the bench. Nonetheless, even with Canton playing an overmatched team, 895 fans, an encouraging number by pro football standards, confessed their love for the game by purchasing tickets. They turned out to see Canton perform similarly to Massillon the day before, with a 58–0 drubbing of Fredericksburg that was shortened by the teams' mutual agreement shortly after halftime. "Going through the visitors' line like water going through a sieve, the wearers of the red and white had little trouble in piling up a good sized score in thirty-five minutes of play," the *Canton Morning News* reported the next day.

Detailed accounts of both games again showed no indication of an attempted forward pass. However, the *Morning News* believed that another new rule requiring a gain of 10 yards, instead of 5, in three downs "made the Fredericksburg boys pitifully handicapped … against such bulk it was well nigh impossible and they were compelled to surrender the pigskin after a few futile attempts to gain the required number of yards."

That night, before returning home from his own Pennsylvania recruiting trip to continue negotiations with Canton, Stewart stopped in Latrobe to verify that Wallace executed a contract for a game with Latrobe on Thanksgiving Day. As the *Latrobe Bulletin* reported on October 8, Stewart confirmed that Wallace was dead serious:

> The Massillon manager found out that it was no bluff, and that Latrobe was going to have a team worthy of meeting Canton's galaxy of stars.… When Mr. Stewart gets home he will probably see the Cantonian management and will agree to play Canton two games prior to Thanksgiving. It is also likely that he will agree to give Canton the percentage of the gate receipts that Canton has been demanding. For he has learned thru his visit here that Canton has him at a disadvantage, having the game arranged with an attraction like Latrobe.

Undeterred, and leaving no stone unturned, Stewart unleashed a torrent in the *Gleaner* the day after his return:

> While the loss of Schrontz and Lang was unexpected at the time … I want to say to the fans who have subscribed so liberally, that the Tigers

will not be weakened one bit by these desertions, but instead will be strengthened. Immediately upon hearing that the two men mentioned above turned us down at the last moment, I determined to go to any expense to secure the best tackle and end in the land. I succeeded, but at a big outlay of funds. All I ask of the fans now is to assist with their moral support, if not financial, in proving to Canton or other teams, that the Canton management made a big mistake when they violated their agreement and signed players from the Massillon team. Massillon has stuck closely to her promise to avoid negotiations with Canton players, and in addition will attempt to demonstrate conclusively that such duplicity does not pay.

Stewart went further to boast, "Although it is not known generally, every player who has ever played on a Massillon team was chosen by me personally." His self-righteousness ignored the implications of one very important choice: his signing of Walter East. A headline in the *Gleaner* on September 7 announced, "'Boy Manager' of the Akron O&P League Base Ball Team Has Signed With Wallace," along with a comment that East could have been secured for Massillon's team. A month later, on October 7, the *Pittsburg Press* announced in a brief post that East had joined the Tigers:

> Canton will not have the football services of the Akron baseball team manager, Walter East, this fall, despite the fact that Coach Wallace announced he had the boy manager under contract. It now develops there existed but a verbal agreement between Wallace and East, which the latter broke by signing with the Massillon Tigers for the season.

It is highly indicative that neither the *Gleaner* nor any Canton newspaper covered Stewart's move, though it was noticed in Pittsburgh. The Canton crowd did not want to touch the issue given Wallace's recruiting behavior and, in Massillon, this kind of underhandedness did not fit Stewart's noble narrative. It is possible that East's performance may not have been up to the Bulldogs' standard, as Wallace's group was loaded with talent. Based on his collegiate history, East's character may also have led Wallace to disqualify him. On the other hand, East and Wallace could have been a good fit for each other, as they were cut from the same cloth as rule breakers. Most likely, though, Stewart offered more money to East in retaliation against Wallace for his loss of other players, and it would not be a surprise that East accepted given his mercenary past. Or was something more sinister in the works?

Although Doc McChesney initially committed to return to Massillon from Pittsburgh for the 1906 season, with unnamed reinforcements on the way to Massillon, he decided to stay in the Smoky City. As a married man, he preferred to play for the Lyceum and keep his secure steel mill job, paying him $8 per day, rather than risk losing it to play for the Tigers for two months. Stewart obliged and released McChesney from his contract, which left Shiring as the only one of the original four ringers from Pittsburgh in Massillon.

As Shiring had been on the pro Tigers the longest, he was the logical candidate for team captain. The popular choice was relayed by the media across Stark County, including in the *Canton Morning News* on October 11:

> Bob Shiring was chosen captain for the Massillon Tigers for the season of 1906 on Tuesday evening. Shiring has been playing with the Tigers for the past three seasons and his return to Massillon for the fourth season has been hailed with delight by enthusiasts in that city. Bob has played in every championship battle which the Tigers have played since the first year of their organization and his selection as captain of the team is a merited one and meets with the approval of almost every fan in the western suburb.

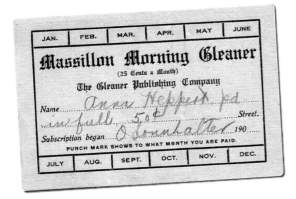

Surrounded by renowned college football players, some trained by legendary coaches from many top academic institutions, it is remarkable that Shiring, a young man with an eighth-grade education and from a blue-collar background, earned his peers' respect to rise to these heights. Such was his character.

With roster disputes having played out, it was time to move on with the season. Reflecting on the dealings, the *Morning News* had a final comment about loyalty in professional sports on October 10:

> It seems that the Massillon management is of the opinion that when they once sign a player that they have a claim upon his services for the balance of his life.... The dealings that Coach Wallace have had with Lang and Schrontz [have] been entirely honorable and within the rights of football law, as neither player had made any agreement to sign with the Tigers for this season and both players were free to sign with any team that they pleased.

As for Stewart, whose grief finally reached the acceptance stage, he took his own parting shot in the *Gleaner* on October 12:

> Schrontz and Lang are already sorry they joined the forces of the Canton players, or rumors are untrue … and if a player is out after the money alone regardless of past friendships, regards of a people with whom he

was a favorite, etc., the player is to be excused. Money will influence many people to do many things which they would not think of if it was left to their own judgment, and this is probably Lang's and Schrontz's predicament…. There is no sentiment among the players against him [Schrontz], as they realize that Schrontz looked upon the season's playing as a cool financial proposition, regardless of former associations, hence his act is excusable to the hard money world inhabitants.

Forgiven, but not forgotten.

⊱ A Tumultuous Season ⊰

Saturday, October 13, 1906, was a landmark day in pro football history due to a watershed event, contrary to the official record in every detail at the time of this publication. The Tigers traveled to Wheeling, West Virginia, to play a strong Benwood team, on which local gamblers accepted wagers at odds of only 10-to-7 as an underdog, according to the *Gleaner*.

It has long been accepted as a historical fact that Massillon quarterback George "Peggy" Parratt threw the first pro forward pass on October 25, 1906, to Dan "Bullet" Riley. New research presented here reveals a different set of facts amid intriguing circumstances. The earlier date for the first pro pass, which the *Gleaner* clearly stated in its Monday, October 15, issue, may have escaped notice because the daily editions of the *Gleaner* from 1906 have neither been transferred to microfilm nor digitized for research access. However, the Massillon Booster Club preserved perhaps the only remaining originals in its private archives. Club leaders allowed the author access to its archives in 2013 before recently transferring the club's assets to the Massillon Museum. Club videographer and Massillon native Ron Prunty explained his discovery and rescue of the originals:

> The Booster Club moved its archives four times over the years in Massillon. The last time was to the York Elementary School. The public library was temporarily storing things there, including the newspapers. They were going to be thrown out. I asked if we could have them, and they said "yes." I didn't realize that nobody else had them.

When asked why the club had not shared the discovery with the Pro Football Hall of Fame in Canton, Prunty said with a chuckle, "Maybe laziness. Maybe the rivalry. Maybe a little bit of both."

The author detailed the history-changing account of the earlier forward pass in an article in *Coffin Corner*, the magazine of the Pro Football Researchers Association (PFRA), in early 2020:

The First Pro Forward

**George "Peggy" Parratt,
1906 Massillon Tigers**

A recently discovered article in the *Massillon Morning Gleaner*, chronicling a game between the Massillon Tigers and the Benwood (West Virginia) team, references forward passes by Tigers quarterback Charley Moran on October 13, 1906. This discovery pushes back the date of this historical pro football milestone by one day.

In the previous end-of-year issue of the *Coffin Corner* (Volume 41, Number 6), Ohio researchers documented evidence from two Ohio newspapers that an unnamed pro player representing the Franklin (Ohio) Athletic Club legally hurled a pigskin forward on October 14, 1906, in a Shelby Blues home game. The Franklin pass was 11 days before one made on October 25, 1906, put forth by the PFRA in its 1979 article that set this historical marker until the end of 2019. That article cited Massillon QB George "Peggy" Parratt as the holder of this distinction while playing against the combined Benwood-Moundsville (West Virginia) team in Massillon. As the major professional teams in Ohio and Pennsylvania played a few games with this new rule before October 14, the researchers correctly added that it is still possible that an earlier instance of an attempted forward pass occurred. It turns out that an amendment to the date of the event is already necessary, in much less time than the previous 40-year interval.

One day before Franklin's game at Shelby, on Saturday, October 13, 1906, Massillon faced the standalone Benwood team at Island Ball Park in Wheeling, West Virginia. Benwood subsequently combined with its neighboring Moundsville team, hoping to provide a better challenge to the Tigers in their return match in Massillon 12 days later. An article in the *Gleaner* the following Monday, October 15, was titled "TIGERS SWAMP BENWOOD AT WHEELING SO EASY." Subtitle: "Forward Pass Worked Like a Charm—Game Rather Slow On Account of Warm Weather—Score 46–0."

Early in its game description, the *Gleaner* made a definitive statement regarding this monumental event:

For the first time this season, the Tigers attempted the forward pass and they demonstrated beyond a doubt that it could be done. Twice did the new play work for touch downs and on two more trials it netted good gains.

Excerpted from the January/February 2020 issue of the Pro Football Researchers Association's *Coffin Corner* (Volume 42, Number 1).

Pass Revisited ... Again

Then came a surprise. Before the season, Massillon's management expected the newly signed Parratt and Jack Hayden, who returned from its '05 team, to compete for the Tigers' starting QB position, according to the *Gleaner*. But Hayden had yet to report to camp as of their first game due to a mid-September injury incurred while playing baseball for the American League Boston Americans, involving a teammate kicking Hayden in the face after accusing him of lackadaisical play. Toward the end of the football season, Hayden instead signed for more money with Canton and its infamous coach "Blondy" Wallace, all of which made Parratt his apparent successor.

The Tigers played two games before the Benwood game against amateur teams, with Parratt starting at QB in the first 19–0 win against a strong Pittsburg Lyceum team on September 29 in Massillon. The announcement in the *Gleaner* on October 4 that Wallace had lured Tigers end Clark Schrontz and tackle Jack Lang into joining Canton then threw their roster into a bit of disarray. But the Tigers proceeded to trounce local Muskingum College, 96–0, with Parratt again at the helm as the starter and Charley "Rebel" Moran also getting some playing time in a backup role.

Moran had just finished the summer playing baseball for Cleburne of the Texas League. He sent a letter to Tigers management from his home in Nashville before reporting for camp, assuring them that he was "feeling like a fool for fighting" regarding his readiness. On September 13, a *Gleaner* article stated about Moran, "As a back field general he is good and his dodging runs, lightning plunges and his punting will be called into use this fall."

Heading into the next game against a Benwood team that the press expected to be competitive, Tigers coach Sherburn Wightman experimented by moving Parratt to end. His replacement at QB was Moran.

After a few weeks of practice without the great Schrontz at end, the *Gleaner* made Coach Wightman's plans clear the day before the Benwood game:

> Parrott [*sic*] makes a great showing at end, working in better
> than anyone else in the forward pass. This is owing to his
> basketball ability as he has the natural nack [*sic*] of handling

Shiring collection

**Charley Moran,
1905 Massillon Tigers**

the flying ball while on the dead run, and his passes and catches are sure. Moran at quarter works smoothly, owing to his long experience in the game. He handles the ball well, pulls the team together, and gets away with quarterback runs and kicks in pleasing shape.

In its post-game writeup on October 15, the *Gleaner* continued with no uncertainty about who executed Massillon's first forward pass:

Moran's passing to Peggy Parrot [*sic*] was perfect and the speedy little end made no delay getting away for long gains.

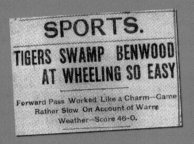

Headline in the *Massillon Gleaner* about the team's first forward pass on October 13, 1906, which is the earliest documented pro forward pass

So, the mantle has officially been passed, at least for now, from Parratt to Moran, just as Moran passed the pigskin to Parratt on that fall afternoon early in the 1906 season. Not only does the *Gleaner* document Moran as holding the honor of attempting the first pro forward pass, but it also establishes him as the first to complete a pass and touchdown pass at the pro level.

With the *Gleaner*'s statement that this was the Tigers' first forward pass of the season, this forever ends the debate regarding any possible earlier attempt from the Massillon squad. The Tigers also started playing earlier than most of the few other pro teams that season since they had kept most of the team together from 1905. Other teams, including Akron, were waiting to assess the Tigers' strength to see if it would be worth spending money to challenge them, which also hinged on acquiring Tigers' castoffs.

Among candidates for other pro teams that could have thrown the forward pass earlier, Canton played its first game on October 7 and its second also on October 13. Detailed accounts of these games in the *Canton Morning News* do not indicate that a forward pass was attempted.

Elsewhere in Ohio, no stories are available in some of the primary online newspaper databases suggesting that neither Franklin, Shelby, nor any pro team other than Canton played games before or on October 13. In Pennsylvania, Latrobe was the only remaining overtly pro team, while squads such as Steelton and the remainder of the '03 Franklin (Pennsylvania) champs were likely semi-pro at best. According to the *Gleaner*, Latrobe organized its pro team on October 9, with John Brallier as manager and coach. However, it had a reserve team with some pro-caliber players that played its first game on October 6 against the Lyceum. A *Pittsburg Press* article from the next day states explicitly that neither team attempted a forward pass due to muddy conditions. Brallier's team played its first game on October 22 with Turtle Creek.

Moran's tenure as the Tigers QB was short-lived, as he incurred a badly bruised knee in the Benwood game that forced him to miss the Tigers' next few games until he returned on November 3 to rotate at the "full back" position for the rest of the season. Meanwhile, Coach Wightman reinserted Parratt at quarterback and added Cornell's "Cooney" Rice the following week as his backup.

The *Gleaner* commented on the following Monday, October 22, regarding the Tigers' 57–0 win over Shelby on October 20:

> Parrot [*sic*] at quarter handled the team well. His judgment on plays was excellent, while several times he worked in the forward pass with East, and twice this play resulted in touchdowns.

Nonetheless, as the representative of the distinction of the first pro player to throw a forward pass, potentially for perpetuity, Moran is a well-deserving and honorable character. After his two-year stint with the Tigers, he continued on a distinguished and well-documented career as a college football coach at Texas A&M from 1909 to 1914 and as an assistant with "Pop" Warner at Carlisle in 1915. Known for inspirational pep talks and pre-game prayers, Moran had his greatest coaching achievement leading the Centre College Praying Colonels (Kentucky), with a student body of 275, to a 10–1 record in 1921 while ending defending national champion Harvard's 25-game unbeaten streak in mid-season. In 1950, the *New York Times* called it "arguably the greatest sports upset of the first half of the twentieth century." In 2005, the *Times* called it "arguably the greatest upset in the history of college football."

In baseball, Moran also had brief stints with the St. Louis Cardinals as a pitcher in 1903 and catcher in 1908. He retired as a minor league player in 1913, began umpiring in the Texas League in 1915, and became a National League umpire from 1918–39. In this role, he was so well-liked that he became known as "Uncle Charley." In 1927, Moran also briefly tried his coaching hand at the NFL level as co-coach of the Frankford Yellow Jackets.

My discovery of this historical milepost is a step along the way in a much longer journey. Some PFRA members may recall my presentation at its 2014 conference in Cleveland, at which I presented my research on the pre-NFL career of my great-grandfather, Bob Shiring. "Big Bob" played center for the pro championship teams of Homestead in 1901, Pittsburg Stars in 1902, and Massillon Tigers from 1903–06. Since that presentation, my journey has continued, including many more discoveries that will add to the sport's official records with the release of my forthcoming book, *Gridiron Legacy: Pro Football's Missing Origin Story.*

As the Tigers' starting center in their 1906 game with Benwood, "Smiling Bob Shiring," as the *Gleaner* called him, may again be smiling as he rests in peace, holding the honor of having snapped the ball for the first pro forward pass … until further research may indicate otherwise.

—*Gregg Ficery*

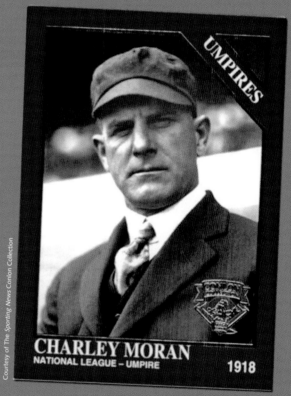

UMPIRES

CHARLEY MORAN
NATIONAL LEAGUE – UMPIRE   1918

Courtesy of The Sporting News Conlon Collection

On that same weekend of October 13, Canton played back-to-back games on Saturday and Sunday. According to the *Morning News,* Wallace's bunch conserved their energy in the first game in a 14–0 win at home against Moundsville from West Virginia. The Toledo Athletic Club was then supposed to provide stiff competition on Sunday but did not gain a first down in Canton's 31–0 victory. The most consequential development of the weekend for Canton was that Stevenson aggravated a lingering knee injury that would keep him out of the lineup at quarterback for a few games, raising questions about his durability for the season.

Ultimately, it was in the financial interest of both organizations to agree to play each other, whether Massillon got its home game with Canton on

Thanksgiving Day or not. Despite Stewart's bizarre last-ditch insistence that Wallace's agreement with Latrobe was invalid since it was not made with an official representative of the opposition, he knew he had the weaker hand and folded.

On Friday evening, October 19, the brass from both sides, including Wallace and Stewart, met in the parlors of the antebellum Hotel Conrad in Massillon to sign the inevitable deal. The management groups agreed to play at Canton on Friday, November 16, and at Massillon on Saturday, November 24, the weekend before Canton's Thanksgiving Day

The Hotel Conrad in Massillon was the meeting place for some of the negotiations between the Massillon and Canton football management teams.

game with Latrobe. The *Gleaner* conceded the next day that its home team failed in its posturing:

> To the Massillon management it is humiliation to feel compelled to give in to the Canton management, but the proposition was assuming more than a question of principle. From a financial standpoint, the Canton games were necessary…. Those who fear that Canton will not play here, should they happen to win the first game, need not worry as a $3,000 certificate of deposit will be placed in the hands of reliable bankers to bind the two teams to both games…. There will be as much satisfaction in seeing the Canton team defeated on both of these dates as there would have been to see them vanquished on Turkey Day.

Competition on the field stiffened for both teams on the weekend of October 20. Massillon lined up against Shelby on Saturday, and Canton signed up for another pair of games, with the Lyceum on Saturday and

Benwood on Sunday, all in Stark County. Never lacking in hyperbole, the *Gleaner* exclaimed before the Shelby game, "It will be for blood."

Shelby had made a late decision to field a team a few weeks into the season by rounding out a roster with castoffs from Massillon's and Canton's 1905 teams, with Charles Follis still running the ball for the Blues. Its young quarterback, Homer Davidson, was also considered the best punter and placekicker in Ohio. However, with the team's delayed start, Shelby was unprepared for the onslaught of Massillon's machinery.

Captain Shiring and Coach Wightman predicted to the *Gleaner* that the Tigers would win by three or four touchdowns, far short of the eventual 57–0 rout. In a laugher at the end, Coach Wightman himself entered late in the game and took off on a few long runs to remind everyone that he could still play. All 275 pounds of Tiny Maxwell also sped 65 yards around end for a touchdown, "shaking off tacklers like a dog would after a swim," according to the *Beacon Journal* on October 22.

East also got into the action for the first time for the Tigers, earning rave reviews from the *Gleaner*'s Monday column:

> Not a spectator doubts today that East is one of the best ends in the country…. East never failed to down his man on runs around the end, and was everywhere when the ball was in the air on punts. He made good with a vengeance, and the remarks of the crowd indicate that Schrontz will not be missed so much as was feared.

Wallace applied the same strategy as he did the previous weekend. His Giants, as the local media still referred to them, played cautiously in an 8–0 win over the Lyceum in Pittsburgh. Then they set about their primary goal for the two-game set, demonstrating their superiority to Massillon by outscoring Benwood by more than the Tigers' 46 the week before, which they did by three points in a 49–0 whitewash.

With the first Canton-Massillon battle less than a month out, both managers went into overdrive to outdo and, thereby, outspend each other in securing the ultimate roster for their duels. Wallace made the first move. He stayed in his comfort zone by bringing back four from his 1905 team, including Bull Smith and Marshall Reynolds from Penn and "Little Eva" Turner from Dartmouth. Then, he gambled once again by re-signing Willie Heston, whose poor conditioning and performance let Wallace and Canton down so badly in the 1905 game against Massillon.

Stewart countered by pulling in Otis Lamson, a consensus All-America tackle on Penn's 1904 national championship team. Since Wallace coached Lamson at Penn, Stewart gained inside information, as well as a measure

All-America tackle Otis Lamson was the only former Penn player to sign with Massillon in 1906 instead of joining Blondy Wallace and other Quakers in Canton.

of retribution. He would not stoop to signing players away from Canton after the uproar over Lang and Schrontz, but getting one of Wallace's Penn Quakers stars to flip was a nice counterpunch for Stewart. Also signed for Massillon was another All-American, the "famous" Cornell halfback Laurence "Cooney" Rice, who was also versatile enough to fill Schrontz's shoes at the end position, if necessary.

Though it seemed as if the Tigers' lineup had no holes left to fill, an injury to one of their running backs made them vulnerable. Leaving nothing to chance, Stewart ventured on a recruiting trip westward and made a package deal for the entire University of Wisconsin backfield: fullback Leonard Roseth and halfbacks Albion Findlay and E.J. Vanderboom.

The off-field drama continued to outweigh the one on-field in the weeks leading up to the clash of the titans. On October 23, the *Gleaner* circulated rumors that Wallace had made overtures to Doc McChesney after Canton's game with the Lyceum. Stewart was fine with letting his former star work in Pittsburgh and play for the Lyceum, but he made it clear that he would pull out Doc's contract with the Tigers if it came down to McChesney playing for Wallace.

Most concerning, from the same article, were rumors circulating among local cynics that the two-game series was arranged as part of a scheme to devise a third game for the teams' mutual financial benefit:

> The "knockers" say that the Tigers will "allow" Canton to win the first game. Such nonsense is disgusting to the management, players and supporters. It means that every player, official and opponent must be "crooked," that the Tiger management would "turn down" the men who make it possible to organize, and that half of the players would have to be "wise" to any "deal" all of which are impossibilities. It may prove of consolation to these disgruntled people to know that the players will bet their own money on the first game, and the second game, and that there will be no third game.

Insiders believed that the Tigers had a leg up on Canton as their clashes approached. Even the day before Massillon pounded Benwood again (now Moundsville-Benwood after a merger to strengthen the team), the opposing captain said, "If Massillon and Canton were to play tomorrow, I would bet every cent I own that Massillon would win by a score of at least 30 points." Massillon repaid the compliment the next day with a 60-point shutout. An unidentified Canton player also told the *Gleaner* after the Wisconsin backs made their debut in the game, "Wish we had that back field at Canton."

Next up for Canton was a rematch with the Lyceum on October 27. With the teams having this common opponent, fans and gamblers alike awaited the result for insight on Canton's and Massillon's relative strength. According

All-America halfback Laurence "Cooney" Rice, 1906 Massillon Tigers

Shiring collection

Courtesy of the Massillon Museum

Massillon recruited the entire 1905 University of Wisconsin backfield for its 1906 team: Albion Findlay (left), Leonard Roseth (middle), and Edward Vanderboom (right).

to the *Pittsburg Post*, Massillon tried to assist the Lyceum's cause by offering the team a few of their Tigers, but the Lyceum rejected the offer on principle. Canton won 12–0, which was less than the Tigers' margin of 19–0 against the Lyceum in the season's first game, but Canton had the habit of holding back in the first of its back-to-back games. It followed by battering the Broadway Athletic Club of Cleveland 57–0 the following day on a field that "in appearance rivaled the mud baths of Hungary," according to the *Morning News*:

> Several players narrowly escaped drowning, when after plunging through the surf, the mighty waves overpowered the sturdy athletes and several were forced to risk their lives to save them. Numerous times were heard cries of "Assistance! Assistance!"

Massillon strolled through Toledo 49–0, on October 29, but expected a challenge to its throne when the tough-talking Orange AC (relocated from New Jersey to Wilmington, Delaware), the "Champions of the East," came to town on Saturday, November 3. As the calendar flipped and the weather turned for the worse, Orange manager Crawford was full of northeastern bluster in the *Gleaner* the day before the game:

> You can say for me that we are coming out here to win. We have larger men whom we could put in and will if necessary, but we are playing the new rules to the limit and have cut out some of the beef to make way for the rugged active type player. We have been beaten but once in four years, and hope to keep our record clean in spite of the great reputation

This early 1900s football sweater is similar to the one worn by Bob Shiring in the image below.

Massillon fans were stunned when Blondy Wallace was able to lure popular Herman Kerkhoff (right) away from the Tigers to sign with Canton for the end of the 1906 season. Kerkhoff is pictured with Tigers Frank Botoner (left) and Bob Shiring (middle) circa 1904–05.

of your team here. I don't care how big your team is. We have beef enough to hold you for downs on the ten yard rule, and are speedy enough to get away with the plays possible under the new rules.

Crawford even told Stewart that night that he would give him $250 of his team's $1,000 guarantee if the Tigers could defeat his squad by 20 or more points. He should have asked for a much bigger spread. The Tigers crushed the Orange 77–0 in front of 2,200 fans, making the visitors look like amateurs. Crawford was not heard from afterward.

Since Canton did not have a game scheduled, the Tigers' management hosted the Canton players and staff for an open display of Massillon prowess, allowing them to watch from the sidelines. The *Morning News* also noticed that Canton gamblers were allowed sideline access, a courtesy previously shown only to journalists and officials.

After the game, wagers on the Canton-Massillon match started flowing in favor of the Tigers. "The action of the 'poker fraternity' of this city, betting against the Canton team, will no doubt be looked upon with suspicion especially after they have been received with open arms by the Massillon management," said the *Morning News* on the Monday after the game.

Wallace's work was not yet done, however. He again made waves by convincing Herman Kerkhoff, a hero of the 1905 Tigers, to renege on a conditional verbal commitment to join the Tigers after his unsuccessful

Courtesy of the Massillon Museum

run for sheriff of Tippecanoe County in Indiana. Kerkhoff's affable nature and bond with the Massillon community made this surprising move a gut punch to Tigers loyalists and the team's spirit.

Stewart pressed ahead with a more subtle recruiting ploy the next day, as he loaned Shiring, Ted Nesser, and Jack Nesser to the Shelby Blues for their game with Toledo. More than strengthening the Blues in their 16–0 win, their plan may have been to strengthen their relationship with Blues star quarterback and kicker Homer Davidson in hopes of the Tigers securing him for their upcoming games against Canton.

After dispatching the Deering Maroons (aka the Chicago Athletic Club) 57–0 the same day, the Canton battalion embarked by train on an extended retreat to Bellefonte, Pennsylvania, near State College, to prepare for its first game with Massillon 12 days away. As many blamed Canton's 1905 loss to the Tigers on weaker teamwork, Wallace figured it would be perfect to isolate the squad in Central Pennsylvania, an ideal site to coordinate his team's play. To take the group's game to the next level, he also imported Michigan coach Fielding Yost all the way from Ann Arbor to provide instruction and strategy on the forward pass and other new rules.

Back in Massillon, comfortable with the Tigers' approach and results, Stewart maintained the team's routine. After a solid week of practice at their home park, the Tigers traveled to Pittsburgh for a final tune-up game against Doc McChesney's Lyceum at Exposition Park on Election Day, November 6. Their 32–0 win meant that, going into their first matchup, Massillon and Canton had not conceded a single point during the entire season. Following the game, McChesney agreed to rejoin the Tigers for the remainder of the season, with his old friend, Shiring, accompanying him on the train back to Massillon later in the week.

Canton kept training. With Stevenson's early season knee injury continuing to drag on, Wallace needed an insurance policy at quarterback. It would have twice the impact to pluck 1905 Tigers quarterback Jack Hayden from Massillon before he rejoined the Tigers after his professional baseball season. So, Wallace did, despite Stewart's threat to file an injunction against Hayden alleging that the quarterback had signed a contract with Massillon.

Hayden and Kerkhoff then headed to Bellefonte to join the Canton retreat, but not before Kerkhoff made an unexpected stop in Massillon along the way to visit some of his former teammates. He was received warmly, according to the *Gleaner*, with the expectation that he would stay on and play for the Tigers. "Kerky" insisted, though, that no money could make him break his contract with Wallace for $400 for the remainder of the season, so his pals brought no further pressure to bear on him.

HAYDEN, INDIANAPOLIS

Jack Hayden, 1906 Boston Americans (major league) and 1909 Indianapolis Indians (minor league)

More disturbing was Kerkhoff's comment to the *Gleaner,* on November 10, that he was misled about the state of the Massillon team:

> Kerky made the surprising statement while here that he had been led to believe by Massillon people that the Tiger team was on the verge of disorganization, and that he would be wise to accept Canton's proposition rather than come here. He was considerably chagrined to find out that the statements were but malicious without foundation.

With Game 1 just days away, crisis hit both teams. On Monday, November 12, the *Morning News* reported that both Canton quarterbacks, Stevenson and Hayden, went down in practice over the weekend. Stevenson wrenched his knee again, and his season was said to be over. Hayden reinjured his jaw, which was initially wounded by a spiteful kick from a baseball teammate in a dugout spat. Wallace quickly signed quarterback Wilmer Crowell from nearby Swarthmore as a backup, expressing confidence that his team would beat Massillon regardless of the casualties.

Later that day, the *Evening Independent* made the surprising announcement that Massillon had released Walter East. Given East's strong play with the Tigers, the ambiguity of the newspaper's comment raised suspicion: "Although East is a star player it was decided that under existing circumstances his services would no longer be needed by the Tiger team."

Readers of the related story in Stewart's *Gleaner* that morning received more detail:

> Many and various rumors are current concerning the reason for the sudden departure, but none are correct. East's condition was not such as to warrant the management retaining him on the pay roll and the Akron man, who is undoubtedly a star player, was perfectly willing to sever his contract with the club under the circumstances.

However, the story in the next column on the same page had far darker undertones:

> Owing to the possibility that Canton may have a spy in Massillon, or in some other way may have acquired the Tiger signals and plays, Coach Wightman dished out to his proteges Saturday evening a brand new set of signals…. Treachery is a thing which all big foot ball teams have to fortify themselves against during a long season…. Today's practice will be as secret as possible. No one will be allowed on the grounds, and from this, until Friday, not a man who is not in uniform will be allowed on the field of play during practice, while scouts will be stationed in the woods east of the grounds to ward off the use of spy glasses from that vicinity.

⊱ Let the Games Begin ⊰

As the final weekend before Game 1 passed, the press's focus shifted to questions surrounding the games themselves. Fans began to consider possible outcomes and obvious questions. What would happen if the teams split the two games? Would there be a third one for the world championship of professional football?

The *Morning News* reported Wallace's definitive answer in all capital letters on November 12: "THERE WILL POSITIVELY NOT BE THREE GAMES BETWEEN CANTON AND MASSILLON THIS YEAR." The implication was that Massillon would retain the title as "world champions" if they won one of the two games since they held the honor the previous year. Canton would need to win both games to claim the championship.

Sentiment on both sides of Stark County, including an opinion from former Canton captain Bill Laub, suggested that neither team would likely cross the other's goal line and that the outcomes might hinge on the kicking game. As Canton's new acquisition, Crowell, was also known as the best kicker in the east, Stewart executed on his earlier plan to bring on Shelby's young Homer Davidson, who could also fill in at quarterback in a pinch.

Regardless of the outcome, Wallace earned the respect of his players and the media for his diligence and collaborative coaching style. A *Cleveland*

THE CANTON MORNING NEWS, CANTON, OHIO.

THE COMING GAMES.

CANTON

"Watch Me Swat Him."

Canton newspapers and fans anxiously awaited their team's championship games with Massillon in 1906.

News special correspondent accompanied Wallace's team to Bellefonte, and his report was reprinted in the Monday issue of the *Gleaner*:

There is one coach for the team. Blondy Wallace, one of the greatest of the old famed Pennsylvania warriors, who grabbed glory in huge chunks the last few years, is the man behind. He's Blondy to the whole bunch and every one of them is working might and main to perfect themselves in the style of play and what he believes will produce a winner. He's a coach who has the complete confidence of the squad, and this is half the battle.

But in a way every man in the squad is a coach. One thinks out a play which might turn out to be a corker. He explains his idea and Wallace has the men try it, every man is asked to use his brains in doing out newfangled plays, in conjunction with Blondy.

Canton's outlook is not at all gloomy. It's a wonderful team that will hurl itself against the powerful champions. It's a team of beef, of strength, of pluck, of proved prowess, of skill, a bunch of strategists who have primed themselves for the possibilities of the new rules, clever foot ball men in every way—this Canton machine that will grapple with Massillon.

Stories of wagers abounded, but the *Gleaner* surprisingly stayed neutral:

Some foolish bets have been made on the Canton-Massillon game so far, and the foolish ones, although few, are Massillon bettors. There is but one bet that is at all warranted by the conditions in this game Friday, and that is even money. Bets on the score are foolish as are bets that Canton will not score, and such bettors are establishing a bad precedent as well as taking on a foolhardy chance.

⇒ Long Live the Bulldogs ⇐

From a historical perspective, the most significant development on Monday, November 12, was the first appearance in print of the Canton professional football team's nickname that would become legendary: the Bulldogs. Oddly, the *Canton Morning News* included it in a front-page story on Canton's upcoming game with Massillon without any explanation:

Four more days and Canton will be on the eve of the biggest event in her history. The first game between the Canton and Massillon world famous football teams will be played at Athletic Field for the championship of the world.

The presidential campaign of 1896 and other events that stand out in Canton's history will be nothing compared to the coming melee … the question that supplants all others, will be: "What will the Bulldogs do next Friday?"

Nov. 14 1905

The Canton Bulldog and the Massillon Tiger Will Soon be Face to Face

Whether Canton or Massillon will pass into history hand in hand with Chicago as holders of the football championship is unknown, but one or the other is sure to rank with the White Sox, either the Bulldogs or Tigers as the pigskin and the Windy City boys as the baseball champs.

As the inspiration for Massillon's nickname came from the prominent Princeton Tigers, though only due to the local availability of replica jerseys, it is possible that Wallace may have continued trying to trump Massillon by claiming the name of the only college team arguably as prestigious and successful as Princeton: the Yale Bulldogs. It would make sense for him, or anyone else associated with the Canton Athletic Club, to transfer the visceral intensity of college football's top rivalry to the professional level, further stoking the fire with Massillon.

On Wednesday, an image of Canton's bold new bulldog mascot made its inaugural appearance atop the *Morning News'* sports page, facing off with a somewhat less intimidating tiger, two days ahead of a historic clash. The battle lines were officially drawn, and one of the greatest rivalries in the history of football became animated, forever.

⇋ Game 1: Fighting Like Cats and Dogs ⇌

The *Canton Morning News* weighed in with caution on a thorough position-by-position analysis of Game 1:

> Canton's team, just the same as 1905, will outshine the Tigers in individual brilliancy…. In Maxwell the Tigers have an All-American man. Aside from "Max" there is not a player who was picked for this mythical eleven after the season of 1905. Hence it is but natural that Canton should be the favorites.

On the other hand, Massillon's team is picked from colleges throughout the west … imbued with that spirit which wins when worked as a team, and determined to fight to the last ditch. Compared individually Canton excels.

While mostly emphasizing the Bulldogs' advantages, the main area in which Canton's scribe gave the Tigers the edge was at the center position:

Sweet, reputed to be the only man who ever "put it over" on Shiring is said to be the best professional center in the business. We dispute the claim and rely on Bob to uphold us. Watch.

Likewise, the *Gleaner* pointed to the center of the line as a key to the battle:

Once upon a time, so the story goes, Sweet and Bob, two well known foot ball players, each vying with the other for honors as the champion center in foot balldom, met in a game. There were various conditions attending to the game which gave the lighter man an advantage in getting down the field. After the game, it was said by some critics that the big Turtle Creek man was slightly outplayed. It was untrue as no gains had been made through the center position, but Sweet had made some tackles down the field which looked more brilliant than anything Bob had done.

Bob has ever since felt the sting of that one criticism. He will meet his old rival for top notch honors today under other conditions…. WATCH BOB.

Courtesy of Rod Winzinek

In Tuesday's *Morning News,* Wallace's analysis expressed humble confidence that his group had done everything possible to prepare for victory: "Massillon may beat us; it's a great team they have down there, but I don't see how they can do it. I can't understand how they can score on us except by fluke or kicks."

The next day, Wallace may have been given an extra boost in his outlook when Coach Wightman commented that the Tigers had a poor practice, mostly due to spying concerns. As the newly minted Bulldogs broke camp in the woods of Bellefonte, on Wednesday, November 14, to travel back to Canton, Wallace gave the *Morning News* his prediction for the team's faithful: "Put me on record as saying that our present bunch of fighters is positively the best football team I have ever seen gathered together and I feel certain that Massillon will go down hard before our splendid team."

Tigers leadership made their calls on the same day in the *Gleaner*:

Coach Wightman: We will win. I believe we have one of the best aggregations if not the best which was ever gathered together. If Canton can stop our offense, it is more than I believe they are capable of, while I believe our line is heavy enough to prevent the team from gaining consistently, owing to the ten yard rule. Therefore I believe that Canton's chance lies in the punting or drop kicking ability of her backs.

Captain Shiring: It will be a hard battle. Canton's team is stronger than that of last season by 50 per cent. So is ours. I don't look for more than two touchdowns in the game, and I hope we get both of these.

Manager Stewart: I believe we will win. I have every confidence in the team. Know it is coached to the limit and in almost perfect physical condition, while the players have never been forced to fight as they will. As for the betting, I will say that while this is a part of the game which makes the coming battle a responsible one, and in case of defeat a very trying one, I believe we will win…. If the bettors are willing to risk their money on the strength of the Tigers as compared with that of Canton, I will stand responsible for the statement that the Tigers will win if it is within the bounds of possibility.

Beyond his prognostication, Stewart felt it necessary to address brewing rumors of scandal proactively:

Reports as to "fixed" games, etc., originate in the statements of irresponsible parties whose ambition it is to see the Tigers lose, regardless of home pride. It would be impossible to "fix" the coming foot ball game. It would mean that the management was rotten to the core, that the Canton management was hand-in-hand with any such dishonesty and that forty or more players under contract to the two managements must be dishonest and minus all sense of honor. Such suspicion does discredit to an honest sport, and is certainly an injustice to those connected with the teams.

The idea of such old reliables as Captain Bob Shiring, Coach Wightman, McNulty, Moran, Riley, Nesser and others, all well known from last season's team, being engaged in such duplicity is as ridiculous as it is disgusting.

Final preparations were made for the most momentous game in pro football history up to that time, with the most talent ever assembled by two teams on one field. More grandstands were built to accommodate an expected crowd upwards of 8,000 fanatics, including 2,500 expected from Massillon. Extra trains were prepared to transport the Massillonians on the eight-mile trip. Forty deputy sheriffs were sworn in to provide additional security.

Each team chose an official, with Massillon selecting legendary Big Bill Edwards from Princeton and Canton deciding on Cornell's Edward Whiting. CAC's maintenance crew covered the field with straw to protect it from ongoing snow and rain that muddied the part of the field that doubled

As a referee, Princeton alum Big Bill Edwards kept matters under control on the field.

CANTON CONSUMED BY FOOTBALL FEVER

Becomes Delirious When Blondy's Bunch of Brawny Braves Bustle into The Hysterical City Bringing Big Bales of Bellefonte Hope Along.

CANTON'S BIG SQUAD

Name.	College.	Position.	Wgt.
Schrontz	W. & J.	Left End	180
Lang		Left Tackle	215
Riley	N. Y. University	Left Guard	255
Sweet	Bucknell	Center	183
Kerchoffe	Purdue	Right Guard	260
Ernst	Lafayette	Right Tackle	220
Thorpe	Columbia	Right Tackle	210
Gilchrist	Columbia	Right End	190
Stevenson	Pennsylvania	Quarterback	145
Reynolds	Pennsylvania	Left Halfback	168
Steinberg	Syracuse	Right Halfback	175
Cure	Lafayette	Fullback	213
Hayden	Pennsylvania	Quarterback	168
Heston	Michigan	Halfback	180
Smith	Pennsylvania	Fullback	203
Farabaugh	Lehigh	Halfback	185
Townsend	Columbia	Halfback	180
Sheldon	Carlisle	Halfback	175
Crowell	Swarthmore	Quarterback	165
Wallace	Pennsylvania	Tackle	225
Reemsnyder	Ohio State	End	165
Murphy	W. & J.	Halfback	218
Heimberger	W. & J.	Guard	205

MASSILLON'S CHAMPION SQUAD

Name	College	Position	Wgt.
Riley	Canton	Left End	178
King	Purdue	Left End	188
McNulty	Notre Dame	Left Tackle	192
Nesser	Heidleberg	Left tackle	208
Haag	Massillon	Left Guard	246
Shiring	P. A. C.	Center	250
Maxwell	Chi-Swarthmore	Right Guard	260
Lamson	Pennsylvania	Right Tackle	204
Kirby	O. S. U.	Right End	184
McChesney	P. A. C.	Right End	188
Parrott	Case	Quarter Back	162
Rice	Cornell	Quarterback	164
Davidson	Case	Quarterback	144
Moran	Vanderbilt	Right Half	166
Thomas	Purdue	Right Half	182
Robison	Dickenson	Left Half	178
Findlay	Wisconsin	Left Half	178
Roseth	Wisconsin	Full Back	176
McAllister	Cornell	Full Back	188
Vanderboom	Wisconsin	Left Back	196
Wightman	Chi-Swarthmor	Full Back	192
Botoner	Massillon	Right Tackle	212
Bast	Massillon	Right End	160

MASSILLON, OHIO, FRIDAY, MORNING NOVEMBER 16, 1906.

OH JOY! THERE'S LITTLE WILLIE HESTON

BLONDY

HASTE! BLONDY! HASTE!	OH! LET ME HAVE A LUNCH	WEE WILLIE HESTON
WHY DO YOU MAKE ME WAIT?	UPON THY BLOOMIN' BUNCH,	WILL BE THE BEST ONE,
YUM! YUM! LET ME TASTE	AND RAPTUROUS CRUNCH,	DON'T PROCRASTINATE
SOMETHING TO SATIATE	KERCK, SCHRONTZ AND LANG!	I'M IN THE MOOD
MY CLAMOROUS FANG!	AND FOR DIGESTION	TO MASTICATE
		THE FOOTBALL FEUD.

Among an unprecedented group of talent on both sides, famed Willie Heston appeared on Canton's roster but not in its starting lineup for Game 1.

OFFICIAL SOUVENIR PROGRAM

Rare program from Game 1 of the Canton-Massillon 1906 "world championship"
matchup that took place in Canton on November 16, 1906

as a baseball infield. Plans were made to burn the straw with gasoline the morning of the game in hopes of drying the mud.

The Bulldogs arrived home in Canton the night before the game to a raucous welcome, according to the *Gleaner*:

> Last season's experiences and enthusiasm was but a pink tea party compared to the wild, unrestrained spirit which was cut loose with the return of the Canton team late Thursday night. With the Canton band, a crowd of five hundred mad rooters with flaring torches, Roman candles and red fire, and a thousand spectators, the Canton team was received at the Pennsylvania depot at 10 o'clock…. They were bundled into an omnibus and carted to the Courtland Hotel where hundreds jammed the corridors for a peek at the athletes, who will either win fame and glory for the red, with countless thousands of dollars, or will suffer the Canton colors to be dragged in the dust by the orange and black.

As morning broke on game day, Friday, November 16, the last hope for a solid field vanished under a heavy snow the day before. The *Beacon Journal* described the field at Canton's Myers Lake as a miniature lake of its own, though the weather was not expected to affect attendance.

For the first time, though, fans across the country would enjoy the game practically in real time, thanks to Bell Telephone, a company that stationed staff on the grounds to call updates to major cities' news outlets. Adding phone capabilities to the game's broadcast was a quantum leap from using carrier pigeons a year earlier.

The lineups announced in the papers settled the coaches' decisions on the quarterback positions. Parratt got the nod for the Tigers, and Stevenson, apparently sufficiently recovered from his injury, for the Bulldogs. There was one glaring omission. Without explanation, Willie Heston was not listed for Canton. He either did not show well in practice or Wallace decided he could not risk making the same mistake with Heston that cost him the title in 1905.

In a final boast before kickoff, Friday's *Morning News* expressed the true feelings of many of Canton's followers: "This is the day that the Canton 'Bulldogs' take the conceit out of the Massillon 'Tigers.'"

Fans began arriving at 12:30 p.m. for the kickoff scheduled at 2:00. However, major events rarely went off like clockwork in the early 1900s, especially given the state of public transportation. A breakdown on the city's rail car line delayed the Canton players from reaching the field until after 2:30. The *Beacon Journal* described the Bulldogs' appearance:

> "Blondy" Wallace and his players were greeted by deafening cheers as they trotted onto the field, and the bands struck up Canton's battle song,

Willie Heston's absence from Canton's lineup in Game 1 against Massillon was a mystery.

"C.A.C." The crowds rushed onto the field, and seizing the Canton players, carried them around the field on their shoulders.

Wallace caused further delay by refusing to abide by his previous agreement for an independent head linesman to be selected by newspaper men. He got his man, but only after Stewart got Wallace to concede that the new linesman, whom Stewart alleged to be Wallace's friend, would have no authority to call penalties. After all that, the Bulldogs still needed time to warm up, while the visiting Tigers, ready for more than an hour, grew impatient and stiff.

The weather was fan-friendly, a sunny and warm day for mid-November. Maintenance efforts were futile, though, and at least three inches of heavy, slippery mud spread across the middle of the gridiron. Canton suffered its first blow during warmups when Stevenson slipped on the slick surface, again twisting his faulty knee while fielding a punt. Much to the disappointment of Tiny Maxwell, who was preparing for payback from their encounter in the 1905 Penn-Swarthmore game, Stevenson was carried off the field and unable to play. Wallace turned the field general role over to Hayden, who had defeated his forces from the other side of the line the prior year.

Canton won the coin toss, and Shiring started the action by kicking off into the wind for Massillon at 3:00. The highly anticipated struggle for the world's pro football title was finally underway. Hayden instantly circled the Tigers' right end for 20 yards, with new Bulldogs end Clark Schrontz bowling over his former teammate, Doc McChesney, along the way. Massillon's defense then stiffened, and Canton's star punter, Marshall Reynolds, averted disaster by scooping up a poor snap and launching his kick "while bearing under the weight of four hungry Tigers," according to the *Beacon Journal*.

Former Penn Quakers All-American Marshall Reynolds was the star of Game 1 for Canton.

After an exchange of punts, strong running and penalties helped Canton advance to Massillon's 18-yard line. A loss of yards forced Hayden to attempt a 32-yard dropkick from a difficult angle 10 yards from the sideline, which he neatly converted for an early 4–0 lead for the Bulldogs.

By the rule at the time, the Bulldogs received the ensuing kickoff after their score and, after a return beyond their 30-yard line, chose a defensive tact by punting on first down, pinning the Tigers in their end. After conceding their first points of the season, the Tigers responded with the interior of their offensive line clawing huge rips in the Bulldogs' defensive front. "King and Maxwell opened up holes through Kirchoffe [*sic*] and Riley which looked large enough to drive an automobile through," the *Beacon Journal* recounted. Massillon drove Canton back to its 6-yard line on runs by former Wisconsin stars Leonard Roseth and Albion Findlay.

With 2 yards to go for a first down on their third and final down (the four down rule passed in 1912), the Tigers elected to go for it. Roseth was forced out of bounds a yard short, sending a shock wave through the Massillon side of the bleachers and giving Canton possession.

Reynolds bailed the Bulldogs out of trouble with his foot, as he would do all day. From beneath the crossbar of Canton's goalpost, again on first down, he masterfully booted a perfect snap 50 yards to near midfield. Massillon barely advanced past the 55-yard line on its next three drives, while Wallace continued ordering up booming first-down punts by Reynolds, most over 50 yards, challenging their rivals to execute a long scoring drive.

Another factor in Wallace's defensive punting strategy was that Hayden, who signed with Canton less than two weeks earlier as a backup quarterback, had difficulty remembering Canton's signals. As they were still new to him, he consistently paused at the line before plays to ask Reynolds for help. To minimize the risk of a disastrous turnover, made worse by the sloppy field, Wallace left little to chance with Canton ahead.

As the Bulldogs protected their lead, the Tigers again found their footing, plunging their backs viciously into the opposing trenches. Even Maxwell leveraged his girth to run the ball through the muck on Massillon's advance deep into Canton territory. A first down on Canton's 13-yard line had the Bulldogs on their hind legs and the crowd on its tiptoes. Two short gains left the offense with another tough decision on third down with 4 yards to go. Once again, the Tigers decided to go for it and, once again, they failed. A trick play of sorts collapsed, and Parratt fumbled, with former Tiger Clark Schrontz gaining possession for Canton. Reynolds's 60-yard punt on first down pulled Canton out of the field position hole again. Peggy Parratt fielded Reynolds's punts magnificently, but a gang tackle after this long blast jammed the plucky quarterback's knee, knocking him out of the game and dimming Massillon's hopes a few shades just before the half.

Coach Wightman replaced Parratt with Cooney Rice, who failed attempting the new forward pass on the last play before halftime, turning the ball over by rule to Canton. The risk of a turnover on an incomplete forward pass was generally not worth the potential reward of likely no better than a short gain on the new play.

Tiny Maxwell (left), Cooney Rice (middle), and Otis Lamson (right) each did his part to keep Massillon in Game 1, with Maxwell scoring the Tigers' only TD.

Courtesy of the Massillon Museum

At the start of the second half, Wightman substituted both Tigers ends, trying to open their outside running game. Their first drive started well but ended on their 45-yard line when Roseth fumbled. With good field position, Wallace could let his offense operate again. Runs by Reynolds, Kerkhoff, Cure, and Hayden landed the Bulldogs on Massillon's 7-yard line. On second and goal from 3 yards out, the Bulldogs' Bull Smith was held to no gain by Otis Lamson, one of Wallace's former Penn pupils. This time, rather than attempting another field goal, Canton decided to go for the end zone on their third and final down.

A deceptive delayed handoff by Hayden sent Reynolds around the left side for a touchdown, marking the first time that a team crossed the Tigers' goal line all season. With the goalpost placed on the goal line at the time, and given the rule requiring that the extra point kick be attempted from the spot at which the runner crossed the line, the two-part extra point try was necessary given the sharp angle. Reynolds kicked the ball out from the point at which he crossed the goal near the sideline toward the middle of the field at the 23-yard line, where Hayden successfully fielded it. From there, Reynolds secured the point, booting the oval between the uprights for a 10–0 lead with just over 20 minutes to play.

Tackling Tiny Maxwell was an unenviable task.

Ten more minutes elapsed, with still no scoring by Massillon, leading Wightman to relieve running backs Roseth and Findlay for the fresh legs of Ted Nesser and Butch McAllister, without impact. An unworldly punt of 68 yards by Reynolds on a Bulldogs first down put another nail in the Tigers' coffin. As tension grew in the air and desperation on the field, the personal battle between Shiring and Sweet overheated. Officials ejected both from the game for slugging each other. Impending doom and darkness were setting in on the Tigers, as dusk approached due to the game's late start.

When Canton's Hayden struggled to field a Tigers punt near midfield, Massillon's Maxwell capitalized on the shadows while charging toward Hayden. Controversy ensued after Hayden gained control of the ball and believed that the play was dead. According to the *Beacon Journal*:

> Hayden failed to get his lunch hooks on the ball. Big "Tubby" Maxwell coming up the field a la [famed trotting horse] Lou Dillon grabbed it, and

sprinted the remaining 60 yards for a touchdown. Hayden claimed that Maxwell took the ball away from him, and it had become so dark that few saw the play. The touchdown, however, was allowed, and the goal was missed.

The missed extra point left the Tigers with a deficit of 10–5, more than a four-point field goal behind, but with still over eight minutes remaining. The Tigers were back in the hunt until the Canton crowd inserted itself into the game, and chaos ensued following the missed kick. According to the *Morning News*:

> Only once did the crowd encroach on the playing space. Near the close of the game after Maxwell made Massillon's touchdown, the ball was lost. Maxwell attempted to kick goal and the pigskin went into the crowd. The ball was not sent back and a search for it was started. It could not be found; neither could a practice ball be located. Then it was that the police lost control of the crowd. They scrambled over and tore down fences, all eager to reach the center of the field, where the players and officials were discussing the lost ball.

Massillon fans insisted that Canton bandits absconded with the ball. After several minutes ticked away with the game clock running, even while the pigskin was missing, an unidentified Bulldog received the ball from someone near the goalpost and brought it forward to the officials at midfield. Police escorted the hooligans off the field, but the disturbance accomplished the mob's goal. By the time play restarted and Massillon kicked off, darkness was setting in, and the game was called. Between 1:30 and 4:45 remained on the clock, according to various newspaper accounts, but the point was moot. Canton secured a 10–5 victory in a must-win game, the defending champions were no longer invincible, and Game 2 of the Bulldogs-Tigers matchup on November 24 would be played for the professional football championship of the world.

⊱ King of the Hill ⊰

Wallace had his day, and his week ahead, in the sun. He was on top of his game and on top of the world, or at least the pro football world. "The sports of [Canton] have gone completely daft tonight because the Canton Bulldogs have wrested the championship from the Massillon Tigers," gushed the *Pittsburg Post*. Headed by a marching band, 22 red-blanketed bulldogs of the canine sort, each adorned with the name of one of Wallace's warriors, paraded the city's streets the following Tuesday.

Stewart stewed in the *Gleaner* that Massillon was the better team and lost due to misfortune. He argued that the Tigers outgained the Bulldogs by

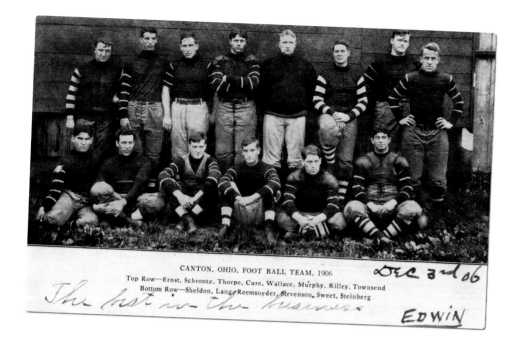

CANTON, OHIO, FOOT BALL TEAM, 1906
Top Row—Ernst, Schrontz, Thorpe, Cure, Wallace, Murphy, Rilley, Townsend
Bottom Row—Sheldon, Lang, Reemsnyder, Stevenson, Sweet, Steinberg

Dec 3rd 06

The best in the business

EDWIN

218 yards to 29, which seems unlikely given Canton's two scoring drives, and that Massillon was penalized 90 yards to Canton's 30. Regardless, Wallace's defensive scheme worked to perfection given the rules of the time, as his team bent but did not break. It was vindication for all of his efforts and must have been euphoric.

It was only the first step, however. Wallace's glory would be short-lived unless his Bulldogs could also win Game 2 eight days later. Financially, it may have tempered his joy that the official attendance was only 5,502, which was healthy but less than the 7,000 or more expected. Succumbing to late pressure to add players to bolster his lineup may have caused Wallace buyer's remorse when thinking about how much he would need to pay them at the season's end.

Regarding Game 1's aftermath in Massillon, the November 20 edition of the *Gleaner* expressed appreciation for the community's support and the team's attitude in defeat:

> Not a man on the team Friday night had other than the greatest gratitude for those who received them so royally, and for those people they will fight Saturday. Not for the paltry salaries which induced them to come here, but for a principle.
>
> Defeat was more of a humiliation to every player in that game than it was for the most disappointed fan. It meant more to those big western men to down the haughty eastern squad of "Blondy's" than would the reward of a thousand dollars. It was galling to those stars of the west and middle west to have to admit even if for a week that eastern style of play excelled that of the west.

Meanwhile, Stewart continued to rage against persistent rumors of a game-fixing scheme that would supposedly lead to a Game 3:

> Rumors that … a third game be made possible by this tie were numerous before the first game and are now being circulated with a vengeance…. We have been contemptibly lied about and vilified from the moment that the team was formed. There were those who thought it impossible to form a winning combination without the complete assortment of stars of 1905, and many of these were poisoned against the 1906 management in various and underhand methods, making it impossible to secure them at any price…. THERE WILL BE NO THIRD GAME IF THE TIGERS DO WIN ON SATURDAY.

However, the *Gleaner* dropped a hint of pending drama the following day, mixed with a message of reassurance to Tigers fans:

> To those friends of the Tigers coach, management and backers, who have remained faithful in spite of the defeat at the hands of Canton Friday, and the nasty rumors which followed, the management hereby extends the thanks of the players, coach, backers and management, and only asks that confidence be continued until next Monday, when the most convincing of proof as to the absolute fairness of the team can be furnished and will be.

Canton team physician Dr. Harry March became prominent as an early NFL executive and later for his book on early pro football.

On the east side of Stark County, the Bulldogs maintained their successful routine and returned by train on Sunday for another week of practice in Bellefonte. Stevenson, though, remained in Canton to convalesce in his room in the Courtland Hotel. Although he received the best treatment from prominent Youngstown physician John "Bonesetter" Reese, his ability to play in Game 2 was highly doubtful.

Massillon followers suspected a ruse in Game 1, hiding Wallace's intention to play Hayden at quarterback all along, given Hayden's knowledge of the Tigers' system. So much speculation endured that the Bulldogs' team surgeon, Dr. Harry March, made an official statement in the *Evening Independent*, on November 21, concerning the injury's medical specifics and seriousness. Soon afterward, Stevenson ventured to Bellefonte to help Wallace coach from the sidelines.

On the upside for Canton, Wallace announced that the famed Willie Heston would return to the Bulldogs for the next game and join the team for practice in Bellefonte. Wallace wired home from camp to the *Morning News* on November 22: "I never before went into a game so brimful of confidence as this."

In terms of strategy, the *Gleaner* defended Massillon's Coach Wightman for failing to use Homer Davidson's punting and kicking prowess, which was the primary reason he recruited the local Shelby star days before the game. At the same time, the paper acknowledged that Hayden and Reynolds decided the game for Canton with their kicking and that Wightman planned to insert Davidson into the Tigers' lineup in Game 2.

After a few days licking their wounds, the Tigers regained their optimism. They recognized that they controlled the essential interior line play and believed that improved conditions on their home field would benefit their stronger running game.

"Lamson made Lang quit long before the game was over and Maxwell's superiority over the hitherto invincible Kerkhoff was apparent to the eye of every fan," the *Gleaner* emphasized. Lamson, himself, added, "If we can't beat that bunch Saturday, I miss my guess by a mile."

Kerkhoff made another trip across enemy lines to visit his friends in Massillon on Saturday night after the game and reflected on his performance soberly. "I know 'Max' outplayed me," he said to the *Gleaner*, "but wait until next Saturday. Not another drop of liquor until that last game."

Countywide, fans debated the outcome of the duel between Shiring and Canton's "Peerless Sweet" at center, with the final decision still in the balance. "It will be renewed Saturday, and the writer ventures the opinion that Sweet will never thereafter be regarded as the best center playing the game today," wrote the *Gleaner*.

Wightman's decision to hold the Tigers' first-full speed intrasquad scrimmage of the season, on the Wednesday before Game 2, seemed ill-advised, and it turned out to be a disaster. Davidson, signed for his kicking abilities, wrenched his knee and broke a bone in his left hand in a pileup while working out at the quarterback position. Also, starting running back Leonard Roseth dislocated a shoulder plowing through the line and was ruled out for Saturday's game.

Canton fans strutted around town with an extra spring in their step and red feathers in their hats all week in support of their victors. The *Gleaner* interpreted the feathers as red capes waved in the faces of angry bulls. Cantonian spirits were taken down a notch, though, with the news that their starting running back, Bull Smith, would be unavailable for Game 2 because he had committed to coaching the backs at Penn. He was allowed one week of vacation, and he used it for the week of the first game. Smith was a "tower of strength" in Game 1, according to the *Gleaner*, especially on defense. Wallace had been hedging on whether he wanted to give Heston a shot at redemption from his 1905 debacle by putting him in the lineup at running back. Now, Smith's absence forced his hand.

Andy "Bull" Smith, another former Penn All-American, was a difference-maker in Game 1 but was unavailable for Canton in Game 2.

Wallace's final roster move before Saturday's Game 2 was a curious one. On Wednesday, he wired to nearby Latrobe asking for their star end, Eddie Wood, to join the team for practice in Bellefonte. The Bulldogs had a decided edge at the end position in Game 1, so it was unclear why they needed Wood. Further, Canton needed to prepare to play Latrobe five days after Game 2, on Thanksgiving Day. It seemed unusual that Wallace would be willing to confide the Bulldogs' signals and strategies to an upcoming opponent, especially if the Bulldogs beat Massillon again and a claim on the world championship was still at stake.

In Massillon, Stewart made last-ditch efforts with solid offers to Notre Dame's Red Salmon to reprise his dominating 1905 running performance, and to famed University of Chicago quarterback Walter Eckersall, the best man ever to play the position in the West. Both turned him down.

While there was plenty of bluster about huge gambling totals tossed about in the papers before and after Game 1, it is notable that there was virtually no such commentary leading up to Game 2. Where there was, the line was even money. Concerns about the perception of a predetermined outcome may have discouraged such discussion.

Instead, the focus was on how the game would play out. Most of the teams' strengths and weaknesses made themselves apparent in Game 1. The Bulldogs stood pat with their roster other than the loss of Smith at running back. Again, though, Heston did not appear in the lineup. For Wallace, it was once bitten, twice shy. The Tigers knew that they needed better play at the quarterback, kicking, and end positions. Wightman moved Parratt from quarterback to end, leaving an open question on who would run Massillon's show at quarterback.

Assuming Wightman had addressed these issues, Massillonians pinned their hopes on their leader to rise to the moment at the "keystone" center position, per the *Gleaner* the day before the game:

Captain Bob Shiring, the most popular foot ball player on the squad, will be right there again for Sweet. Sweet will be right there again for Bob, and we might predict right here that the fur will fly this time. Both were put out of the game last week, but it is safe to say that the same will not take both to the sidelines Saturday. It remains to be seen which will leave the game, however, in order to put in a better man, and we believe we know.

For the Tigers and their growing legions of fans, their battle call was clear: "Sweep that aggravating Bull Pup from the face of the earth!"

1906 Canton Bulldogs watch given as a gift to one of their players

(Courtesy of the Pro Football Hall of Fame)

HE WILL BE ALL IN TODAY.

With Game 1 in hand, Canton fans hoped that their Bulldogs would finish off the Tigers in Game 2 to win their first "world championship."

⤞ Game 2: One for the Ages ⤝

"Again was the tale of two cities told on the Massillon gridiron on Saturday afternoon, when the Tiger and the Bull Dog met in mortal combat for championship honors," hailed the *Massillon Evening Independent*. A clear sky, a cool breeze, and a perfect field greeted the occasion on game day. "The entire east side of the field was one waving, fluttering, mass of humanity with colors flowing in the wind, while a deep circle of spectators completely fringed the field," the *Gleaner* described, with fans "waiting with bated breath for the referee's whistle." Traffic delayed the teams' train arrivals until 1:40, just before the 2:00 kickoff, but not enough to delay the start.

The only delay was caused by Stewart's shenanigans that the *Morning News* called deliberate, malicious, and premeditated. The contract between the teams stipulated that the home team would provide the game ball. After the coin toss at midfield, Coach Wightman produced an overinflated official intercollegiate Victor brand ball, smaller than the standard Spalding variety. Wallace strongly objected. When Wightman argued that Canton would forfeit if Wallace rejected the ball, Wallace knew he was cornered and consented to play.

Captain Shiring won the toss, and the Tigers chose to defend the south goal with the wind at their back. Advantage Tigers. Canton kicked off, hoping Reynolds could pin the Tigers deep in their end. In a surprising move, Wightman gave young Homer Davidson the Tigers' reins at quarterback.

Massillon manager E.J. Stewart's ploy to use the smaller Victor brand ball confused the Bulldogs in Game 2.

Among a sea of collegiate stars, the frail-looking 22-year-old, 145-pound Davidson did not attend college. After graduating from Central High School in Cleveland, he gained acclaim instead by going pro and playing for the nearby Shelby Blues.

Davidson started the Tigers' first drive without fear or hesitation, slamming into the line for two short gains before scooting around end for a first down on a risky third-down play. After stalling near midfield, the baby-faced local boy showed off his punting skills with a 50-yard boot to near the Canton goal line.

For 20 minutes, the athletes treated awestruck fans to a tense set of series with more power, speed, and open-style football than had previously been witnessed. One exciting 30-yard run by the Bulldogs' Reynolds was stopped by a gritty defensive play by the agile Davidson. The Tigers again seemed vulnerable on the outside until a knee injury to Canton's end, former Tiger Clark Schrontz, solved that problem for Massillon, forcing Wallace to retreat to his previous first-down punting strategy. Davidson and other Massillon backs, including Roseth, Parratt, and former Purdue captain Homer "Sandy" Thomas, continued to break away for large chunks of yardage and multiple first downs through the line. Wallace's punting ploy nearly worked, though, when the Tigers fumbled three times but recovered each of them.

When their teams' drives halted, Davidson and Reynolds engaged in an unprecedented punting exhibition, launching missiles up to 70 yards. Long kicks also opened the field for breathtaking returns, often by the same pair, in what started to resemble an individual battle between a heralded All-American and an unlikely local counterpart. Reynolds's experience and physique, and Davidson's lack thereof, made the Bulldogs the favorite to prevail.

Courtesy of the Pro Football Hall of Fame

Consecutive runs of 20 and 5 yards by Massillon's Roseth, after a rare short punt by Reynolds, set up the Tigers on second-and-5 on the Bulldogs' 16-yard line. Bulldogs defender Jack Ernst slammed Davidson on his head, destroying an end run and doubling the youngster's head against his chest. Davidson lay limp and silent as the girth unpiled, requiring a delay for medical attention to the quarterback's twisted neck. The skinny lad staggered to his feet and, while still dazed, attempted a field goal from 20 yards out. He struck it well but missed wide by a few feet.

Another long spiral punt by Reynolds on first down relieved Canton's stress momentarily until Davidson returned the favor on the next play. With the wind still at his back, Davidson's 50-yard launch from the Tigers' 25-yard line sailed over Hayden's head and bounced toward the Bulldogs' goal line. The *Gleaner* portrayed a mad dash ensuing, initially with Reynolds and Hayden in hot pursuit, attempting to retain possession for the Bulldogs:

> Suddenly a flash … shot out of the mass of players from scrimmage and fairly flew down the field after the two opposing players and the elusive ball. It was Findlay, the Wisconsin half back, and the way that westerner covered the ground was thrilling. As the ball neared the goal line, Findlay gained on the two players with it, and as it crossed the side line, two yards from the goal line, "Finke" brushed aside Reynolds and dove for the ball just as Hayden grabbed for it. Findlay's speed carried him in a long slide over the ground and into the fence where he tangled with Hayden and the ball, emerging a moment later with the ball tucked securely under his arm. Referee Whiting carried the ball in fifteen yards, and when Massillon formed on the offensive and it was realized for the first time that the Tigers had the ball within striking distance of the Bull Dog's goal line, the crowd broke loose.

The passion was palpable as fans, anticipating a climactic score, pressed up against the goal line from behind the field, which lacked a defined end zone, unlike today's fields. The *Gleaner* continued:

> A fumble without gain sent the shivers down the backs of the Massillon fans, but Davidson made a good recovery and the next moment Roseth plunged over the goal line for the touchdown which looked like the winning score then. It was off to one side of the field, and a kick out was necessary. McNulty sent a pretty spiral fairly into the arms of a waiting Maxwell, who heeled the ball and then tried for the goal. The ball went wide by a few inches and the score stood at five to nothing in favor of the Tigers.

With five minutes remaining in the half, the action did not stop. After the Tigers received the kickoff, Davidson took off on a 40-yard jaunt around the left side, but it was called back for an offside penalty. A short punt by Davidson, and Canton's initial first down of the game, put the Bulldogs within reach of a score on Massillon's 18-yard line. But on the next play, Eddie Wood, in the game on loan from Latrobe to replace the injured Schrontz, turned it over with a fumble. Given Wood's lack of experience with the Bulldogs, it was a curious move by Wallace to give Wood the ball in that crucial situation.

The half ended without further ado and Massillon clinging to a 5–0 lead. During the break, the Tigers rested on warm straw piled on the cold ground on their sideline, where they were served hot coffee and broth. The Bulldogs were escorted back to their rail car, outside the grounds, to regroup and make adjustments for the second half.

As a strategist, Wallace was not a one-trick pony. Playing from behind for the first time with the new rules, Wallace knew that continuing to punt on first down was a low-percentage ploy. Schrontz's injury also ended the Bulldogs' edge in the outside running game. Thus, he made the bold but logical move to break out the forward pass, which they had practiced diligently at Bellefonte under Coach Yost's tutelage.

After an exchange of punts to start the half, two Hayden passes over the line with quick Tiger tackles resulted in gains of over 10 yards each and a first down near midfield. A successful quarterback kick by Hayden, allowed by rule to be caught in the air by a fellow Bulldog, advanced the ball another 25 yards, and Canton was in business in Tiger territory. The Tigers held strong on first down, with left guard Pratt King of Purdue stonewalling a Bulldogs runner, though King was knocked unconscious on the play and taken off the field. A 14-yard run by Lehigh legend Andrew

EDWARD WOOD   RE

Eddie Wood's one-game role on the Bulldogs after a long career at Latrobe has become a topic of historical controversy.

Farabaugh and another forward pass from Hayden to Jack Ernst for 9 more moved the ball just outside of the Tigers' goal on the 3-yard line. On second down, Reynolds wormed over for the score. For the conversion attempt, he kicked the ball out from the spot of the score to Hayden, who fielded it cleanly on the 15-yard line. Hayden then held the ball for Reynolds's successful extra point, giving the Bulldogs a 6–5 lead. With Reynolds's toe and solid defense, and 20 minutes to play, they were in position to run out the clock and claim the title.

After Canton received the following kickoff by rule, both teams failed to maintain a drive and Davidson blasted another Tigers punt from the 55-yard line toward Canton's goal line. For the fourth time in the game, Reynolds and Hayden underestimated Davidson's power, and the power of the Victor football that Stewart supplied, and chased a kick that sailed over their heads. This time, Reynolds covered the ball on the Bulldogs' 2, calling for another Reynolds first-down punt to escape a precarious situation.

Standing against the fence behind his goal line on the loosely bordered field, Reynolds needed to release a kick quickly on first down to prevent being trapped for a safety. "The pass was fair," said the *Gleaner*, "but with a rush Maxwell swept the mighty (once) Kerkhoff to one side and plunged into the kicker, knocking the ball over the fence into the crowd."

Havoc ensued once again, as comically depicted by the *Beacon Journal*:

> "Tubby" Maxwell and his 250 pounds of avoirdupois cleared the four-foot picket structure with a mighty leap, and the big fellow floundered through the crowd until he found the ball. He descended squarely on the heads of several of the people who were packed against the fence, and more than one good hat was smashed in breaking his fall.

Captain Shiring argued for a touchdown, but the officials declared a safety, giving the Tigers back the lead at 7–6 with just over five minutes remaining.

With the clock winding down, Reynolds punted to the Tigers from the Bulldogs' 20-yard line following the safety, giving Massillon control just behind midfield. Instead of grinding the clock, Davidson surprised the Bulldogs with a short forward pass that Thomas took around the end for 20 yards. The Tigers then double-teamed their former teammate, Herman Kerkhoff, blasting holes through his spot on the line on four consecutive plays and moving 30 yards to the shadow of the Canton goalposts. With a round, bald head like a bowling ball, Roseth again got the call to carry the pigskin over the goal line to glory. He answered it with a thundering crash for a touchdown through Canton's desperate last defensive stand. Shiring held the ball for Davidson's good kick, and the Tigers staked an insurmountable 13–6 margin.

Tiny Maxwell (back right) was exceptionally fast and athletic considering his size. He is pictured here with Swarthmore track teammates at the 1905 Penn Relays.

The Bulldogs appeared to lose heart, and after the Tigers again received the kickoff following their score, Findlay sprinted for a 40-yard run with little resistance. Then, as described by the *Gleaner*, a crowning moment transpired:

> Sweet, the wildly heralded star of the Canton team, was outplayed in both games and before the second contest was more than half over, he was ready to quit, finally leaving the game in favor of Hoskins, while on Bob that glad smile broadened.

In a moment of exhalation and exaltation, the titles of "greatest center" and "greatest team" of the era were settled.

With the conflict decided on the field, the coaches emptied the benches and sent in their substitutes. Hayden botched another Davidson punt, and Davidson missed a 30-yard dropkick attempt before the clock expired.

In postgame comments to the *Cleveland Plain Dealer*, Coach Wightman credited the whole team and its concept:

> Every man of ours showed up his opponent…. I knew we would do it. Our training and system is what did it. We were unlucky in the first game or we would have won that. Davidson played a wonderful game for us.

Stewart spread praise generously in the *Gleaner* to the Tigers' unexpected heroes. Davidson's revelation as a prodigy, climbing off the dirt from injury three times and matching the great Reynolds's punting average of 45 yards, was mind-boggling. Less obvious were Parratt and Nesser shoring up the ends and "Iron Man" Max McNulty playing through a separated shoulder at tackle to fend off Canton's Jack Ernst. The statistics once again justified the line's accolades, with the Tigers outgaining Canton 222 yards to just 48 for the Bulldogs.

Stewart saved his highest praise for the Tigers' leader, who made good when it was needed most:

> Captain Bob Shiring is one to be congratulated above all others. All season Bob has worked, almost as hard as the coach, to get the players working smoothly. He showed great interest in the team, and by getting into physical condition better than he ever had been before, managed to show the entire foot ball world that he is in a class by himself at center.

On the losing side, Wallace felt disconsolate and deceived, as quoted by the *Morning News:*

> I am torn to pieces over the result, as I was very confident of victory. The real cause of our defeat was that the Massillon management insisted

Young local boy Homer Davidson, pictured with the Cleveland Naps of the American League in 1908, stole the show for Massillon in Game 2.

on using what is called a "phony ball" in the game. When we arrived in Massillon to complete the preliminaries for the game, we were told a Victor ball would be used in the game. We have been in the habit of using and also practicing with a Spalding ball, which is recognized all over the country as the official ball. The Victor ball is much lighter in weight and therefore can be kicked a great deal further, and when it alights on the surface it bounds about three times as far as a Spalding ball. Our team has done all its practice work with a Spalding ball, and of course was not accustomed to the other. I insisted on using the Spalding ball but our opponents were just as obstinate and told me plainly that unless the Victor ball was accepted there would be no game. In view of the fact that we had a $3,000 guarantee posted in a Massillon bank, and that the receipts of the game were required to meet expenses already incurred, I with much reluctance consented.

Beyond bitterness over gamesmanship, Wallace began to reveal his personal animosity toward Massillon's administration for the first time:

I believe I have been imposed upon by the Massillon management from the very time when negotiations commenced last fall for the games. In the first place, they wanted the earth, so to speak, in the division of gate receipts…. It was not until I went east and signed Latrobe for a Thanksgiving day game that I was able to do any business with the Massillon management. I have been treated in a very discourteous manner on several occasions, but have borne it all without comment until now.

While venting, Wallace then felt it necessary to address the lingering whispers of corruption:

And now to the people of Canton, there have been many rumors as to sell out and laying down. To those people I invite the most explicit publicity. I believe that the columns in the public press are open to any person to make statements, and I repeat again that I want them to show if they can where any signs of a lay down are evident.

In fact, many Bulldogs lost significant coin wagering on themselves, according to the *Morning News*. The article also described that when one unwise local insinuated to one of Wallace's troops that the game was not on the level, "it was to his subsequent sorrow, for the player resented it, and in a manner that will be remembered."

Despite the rancor, it was a spectacular display of football heralding the game's future under the new rules. On a firm field, the country's best

Courtesy of the Massillon Museum

This handwritten 1906 Massillon Tigers schedule shows that the team's late-season plans were in flux due to the turmoil surrounding its games with Canton.

teams showed off their full set of artistry: inside and outside running, forward passes, dropkicks, placekicks, quarterback kicks, and booming punts, all wrapped in a close game with lead changes until the final minutes and a championship atmosphere. The exhibition was cause for celebration.

Before the postgame revelry could start in Massillon, the partisans needed to separate from the park. It was wise that the cheering sections of both sides were set across the battlefield from each other during the game, but conflict afterward was harder to prevent. The *Morning News* described how one fan defended her Bulldogs' honor:

> Just after the game was over … two women, one of Canton and the other of Massillon, engaged in a dispute about the result of the game. It is said that the Massillon woman started the argument by making some disparaging remarks about the Canton team, which the lady from Canton resented. Then ensued a hair-pulling battle, with wordy scrimmages interspersed. The lady of the Bulldogs was getting decidedly the best of the argument when a peace-loving male interfered. Had a decision been given, it would probably have been in favor of the Canton lady.

In a tradition that continues today, crowds poured into the heart of Massillon to share the spoils of gridiron victory. Revelers gathered barrels of wood, straw, and shavings to light towering bonfires. Horns tooted, whistles blew, and masses screamed in a united festival. "Sunday had crowed Saturday off the map long before the celebration ceased," according to the *Morning News*.

In Canton, all hell broke loose.

A 16-year-old Bulldogs fan named Jack Cusack was an eyewitness to what transpired in Canton at the watering hole where many of the home team came to drown their sorrows after the game. He recounted the story in his 1963 book, *Pioneer in Pro Football*:

> One of my neighbors, Victor Kaufmann, who later became a physician in Canton, had lost a heavy bet on the disputed contest … and on that evening he took me with him to the Courtland Hotel bar, where most of the Bulldogs had congregated to post-mortem the game. Arriving at the hotel, we went directly to the bar, where Kaufmann lost no time in making his feelings known, loud enough for all to hear.
>
> "If you want to know what I think," he said. "I'll tell you—I think that game was crooked!"
>
> The fight that started in that barroom was as spontaneous as the lighting of a fuse on a powder keg. Somebody swung out at Victor, and men who had been arguing over the matter only a few minutes before

began punching each other all over the place. Tables were overturned, and the surging crowd crashed through the plateglass window and continued the battle on Court Street until the coppers arrived with their night sticks, to quell the rioters and haul some of them away to the pokey. Victor and I managed to slip out of the crowd and get away, but my friend went home in high satisfaction—because he had gotten in some punches in the right places.

After a long, slow boil throughout the season, the pressure cooker finally exploded. The nefarious forecast of a split series came true. The results seemed too convenient to skeptics, who believed that they would be suckered into buying tickets to a deciding third game to line the teams' pockets. People wanted answers.

Based on the clue that Stewart left in the *Gleaner* the previous Wednesday, he already planned to drop a bomb.

SCANDAL THREATENS TO END PRO FOOTBALL

The tragedy of life is not that man loses but that he almost wins.
—Heywood Broun, *Sport for Art's Sake*, 1921

On Monday morning, November 26, 1906, following Saturday's Game 2 of the championship series between Canton and Massillon, the people of Stark County awoke to a shocking front-page headline in the *Massillon Morning Gleaner:* "THEIR HONOR INVIOLATE"

Strapline: "THE FAMOUS MASSILLON TIGERS OF 1906 COULD NOT BE BOUGHT OFF WITH A PRICE"

Second strapline: "Details of a Plot to Disrupt and Corrupt the Tiger Team and Management Which Failed.—$5,000 In Cash and a 'Sure Thing' in a $50,000 Betting Pool Offered But Never Considered."

The declaration of an attempted bribe to influence the Tigers' performance was jaw-dropping. This was not going to end well.

Tigers manager E.J. Stewart and Massillon Athletic Club president H.A. Croxton affixed their names to a lengthy statement detailing accusations of a complex scam and subterfuge.

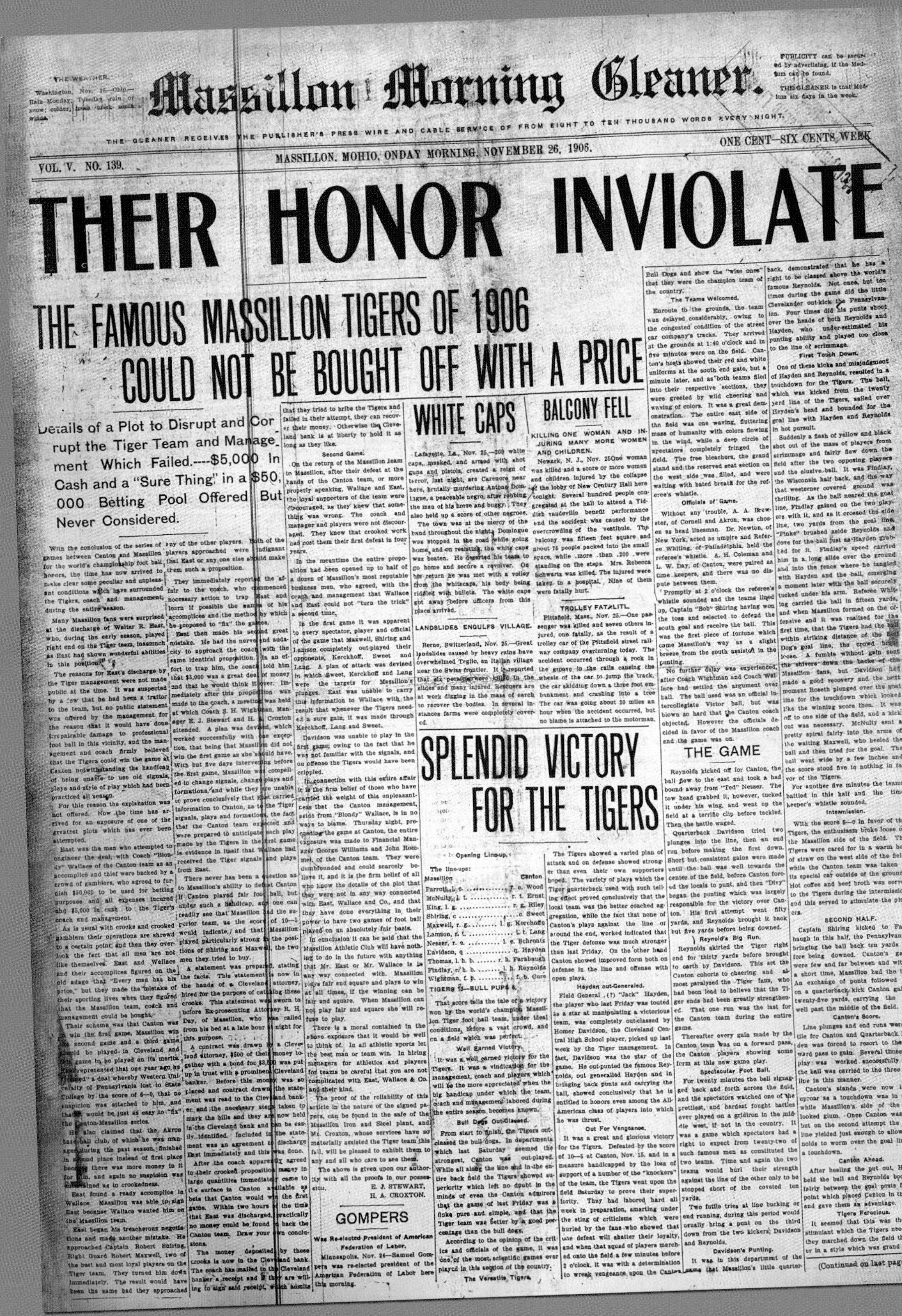

THE WEATHER.
Washington, Nov. 26—Ohio—
Rain Monday; Tuesday rain or
snow; colder; fresh brisk south and

Massillon Morning Gleaner.

THE GLEANER RECEIVES THE PUBLISHER'S PRESS WIRE AND CABLE SERVICE OF FROM EIGHT TO TEN THOUSAND WORDS EVERY NIGHT.

PUBLICITY can be secur-
ed by advertising, if the Medium can be found.

THE GLEANER is that Med-
ium six days in the week.

VOL. V. NO. 139.　　　MASSILLON, MOHIO, ONDAY MORNING, NOVEMBER 26, 1906.　　　ONE CENT—SIX CENTS WEEK

THEIR HONOR INVIOLATE

THE FAMOUS MASSILLON TIGERS OF 1906 COULD NOT BE BOUGHT OFF WITH A PRICE

Details of a Plot to Disrupt and Corrupt the Tiger Team and Management Which Failed.—$5,000 In Cash and a "Sure Thing" in a $50,000 Betting Pool Offered But Never Considered.

With the conclusion of the series of games between Canton and Massillon for the world's championship foot ball honors, the time has now arrived to make clear some peculiar and unpleasant conditions which have surrounded the Tigers, coach and management, during the entire season.

Many Massillon fans were surprised at the discharge of Walter E. East, who, during the early season, played right end on the Tiger team, inasmuch as East had shown wonderful ability in this position.

The reasons for East's discharge by the Tiger management were not made public at the time. It was suspected by a few that he had been a traitor to the team, but no public statement was offered by the management for the reason that it would have done irreparable damage to professional foot ball in this vicinity, and the management and coach firmly believed that the Tigers could win the game at Canton notwithstanding the handicap of being unable to use old signals, plays and style of play which had been practiced all season.

For this reason the explanation was not offered. Now the time has arrived for an exposure of one of the greatest plots which has ever been attempted.

East was the man who attempted to engineer the deal, with Coach "Blondy" Wallace of the Canton team as an accomplice and their were backed by a crowd of gamblers, who agreed to furnish $50,000 to be used for betting purposes and all expenses incurred and $5,000 in cash to the Tigers' coach and management.

As is usual with crooks and crooked gamblers their operations are shrewd to a certain point, and then they overlook the fact that all men are not like themselves. East and Wallace and their accomplices figured on the old adage that "Every man has his price," but they made the mistake of their sporting lives when they figured that the Massillon team, coach and management could be bought.

Their scheme was that Canton was to win the first game, Massillon win the second game and a third game should be played in Cleveland. This game to be played on its merits. "Blondy's" deal whereby Western University of Pennsylvania lost to State College by the score of 6—0, that a suspicion was attached to him, and that it would be just as easy to "fix" the Canton-Massillon series.

He also claimed that the Akron base-ball club, of which he was manager during the past season, finished in second place instead of first place because there was more money in it for him, and again no suspicion was entertained as to crookedness.

East found a ready accomplice in Wallace. Massillon was able to sign East because Wallace wanted him on the Massillon team.

East began his treacherous negotiations and made another mistake. He approached Captain Robert Shiring, Right Guard Robert Maxwell, two of the best and most loyal players on the Tiger team. They turned him down immediately. The result would have been the same bad they approached

that they tried to bribe the Tigers and failed in their attempt, they can recover their money. Otherwise the Cleveland bank is at liberty to hold it as long as they like.

Second Game.

On the return of the Massillon team to Massillon, after their defeat at the hands of the Canton team, or more properly speaking, Wallace and East, the loyal supporters of the team were discouraged, as they knew that something was wrong. The coach and management and players were not discouraged. They knew that crooked work had cost them their first defeat in four years.

In the meantime the entire proposition had been opened up to half of a dozen of Massillon's most reputable business men, who agreed, with the coach and management that Wallace and East could not "turn the trick" a second time.

In the first game it was apparent to every spectator, player and official of the game that Maxwell, Shiring and Lamson completely outplayed their opponents. Kerckhoff, Sweet and Lang. A plan of attack was devised in which Sweet, Kerckhoff and Lang were the targets for Massillon's plunges. East was unable to carry the information to Wallace with the result that whenever the Tigers needed a sure gain, it was made through Kerckhoff, Lang and Sweet.

Davidson was unable to play in the first game, owing to the fact that he was not familiar with the signals, and on offense the Tigers would have been crippled.

In connection with this entire affair it is the firm belief of those who have carried the weight of this unpleasantness that the Canton management, aside from "Blondy" Wallace, is in no ways to blame. Thursday night, preceding the game at Canton, the entire exposure was made to Financial Manager George Williams and John Rommel, of the Canton team. They were dumbfounded and could scarcely believe it, and it is the firm belief of all who know the details of the plot that they were not in any way connected with East, Wallace and Co., and that they have done everything in their power to have two games of foot ball played on an absolutely fair basis.

In conclusion it can be said that the Massillon Athletic Club will have nothing to do in the future with anything that Mr. East or Mr. Wallace is in any way connected with. Massillon plays fair and square and plays to win at all times, if the winning can be fair and square. When Massillon can not play fair and square she will refuse to play.

There is a moral contained in the above exposure that it would be well to think of. In all athletic sports let the best man or team win. In hiring managers for athletics and players for teams be careful that you are not complicated with East, Wallace & Co. and their kind.

The proof of the reliability of this article in the nature of the signed papers, can be found in the safe of the Massillon Iron and Steel plant, and Mr. Croxton, whose services have so materially assisted the Tiger team this fall, will be pleased to exhibit them to any and all who care to see them.

The above is given upon our authority with all the proofs in our possession.

E. J. STEWART.
H. A. CROXTON.

WHITE CAPS

Lafayette, La., Nov. 25.—200 white caps, masked, and armed with shot guns and pistols, created a reign of terror, last night, are Carenora near here, brutally murdering Antona Domingue, a peaceable negro, after robbing the man of his horse and buggy. They also held up a score of other negroes.

The town was at the mercy of the band throughout the night. Domingue was stopped in the road while going home, and on resisting the white caps he was beaten. He requested the team to go home and secure a revolver. On his return he was met with a volley from the whitecaps, his body being riddled with bullets. The white caps got away before officers from this place arrived.

BALCONY FELL

KILLING ONE WOMAN AND INJURING MANY MORE WOMEN AND CHILDREN.

Newark, N. J., Nov. 25—One woman was killed and a score or more women and children injured by the collapse of the lobby at New Century Hall here tonight. Several hundred people congregated at the hall to attend a Yiddish vaudeville benefit performance and the accident was caused by the overcrowding of the vestibule. The balcony was fifteen feet square and about 75 people packed into the small space, while more than 200 were standing on the steps. Mrs. Rebecca Schwartz was killed. The injured were taken to a hospital. Nine of them were fatally hurt.

TROLLEY FATALITY.

Pittsfield, Mass., Nov. 25.—One passenger was killed and seven others injured, one fatally, as the result of a trolley car of the Pittsfield street railway company overturning today. The accident occurred through a rock in the path of the car skidding down a three foot embankment and crashing into a tree. The car was going about 30 miles an hour when the accident occurred, but no blame is attached to the motorman.

LANDSLIDES ENGULFS VILLAGE.

Berne, Switzerland, Nov. 25.—Great landslides caused by heavy rains have overwhelmed Teglio, an Italian village near the Swiss frontier. It reported that six persons were killed in the slides and many injured. Rescuers are at work digging in the mass of earth to recover the bodies. In several instances farms were completely covered.

SPLENDID VICTORY FOR THE TIGERS

Opening Lineup.

The line-ups:

Massillon	Canton
Farrell, l. e.	F. Wood
McNulty, l. t.	F. t. Brist
King, l. g.	r. g. Riley
Shiring, c	c. Sweet
Maxwell, r. g.	l. g. Korchoff
Lamson, r. t.	l. t. Lang
Nesser, r. e.	l. e. Schrontz
Davidson, q.	q. Hayden
Thomas, l. h. b.	r. h. Farabaugh
Findlay, r. h. b.	l. h. Reynolds
Wightman, f. b.	f. b. Curs

TIGERS 8—BULL PUPS 0.

That score tells the tale of a victory won by the world's champion Massillon Tiger foot ball team, under ideal conditions, before a vast crowd, and on a field which was perfect.

Well Earned Victory.

It was a well earned victory for the Tigers. It was a vindication for the management, coach and players which will be the more appreciated when the big handicap under which the Tiger coach and management labored during the entire season, becomes known.

Bull Dogs Out-Classed.

From start to finish, the Tigers out-classed the bull-dogs. In departments which last Saturday seemed the strongest, Canton was out-played. While all along the line and in the attack the Tigers showed a superiority which left no doubt in the minds of even the Canton admirers that the game of last Friday was a fluke pure and simple, and that the Tiger team was better by a good percentage than the bull dogs.

According to the opinion of the critics and officials of the game, it was one of the most scientific games ever played in this section of the country.

The Versatile Tigers

The Tigers showed a varied plan of attack and on defense showed strong or than even their own supporters hoped. The variety of plays which the Tiger quarterback used with such telling effect proved conclusively that the local team was the better coached aggregation, while the fact that none of Canton's plays against the line or around the end, worked indicated that the Tiger defense was much stronger than last Friday. On the other hand Canton showed improved form both on defense in the line and offense with open plays.

Hayden out-Generaled.

Field General (?) "Jack" Hayden, the player who last Friday was touted as a star at manipulating a victorious team, was completely out-classed by Homer Davidson, the Cleveland Central High School player, picked up last week by the Tiger management. In fact, Davidson was the star of the game. He out-punted the famous Reynolds, out generaled Hayden and in bringing back punts and carrying the ball, showed conclusively that he is entitled to honors even among the All-American class of players into which he was thrust.

Out For Vengeance.

It was a great and glorious victory for the Tigers. Defeated by the score of 10—5 at Canton, Nov. 15, and in a measure handicapped by the loss of support of a number of the "knockers" of the team, the Tigers went upon the field Saturday to prove their superiority which had labored hard all week in preparation, smarting under the sting of criticisms which were hurled by the fans who showed that one defeat will shatter their loyalty, and when that squad of players marched ed onto the field a few minutes before 2 o'clock, it was with a determination to wreak vengeance upon the Canton

Bull Dogs and show the "wise ones" that they were the champion team of the country.

The Teams Welcomed.

Enroute to the grounds, the team was delayed considerably, owing to the congested condition of the street car company's tracks. They arrived at the grounds at 1:40 o'clock and in five minutes were on the field. Canton's hogs showed their red and white uniforms at the south end gate, but a minute later, and as both teams filed into their respective sections, they were greeted by wild cheering and waving of colors. It was a great demonstration. The entire east side of the field was one waving, fluttering mass of humanity with colors flowing in the wind, while a deep circle of spectators completely fringed the field. The free bleachers, the grand stand and the reserved seat section on the west side was filled, and were waiting with bated breath for the referee's whistle.

Officials of Game.

Without any trouble, A. A. Brewster, of Cornell and Akron, was chosen as head linesman. Dr. Newton, of New York, acted as umpire and Referee, of Philadelphia, held the referee's whistle. A. H. Coleman and L. W. Day, of Canton, were paired as line keepers, and there was no dispute between them.

Promptly at 2 o'clock the referee's whistle sounded and the teams lined up, Captain "Bob" Shiring having won the toss and selected to defend the south goal and receive the ball. This was the first piece of fortune which came Massillon's way as a slight breeze from the south assisted in the punting.

No further delay was experienced, after Coach Wightman and Coach Wallace had settled the argument over ball. The ball used was an official intercollegiate Victor ball, but was blown so hard that the Canton coach objected. However the officials decided in favor of the Massillon coach and the game was on.

THE GAME

Reynolds kicked off for Canton, the ball flew to the east and took a bad bound away from "Dutch" Nesser. The tow head grabbed it, however, tucked it under his wing, and went up the field at a terrific clip before tackled. Then the battle waged.

Quarterback Davidson tried two plunges into the line, then an end run before making the first down. Short but consistent gains were made until the ball was well towards the center of the field, before Canton forced the break to punt, and then "Dizzy" began the punting which was largely responsible for the victory over Canton. His first attempt went fifty yards, and Reynolds brought it back but five yards before being downed.

Reynolds Big Run.

Reynolds skirted the Tiger right end for thirty yards before brought to earth by Davidson. This set the Canton cohorts to cheering and almost paralyzed the Tiger fans, who had been lead to believe that the Tiger ends had been greatly strengthened. That one run was the last for the Canton team during the entire game.

Thereafter every gain made by the Canton team was on a forward pass, the Canton players showing some form at this new game until the Tigers would harass them.

For twenty minutes the ball zigzagged back and forth across the field, and the spectators watched one of the prettiest, and hardest fought battles ever played on a gridiron in the middle west, if not in the country. It was a game which spectators had a right to expect from twenty-two of such famous men as constituted the two teams. Time and again the two teams would hurl their strength against the line of the other only to be stopped short of the coveted ten yards.

Two futile tries at line bucking or end running, during this period would usually bring a punt on the third down from the two kickers, Davidson and Reynolds.

Davidson's Punting.

It was in this department of the game that Massillon's little quarter-

back, demonstrated that he has a right to be classed above the world's famous Reynolds. Not once, but ten times during the game did the little Clevelander out-kick the Pennsylvanian. Four times did his punts shoot over the heads of both Reynolds and Hayden, who under-estimated his punting ability and played too close to the line of scrimmage.

First Touch Down.

One of these kicks and misjudgment of Hayden and Reynolds, resulted in a touchdown for the Tigers. The ball, which was kicked from the twenty yard line of the Tigers, sailed over Hayden's head and bounded for the goal line with Hayden and Reynolds in hot pursuit.

Suddenly a flash of yellow and black shot out of the mass of players from scrimmage and fairly flew down the field after the two opposing players and the elusive ball. It was Findlay, the Wisconsin half back, and the way that westerner covered ground was thrilling. As the ball neared the goal line, Findlay gained on the two players with it, and as it crossed the side line, two yards from the goal line, "Finke" brushed aside Reynolds and dove for the ball just as Hayden grabbed for it. Findlay's speed carried him in a long slide over the ground and into the fence where he tangled with Hayden and the ball, emerging a moment later with the ball securely tucked under his arm. Referee Whiting carried the ball in fifteen yards, and when Massillon formed on the offensive and it was realized for the first time, that the Tigers had the ball within striking distance of the Bull Dog's goal line, the crowd broke loose. A fumble without gain sent the shivers down the backs of the Massillon fans, but Davidson had made a good recovery and the next moment Roseb plunged over the goal line for the touchdown which looked like the winning score. It was off to one side of the field, and a kick out was necessary. McNulty sent a pretty spiral fairly into the arms of the waiting Maxwell, who heeled the ball and then tried for the goal. The ball went wide by a few inches and the score stood five to nothing in favor of the Tigers.

For another five minutes the teams battled in this half and the time keeper's whistle sounded.

Intermission.

With the score 5—0 in favor of the Tigers, the enthusiasts broke loose on the Massillon side of the field. The Tigers were cared for in a warm bed of straw on the west side of the field, while the Canton team was taken to its special car outside of the grounds. Hot coffee and beef broth was served to the Tigers during the intermission, and this served to stimulate the players.

SECOND HALF.

Captain Shiring kicked to Farabaugh in this half, the Pennsylvanian bringing the ball back ten yards before being downed. Canton's gains were few and far between and within a short time, Massillon had the ball. On an exchange of punts followed and on a quarterback kick Canton gained twenty-five yards, carrying the ball well past the middle of the field.

Canton's Score.

Line plunges and end runs were futile for Canton and Quarterback Hayden was forced to resort to the forward pass to gain. Several times this play was worked successfully and the ball was carried to the three yard line in this manner.

Canton's stands were now in an uproar as a touchdown was in sight while Massillon's side of the field looked glum. Once Canton was held but on the second attempt the Tiger line yielded just enough to allow Reynolds to worm over the goal line for a touchdown.

Canton Ahead.

After heeling the put out, Hayden held the ball and Reynolds booted it fairly between the goal posts for the point which placed Canton in the lead and gave them an advantage.

Tigers Ferocious.

It seemed that this was the very stimulant which the Tigers needed, as they marched down the field thereafter in a style which was grand to see,

(Continued on last page.)

GOMPERS

Was Re-elected President of American Federation of Labor.

Minneapolis, Nov. 24—Samuel Gompers was re-elected president of the American Federation of Labor here this morning.

The *Massillon Morning Gleaner* blew the lid off of the Bulldogs-Tigers gambling scandal on the Monday after Game 2 of the 1906 world championship series.

It began:

With the conclusion of the series of games between Massillon and Canton for the world's championship foot ball honors, the time has now arrived to make clear some peculiar and unpleasant conditions which have surrounded the Tigers, coach and management, during the entire season.

Names were not spared:

Many Massillon fans were surprised at the discharge of Walter R. East, who, during the early season, played right end on the Tiger team, inasmuch as East had shown wonderful abilities in this position.

E.J. Stewart, 1917

The reasons for East's discharge by the Tiger management were not made public at the time. It was suspected by a few that he had been a traitor to the team, but no public statement was offered by the management for the reason that it would have done irreparable damage to professional foot ball in this vicinity, and the management and coach firmly believed that the Tigers could win the game at Canton notwithstanding the handicap of being unable to use old signals, plays and style of play which had been practiced all season.

For this reason the explanation was not offered. Now the time has come for an exposure of one of the greatest plots which has ever been attempted.

If Stewart had the best interests of pro football at heart, as he suggested, it is not clear how blowing the story open at this point would have limited the destruction. The only thing he accomplished by holding the story back was preserving the Tigers' self-interest, ensuring that fans attended Massillon's two games with Canton. The Bulldogs' final contest with Latrobe seemingly meant nothing to Stewart. But he purposely tried to devastate Wallace on two levels, accusing him of collusion in the scheme, while simultaneously hitting him in the wallet by discouraging headcount at the game:

> East was the man who attempted the deal, with Coach "Blondy" Wallace of the Canton team as an accomplice and thief [*sic*] were backed by a crowd of gamblers, who agreed to furnish $50,000 to be used for betting purposes and all expenses incurred and $5,000 to the Tiger's [*sic*] coach and management.
>
> As is usual with crooks and crooked gamblers their operations are shrewd to a certain point, and then they overlook the fact that all men are not like themselves. East and Wallace and their accomplices figured on the old adage that "Every man has his price," but they made the mistake of their sporting lives when they figured the Massillon team, coach and management could be bought.

The misspelling of the word "they" as "thief" seemed more than co-incidental, though the *Gleaner* later issued a retraction that it was a typo. Regardless, Stewart had decided to turn an intense sports rivalry into a crime drama. The details of the allegations were compelling:

> Their scheme was that Canton was to win the first game, Massillon win the second game and a third game should be played in Cleveland and this game to be played on its merits. East represented that one year ago he "framed" a deal whereby Western University of Pennsylvania lost to

State College by the score of 6–0, that no suspicion was attached to him, and that it would be just as easy to "fix" the Canton-Massillon series.

He also claimed that the Akron baseball club, of which he was manager during the past season, finished in second place instead of first place because there was more money in it for him, and again no suspicion was entertained as to crookedness.

East found a ready accomplice in Wallace. Massillon was able to sign East because Wallace wanted him on the Massillon team.

East and Wallace had a lot of explaining to do. Stewart went on to describe how East initiated the attempt to drag the Tigers into the plot:

> East began his treacherous negotiation and made another mistake. He approached Captain Robert Shiring, [and] Right Guard Robert Maxwell, two of the best and most loyal players on the team. They turned him down immediately. The result would have been the same had they approached any of the other players. Both of the players approached were indignant that East or anyone else should make them such a proposition.

Shiring and Maxwell demonstrated the high character for which they were known and made the right decision together on their next step. Choices made at the next levels were more questionable:

> They immediately reported the affair to the coach, who commenced necessary action to trap East and learn if possible the names of his accomplices and the method by which he proposed to "fix" the games.
>
> East then made his second great mistake. He had the nerve and audacity to approach the coach with the same identical proposition. In an effort to trap him, the coach told him that $5,000 was a great deal of money and that he would think it over. Immediately after this proposition was made to the coach, a meeting was held at which Coach S.H. Wightman, Manager E.J. Stewart and H.A. Croxton attended. A plan was devised, which worked successfully with one exception, that being that Massillon did not win the first game as she should have. With but five days intervening before the first game, Massillon was compelled to change signals, change plays and formations, and while they are unable to prove conclusively that East carried information to Canton, as to the Tiger signals, plays and formations, the fact that the Canton team expected and were prepared to anticipate each play made by the Tigers in the first game is evidence in itself that Wallace had received the Tiger signals and plays from East.

Charges and Counter Charges Flying Fast.

Alleged Attempts at Bribery in the Present Football Controversy. Full Details.

Massillon Tigers teammates Bob Shiring and Robert "Tiny" Maxwell in 1906

Stewart's claim that East made offers to Shiring, Maxwell, and Wightman in person was convincing based on the objective experiences of the
respective parties involved. However, it was an incredibly bold leap for him
to vilify Wallace based solely on his perception that the Bulldogs anticipated
the Tigers' plays too effectively in Game 1.

The Tigers' plan to entrap East then became a tangled web of deceit:

> A contract was drawn by a Cleveland attorney, $500 of their money
> together with a bond for $3,500 was put up in a trust with a prominent
> Cleveland banker and the necessary steps taken to mark the bills and
> they are now held in the Cleveland bank and can easily be identified.
> Included in the statement was an agreement to discharge East immedi-
> ately and this was done.
>
> After the coach apparently agreed to their crooked proposition
> money in large quantities immediately came to the surface in Canton
> available as bets that Canton would win the first game. Within two hours
> of the time that East was discharged, practically no money could be found
> to back the Canton team. Draw your own conclusions.
>
> The money deposited by these crooks is now in the Cleveland bank.
> The coach has mailed to the Cleveland banker a receipt and if they are
> willing to sign said receipt, which admits that they tried to bribe the Tigers
> and failed in their attempt, they can recover their money. Otherwise the
> Cleveland bank is at liberty to hold it as long as they like.

Stewart did not implicate anyone else associated with the Canton
organization and proactively made its management aware of the situation
before their games:

> In connection with this entire affair it is the firm belief of those who
> have carried the weight of this unpleasantness that the Canton man-
> agement, aside from "Blondy" Wallace, is in no ways to blame. Thursday
> night, preceding the game in Canton, the entire exposure was made to
> Financial Manager George Williams and John Rommel of the Canton
> team. They were dumbfounded and could scarcely believe it, and it is the
> firm belief of all who know the details of the plot that they were not in
> any way connected with East, Wallace and Co., and that they have done
> everything in their power to have the two games of foot ball played on
> an absolutely fair basis.

While Stewart added that he and Croxton had a Cleveland attorney
prepare a legal statement stating the facts "for the purpose of catching

1907–08 Jewel automobile built by Massillon's Forest City Motor Company, which was co-owned by Massillon Athletic Club president Herbert Croxton

these crooks," he did not make clear which law he believed the accused had broken. Stewart distilled the purpose of his attack in his conclusion:

> There is a moral contained in the above exposure that it would be well to think of. In all athletic sports let the best man or team win. In hiring managers for athletics and players for teams be careful that you are not complicated with East, Wallace & Co. and their kind.

More than anything, he wanted to destroy their reputations and athletic careers. It was personal.

As if Wallace did not have enough on his plate, Stewart piled on by revealing his financial crisis on page four of the same edition:

> Many Massillon people were surprised this fall when Kerckhoff [*sic*], Hayden, Lang and Schrontz signed with Canton. Many criticisms were

tendered to the local management for permitting these players to escape from the Tiger fold.

These many critics were not aware of the conditions under which the men went to Canton, and neither were they aware of the impossible and fabulous sums offered by Manager Wallace of the Canton team. The fact that the Massillon management will probably be able to pay every cent of salary and expense and the announcement Sunday that the Canton team would be in debt many thousands of dollars at the close of the season, will explain matters very easily, and give these critics an idea of the absolute unreliability of Wallace and his promises…. It can now be seen that Wallace's fancy offers were made without intent of paying them, but merely to induce the players to jump their Massillon obligations.

As soon as the news broke, Wallace and the entire Bulldogs team met with Canton Athletic Club president John Rommel and financial manager George Williams on Monday morning. At 1:00 p.m., Wallace issued the following statement:

CANTON'S SIDE OF THE STORY

Additional Statements are Given the Public.

MANAGER WILLIAMS WAS HERE

An article appeared in the *Massillon Morning Gleaner*, accusing me of attempting to assist in engineering a deal whereby Canton was to win the first Canton-Massillon game and Massillon the second.

This article named me as an accomplice. The Massillon statement was signed by H.A. Croxton and E.J. Stewart. I wish to state that as far as I am concerned the statement is unqualifiedly and absolutely false. I am not a party of fraud or questionable actions concerning the Massillon games.

I expect to hold all parties strictly accountable for their accusations. It has been my sole aim to be fair and honest in this affair. Further developments will vindicate me, and establish the fact that I have been cruelly misrepresented and maliciously attacked.

I have placed the matter in the hands of attorneys, and all future actions will be handled by them.

CAC financial manager Williams added his statement:

I intend going over to Massillon at 1:30 o'clock. I understand the Massillon management will allow any person to peruse the document upon which charges are made. I have arranged with the Massillon management to see and examine them and will get a copy if possible.

The first idea I had of any attempt at "fixing" the games was when Manager Stewart, of Massillon, came to me on Thursday before the first game. He told me of some alleged facts that were supposed to have happened days before. I became eager to learn of the matter, but he finally assured me that the trouble had been settled, as the man who had attempted to do the negotiating had been discharged from the team. "Very well," I then said. "It's all right, now, and the games will be played on the square."

He told me they would be as far as he knew. I had no other thought of unfair play thereafter.

Williams dutifully traveled to Massillon to meet Croxton and Stewart to execute the agreed-upon revenue sharing and view the contract documenting the phony deal. Conveniently, Stewart was out of town. Williams made the following statement after returning to Canton:

> After my arrival, after promising in strict confidence not to divulge the name of the Akron business man, who is supposed to be a party to the deal, and whose signature appears on the contracts with the name of Walter East, who is charged with having engineered the deal, … I was shown the papers and the contract. I carefully examined the same and I want to state to the public that on no paper did I find the name of "Blondy" Wallace, or any official of the Canton Athletic Club. In fact, no other name appeared besides those already publicly mentioned and the name of the Akron business man whose name I am pledged not to divulge…. Now as to Mr. Wallace, I have found him absolutely square in our business dealings and I am loath to believe that he would be party to such a deal.

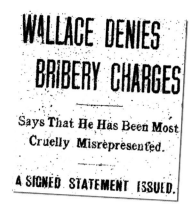

Later Monday evening at the Canton team residence, at the Courtland Hotel, Wallace displayed affidavits signed by all of his players who remained in the city, asserting that they had not been in any way approached to throw the games. They added that, if anything, they thought Wallace's discipline had been too strict before and during the two contests. When asked directly by reporters if he had ever been approached by any of the Massillon parties or East about a fix, Wallace added more intrigue:

> No member of the Massillon management ever approached me on the subject, but one of the parties and I had a talk in the Courtland Hotel lobby some time before the games in which it was intimated that a deal could be made whereby the game could be "throwed." I gave the party no direct reply as I believed at the time that it was only a scheme to draw me into a trap so as to get even with me for signing the Latrobe team for the Thanksgiving day game. I have arranged to employ an attorney and will at once institute a suit for damages against the parties who have so

foully assailed me. In my opinion, it is nothing but a scheme to kill off the attendance at the Thanksgiving day game. If the public are going to be deluded by this trick, why all well and good, but I want to say to the people of Canton that win or lose, I intend to become a resident of this city and earn my livelihood in an honorable manner if I have to go down to the ditch with a pick and a shovel to do so.

Wallace's need to clear his name became more apparent with his stated desire to reside in Canton for the long term. It was time for him to go on offense and provide theories of his own to cast doubt on the other side:

I do not want to make any open charge, but it might be that the Massillon people wanted to do the fixing and then after seeing that they could not buy me, to protect themselves they tried to throw the deal onto me. From what I understand the papers in the possession of the Massillon management are supposed to have been signed by Walter East and a man from Akron who was indicted by a grand jury of Summit County for alleged bribery some time ago. I never met the man referred to, but I will say that Walter East promised to sign a contract with Canton last summer and the Massillon management went behind my back and signed him after he agreed to come to Canton. This will show where Walter East's interests are most likely to be…. I might add that Coach Wightman's name appears on the so-called "throw down" and this talk of honesty on the part of Massillon management doesn't look very good after they allow one of their own players to become party to the deal.

It was a whirlwind day. Staggering charges and countercharges opened questions that would take time to address. The *Canton Morning News* displayed patience in its reaction, allowing Wallace the presumption of innocence until proven otherwise:

The sports throughout the city were in very remorseful spirits yesterday, and, while most of them are inclined to be fair in the matter they are all unanimous in saying that they "have got to be shown" before they decide to take sides in the controversy, and that if the Massillon management is guilty of the charges made by Manager Wallace, the Canton manager is a victim of one of the dirtiest plots ever attempted in athletic history.

East had not yet responded, as he was in Pittsburgh recruiting players for his Akron baseball team's upcoming season, but he would have to face the music soon enough. The stage was set for a legal battle that could forever determine pro football's fate. The neighboring *Cleveland Plain Dealer* on Tuesday, November 27, summarized the public's perception of the present and future of the pro game:

> The charges made by the Massillon managers and backers against Canton and a coterie of gamblers is only what could be expected of the professional game and as long as such games are made an object of interest by the gamblers, there will always be the cry of "Fake" and "Sold out." For that very reason, professional football will never become popular throughout the country and the proposed league which was intended to include Cleveland probably will never be formed. Football is a true college sport and the college game will never be supplanted by the exhibitions of the "pros." No scandals have ever been attached to the college games and the only instances of where the honor of the great national game of baseball has been impugned has been where gambling was sanctioned in the stands.

With anxiety swirling, both teams still had to refocus on their final games on Thursday, Thanksgiving Day. These last bouts may have seemed anticlimactic, but they were not without consequence. Latrobe had defeated Canton in 1905, and Wallace wanted to demonstrate that his team was legitimate, both competitively and ethically. In Chicago, having been cast off from Canton, Willie Heston put together an impressive team of western all-stars and challenged Massillon for a visit.

Wallace promptly retaliated against his accusers by initiating a libel lawsuit against Stewart, Croxton, and the *Gleaner* on the day before Thanksgiving, suing them for a tremendous amount of money by 1906 standards. According to the *Morning News* on Thanksgiving morning, "Wallace in his petition claims that by reason of the libelous publication he has been injured in his business and profession and that his good name and professional credit have been ruined, wherefore he asks a judgment against the defendants in the sum of $25,000."

Although it was a further distraction to file suit rather than prepare for the game against Latrobe, Wallace remained steadfast. "The Thanksgiving day game will be played regardless as to what the public say or do. I have guaranteed the visitors $1,500 to come to this city and I will fulfill my obligations no matter whether one or ten thousand attend the game," he said to the *Morning News*. The official Game 2 attendance tallied less than expected at under 5,000, and he needed to maximize remaining ticket revenue to pay his obligations to his players and opponents.

**Paul "Twister" Steinberg,
1906 Canton Bulldogs**

Despite any initial reservations, the Canton community seemed ready to support Wallace, as the *Morning News* observed:

Hundreds of people who expressed themselves as not desiring to attend the game with Latrobe today, announced last night that the whole affair had the appearance of a dirty trick and that they would witness the game today regardless of the weather conditions and to thus give the so-called conspiracy a stinging rebuke that they will not soon forget.

With their pride wounded by their loss to Massillon and attacks on their character, the Bulldogs showed up motivated and angry to face Latrobe's Miners. With legend John Brallier still at quarterback, playing in the last game of his career, and defending a four-year unbeaten streak, the Miners had plenty of incentive themselves. The Bulldogs, aided by the return of Bull Smith, took out their collective frustration with a convincing 16–0 win over the Pennsylvania champions, who had not relinquished a point during their four-year winning streak. The game's highlight was provided by Marshall Reynolds, who scored the first points by bolting for a 90-yard touchdown on a fake punt late in a taut first half.

The star of the game, though, was Bulldogs halfback Paul "Twister" Steinberg. The former Syracuse standout performed tremendously earlier in the season but was squeezed out of the team's two games with Massillon, given Wallace's preference for Smith and Reynolds in the backfield due to his familiarity with them from Penn. Since end Eddie Wood returned to play for Latrobe, Wallace moved Smith to end, opening a spot at running back. Given a chance to shine, Steinberg reeled off several long inside and outside runs and had the *Morning News* expressing that the outcome of Game 2 with Massillon may have been different if he had played.

Wallace was proud of his men. Unfortunately, he was not rewarded by the turnout at the game that he needed to break even. Only 939 fans showed up, and 300 of them had ventured from Latrobe. The weight of the situation began to wear on Wallace, as he expressed to the *Morning News*:

> I consider the game today to be a good one in which almost every player on the team was a star in his respective position…. I am satisfied that in all the games played by the Canton team this year, every player did his best to win, and am sorry that the football public was deluded by the malicious stories that were peddled out by some of the Massillon people. I have done my best to secure for Canton the best football aggregation that was ever organized, and I believed that I had succeeded, and now that the games have all been played, and I have lost a large amount of money in my undertaking, I naturally feel embarrassed that I was not backed up as I should have been by the people in general.
>
> I wish to add that I am surprised that any person who had the interest of Canton at heart, knowing at the same time how some of the people of Massillon acted towards Canton in the past, should pay any attention to the libelous stories that originated in that city concocted by a few individuals who were only jealous of me because I would not submit to unreasonable terms for a Thanksgiving Day game.

Despite not being able to collect his team's $1,500 guarantee from Wallace after the game, Latrobe manager Harry Ryan was sympathetic to Wallace's plight:

> I have no excuse to offer for our defeat. The terrible on-slaughts of the Canton players … told on our players to such an extent that I was compelled to add other players to my line-up in place of some of my stars who were injured. I consider the Canton team the best that I have ever played against, and I cannot understand why the people of Canton did not turn out in larger numbers to witness the game today.

On the same afternoon, the Tigers lined up at Chicago's South Side Park, where the 1906 White Sox, nicknamed "the Hitless Wonders," upset the cross-town Cubs in the World Series weeks earlier. Roughly 2,000 fans paid to see the hastily arranged game with Heston's all-stars that Massillon used to fill its open date. Heston performed sensationally, especially on defense. Down 4–0, his forces battled back to tie the game at 4–4 midway through the second half. Heston's bad luck continued, though, when his leg was broken under a pileup. Without Heston to back the line on the defensive side, the Tigers roared on a game-winning drive, completed again by a short run by Leonard Roseth for a touchdown and a 9–4 win that sealed their undisputed world championship.

Courtesy of the Massillon Museum

The Massillon Athletic Club housed the Tigers during the football seasons in their early 1900s professional era. Stone tigers still hang adjacent to the doorway on the current building.

After the last beans were counted, Wallace was in the hole roughly $3,000, including player salaries and Latrobe's guarantee, plus an unknown amount promised to quarterback Vince Stevenson. Swallowing their pride, Bulldogs financial manager Williams and guard Tom Riley trekked to the Tigers' residence at the Massillon Athletic Club on Friday evening to beg for help. They proposed a benefit game to Stewart and the Tigers players between Canton and Massillon on Sunday, December 2, in Canton, to help pay for railroad fares for those Bulldogs stars who had been recruited to travel to Canton and found themselves left stranded. To keep the game friendly and add entertainment, under the proposed format, teams would be mixed, with some Bulldogs playing for Massillon, some Tigers playing for Canton, and players from both sides playing in unfamiliar positions. Massillon's Stewart and Canton's Williams would officiate. To avoid any problems, Wallace would not be on site. All proceeds would be split evenly among Canton's participating players. Out of a spirit of camaraderie, the Tigers readily agreed.

It was not the dramatic Game 3 that might have made sense if cooler heads had prevailed all along. A sparse pack of 600 good-hearted supporters turned out to take in what the *Morning News* called a burlesque. Generally, linemen played in the backfield and vice versa. Maxwell tried his hand at quarterback for the first time in his career for the "Massillon" team. Shiring moved to end. Massillon's backup halfback, William Robison, scored a touchdown for "Canton." Pratt King did not switch teams and scored for the so-called Tigers in a 5–5 tie that seemed predetermined. Rules were loosely followed. As the referee, Stewart used a revolver instead of a whistle to keep things in line, hopefully firing blanks. The event raised enough cash to provide each player with $15, sufficient to purchase a rail ticket home "with a glad remembrance that after he returns there he was a lucky man he didn't have to walk," as the *Morning News* put it.

As spokesmen for the Bulldogs, Jack Ernst, Paul Steinberg, and Tom Thorpe issued a final statement to their hometown journal on behalf of their teammates:

> To the foot ball public of Canton:
>
> We the players of the Canton foot ball team, wish to extend our thanks to those Cantonians who so loyally supported us during the season just closed, and we also wish to acknowledge our gratitude toward the players of the Massillon foot ball team for their services in Sunday's benefit game, and to the *Morning News* for the fair and impartial treatment given us during the last season.

On the personal front, Canton's Pop Sweet took the opportunity to announce his retirement. "This is my last year of foot ball," declared Sweet. "Getting old enough to know better." Bulldog Tom Riley added, "Well, it's been a good experience anyway."

The next evening, according to the *Gleaner*, 13 Tigers still in Massillon and one surprise guest were celebrated by a group of over 40 members at the local Elks lodge. Herman Kerkhoff received the warmest of welcomes from his former comrades-in-arms when he unexpectedly joined the party:

> "Kerky" returned like a prodigal son, a lost lamb, to the fold. He was welcomed back

IT WAS A TIE

Burlesque Game Between Players of Canton and Massillon.

CROWD DISAPPOINTED

Lynn "Pop" Sweet,
1906 Canton Bulldogs

Herman Kerkhoff's Legacy

I am proud to say that my great-great-grandfather was Herman C. "Bumper" Kerkhoff, a professional football player at the turn of the twentieth century. Herman's 6-foot-4, 240-pound frame, superior athletic ability, and extraordinary footspeed enabled him to achieve superstar status on the gridiron for 10-plus years.

"Hermie" (his family nickname) was raised in the middle of the pack as one of 10 children on the family dairy farm just south of Lafayette, Indiana. His daily deliveries introduced him to local club "foot ball" teams. In 1890, the 20-year-old farm boy phenom was a monster on the gridiron for one of Lafayette's many teams, the Oakland Hill Bumpers.

Hermie's prowess as a footballer allowed him to enroll at Purdue University in 1895 as a non–high school graduate "special student." No official records exist, but family oral tradition claimed he also played for the school in 1893 and 1894. Three months and six games later, Bumper (his Lafayette nickname) left PU with some touchdowns and football photos, but no official transcript.

For the next 11 years, Kerkhoff's pro football services were brokered to the highest bidders from Denver to Pennsylvania. Highlights include frequent "guards back" line bucking, carrying three to six tacklers for 10-plus yards, picking up a 200-pound ball carrier and throwing him over the goal line for a touchdown in Madison Square Garden, and lifting a fallen horse upright on an icy street.

Three seasons for the yellow-clad Indianapolis Athletic Association from 1896 to 1898 included a 10–1 season in '97, with only a loss at Yale, and catapulted Kerkhoff to the Chicago Athletic Association Cherry Circle in '97. The Denver Athletic Club's Cherry and Black gridders lured "Kerky" (his national moniker) westward from 1899 through 1901, where the dominating guard earned bonuses paid in gold and All-Denver accolades.

In 1902, Kerkhoff and Bob Shiring anchored the champion Pittsburg Pros line, and in 1904 and 1905 the two linemates were reunited in football's earliest holy land, Massillon, Ohio. Their three seasons together all resulted in championships. While playing side by side for the Tigers, ne'er a game was lost or tied. The two pals who lined up next to each other on the gridiron were also frequently alongside each other in team photographs.

Bumper was not just a gargantuan strongman. He endeared himself to locals with his kindness and jovial nature at each stop on his football tour. At one point, Kerkhoff accumulated great wealth and prestige as a professional when professionalism was generally derided. He later married and provided for his small family by working his land. The loss of all his wealth on a failed southeast Missouri farm and land deal, plus only three grandchildren, seemed to erase Bumper's legacy mere decades after his passing.

When I received the collection of family photos, notes, and genealogies in the mail from Aunt Diane Terrell with a note stating I "seemed like the only one who showed any interest in family history, so enjoy!" I was ecstatic. The old pictures that I would beg great-grandma to bring out from her drawer were now mine!

"The famous grid star," as Bumper's obituary read in the *Lafayette Journal and Courier*, was added to the Purdue media guide's letter winner list in 2019 as a result of nearly 100 pieces of evidence my daughter Claire and I submitted to its athletic department. These efforts are a first step to restoring Bumper's athletic legacy, as I also hope to rekindle a connection with communities from his other teams: the Chicago Athletic Club, Denver Athletic Club, Franklin (PA) Athletic Club, Canton, and Massillon—"the City of Champions."

— Billy Fusiek, Lafayette, IN

Herman Kerkhoff with Massillon Tigers manager J.J. Wise in 1905

in such a demonstrative manner that tears trickled down his hardened cheeks and words failed him when he attempted to explain his gratitude for the reception.

"I just sort of sneaked up here," he began, when speaking, "and didn't think I'd be seen. I don't know why I came, but I guess it was because I feel at home here."

After the turkey feast, the Elks and Tigers passed the hat and raised another $38.50 for the Bulldogs. Shiring, Maxwell, Stewart, and others then took turns at the front of the room, reflecting on their experiences with the team. Shiring spoke of his feelings for Massillon, how he was introduced to society there, and became so fond of the place that he never thought of playing elsewhere. "I'll be back next year if you want me," he concluded, receiving the loudest ovation.

The following afternoon, old friends Shiring and Doc McChesney boarded the train together for Pittsburgh, just as they had arrived together before the title games. It was an emotional goodbye, according to the *Gleaner*:

> Bob hated to tear himself away from Massillon almost as much as did the Massillon people, players and officials have him go. He was accompanied to the train by a few of the players and management, and as the train pulled out of the depot, there were tears of genuine regret in his eyes.

⇋ East's Countercharges ⇋

After their football players returned home, it was left for the Canton-Massillon legal game to be played out. Though East had his witnessed signature on a contract committing to fix the 1906 championship games, it remained to be seen if his reputed cleverness would lead him to deliver an alternate story. Indeed, it did. In his sensational version of reality, it was the Tigers who entrapped him. Upon his return from Pittsburgh on Wednesday, December 5, East released a signed statement to the press turning the tables on the Tigers:

> In justice to myself and for the enlightenment of the public, I herewith present a statement of the case, without reserve…. Suffice it to say that the entire matter originated with, and was directed by Mr. Wightman; that it was Mr. Wightman who first suggested the matter to me; that I at first declined to enter into the affair, but consented at a later interview; that it was at Wightman's request that I saw the Massillon players, Shiring and Maxwell; that it was at his suggestion I looked up a party to furnish the money; that it was at his request a meeting was arranged at Pittsburg, and that after the terms demanded by Wightman had been turned down, it

was at the suggestion and urgent request of Wightman that negotiations were reopened and a meeting at Cleveland, O., arranged. A reference of the local telephoned exchange will corroborate these statements, the same showing that Wightman repeatedly called up … for the purpose of arranging those meetings.

While not denying that he engaged in the scam, East took another shot at Massillon management's virtue by entirely exonerating Wallace:

I notice further that Wightman and the management of the Massillon foot ball team, charge Mr. Wallace … with being a party to the deal. If he was, it was wholly without any knowledge on my part.

No member of the Canton foot ball team or of the Canton Athletic Association were, so far as I know, connected with the deal in any manner whatsoever. If Wallace was connected with the matter, as Wightman and the Massillon foot ball management assert, they, and not I are aware of the fact.

As an excuse for the loss of the first game, Massillon charges that I gave their signals to the Canton players, and then say that they were obliged to change their signals to play with an entirely new set…. None of the signals, plays, or formations were divulged by me, either to the Canton players or anyone else.

As to whether Mr. Wightman was acting in good faith when he made the original proposition or was simply acting for the Massillon management in feeling out his team, I leave under all the circumstances of the case for the public to judge.

Walter East, 1904 Western University of Pennsylvania

While also denying Stewart's and Croxton's claim that he had admitted to fixing a WUP football game and games of the Akron baseball team, East let the cat out of the bag about who financed the Canton-Massillon deal. Stunningly, the other signature on the contract belonged to John T. Windsor, Akron baseball club vice president, also secretary and treasurer of the Windsor Brick company in Akron. The commingling of corruption within the Ohio sports world, especially originating from the management of East's other team, added levels of complexity to the plot.

East added that, on the morning Massillon released him, Coach Wightman sent him to Akron to demand Windsor return all copies of the agreement, which Windsor refused to do. Thus, East provided the full text of the contract to the press, which the *Morning News* included in its article on Thursday, December 6, after East's conclusion:

Knowing that neither Mr. Wightman nor myself have any justification for our actions in the foot ball matter, but being willing to bear my share of the blame, without attempting to screen myself, by besmirching the reputations of innocent parties, I am submitting all the facts to the public for their consideration.

All things considered, East's account was convoluted but not out of the realm of possibility. His portrayal of Wightman as the mastermind seemed odd, though. Stewart's name was not on the contract, but given his extreme ambition, competitiveness, and paranoia, Wightman appeared more likely Stewart's pawn. However, the first sentence of the agreement cast doubt on East's entire case:

> Whereas, East, a member of the Massillon foot ball team, has proposed to the parties that the foot ball game to be played between the Massillon team and the Canton team on November 16th, 1906, at Canton, O., be permitted to be won by the Canton team, and if so won, Wightman will be paid the sum of $4,000, and Windsor has offered and is willing to insure and guarantee payment of said sum to Wightman.

It is baffling why East, while claiming Wightman was the plot's architect, would have provided the contract to the press, given the statement therein that "East … proposed" the deal.

As the case also pertained to East's standing in the Ohio and Pennsylvania baseball league, O&P president Charles Morton expressed cautious relief in the *Akron Beacon Journal* the same day:

> I am glad to hear that East has denied having kept Akron behind Youngstown in the O&P league because he received any consideration for it. The Massillon business, of course, looks bad, but I don't want to say anything about it until after I get the facts. He should have a fair hearing before he is criticized.

Perhaps the truth rested somewhere in between. As many expected, Coach Wightman assigned responsibility to his superior. From his parents' home in Cleveland, Wightman said his piece to the *Plain Dealer* in its December 7 issue:

> Anything and everything I did in conjunction with East and Windsor was done in accordance with instructions from Manager Stewart and the backers of the Massillon team. When East first came to me with his scheme, I reported his proposition to my employers and they told me to go ahead with it and see what lengths East and his fellow conspirators would go. Consequently, I strung them along until I had the signatures of East and Windsor down on paper. When that was done East was released

Coach Sherburn Wightman, 1906 Massillon Tigers

and the conspirators saw that we had goldbricked them. Consequently, the great plunging on the first game on the part of the bettors did not take place.

East's statement does not worry me in the least, for I am innocent of any intent to pull off any dishonesty.

With all of those involved having weighed in, except Windsor, CAC's management had heard enough to decide that "some gross wrong had been committed" by the Massillon side:

When the alleged sell out of "Blondy" Wallace was printed in a Massillon paper, a great many people in Canton were inclined to believe the truthfulness of the story…. This caused a loss of no less than $5,000 to Mr. Wallace and placed him in a position that would not be envied even by a prisoner in the Ohio penitentiary, but since the facts and motives of the conspirators are being ferreted out, the people of Canton are finding out that they have been duped by the Massillon management and many of them have gone to Mr. Wallace personally and apologized for their actions, and it is confidently believed that after the courts and the grand jury gets through with certain people, there may be some developments that will even surprise some persons in Massillon.

The consequence of CAC's decision, according to the *Morning News* on December 8, was that in any sport, it "would in the future refuse to have any contests with Massillon." Without mentioning Stewart by name, CAC managed to point its finger at whom it believed to be the source of the problem:

So long as Jake Wise had charge of Massillon's interest in sport, every statement made by him was always made good and when he stepped down and out, in Massillon sporting circles, the people of that city lost the services of one of the cleanest and truest sportsmen that ever headed any organization. In the future, the management of the C.A.C. will be confined to baseball and basketball contests only, but no games with Massillon with the present crowd at the head of their affairs.

Stewart did not take kindly to the news, accusing CAC of being ungrateful for his club's assistance in providing its players complimentary services to rescue CAC's stranded men. CAC shot back hard, referencing previously unpublished innuendo that some parties in Massillon may have bought off two Canton players in the 1905 championship game. Heston was not mentioned directly, but his aggressive pursuit of top dollar from both teams and poor performance in the game could explain Wallace's lack of confidence in rehiring him in 1906.

At last, Windsor stepped out of the shadows with his account. Everything he said supported East's story, only in greater detail for clarification:

> My name having been made public as a party to the deal … I desire to present my side of the case.
>
> The first intimation that I had with reference to the matter was on November 4, when I was solicited by East, at the request of Wightman, to become a party to such a deal. At that time I turned down the proposition.… East came again to see me, and said that Wightman wanted to see me personally and requested a meeting at Pittsburg the following day, upon which date the Massillon foot ball team was to play the Pittsburg Lyceums. In compliance, I went to Pittsburg, and met Wightman and East at the Seventh Avenue hotel. Wightman there suggested that he was in the game for the money there was in it and said that he could make arrangements for Massillon to lose the first game, naming the players whom he thought could be fixed, and proposed to have such officials selected as would do his bidding, but demanded $4000 in cash to be paid him before the game and the further stipulation that he wanted it arranged to have Massillon win the second game. He gave as his reason for wanting so large a sum that it would not pay for him to take less, for if it was ever discovered it would ruin his reputation. I refused to consider the proposition and so informed him.

ON WIGHTMAN

Windsor, of Akron, Puts Blame For the Foot-ball Scandal.

MAY GO INTO COURTS

Windsor continued by saying that Wightman then reached out to him directly by phone the next evening requesting a meeting in Cleveland to present a revised offer. East and Windsor accepted the appointment, at which the parties discussed a couple of iterations before reaching an agreement on terms in the signed contract. East returned to visit Windsor the next day, with news that Wightman released him, demanding that he return all copies of the signed contract. Windsor concurred with East that he would do no such thing:

> I immediately called up Wightman by 'phone and told him that I would not return any papers in my possession with his signature attached, and that so far as I was concerned the entire agreement was cancelled, and he could make the same public at once if he so desired.
>
> On the 22d day of November I received a letter from Wightman informing me that I could get the money which had been deposited at Cleveland, O. by signing a receipt for the same. Later he went to Cleveland and demanded money. We were informed that we could not have the same unless we signed the receipt which had been prepared by either Wightman

or someone in his behalf, completely exonerating him and putting blame for the entire deal on us as is shown by the receipt which was presented to us for our signatures and of which the following is a copy:

Cleveland, O.

Received of J.H. Kusel, of Cleveland, O., the sum of five hundred ($500) dollars, which was deposited with him for the purpose of bribing S.H. Wightman and the Massillon foot ball management in such manner that they would permit the Canton team to win the first football game to be played at Canton, November 16, 1906.

I acknowledge that such a bribe was attempted and further acknowledge that such bribe failed.

This receipt we refused to sign and before I will ever sign the same or any document concerning Wightman, the man who had repeatedly solicited East and myself to go in with him on his numerous propositions, I will go into court and let the matter be decided there. Wightman cannot use the $500 as a club for the purpose of compelling me to give him a statement clearing him of the part he took in the matter. Every proposition from the time I first met Wightman, including the final agreement entered into at Cleveland and prepared by his attorney, was made, proposed and outlined by Wightman, the same man whom I see by the daily press later attempted to buy from a player the plays devised by and belonging to Coach Stagg, of Chicago University, without his knowledge and consent.

In concluding, Windsor also cleared Wallace:

So far as Wallace or any other member of the Canton foot ball team or the Canton Foot Ball Association are concerned, they had no dealings either directly or indirectly with me. I did not know Wallace at the time, do not know him now, and never had any communication with him.

(Signed) J.T. Windsor

⪦ Waiting in Suspense ⪧

E.J. Stewart stubbornly assumed that business would go on as usual for him at the Massillon Athletic Club in 1907. He made several attempts to secure basketball games with CAC, which quickly fell on deaf ears. Stewart found out CAC management meant what it said about refusing to play any sport with Massillon under its present management.

On March 8, the *Dayton Herald* reported:

> Without sporting relations with Canton A.C., which always has strong or-
> ganizations in every branch, Massillon can not support professional sports.
> News was received here today that Manager Ed Stewart, of the Massillon
> Athletic Association, has resigned, but it is not likely to help matters.

Within months, Stewart was gainfully employed again as the head
football coach at Mount Union College in Alliance, Ohio, still within the
limits of Stark County.

With the 1907 baseball season approaching, Walter East's dilemma
created immediate concerns for him about his career as Akron's manager.
He had more support in Akron than elsewhere, given his mostly successful
stretch over his two seasons managing the team. Based on their observations
and experiences, Akron sportswriters and players came out in support of
East, as Ohio's *Mansfield News-Journal* related in an interview with Akron
first baseman Bill Schwartz on December 12:

**Walter East retained
his position as Akron's
baseball manager in 1907
despite his role in the
football scandal.**

> Any talk of last season's race being "fixed" is bosh and I believe I can
> reasonably prove it, though I must divulge a secret with a friend in doing
> it, but if any good will come out of what I say I believe I am justified.
> Never did I see a more dejected man than Walter East after a game in
> Youngstown toward the close of the season that settled the pennant
> against Akron. East did not speak to a single man on the team for two
> hours after the game. He did not eat supper and the first train out of
> Youngstown he boarded leaving the team for three days, although we
> were playing every day, and he was needed. That is how East felt about
> losing first place. His absence was kept quiet at home beyond his state-
> ment that he did not feel like playing. Well, he certainly didn't.

If East had intentionally lost the 1906 O&P championship for Akron, as
Stewart alleged East had told him, he was an extremely good actor. Nonetheless, a more objective opinion from outside Akron considered a broader
perspective, per an editorial in the *Pittsburg Press* on December 15:

> East is a college man, whose advantages and associations have been better
> and higher than those of the average ball player, and while all deplore
> his downfall, none, with the welfare of baseball at heart, can condone
> his offense and consent to his return to the game as manager or player.
> It is of little moment whether he was principal or accomplice in the plot,
> to which, according to his statement, he, Wightman, the Canton coach,
> and Windsor, vice president of the Akron Baseball Club, were parties.

His connection with the nefarious affair is admitted and the man who would cheat at football is not up to the standard of integrity that exacting baseball patrons demand of the exponents of their favorite sport. Vice President Windsor, of the Akron Club, who guaranteed the payment of the sum of $4,000 to have the Canton-Massillon game "fixed," should dispose of his stock and close his baseball career.

In response, East was quoted by the *Press* as saying:

Of course, I believe that my case should come before the league, but as regarding my integrity on the diamond no one can rightfully say I have done anything wrong. I worked hard to win for Akron, and always will as long as I am connected with that team.

Meanwhile, in Canton, with public sentiment shifting in his favor, Wallace directed his attorneys, Homer Briggle and Oscar Abt, on December 18, to file a supplemental petition seeking an additional $6,400 in damages based on amounts due to his players, the Latrobe team, and the lost attendance from the Latrobe game.

Christmas passed, and 1906 ended with Wallace still waiting in Canton for his turn in court. All he could do was watch the wheels of justice turn slowly. Without funds to settle his debts, though, it was unclear how Wallace could afford his mounting legal bills unless a contingency arrangement existed.

Shortly after the calendar turned to 1907, the *Cleveland Plain Dealer* reported a development that delayed the matter further. It was bad news for Wallace but very good news for East:

[O&P League] President Charles Morton received a letter today from the attorney of S.H. Wightman, the Massillon foot ball coach, which, it is believed, will mean the certain retention of Walter East as manager of the Akron base ball team. The communication to Morton, which came from Attorney Wallace I. Knight, of Cleveland, says that owing to the fact that Wightman is to be an important witness in the damage case brought by "Blondy" Wallace against Wightman, it will be impossible for the latter to appear before the league magnates at their meeting this month and give any testimony as to East's connection with charges that have been made. The letter is regarded as a virtual refusal on Wightman's part to back up his charge, and since there can be no hearing without Wightman, it is taken that there will be no investigation and East will be allowed to remain as manager. It is unlikely that East will be displaced, since the damage case will most likely drag through the summer.

Massillon Coach Wightman was ultimately never deposed, damaging Blondy Wallace's case.

On January 28, the *Massillon Evening Independent* printed a vague one-paragraph update on the case. It said that the judge struck out parts of Wallace's petition and that the defendants filed a demurrer objecting that Wallace's petition failed to allege facts sufficient to support some of his claims.

With no news to report for over a month, the media's attention began to drift away from the case. The headline of another brief article in the *Beacon Journal* on March 2 read, "An Echo of the Scandal." It mentioned that Wallace amended his petition to document Croxton's net worth at $500,000, ostensibly to demonstrate the ease with which Croxton could pay Wallace's damages. Wallace also added two attorneys, making his legal team "four of the ablest lawyers in Canton."

East proceeded to manage through challenging issues on and off the baseball field as 1907 progressed. In January, he avoided any charges at an O&P League meeting. His father passed away in February. After a brief time at home in Illinois, he then met with Akron's baseball directors to do "some salve spreading in a tete-tete [*sic*]," according to Ohio's *Marion Daily Mirror* on March 9, to keep a tenuous hold on his job. Newspapers from across O&P League towns predicted that East's team, now called the Akron Rubbernecks, would win the league's pennant in 1907, adding to his pressure.

In April, Wallace's legal team subpoenaed East for a pretrial deposition and a withering cross-examination that took place on the 22nd. For his own well-being, East skipped his team's preseason road trip to play the Canton baseball club. "He stated that he did not think it would be safe nor healthy for him to come to Canton," the *Stark County Democrat* remarked on May 3, "and instead went to Columbus, where the deposition was taken." Highlights of East's deposition were leaked to the *Canton Morning News* and published in its May 7 issue. Without direct quotes, it was not possible to know whether the leaker's report was accurate. Regardless, East's accusations were reportedly consistent with his previous statements, although with a new twist about his connection with Wallace:

> From the statements made in this deposition the parties who made the deal framing up the games with him were S.H. Wightman, coach of the Massillon Tigers, J.T. Windsor, Maxwell, the giant guard of the Tigers, and Shiring, their strong center. East claims that several times he had attempted to get Wallace in on the deal, but at no time could he get him to sign any agreement.

By mid-May, Pennsylvania's *New Castle Herald* reported that East lost his previously prolific head of hair, calling him "Baldy," and suffered a subsequent case of flu-like grippe. In June, the heat of daily battles on the diamond led the typically supportive *Beacon Journal* to call him out for turning into the worst umpire-baiter at any level in baseball. At midseason, in late July, Akron stood in second place in the eight-team league, though the *Pittsburg Post* echoed the *Herald*'s preseason expectation that East's squad would still come out on top.

With the season entering the home stretch and the Rubbernecks' prospects not improving, tempers flared at the team's director level, according to the *Daily Mirror* on August 6:

> Both Manager East and Mr. Windsor have been in a measure exonerated since [the football scandal]. East, it came to light, allowed himself to be duped into making arrangements for an official of the Canton team and another on the Massillon team. Mr. Windsor's part was to come to East as a friend with the necessary capital to put the scheme through.
>
> Director Campbell, it seems has desired the removal of East and resignation of Mr. Windsor on account of the scandal. He brought up this topic at the directors meeting. Hot words passed and while alone Mr. Windsor hit Campbell, breaking his nose and badly discoloring his left eye. Mr. Windsor has resigned and offers his baseball stock which Campbell says he will take. President Gibbs, who has been on Windsor's side of the controversy as have the other directors, will also offer his stock. Mr. Campbell by purchasing the holdings of these two will control the club and in that event is sure to release Manager East.
>
> Campbell says he will cause Windsor arrest for assault and battery and will sue him for $10,000 damages.

Legend holds that a Lancaster, Pennsylvania, newspaper whimsically editorialized, "It was the first time two men got into a fight over another man."

By late September, the Rubbernecks slipped to third place after a loss at fifth-place New Castle. Despite support for East from Akron newspapers, the team's attendance declined due to suspicions over his role in the Canton-Massillon disgrace. With the Rubbernecks falling out of contention, rumors of corruption again circled East and his players. Fans accused an Akron pitcher of selling out in a Youngstown game, getting "500 bones to put 'em straight over," according to the *Herald* on September 30. The following day, a *Herald* writer asserted, "It is not believed a straight [*sic*] jacket would make Walter East any less crooked."

At this point, it could be said that East's life went south, again literally, as well as figuratively. On October 17, the *Herald* reported that a deal was in place to move East to Little Rock's Southern League team. East initially refused the assignment and, after a change in Akron's ownership, the Rubbernecks surprisingly appealed to the O&P president for his return. As the *Herald* sarcastically commented, "Akron felt it could not struggle along through another season without East, the boy wonder and all that."

Walter East's Akron baseball teams never won a championship until he left the team.

The appeal was denied, and East served out his season in Little Rock. The team's fans jeered him mercilessly after he spiked an opposing catcher on a play at home plate early in the season.

Ironically, with former Massillon quarterback Homer Davidson playing right field, the Akron Rubbernecks acquired the official honor, as was the annual O&P custom, of being called the Akron Champs after winning the 1908 league championship without East at the helm. The Champs then continued to win consecutive pennants through 1911.

⪤ Wallace's Woes ⪥

While stuck in legal limbo during the spring and summer of 1907, Blondy Wallace continued living at the Courtland Hotel in Canton and took on odd jobs, including one as a cashier at a racetrack. The related article in the *Herald* stated that he was just as popular with the ladies there as he was when he was on the gridiron.

Pro football was not going to recover any time soon in Ohio after the 1906 uproar. With incredible resilience and time on his hands, Wallace went back to work, organizing a semi-pro league in the state while waiting to learn his legal fate. As CAC was under new management heading into the 1907 football season, Wallace somehow convinced the club's new manager to allow him to coach its team, which was composed mostly of local amateurs plus a few players compensated with reasonable salaries. Teams in the league included Toledo, Akron, Cleveland, Alliance, and Massillon, among others.

Negotiations between new CAC manager Markling and new Massillon Athletic Club manager Rodway for a renewal of the towns' football rivalry went on unsuccessfully for weeks until Wallace and Markling "dropped in" on Rodway in Massillon on Tuesday, October 28. According to the *Beacon Journal*, the parties agreed to a game the following Sunday at Canton's Lakeside Park. However, no record exists of the game, nor can a report be found explaining why it was canceled. It is reasonable to assume that the teams' failure to get together may have had something to do with Sherburn Wightman continuing to coach the Massillon squad. As Wightman somehow avoided being deposed in Wallace's case, he may have also chosen to avoid him on the field. The All-Massillons won the league championship with a record of 7-0-1, capped off by a 13–4 win over the Columbus Panhandles on Thanksgiving Day. Bob Shiring was among the Massillon players, making the trip from Pittsburgh to play his only game that season for the Tigers.

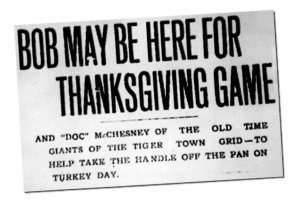

BOB MAY BE HERE FOR THANKSGIVING GAME

AND "DOC" McCHESNEY OF THE OLD TIME GIANTS OF THE TIGER TOWN GRID—TO HELP TAKE THE HANDLE OFF THE PAN ON TURKEY DAY.

FOOTBALL SCANDAL OVER

Without news regarding Wallace's case for months after the 1907 season, the *Evening Independent* reported on May 4, 1908, in a one-paragraph blurb near the bottom of the front page, that the case had been dismissed:

> Dismissal has been made in the celebrated damage case brought by C.E. Wallace, coach of the Canton football team for two years, against H.A. Croxton, et al. of Massillon. The plaintiff sought to recover damages for alleged slander and libel used by the defendants, previous to the championship contests in the fall of 1906. Entry of dismissal was made Monday morning before Common Pleas Judge Ambler by Attorney Luther Day, counsel for the defendant. Plaintiff, it was claimed, had failed to furnish security for costs. Attorney Homer Briggle, counsel for Wallace, said that he was not in a position to oppose the dismissal. "My client failed to secure costs and that was the end of the matter," said Briggle. Wallace is now living in New York City.

On the surface, at least, in an all-too-common outcome, the parties with the deeper pockets outlasted the less wealthy legal opponent, justice aside. There were no quotes from Wallace or anyone else, either justifying or qualifying the outcome. The only point that can be concluded to have affected the result was that Wallace's residence outside of Ohio forced the judge to demand payment of the court costs, just as he was excused from paying them at the beginning of the trial while he lived in Ohio. It was an oddly anticlimactic end to his personal crusade for justice and to the drama that Stewart had called in the *Gleaner* "one of the greatest plots which has ever been attempted."

The consequences of Stewart's decision to implicate Wallace had eventually followed their logical course. The only way for Wallace to clear his name and preserve his future was to pursue legal action against his accusers. Yet, he must have recognized that he was up against long odds on more than one front. Wallace initially filed his libel claim in Stark County against Croxton, Stewart, and the Gleaner Publishing Company on November 28, 1906. As the case proceeded, he realized local bias was likely against him, possibly preventing him from receiving a fair trial. Thus, rumors swirled in legal circles in March 1907 that his attorneys would likely file a motion to move the case to another jurisdiction in a nearby county. After piling up legal expenses for over a year, it is reasonable to expect that Wallace could no longer afford to pursue the justice that he believed he deserved against the bankroll of his multiple well-established opponents. Croxton and the *Gleaner* could certainly fend for themselves. If Stewart did not receive financial support from either of his employers, at least he had held jobs for several years to build a war chest for himself.

If, in truth, the facts supported Wallace's innocence in this matter, it would seemingly never be known without a public hearing. Or he may have been forced to calculate that it was simply expedient to drop the case, leaving a shadow of doubt as to his involvement, if he knew that he was guilty or determined at some point that he was unlikely to win, or both. So, better for him to cut his losses before he became financially crippled. Or it may be that one or more of the accused cut Wallace a back-room deal to bail him out of his legal and other debts and make him go away while preserving all of their reputations. If they could pay Wallace off by making him an offer he could not refuse so he would disappear without further slandering these pillars of the Massillon community, it may have been in the best interest of all parties involved to settle out of court. Why else would he have left Ohio without a parting shot after all that he had been through? Unless Wallace was guilty or threatened somehow, why would he have decided to go quietly and accept any of these scenarios that would likely end his career as a football leader and, worse, amount to selling his soul?

This is how the end of the story sat for decades, with no decision on the great Wallace's complicity in the scandal that rocked and wrecked pro football just as the game sparked the fire of America's passion for the first time. It was hardly a satisfying conclusion for the curious fans and sleuths who followed the drama during the season and after the anticlimactic Canton-Massillon charity game in December 1906. But without his day in court, Wallace's career and legacy would be left to the court of public opinion. Although the evidence presented by Stewart in the *Gleaner* was entirely circumstantial, Wallace's reputation as a rebel tipped the scales against him, as he was effectively blackballed out of any significant form of participation in the sport that he loved.

⊱ "Doleful Doc" Stewart ⊰

From Mount Union College, E.J. Stewart continued to build a highly successful career coaching various combinations of football, basketball, baseball, and track and field at an impressive list of schools, including Purdue, Oregon State, Nebraska, Clemson, Texas, and the University of Texas at El Paso through 1928. In the 1923 season, he led the Texas football team to an 8–0–1 record and, months later, guided its basketball team to a 23–0 mark and a Southwest Conference championship. Stewart was also quite the Renaissance man, owning a medical degree, skills as a pianist, and an automobile dealership. Texas also made him an open offer for a position in its English Department due to his literary skills as a former sportswriter. Critics thought he would have done better as a coach without so many interests.

Despite Stewart's success and popularity with students, he carried a pessimistic nature. He always downplayed his teams' chances, claiming that his attitude was a precaution against overconfidence, especially for Texas alumni. This led to a Waco, Texas, sportswriter labeling him as "Doleful Doc" Stewart in 1924, a nickname that stuck throughout the rest of his career. After retiring from UTEP in 1928, Stewart operated a hotel, as well as boys and girls summer camps, in his home of Kerrville, Texas.

Stewart was tragically killed in a hunting accident on November 18, 1929, near his home. According to the *Amarillo Globe-Times*:

> E.J. "Doleful Doc" Stewart, football coach for a quarter of a century, was accidentally killed about 30 miles from his home here yesterday when he was mistaken for a deer.
>
> J.W. O'Byrne of San Antonio, hunting in the same party as Stewart, fired the fatal shot.
>
> O'Byrne had come to Texas recently from Missouri and had never shot a buck. Stewart promised to go into the brakes and scare one out. The veteran mentor evidently could not get through, and he returned by the same route O'Byrne thought the deer would take. O'Byrne saw the brush moving and thought Stewart was the buck. The charge struck Stewart in the chest, killing him instantly.
>
> Stewart was buried in Cleveland, where he was born and raised.

Courtesy of Mike McKee

E.J. Stewart's unfortunate death occurred shortly after the end of his long and successful coaching career.

Walter East clearly appeared to be "the bad guy," at least the main one, in the ordeal, and to a degree, he seemed to embrace the role of a mischievous, if not evil, genius. Even without a legal decision in the case, after owning up to his involvement in the Canton-Massillon scandal in the media, he was also excommunicated from the football and baseball worlds after the 1907 season, at least in Ohio.

East resorted to an extended career in minor league baseball, mostly throughout various southern leagues, where his travels included stints on the Nashville Vols, Memphis Turtles, and Atlanta Crackers. In February 1910, East was acquired from Nashville by the American League's Cleveland Naps, which, at the time, also employed "Shoeless" Joe Jackson. Jackson was later a key figure in the 1919 Chicago "Black Sox" baseball scandal. He was one of eight players banned from baseball for life for participating in a gambling scheme in which the team intentionally lost the World Series to the Cincinnati Reds. It is interesting to consider the possibility that East and Jackson may have had a conversation at some point on their philosophies about sports gambling during East's time with the Naps. However, it is not likely since, after acquiring East, the Naps sent him directly to their Buffalo Bisons minor league affiliate, before trading him to the Montreal Royals four months later, without any time in the big leagues in Cleveland.

In a twist revealing something of the power of East's charisma, he was named captain of the Atlanta Crackers in 1912, shortly after latching on with the team in the early part of the season, as his athletic career neared its end. He endured jokes from his teammates about his advanced age, 29, and his bald head, before the team released him in midseason due to his declining skills. East finished his baseball career with a reprise in Ohio as player-manager for the rest of the 1912 season with the Mansfield Brownies of the Ohio State League. The *Mansfield News* mentioned nothing about his football past. Again, he took over a team expected to win its league title and finished second.

East's character flaws, unfortunately, continued to surface beyond the sporting fields. Almost inevitably, his business endeavors quickly devolved into a criminal incident. On September 7, 1912, just after the Ohio State League baseball season, the *Mansfield News* reported that East purchased an interest in a laundromat in neighboring Ashland, Ohio. On February 11, 1913, Ohio's *Marion Star* added that he and a few business partners secured an eight-year lease on a building in Marion that they planned to renovate into a European hotel and eating-house called the Eastman Hotel. To fund the development, the group cut a deal with the Huebner Toledo Brewing Company in which the brewery advanced the partners $3,000

NASHVILLE BASEBALL TEAM, 1908. FROM COPYRIGHT PHOTO BY W. G. & A. J. THI

The 1908 Nashville Volunteers included Walter East (middle row, third from left), who was comfortable wearing the "black hat."

"Shoeless" Joe Jackson, 1914 Cleveland Naps

with the understanding that their operation was to sell the company's beer. However, the sum was insufficient to complete the work, and the partners demanded more money, which the brewing company denied. One of the partners then denied knowing anything about an offer from a Huebner Toledo rival to finish the buildout.

By early October, the hotel still had not opened, and East was arrested for fraudulently obtaining the funds from Huebner Toledo's president by misrepresenting that he was the owner of the Ashland laundromat. It turned out that the washateria was in East's wife's name, which meant that East had no collateral, making him execution proof. He was released on a $1,000 bond. Before the end of the month, the three-story building formerly occupied by the Eastman Hotel caught fire, initially believed to be caused by a plumber's torch. Within days, the plumber was arrested for arson as an alleged tool of "higher-ups" in an insurance scheme. The case's resolution is lost to history.

Before long, East reversed course from a risky career as an entrepreneur, settling for a more stable and private one as a lawyer, for which he had trained while playing football at WUP. He died at the age of 46, on August 28, 1930, under suspicious circumstances, according to his obituary in the *Beacon Journal*:

Barberton Leader Dies At Hospital

Walter East

When Walter East died mysteriously in 1930, he was representing a client in a political corruption case.

Attorney Walter East, 46, of Barberton [Ohio] died in a Philadelphia hospital yesterday after a brief illness occasioned by uremic poisoning. He had been away from his home here for nearly a month on a business trip friends revealed today and no word of his illness had reached here prior to his death.

Attorney East began the practice of law here shortly after his graduation from the University of Pittsburg [formerly WUP]. He was admitted to the bar in 1909.

He prospered steadily and eventually removed to Barberton where he has made his home ever since. He became active in the civic life of Barberton and has twice been a candidate for public office there. Most recently he campaign [*sic*] for the office of municipal court judge and before that sought to be elected as city solicitor.

In recent months, his name figured recently in court affairs because of his connection with the Chester W. Briggs case. East was counsel for Briggs, former Barberton street commissioner, accused of payroll padding.

When Briggs was indicted, the court authorized attorneys for both the state and the defense to take depositions and East spent six weeks abroad in quest of one of the men said to have been named on payroll reports. The trial of Briggs later resulted in a disagreement by the jury, but Briggs afterwards pleaded guilty to other indictments.

East was married in 1912. His wife who survives him lives in Ashland. His mother, 83, and two brothers, also living, make their home in Colterville [*sic*], Ill.

Effectively, the subtext of East's remembrance was that he was done in while trying to chase down and depose a political grifter associated with his client.

⇋ The Downward Spiral ⇌

For the next couple of years, Blondy Wallace made random appearances on collegiate practice fields for a week each season, helping old friends coach the line at Lehigh in 1908 and Franklin & Marshall in 1909. He then disappeared from the public eye for several years until resurfacing in 1913 as a full-time assistant coach at Wesleyan College in Connecticut. However, Wallace was fired, along with the head coach, after an unsuccessful season that otherwise might have gotten his coaching career back on track. The following year, in 1914, he landed as the line coach at his alma mater, Penn, where he was still held in great esteem for his playing accomplishments there. This role also lasted only one year, though, and Wallace's name was rarely seen in the press again until the days of Prohibition in the early 1920s when bootlegging became a more lucrative career path.

People assumed, like they did with East, that Wallace had a flawed character that guided him to its logical conclusion. Anyone who tracked stories of Wallace's activities in the press in later years would at some point have logically surmised that he had likely been in on the football gambling scam.

Whether Wallace's hand was forced by having limited options, or whether he had a dark side that inevitably drew him, or both, is an interesting question without a certain answer. But as he was well-connected in his home state of New Jersey, where dealing in alcohol in Atlantic City was especially prominent, it created the opportunity for him to leverage his former celebrity for profit. While operating other legitimate businesses, including a café, cabarets, and a brewery (at least as money laundering fronts), he quietly became known as "the King of the Bootleggers." No doubt, the adrenaline rush from being recognized again, as well as constantly being on the lam, fed right into Wallace's need for action and fame that had been stripped away.

A string of progressively serious charges was levied against Wallace throughout the 1920s and 1930s:

- 1922—Arrested for criminal conspiracy in connection with the theft of cases of whiskey valued at $230,000 from the Lexington, Kentucky, courthouse with assistance from a local judge

- 1924—Arrested for conspiracy to transport liquor across Kentucky state lines to Atlantic City, New Jersey
- 1930—Suspected in connection with the murder of a prohibition agent in Elizabeth, New Jersey

On June 21, 1932, the *Evening Courier* of Camden, New Jersey, wrote that Wallace's luck and health were running out:

Blondy Wallace Held In Automobile Case

EDGAR "BLONDY" WALLACE.

Blondy Wallace built a long rap sheet after his football career.

Edgar "Blondy" Wallace, former "right-hand man" of the slain racket king, Mickey Duffy, was admitted to Federal bail in Philadelphia yesterday on a charge of implication in a "beer conspiracy."

Wallace, a former "big shot" in New Jersey and Pennsylvania beer manufacturing interests and well known in Camden, where he has many "connections," was arrested by federal agents in the Chestnut Hill Hospital.

His condition was so critical, however, that he could not be removed from the institution and an armed guard was placed at his bedside until yesterday when U.S. Commissioner Patterson set bail at $5,000, which was furnished by a bonding company over the signature of the ill "beer lord."

Wallace, a former All-American football star at Penn and later a coach there, is said to be suffering from diabetes and a paralytic stroke.

Authoritative sources say "Blondy" has lost most of the fortune he is reputed to have made in the beer business.

At one time he was supposed to have had control of more road-houses than any other person in New Jersey. His places of business were in Atlantic City, where he enjoyed most of his power, Egg Harbor, Camden, and many other South Jersey places.

He was a resident of Camden for a number of years and was known to have been one of the founders of the Hudson Café, recently dismantled by Federal authorities.

Federal agents have been "searching" for Blondy since the killing of Agent John G. Finiello during a raid on the Rising Sun Brewery in Elizabeth, September 19, 1930.

Wallace was believed to be a part owner of the brewery.

He and 20 others have been indicted by a federal grand jury at Elizabeth as organizers of the "Oneida Manufacturing Company," a concern formed to make and distribute beer, it is said.

Federal agents say an agreement was made by which the brewery was to supply beer to the "Oneida" company and the indictment charges that 8700 barrels were made and delivered.

Wallace will be required to appear for a hearing on June 29.

Others named in the indictments include "Al" Silverberg, notorious gunman; Sammy Grossman, who was slain in Philadelphia several months ago after first being accused in the Duffy killing at Atlantic City, and Nick Delmore, another well known beer baron.

Wallace was able to leave the hospital to post $5,000 bail at his hearing with the U.S. Commissioner in Philadelphia on June 29. However, he appeared "white and shaken," according to Camden's *Courier-Post*. As with notorious gangster Al Capone, charging the elusive Wallace with tax evasion was the best the Feds could do. A raid by government agents at his brewery in Egg Harbor supplied records of his total unreported income of approximately $77,000 for 1929 and 1930, leading to his charges.

On June 13, 1933, Wallace pleaded not guilty to the charges before prominent judge John Boyd Avis in U.S. District Court in New Jersey. A trial date was set for June 26. During the trial in the same court, he changed his plea to guilty on July 7. On July 20, Wallace was sentenced to a year and a day in the federal penitentiary in Lewisburg, Pennsylvania. The *Reading Eagle* (PA) found irony in the situation, making a connection with the name of Wallace's alma mater in its headline on the same day: "Former Football Player Sent to 'Pen.'"

At his sentencing, Wallace claimed that he was ill and penniless with little hope of regaining health or financial position, according to New York's *Daily News*. While serving time, in February 1934, Wallace was indicted again for embezzlement related to an incident in which he allegedly passed a fraudulent check in April 1933.

Wallace died on March 5, 1937, at the age of 57, from liver disease, with which he had suffered for 10 years. He passed in an ambulance

Grid Hero's Ashes Strewn On Field Where He Starred

Unique Ritual for Blondy Wallace at Penn Campus Last Monday Revealed by Widow; Calm Climax to Adventurous Life

while being rushed to an Atlantic City hospital from a friend's home in nearby Egg Harbor, where he was also living. New Jersey's *Asbury Park Press* reported that Wallace was survived by his wife, Katie, of New York City, and a nephew, Albert Nubell, of Collingswood, New Jersey.

In a small ceremony conceived by his widow, Wallace's ashes were spread over Franklin Field at the University of Pennsylvania on October 11, 1937, where he likely experienced his greatest joy and where he was remembered most fondly. She shared her reflections of the event with Camden, New Jersey's *Courier-Post* later that week:

Blondy Wallace's Legacy

Blondy Wallace was my great-uncle. As such, he was my maternal grandmother's brother. I knew little about my mother's ancestors until I started doing genealogy research in the late '90s and began questioning her and her living relatives about them.

Much of the public information about "Uncle Blondy" (as he was known in our family) seemed to indicate that he was involved with known criminals in some scandalous and illegal activities, especially during Prohibition. His name is also associated with a football scandal in the early pre-NFL professional football organization that he helped form—the Canton Bulldogs. Newspaper articles published at the time mentioned him by name in connection with some notorious events. However, there is more to Uncle Blondy's story than what the public was told, and it reveals a new side of his character.

Helen Amelia Wallace, Blondy's sister, married a man named Albert K. DuBell and had two children. The two children were my mother, Helen "Franny" DuBell, and my maternal uncle, Albert "Walley" DuBell. At some point

early in the marriage, while my mother and uncle were still young children, her husband, Albert, left the family and did not return. It is not clear if there were any divorce settlements or if this was an abandonment situation. However, family members I talked to all agree that Albert could not be located after leaving his wife destitute with two young children to raise alone with no job or financial support. They also agree that when Blondy found out about his sister's predicament, he immediately stepped in to provide the support, financial and otherwise, that his sister's family needed. This assistance included a small house for them in Atlantic City and a job for his sister, as well as jobs for her two children when they grew older. I have a first draft of an income tax return for my mother showing her income from the Camden County Beverage Co., which Blondy owned.

As far as his reputation is concerned, I think it is reasonable to consider that Blondy was a "victim of circumstances." Much of his soiled reputation arises from his activities during Prohibition and his supposed involvement in

It was a very beautiful and touching ceremony. No man ever had a lovelier tribute from his friends than was paid to my husband and his classmates and teammates. They scattered his ashes along the football field which meant so much to him in his college days. The men conducted the ceremony which they designed themselves.

Because of Wallace's later misdeeds, it was natural to assume that he was guilty of conspiracy in the game-fixing scandal of 1906, at least from a distance. Yet, there had been no definitive proof. Even those close to the

an early football scandal. To begin with, Prohibition should have never happened. It was a failed idea brought about by a radical and illegal movement that disregarded the personal freedoms for which our country is supposed to stand. People, such as Blondy (who owned two breweries), had their businesses seized without proper legal procedure and had their livelihood taken away from them without notice and compensation. Additionally, Gregg Ficery presents new evidence in *Gridiron Legacy* that Blondy may not have been as involved with the 1906 football scandal as previously thought. In both cases, it seems likely that he was unwittingly involved in situations not of his making and just trying to survive them.

For me, Uncle Blondy was a guardian angel for my mother's family. Without his help, who knows what would have become of them? Both my mother and my uncle went on to live very meaningful, successful lives, and Blondy had a major role in making that possible. For him, family came first, and he did the right thing by them.

—Robert W. Ryerson, Pembroke, MA

Courtesy of Robert W. Ryerson

Blondy Wallace (left) continued to live out a risk-taking business career after his football days.

situation had similar opinions. Dr. Harry March, a Canton native and the 1906 team physician, took on the noble task of documenting his recollections of the pre-NFL era in his 1934 book *Pro Football: Its "Ups" and "Downs."* In a series of personal letters to Philadelphia Eagles cofounder Lud Wray during his research for the book, March wrote, "Time someone wrote of the early history of the pro game." In another, he indicated that he knew the truth of the scandal:

> Paul Steinberg was on the [Philadelphia] Athletics too as was Jack Hayden after they played Watertown and knew his ability…. He and Blondy Wallace were accused of framing games in the Canton-Massillon imbroglio and I was there and know it is true. It killed pro football in Ohio for 12 years alright. He was as good as any—crowded Stephenson [*sic*] off the quarterbacking job in Canton, but Stevies [*sic*] habits helped in his downfall too.

Dr. March's addition of Hayden to the mix is interesting since the 1906 Canton quarterback was not part of any related legal proceedings. However, the *Gleaner* did question Hayden's effort and intentions in Game 2 on the Monday following the game in its brief article titled "Did Hayden Quit?":

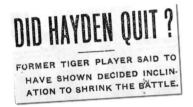

> Many who saw the game Saturday were surprised to see the hitherto daring Hayden, apparently deliberately shirk several scrimmages with Massillon players.
>
> Whether the former Tiger quarterback had cold feet, rheumatic joints, or avoided the contact with Tiger beef from pure politeness is not known.
>
> In Canton Sunday night it was rumored that Hayden had sold out. That Pittsburg capitalists had sent their money to Canton to bet on Massillon, and that it was a sure thing, etc. Kerckhoff [*sic*] and Lang are also accused of selling out, just as were Kauffman and Rayl in the Canton-Massillon game last season. While the sentiment in Massillon is not at all friendly to these men, there is scarcely any doubt here as to the honesty of the men and the stories probably emanated from the imaginations of some losing fans.

Wallace, though, addressed the media's questions, and others prepared by fans, outside the Courtland Hotel that Friday. The *Beacon Journal* reported his defiant comments:

> And as to Hayden throwing the game, or any evidence to that effect: $500 await any man who can give us information which could lead to

his conviction on that charge. Now, boys, those of you who have been making these accusations, come ahead with the proof, or shut up.

Dr. March told another unique account in his book of Wallace's machinations:

> The Canton players had been drawing very little money from Wallace, letting him keep their funds for fear a big poker game or an appetite for "lollypops" and other luxuries would lead them to extravagances. They had asked him to bet it on the first game with Massillon. When the next game resulted in a Massillon victory he told the fellows he had been unable to get it placed for the first.

Historians have criticized Dr. March's work as being based on faulty memory and little research, so it is difficult to assess its veracity. Indeed, some of the facts in his book are inaccurate, including his claim that Eddie Wood, who played all but one game of his career with Latrobe, caught the first forward pass ever thrown in a pro game. If Dr. March attended only Canton games while attending to its players, perhaps the pass he mentioned took place in the one game that Wood played for Canton, which was Game 2 against Massillon. Canton's *Evening Repository* reported, "On a triple forward pass from Hayden to Reynolds to Wood, Canton gained 20 yards." The author's aforementioned research proves that Massillon threw the first pro forward pass six weeks earlier.

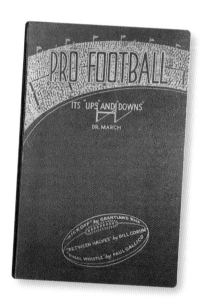

Without mentioning the player by name, Dr. March also relayed an account from the *Massillon Independent* about Wallace having employed a mole within the Bulldogs:

> After the second game, the *Massillon Independent* openly accused Wallace of trying to frame the games with the Massillon players and failing in this, had persuaded one Canton player to deliberately cross up his fellows and throw the game. When accused by his team-mates this player said he simply obeyed orders as he was accustomed to do. At any rate he left town hurriedly, on the first train, in his playing togs-his belongings following later-maybe.

Dr. Harry March's allegations against Blondy Wallace in his 1930s book left Wallace's legacy in disgrace for decades.

According to the *Independent*'s game account, it was Wood who had fumbled deep in Tigers territory just before halftime. Multiple publications also blamed Canton's ends (Wood's position) for the Bulldogs' loss. However, Wood was only forced into action after Clark Schrontz's injury early in the game. Other newspaper accounts indicated that Wood's so-called orders

Dr. Harry March's Legacy

He was my great-grandfather. The family knew him as "Hoddy," a twist on his name as his young grandson and namesake mispronounced it. His grave marker reads:

Harry A. March
1875–1940
Physician, Author, Soldier, Sportsman.

It is in that last role for which Dr. Harry A. March is best known.

Upon Harry's death in June 1940, newspapers across the nation reported the death of "the Father of Professional Football." He built the New York Football Giants, was an active member of the National Football League's executive committee for a decade, wrote the first history of professional football, started a rival league to the NFL in 1936, and doctored pro football players in the first decade of the twentieth century.

Harry was around football all his life. He played on Mount Union College's first varsity team in 1893 and 1894, then coached and refereed high school and college football in and around Canton in the first decade of the twentieth century. When the Canton Athletic Club began paying its football players in 1905, Harry was the team's physician. Providing on-field first aid to Canton's players and their opponents, Dr. March got to know most of the men involved in pro football in Ohio in the game's early years.

He moved to New York City in 1914, living there for 25 years, but remained interested in football. Among his Ohio friends was Joe F. Carr, president of the new National Football League. Carr knew that the NFL must have a successful team in New York City to make it a truly national league. He knew Harry was the guy to deliver that success.

After more than a year of seeking a financial backer, Harry found one in bookmaker Tim Mara. Buying the NFL franchise for $500 in May 1925, Mara asked Harry, "What do I do with it? I've never seen a football game." Harry said, "You leave that to me." Mara hired Harry as his football guru. Within four months, Harry introduced the New York Football Giants to the world. By 1929, Harry became team president. The Giants' success helped make the NFL a success.

The NFL held league meetings twice per year in those days, and Harry attended every one. His knowledge and integrity led him to be elected to the league's executive committee for nearly a decade. Serving alongside men such as George Halas and Curly Lambeau, Harry helped shape pro football in America.

In 1932, Tim Mara appointed his son, John Mara, Giants president to replace Harry. Harry then served on the NFL's executive committee until Redskins owner George P. Marshall ousted him in a power play in 1934. In that year, Harry published the first history of professional football, *Pro Football: Its "Ups" and "Downs,"* subtitled *A Light-Hearted History of the Post-Graduate Game*. The book was a success and became the go-to source for pro football history facts for decades.

Modern historians of the professional game have charged that Harry's book includes inaccuracies. One supposed inaccuracy is the identity of the first pro football player. Dr. John Brallier of Latrobe, Pennsylvania, corresponded with Harry as part of Harry's research. Brallier was quite open about being paid "ten dollars and cakes" to play football for Latrobe's YMCA team in 1895. Thus, in his book Harry reported that Dr. Brallier was the "first confessed professional football player." Thirty years later, a forgotten accounting ledger was discovered in the Pro Football Hall of Fame's archives, proving that William "Pudge" Heffelfinger of Yale had been paid $500 to play football three years earlier than had Brallier. In his 60 years playing, coaching, and writing about football, Pudge never admitted having been paid to play. In fact, in his memoir, *This Was Football*, Pudge explicitly denied having accepted money to play. So, when Harry wrote that Brallier was the first confessed pro, he was correct. No one had publicly admitted being paid to play football before Brallier had.

Harry also wrote about the Canton-Massillon betting scandal of 1906. He suggested he had firsthand knowledge that Canton coach Blondy Wallace was involved in an attempt to fix the outcomes of Canton's two games with Massillon for the 1906 "world championship." The Professional Football Researchers Association refutes that suggestion in its thorough article "Blondy Wallace and the Biggest Football Scandal Ever," which criticizes Harry's work as being based upon faulty memory. Yet, the PFRA quotes him to support other parts of the story.

Fortunately for history, Gregg Ficery puts to rest many questions regarding the Canton-Massillon scandal in his wonderful book *Gridiron Legacy: Pro Football's Missing Origin*

Courtesy of Alan March

Dr. March's early connection to pro football in Canton led to a lengthy career in the sport that has led some to call him "the Father of Professional Football."

Dr. March exchanged several letters with Philadelphia Eagles founder Lud Wray in 1934 to research his book.

PRO FOOTBALL
Its "Ups" and "Downs"

Being a Light Hearted History of the Post Graduate Game from its Inception to the Present;
Published in Accord with King Features Syndicate—Book Out October 1st, 1934.

By DR. HARRY A. MARCH

235 West 103rd Street

New York,..August.23rd....1934

Mr. Lud Wray
409 Flanders Building
Philadelphia, Pa.

Dear Lud:

As per your order at the League meeting, in New York, I am sending you express, collect, one hundred books – fifty bound and fifty leatherette – on "Pro Football Its 'Ups' and 'Downs'".

There seems to be a lot of interest over this book and I am very much pleased with it's reception even before the reviews or other publicity in the newspapers.

Let me have your opinion after you have read it thru. With best wishes for the coming season,

Very sincerely

Harry G. March

per, B. A. Kirwan

HAM:BAK

from Wallace were simply to crash the inside of the line on the defensive side to guard against the Tigers' tendency to run the ball through the middle of the line instead of around the end. Finally, in a postgame quote to the *Gleaner*, Wallace did not even seem to be familiar enough with Wood to call him by his correct first name:

> Our ends, with Schrontz and Gilchrist not able to play the game, certainly weakened us in those positions, although I do not wish to be misunderstood, as I consider Bobby Wood a fine player…. But I still maintain that with Schrontz, Gilchrist and Smith in the game, I can shut out the Massillon aggregation with my present collection of stars.

Story. Gregg's tenacious research reveals the truth behind the specific allegations of corruption against Wallace alleged by the *Massillon Gleaner.* However, Harry's reference to Canton quarterback Jack Hayden's involvement in the scheme, which was not part of the *Gleaner's* story, points to the possibility that he may have been aware of another deal. With gambling so prevalent at the time, it is impossible to know every player's intentions. Harry could have been onto something. He said that he knew this because "I was there."

Another criticism of Harry's book is that he conducted little to no research. Correspondence between Harry and Lud Wray, cofounder of the Philadelphia Eagles, discovered by Gregg, demonstrates the extent of Harry's research. The letters seek information from Wray and mention his outreach to others in the pro football community. Team rosters and photos that appear in the book further display Harry's diligence.

Any first history is likely to have omissions and errors, to be incomplete in some way. It is a foundation upon which others can build. Harry recognized this himself when he wrote these closing words in *Pro Football: Its "Ups" and "Downs."*

"It has been no small task securing old records, line-ups, and photographs.... In later years, may keener minds, younger hands, and more observing eyes go over what is here written, to clarify, amend and add to it, that the next history may be more searching, more accurate, and more entertaining!"

Whether Dr. Harry A. March is the Father of Professional Football is the topic for another book. However, it is clear he was engaged with professional football for decades from its earliest days as a fan, team doctor, organizer, scout, recruiter, promoter, executive, and historian. His work had a positive impact on the sport of professional football that helped it become the multibillion-dollar industry it is today.

—*Alan March, Cincinnati, OH*

Without anyone else stepping up to the task of adding to or challenging the facts in Dr. March's work, it served as gospel to historians for over 50 years until 1979, when the PFRA began changing the historical narrative. As worthy as Dr. March's effort was, though, it branded Wallace as corrupt for generations. In his 1949 volume of books titled *The Stark County Story,* author Edward Heald wrote:

Wallace became king of the beer bootleggers with headquarters in Atlantic City. For awhile [*sic*] he was under Federal indictment. Possessing a potent personality and great ability as an organizer, lack of character ruined what could have been a great career.

STARK COMMON PLEAS

Wallace, Jr. Plaintiff

vs.

Croxton, et al Defendant

Civil Action

Cause *Law*

Disposed of *May* Term, 190*8*

Recorded Vol. _____ Page _____

Taxed for _____ Record

Plaintiff's Attorney

Defendant's Attorney

W. H. Stannago & Co., Blank Book Manufacturers and
Legal Blank Publishers, Cincinnati, Ohio.
The Law Seamless Extension Envelope.—Patented, June 1st, 1894.

The author's discovery of the legal file from Blondy Wallace's libel case that never had its day in court sheds new light on the events surrounding the 1906 pro football gambling scandal and provides closure for those whose legacies hung in the balance.

⇋ Cold Case ⇌

Due to his prominence and the trial's publicity, Blondy Wallace's name became synonymous with the scandal throughout history. With the truth of the matter left to speculation, his legacy had been left suspended in doubt, along with those of the courageous pioneers who ventured to build pro football. However, Wallace's investment in the legal process did proceed for 18 months, and for this, his legal team performed extensive diligence to discover, document, and ultimately preserve the case's facts. Though it seemed likely that the related records would have been purged decades ago, the Ohio press left a trail of clues that could be followed to try to discover what might have been accomplished on Wallace's behalf. In various articles, newspapers mentioned the names of lawyers on both sides of the case and a judge's name. Still, the potential location of related files was unclear due to a possible change of venue.

At the author's request, a Massillon Museum intern searched records held by courthouses adjacent to Stark County where Wallace's case was likely to have been transferred. Nothing was found. Likewise, attempts to trace the file to law firms that had been successors in interest of those involved in the case and to the corporate successor to H.A. Croxton's automobile company also failed. Just when hope was nearly exhausted, and the author's efforts were about to conclude, one last search in the most logical place turned up a find. The entire case file had remained in the archives of the Stark County Courthouse, where the case began, apparently untouched for over a century. The file, containing more than 250 pages, includes Walter East's detailed deposition and statements from Wallace and the defendants, along with those of key witnesses, including one of the Canton players, Ed Murphy.

Filed on November 28, 1906, in the Court of Common Pleas in Stark County, Ohio, by his attorneys Homer V. Briggle and Oscar M. Abt, Wallace's petition summarized his $25,000 claim:

> At the time of the grievances hereinafter set forth, [Wallace] had a good and valuable reputation and credit as a manager and football coach which was very valuable to him in his said business and profession.
>
> Plaintiff says that the defendants on the 26th day of November, 1906, contriving, maliciously and falsely intending to injure the plaintiff in his good name, fame and credit in his chosen profession, and to bring him into business scandal, infamy, disgrace and disrepute among his business and professional associates, and to cause it to be suspected and believed that the plaintiff had been and was guilty of the offense

and misconduct hereinafter mentioned to have been charged against him by the defendants, and to vex, harass and oppress him, the defendants did, on said before mentioned date, falsely and maliciously compose and cause and procure to be published, and did in fact publish in said newspaper called the "Massillon Morning Gleaner," of and concerning the plaintiff, the following false, defamatory, malicious and libelous matters: to-wit:

The full article from the *Gleaner* titled "Their Honor Inviolate" was quoted, followed by Wallace's amended petition for an additional $6,400. Filed December 18, it restated the argument he made in the press that "as a direct result of the libelous publication," attendance at the Canton-Latrobe game was significantly diminished, and that he was unable to pay Latrobe its guarantee and his players their salaries.

The defense countered Wallace's demand for more money with its own effort to prove that Wallace was liable to provide security for court costs as a nonresident of Stark County in the event that he lost the lawsuit. To that end, Dr. Harry March provided the first affidavit in the file, taken by the defendants' attorney, Luther Day, on January 9, 1907. Dr. March's brief statement confirmed that he had known Wallace since his arrival in Canton in November 1905, that Wallace lived in the Courtland Hotel during his time in Canton, and that Wallace had not held employment in Canton other than as a football coach. Day also filed E.J. Stewart's affidavit, stating that Stewart first met Wallace in November 1905 and that, to Stewart's knowledge, Wallace returned home to Philadelphia between the end of the 1905 season and July 1906 without other employment in Canton. Another Wallace acquaintance, Charles Daugherty, provided an affidavit that Wallace had held no employment in Canton since the end of the 1906 season.

Wallace's legal team followed by having six Wallace acquaintances, including CAC president John Rommel, submit affidavits confirming their knowledge of Wallace's plans to establish a business in Canton. The court ruled in Wallace's favor, allowing the amendment for increased damages and denying the defense request for a bond for court costs, and the case proceeded. However, it is notable that the same issue of security for costs later resulted in the court's dismissal of the case in May 1908 when Wallace was residing in New York City, and he either refused or was unable to pay the court's costs at that time. It was a worthwhile attempt on the defense team's part to attack Wallace's weak financial position that could have ended the case early on if successful.

The court considered a few other procedural technicalities of little consequence put forth by both sides over the next few months before the

Walter East's deposition, in which attorneys asked him nearly 500 questions, highlighted Blondy Wallace's libel case file.

issues of substance came to the forefront. Wallace had to know he was going to be in for a long haul. To bolster his position on financial damages, Wallace's team filed an amended supplemental petition on March 16 listing over 500 names from a group of "not fewer than Four Thousand persons…who would, but for the publication of said false and malicious libel, have attended said game and would have purchased said tickets… [having been] wrongfully induced and persuaded by defendants to refrain from attending said game."

The essential issues of the matter began to be exposed when Walter East was deposed on April 22 in Columbus. Attorneys from both sides were present. East was first questioned by defense attorney Arthur J. Rowley of the firm Rogers, Rowley & Rockwell. Rowley did not ask East how he first met Wallace, thereby avoiding exploring how or why East signed with Canton before Massillon for the 1906 season. Instead, as excerpted in the following pages, he started his questioning by asking East to reveal details of how East had attempted to bring Wallace into the game-fixing plot:

DEPOSITION OF WALTER EAST, APRIL 22, 1907

Rowley: *What is your name?*

East: *Walter R. East.*

Rowley: *And how old are you?*

East: *Twenty-four.*

Rowley: *Where do you reside?*

East: *Akron, Ohio.*

…

Rowley: *When did you first see Mr. Wallace, if at all, after you had been signed as a member of the Massillon Foot Ball Team?*

East: *After I had signed?*

Rowley: *Yes, after you had signed as a member of the Massillon Foot Ball Team?*

East: *It was along about the first few days of November.*

Rowley: *And where did you see him?*

East: *In the Courtland Hotel, Canton, Ohio.*

Rowley: *You may state how you met him at that time.*

East: *I went to the hotel—the Courtland Hotel with the intention of meeting him and I found that he was in the dining room in the café there and I, through the bell boy—the elevator boy—*

Witness stopped by objection.

East: *And through the bell boy I got into communication with Mr. Wallace.*

Counsel for Plaintiff objects to any testimony as to what was done through the bell boy.

Rowley: *Where did you finally meet him?*

Question objected to by counsel for the Plaintiff as leading.

Rowley: *I will ask you, Mr. East, if you did meet Mr. Wallace on the occasion of this visit you have mentioned?*

East: *Yes sir.*

Rowley: *And where did you meet him?*

East: *In a room of the Courtland Hotel.*

Rowley: *Who else, if anyone, was present in the room at that time when you first met him?*

East: *There was no one present in the immediate room that we were in.*

Rowley: *At any time: how long were you with Mr. Wallace at that time would you say?*

East: *I was with him for about twenty minutes and later I was with him in another room for about an hour and a half—two hours.*

Rowley: *What room was it, if you know, where you first met Wallace?*

East: *It was in his own room.*

Rowley: *You may state now, in detail, Mr. East, the conversation which took place between you and Mr. Wallace at the time of this meeting.*

Question objected to by Plaintiff.

East: *Relative to matters pertaining to the Canton-Massillon foot ball games?*

East: *I suggested to Mr. Wallace that I might be able to arrange from a Massillon end to have these games go the way we wanted them to in order to make a good gambling proposition.*

Rowley: *What did he say to that?*

East: *He said that he was in favor of such a plan provided that satisfactory arrangements could be made from his standpoint. I further submitted that it was the suggestion or the idea of us, from a Massillon side, that we should win the first game and that he should put up a forfeit of three thousand dollars that he would see that the second game—no, not to win the first game as he was to win the first game and he was to put up a forfeit of three thousand dollars that he would throw the second game. Well, he refused to put up a forfeit of three thousand dollars unless we put up a similar forfeit, and I told him that the Massillon people wanted to win the first game and he pointed out or said that he wanted to win the first game for the reason there was a better betting proposition, as the odds were in favor of Canton, and I told him that I thought that was alright.*

Rowley: *Now you say that the odds were in favor of Canton. What do you mean?*

Question objected to by counsel for the Plaintiff.

East: I mean that the betting was about three to one, something like that, in favor of Canton—the long end.

Rowley: Canton was the long end?

East: No, Massillon was the long end.

…

Rowley: In favor—

East: Of Massillon.

Mr. [James] Rice [attorney for Wallace]: *We object to the former answer because it is not responsive to the question and because it is a supposition.*

Rowley: Go ahead Mr. East.

East: We talked further about it and discussed the possibilities and means of throwing the games and I told him how we intended to do it from a Massillon end and he told me that he had the men he could depend on from a Canton end.

Answer objected to by counsel for the Plaintiff.

East: He advised me—

Rowley: Did he state to you at that time who the men were that he could get from his end or the Canton end?

East: No sir.

…

Rowley: Was the name of a man named Jack Hayden mentioned during that conversation?

East: It was mentioned in this way; that he suggested—Mr. Wallace did—

Rowley: What did he say?

East: He said that they should cut loose from Weightman [sic]; that he didn't have any confidence in Weightman; that he knew him from before and he said to go ahead with two men whom I told him I could get at Massillon and he said if the people can get Hayden, he says, I believe that you can rely on him; I know of him and I believe him to be alright. That was before Hayden signed with Canton.

Answer objected to by counsel for the Plaintiff.

Rowley: Go ahead.

East: He also told me that if it came down to a show-down that he had to put up this three thousand dollars forfeit, that he could arrange, he believed, with a man in Philadelphia, whom he did not mention, to supply him the money and he practically told me he would put up no forfeit unless we did.

…

Rowley: During that conversation, Mr. East, what if anything was there said by Mr. Wallace with reference to what the result would be upon his prospects if Canton should win the first game?

East: He said that the result would be that it would make him popular down there and if he won the first game he could step into a saloon there and the fact that he had beat Massillon would make him popular and help to build him a good business.

Mr. Rice: *I object to the above answer.*

Rowley: You said that you stayed in this room where you first went, about twenty minutes, and later went into another room; where was the other room?

East: I do not remember the number of the other room or what floor it was on but the room in which I first saw Mr. Wallace was his own and he said that he had to get back to his wife and family—some other parties there; I do not recall their names. They were dining in the dining room and he said when he was done, why he would come to my room, which he would find by looking on the register where I put my name, and later he came up there.

Mr. Rice: *I object to the question and the answer.*

Rowley: After you had left this first room or Mr. Wallace's room where you stayed for a period of about twenty minutes, where did you go?

East: I went down to the desk and registered.

Rowley: And in what name did you register?

East: I registered in my own name, W.R. East. I believe it was.

…

Rowley: After you had registered and had gone to the room, what next took place?

Question objected to by counsel for the Plaintiff.

East: *Why, he came to the room about half an hour later; after I went into the room he came up.*

Rowley: *State what took place after he came up to the room which had been assigned to you.*

Question objected to by counsel for the Plaintiff.

East: *Why, we discussed the matter from his side. I do not recall all the conversation in the matter but when finally I left him—why he left—why, we understood or at least I understood from his conversation that he was willing, provided a satisfactory deal could be framed.*

Mr. Rice: *I object to all of the answer.*

Rowley: *State, Mr. East, what was said as near as you can remember, by Mr. Wallace?*

East: *He said that if I could fix this thing up from a Massillon end—get those fellows to throw that first game to Canton, that he would surely see to it that he would throw the second game to Massillon.*

Question and answer objected to by counsel for the Plaintiff.

East: *He said that he had the men to do it; he could depend upon it.*

…

Rowley: *Mr. East, in this conversation that you had with Mr. Wallace, was anything said along the line of who should be the officials of the game?*

East: *I said to him that I thought it might be arranged that we could get officials who would see that these games went which ever way we wanted them to. That plan I suggested, that we were to submit a list of officials to him and the right man we was to tip him up.*

Rowley: *What do you mean by that?*

East: *In order to tell him to pick the official; that he was the right man.*

Rowley: *What did he say to that?*

East: *He said it was a good idea, or words to that effect.*

…

Rowley: *At the time when Mr. Wallace left, what arrangements if any were made with reference to future conferences?*

Question objected to by counsel for the Plaintiff.

East: *Why, I told him when I left that I would keep him informed as to how the matter was progressing and how the details were arranged, and so forth, either by coming over to see him or to write.*

…

Rowley: *Did you see Mr. Wallace again after that night personally?*

East: *I saw him one evening in the bar room of the Courtland Hotel.*

Rowley: *You may state what conversation, if any, took place between you and Mr. Wallace in relation to the matters you had previously discussed with him and concerning matters which you have testified.*

Question objected to by counsel for the Plaintiff.

East: *I saw him there in the bar and when I had an opportunity to talk to him so that it would not be overheard …*

Rowley: *What did he say?*

East: *I told him that things were looking very good over in Massillon and that I did not think that we would have any trouble arranging matters; that at that time I did not know definitely what the details should be.*

Answer objected to by counsel for the Plaintiff.

Rowley: *What did he say, if anything, in reply?*

East: *He said he would let me know as soon as possible.*

Rowley: *How long were you with him probably at that time?*

East: *I was with him probably about five minutes, but that was all because there were other parties around close by.*

…

Rowley: *What was the occasion of your being in Canton at that time?*

East: *I went over there to see the polo game, I believe it was.*

Rowley: *Did anyone go with you?*

East: *Why, two of the Massillon players went with me.*

Rowley: *Who were they?*

East: *Moran and another man by the name of Riley.*

Rowley: *Were they in the room when you had the conversation with Mr. Wallace that you have just related?*

East: *I believe that they were in the bar room there at the time—some place in the bar room.*

...

Rowley: *Do you know how many days it was after you had had the first talk with Wallace at the Courtland Hotel that you had the talk with him in the bar room?*

East: *I do not remember definitely, but I think it was about a week.*

— — — — — — — — — — — — — — — — — — — —

Rowley's questioning and East's testimony under oath established that Wallace had been more involved in early discussions about the plot than either Wallace or East had previously led the media to believe. While the details of East's proposition to Wallace and Wallace's apparent initial willingness to cooperate were surprising, East was not on trial. As the defendants' attorney, Rowley's only job was to document the facts of East's dealings on the Massillon side in efforts to exonerate his clients:

Rowley: *What if anything did you do in pursuance of that talk with reference to taking up the matter with the people who were in with you on the Massillon side of the deal?*

East: *Right after I had this talk with Wallace I went over there and told them that Wallace would be willing—*

Mr. Rice: *Plaintiff objects to witness stating anything that he did with anybody or said to anybody in the absence of Wallace.*

East: *To throw the second game provided Massillon would throw the first game and that he would put up a forfeit to insure us that he would do this, and then with the Massillon people, we started to arrange to get the money to bet.*

Rowley: *Who did you have this conversation with?*

East: *Weightman*

Rowley: *And by Weightman you mean S.H. Weightman of the Massillon Foot Ball Team?*

East: *The coach of the Massillon Foot Ball Team.*

Rowley: *After you had this talk with Wallace … did you have any further talk in pursuance of carrying out the arrangement with any other Massillon parties except Mr. Weightman?*

East: *Yes sir.*

Rowley: *With whom?*

East: *With Mr. Shiring and Mr. Maxwell.*

Rowley: *Who were Mr. Shiring and Mr. Maxwell?*

East: *They were two players on the Massillon club.*

Rowley: *What did you say; what conversation did you have with them?*

East: *I told them that we ought to be able to arrange to have these games go the way we wanted them so we could bet and win some money.*

Rowley: *What if anything was said by you with reference to Mr. Wallace's connection to the matter?*

East: *I told them that I thought that Mr. Wallace would go into the deal.*

Rowley: *Did you tell them that you had a talk with Wallace?*

East: *Yes sir—I don't remember whether I told them or not—those two parties.*

Rowley: *Did you tell Mr. Weightman that you had a talk with Mr. Wallace?*

East: *I did not tell him all of the talk that I had with Wallace but I told him that Wallace would go in for the right kind of a deal.*

Rowley: *Where was this talk with Weightman?*

East: *In the training quarters of the Massillon Foot Ball Club.*

Rowley: *Did you at any time have a talk with Mr. Weightman at any other place?*

East: *Yes sir.*

Rowley: *And whereabouts?*

East: *In a room in the Seventh Avenue Hotel, Pittsburg.*

Rowley: *Who was present at that conversation?*

East: *Mr. J.T. Windsor of Akron, Ohio.*

…

Rowley: *What if anything did you do at about the time of your conference with Weightman and Windsor in Pittsburg with relation to attempting to get into communication with Mr. Wallace?*

East: *I wired him to State College, Pennsylvania, from Pittsburg.*

…

Rowley: *When was it with reference to this conversation that you and Windsor had with Weightman that you telegraphed Wallace?*

East: *When Weightman thought he could not do anything short of three thousand dollars and Windsor told him he would not give him anything* [other than a third of the money won], *the deal was apparently off and my motive for wiring Wallace to meet me in Pittsburg was to see him and see what he could do in the shape of getting some money or securing means to put this Weightman fellow right.*

Rowley: *Did you ever see Wightman and have any conversation with him after the Pittsburg meeting?*

East: *Yes sir.*

Rowley: *Where was that?*

East: *In Cleveland, Ohio, at the Forrest City House.*

Rowley: *Who was present at that conversation?*

East: *Mr. Wightman, Mr. Windsor and myself.*

Rowley: *Up to this time had you received any word from Mr. Wallace notifying you that he was out of the deal or would have no further part of it?*

…

East: *No sir; I have never talked to him after that time when I talked with him at the Courtland Hotel bar.*

Rowley: *Did you ever get any communication from him advising that he was not in the deal?*

East: *No sir.*

…

Rowley: *Did you at any time write any letters to Mr. Wallace?*

East: *I wrote him one letter from Massillon, I believe.*

…

Rowley: *And to whom was it addressed.*

East: *To Blondy Wallace, Canton.*

…

Rowley: *Was it ever returned to you?*

East: *No sir.*

…

Rowley: *You may state the contents of this letter.*

East: *The contents of the letter were to arrange a meeting with Mr. Wallace.*

Rowley's line of questioning then demonstrated that while Wallace was no longer responding to East, East had continued the risky path of pursuing the deal with Wightman, his coach, without revealing the status of his communications with Wallace.

Rowley: *Now you may state the conversation you and Windsor had with Wightman at the Forrest City House.*

East: *The conversation was that Wightman said he thought over the matter in this way … he would take five hundred now to be deposited with anyone in Cleveland that we might suggest and if he did not throw the game the money was to revert to* us, and if he did, he was to get the five hundred dollars and Windsor executed him a bond for thirty-five hundred, stipulating that he would pay the balance provided Wightman went through with the agreement.

Rowley: *After this talk had taken place at the Forrest City House, which you relate and you went to the office of Wallace Knight, the attorney, what was done, if anything, with reference to placing in writing the agreement?*

East: *Why, this Mr. Knight drew up the agreement the way we wanted it and the three of us signed it in triplicate.*

Rowley: *Do you remember what the talk was there at Knight's office?*

East: *The talk was concerning the matter of fixing these games.*

Rowley: *What was said, Mr. East?*

Question objected to by counsel for the Plaintiff.

Rowley: *After you had got up to Knight's office who did the talking and what was said?*

East: *Wightman and I did the talking and our talk was to—as to what he should put in this agreement.*

Rowley: *What did you say about it?*

East: *I told him to draw up an agreement which was to be assured by Windsor's bond, that would assure this fellow Wightman that he was to get his money and it would also insure us that if Wightman did not go through with the deal that we were to get the five hundred dollars.*

Rowley: *Were papers drawn up to that effect?*

East: *Yes.*

Rowley: *And they were signed and executed?*

East: *Yes sir.*

Rowley: *By whom?*

East: *By Windsor, Wightman and I.*

Rowley: *After the papers had been executed, where did you go?*

East: *I went to the Western Union office at the depot in Cleveland.*

Rowley: *I will ask you, Mr. East, where you deposited the money?*

East: *With Mr. Kuzel, the Cashier of the Dime Savings Bank in Cleveland.*

Rowley: *Who went with you?*

East: *Mr. Wightman and Mr. Knight.*

Rowley: *What was done, if anything, with reference to giving you a receipt for the money?*

East: *Mr. Kuzel gave us a receipt for the money.*

Rowley: *After you had deposited the money at the Dime Savings Bank what did you do next?*

Question objected to by counsel for the Plaintiff as incompetent.

East: *I went to the depot to get the train to Massillon and while there I ... wired Mr. Wallace at State College to meet me in Akron at the Empire Hotel.*
…

Rowley: *Did you get any response to the telegram that you sent Mr. Wallace upon that night?*

Question objected to by counsel for the Plaintiff.
…

East: *No sir.*

Rowley: *Up to that time had Mr. Wallace repudiated the agreement that he had entered into with you with reference to the throwing of the Canton-Massillon games at the Courtland Hotel meeting?*

Question objected to by counsel for the Plaintiff as incompetent or irrelevant.

East: *No sir, I never had any communication or correspondence with Mr. Wallace after the talk in the bar room of the Courtland Hotel.*

Rowley: *Did you at any time have any further communication with Mr. Wallace after the telegram which you sent from the Union Station in Cleveland?*

East: *Yes sir.*

Rowley: *In what form was that?*

East: *It was in the form of a message.*

Rowley: *What sort of message?*

East: *Western Union telegram.*

Rowley: *And how was that addressed?*

East: *Blondy Wallace, State College Pennsylvania.*

Rowley: *And when was it sent?*

East: *It was sent, I believe, two days after our—the one I had sent him from Cleveland.*

...

Rowley: *What were the contents of the same?*

East: *"Do not come as the deal is off."*

Rowley: *How was that signed, do you remember?*

East: *I do not recall; I think I signed my name or my initials.*

...

Rowley: *Refreshing your recollection, do you now remember that that telegram was signed "E"?*

Question objected to by counsel for the Plaintiff.

East: *I do not recall whether it was or not. I believe I signed one telegram that way; I do not know whether that was the one or not.*

Rowley: *After you had sent this telegram to Wallace*

from the Union Station at Cleveland, Ohio, where did you go?

East: *I went to Massillon, Ohio.*

...

Rowley: *When did you next have a conversation with Wightman, if you remember?*

East: *The following morning.*

Rowley: *And what was said in that conversation?*

East: *He called me into his office and told me I was a traitor and that he had been playing the detective on me and that his part of the deal had been merely to lead me on and to feel out his team and that he had succeeded at least in feeling me out and since he had found that I was treacherous and could not be depended upon, he would have to give me my release.*

...

Rowley: *When was it with relation to that time that you had this talk with Wightman where he released you, that you sent this telegram from Akron that you have testified to?*

East: *When I got back to Akron, why it was—of course from what Wightman had told me I decided to wire Mr. Wallace and tell him the deal was off, which I did.*

There it was. From the testimony of the primary conspirator, Wallace was innocent of formally colluding in the plot. Ironically, the defense attorney's attempt to defeat Wallace prompted East's statement to clear Wallace of wrongdoing. For reasons that were still unclear, Wallace had played along with East for a while but never followed through. The deal that East attempted to assemble had fallen apart when Wightman called him out and terminated his employment. However, the Massillon side had no direct proof of Wallace's involvement in the scheme. Any assumptions they made were based only on East's representations. It was up to Wallace's counsel, James Rice, in his cross-examination of East, to close the argument and reinforce the point that Wallace was the innocent victim of false accusations to prove Wallace's libel claim:

Rice: *You are a law student in the offices of Roger, Rowley & Rockwell, Akron, Ohio?*

East: *I was, yes sir.*

Rice: *Mr. Rowley of that firm is the same gentleman who has just examined you?*

East: *Yes sir.*

Rice: *As a law student, you are registered with their firm?*

East: *Yes sir.*

...

Rice: *And the first time you ever met [Wallace] to talk with him was when?*

East: *Last summer … the latter part of August.*

Rice: *Where did you meet him then?*

East: *Courtland Hotel, it was—*

Rice: *That was before you were hired to play on the Massillon Football team of 1906, was it not?*

East: *Yes sir.*

Rice: *When were you employed by Coach Wightman of the Massillon team?*

East: *He never employed me. It was the manager— Stewart.*

…

Rice: *When were you employed by Stewart?*

East: *In the latter part of September.*

— — — — — — — — — — — — — — — — — —

It is notable that neither attorney further explored the circumstances under which the *Gleaner* reported on October 7, 1906, that East had signed with Canton before joining Massillon. Also interesting from the transcript is that East was not even aware that the defendants (Croxton, Stewart, and the Gleaner Publishing Company) had hired his former employer to represent them.

Rice: *Who first talked to you about making this deposition?*

East: *Why, Mr. Rowley.*

Rice: *Do you know whether or not Mr. Rowley is retained by counsel for the defendants in this law suit or any of them?*

East: *I do not know that, no sir.*

Rice: *When did Mr. Rowley first talk to you in regard to making this deposition?*

East: *Why, the other day he told me that … he says that the attorneys for the Massillon Football Team want to take your deposition.*

…

Rice: *Now going to the conversation you have testified to in chief with Mr. Wallace at the Courtland Hotel at Canton, state the date of the first conversation you had with Mr. Wallace.*

East: *Regarding this deal?*

Rice: *Regarding anything?*

East: *The first time I talked with Mr. Wallace at the Courtland Hotel … was with reference to signing up some people for a foot ball team.*

Rice: *When was that?*

East: *Along in the summer, I think about the last or middle of August.*

— — — — — — — — — — — — — — — — — —

Again, East also circumvented the fact that he had initially signed with Wallace and Canton.

Rice: *When did you next talk to him?*

East: *I think the next time I had a talk with him was at the Courtland Hotel in the room that I have testified.*

…

Rice: *At that time you were employed by and training with the Massillon Foot Ball team, were you not?*

East: *Yes.*

Rice: *What was your occasion for coming to Canton on this day?*

East: *The occasion for coming over there was as agreed with the Massillon associates at Massillon to come over and see Mr. Wallace to see what he would do in regard to framing these games.*

Rice: *To whom do you refer when you speak of your Massillon associates?*

East: *Mr. Wightman in particular, of course, or the other members of the team who were to be in on the deal.*

Rice: *Who were they?*

East: *Mr. Shiring and Mr. Maxwell.*

Rice: *Mr. Stewart, one of the defendants, was your business manager?*

East: *Yes sir.*

...

Rice: *Was Mr. Croxton or Mr. Stewart consulted with in regard to your going to Canton to talk with Mr. Wallace?*

East: *I think not, no sir.*

Rice: *Not that you know of.*

East: *No sir.*

Rice: *Who got you to go over there?*

East: *I went over there at the suggestion of Mr. Wightman.*

Rice: *Did Shiring and Maxwell know that you were to go on that day?*

East: *They knew—I don't know whether they knew I was to go on that day or not but they knew that I was to go and see Wallace.*

Rice: *Who was the first man to propose seeing Wallace at all on this subject?*

East: *Mr. Wightman.*

Rice: *Were Shiring and Maxwell present at the time he first made the suggestion?*

East: *No sir, I never talked to Mr. Wightman about this matter in the presence of anyone.*

Rice: *You did, however, talk to Mr. Shiring and Mr. Maxwell when Mr. Wightman was not present.*

East: *I never talked with Mr. Shiring or Mr. Maxwell together.*

Rice: *Well, you talked to them separately when no one was present?*

East: *Yes sir.*

Rice: *And about this proposition of Wightman's to throw these games.*

East: *Yes sir.*

Rice: *As a matter of fact, Mr. East, the only proposition ever made to you involving the fixing of a deal to throw the Canton-Massillon games at all in the season of 1906 was made to you by S.H. Wightman, who was coach of the Massillon team, is that not true?*

East: *Do you mean that he was the only man that made this proposition to me?*

Rice: *Yes.*

East: *Well, I would say that he was the only one that suggested to me that we do this.*

Rice: *But you made no objection to joining him in that kind of a venture, did you?*

East: *My only objection was that I would not go and see the other players about it and he wanted me to do that. I at first refused to do it but later did do it.*

Rice: *This second time you made negotiation to talk to Wallace, on which you say you talked to Wallace in the Courtland Hotel bar, who sent you to Canton that time?*

East: *No one. I ... didn't come over that time with the intentions of seeing Wallace. There wasn't much developing to tell him since our previous conversation.*

Rice: *Those were the only two times that you ever talked to Mr. Wallace on the subject of fixing these games?*

East: *Yes sir.*

Rice: *At none of the talks had by you with Wightman, Shiring, Maxwell or Windsor was Mr. Wallace present, was he?*

East: *No sir.*

Rice: *You say that Wightman's plan was to have Wallace put up a forfeit?*

East: *Yes sir.*

Rice: *To guarantee that if Wightman got his team to throw one game Wallace would throw the other?*

East: *Yes sir.*

Rice: *You say you proposed to Wallace that he put up a three thousand dollar forfeit.*

East: *Yes.*

Rice: *Wallace never put it up did he?*

East: *No sir; he said he would not unless we put one up. He agreed to put one up if we would.*

Rice: *Did you put one up?*

East: *No sir.*

...

Rice: *You proposed to Mr. Wallace that an agreement be made and reduced to writing, did you not?*

East: *I don't remember. I believe that I did propose we make an agreement like that.*

Rice: *I will ask you whether or not Mr. Wallace did not say to you that he would sign nothing and sign no such agreement or words to that effect?*

East: *He said that he was against putting his name on a piece of paper and I thought another and more satisfactory arrangement could be made.*

Rice: *Did Mr. Wallace sign a paper or agreement of any kind between himself and anybody else for the framing up or throwing of these games as you have testified concerning, to your knowledge?*

East: *He never signed any with me or with anyone I know of.*

Rice: *At neither of these conversations to which you have testified was any party other than yourself and Mr. Wallace present?*

East: *No sir, that is to say that our second conversation of course, was in the bar room where there were people present but not in the sense that they knew what we were talking about.*

Rice: *You remember Mr. Vanderboom; do you know him?*

East: *Yes sir.*

Rice: *Do you know his first name?*

East: *No sir, I do not.*

Rice: *He was one of the players employed by the Massillon Football Team last season?*

East: *Yes sir.*

Rice: *Trained with you on that team?*

East: *Yes sir.*

Rice: *I will ask you whether or not you talked with him about this proposed frame up of those games?*

East: *Vanderboom?*

Rice: *Yes.*

East: *No sir, I don't remember of ever talking to him about it.*

Rice: *You do not?*

East: *No sir.*

Rice: *I will ask you whether you did not talk to him about Wallace in connection with this proposed frame up?*

Question objected to by counsel for the Defendants.

East: *Not to my recollection, no sir.*

Rice: *And didn't you say to him, "The white headed son of a bitch hasn't got brains enough to frame up a deal," or words to that effect?*

Question objected to by counsel for the Defendants.

East: *I do not remember of ever having said that but I would not be sure that I did not say it for this reason, that there was rumors flying here and there I guess before the teams ever got on the grounds, and if I said that it was with the intention of throwing any suspicion that there was a frame on, and if I gave my opinion about Wallace to that effect, it was for that reason.*

Rice: *There was no frame on was there?*

East: *I think up to the time I got the release that there was.*

Rice: *You think that there was?*

East: *Yes sir.*

Rice: *Mr. Wallace never told you that there was? (No reply.)*

Rice: *You say he never told you that there was.*

East: *No.*

Rice: *But he agreed and said that he was in and willing to put one on?*

East: *Yes sir.*

Rice: *But he never did put one on that you know of?*

East: *No sir, because there wasn't any on; none ever came off.*

Rice: *You desired that Wallace put up a forfeit, didn't you?*

East: *Yes sir.*

Rice: *That was one of the conditions that you imposed on the frame up, wasn't it?*

East: *I told him that was what we wanted so he wouldn't give the double cross; we wanted his money up.*

Rice: *And you would not go into the frame up until he had put his money up?*

East: *I told him that was Wightman's idea, but I told him I thought it could be arranged so neither of us would have to put up a forfeit. He said he would not put one up unless we did. I told him we would not and therefore I did not blame him for doing it.*

Rice: *After that you never talked to him about the arrangement again, did you?*

East: *No sir.*

...

Rice: *You were acting for Wightman then in this matter, is that your position?*

East: *I was acting for Wightman and myself.*

Rice had turned the tables. Stewart's false narrative in the *Gleaner* that East had infiltrated the Tigers' camp with Wallace's support had now been exposed as his conspiracy theory against Wallace. Rice then quizzed East to clarify how John Windsor of the Akron baseball team became involved:

Rice: *You have testified as to a conversation between yourself, Mr. J.T. Windsor, of Akron, and Mr. Wightman, at the Seventh Avenue Hotel in Pittsburg?*

East: *Yes sir.*

Rice: *Who first talked to Mr. Windsor on the subject of fixing these games?*

East: *I did.*

Rice: *Of your own account or at the instance of someone else?*

East: *On my own account and at the instance of Mr. Wightman.*

Rice: *Anybody else?*

East: *No sir.*

Rice: *Who suggested that you talk to Mr. Windsor, you or Mr. Wightman?*

East: *Why, Mr. Wightman didn't know Mr. Windsor and he suggested we try to get someone who had some money to bet, as the proposition was too big a one for our limited capital.*

Rice: *And did you have at that time a personal acquaintance with Mr. Windsor?*

East: *I have known Mr. Windsor for three years.*

Rice: *Have you had any business dealings with Mr. Windsor in that time?*

East: *None excepting that he is one of the directors and Vice President of the Akron Baseball Club.*

...

Rice: *He was Vice President and director of the club in 1906, was he not?*

East: *Yes.*

Rice: *And you were manager of that team in 1906?*

East: *Yes sir.*

Rice: *Was it because of your business relations and intimate acquaintance then with Mr. Windsor that you approached him on the subject?*

East: *That was the reason, that I know that he had the money and if he decided to go in why we would have that end taken care of.*

...

Rice: *Now you have testified, I believe that Mr. Windsor did not make terms with you and Mr. Wightman at this meeting in Pittsburg?*

East: *No sir, he did not.*

Rice: *And you have testified that when that meeting ended you thought any deal with Windsor by you and Wightman was at an end?*

East: *Yes sir, it looked that way.*

Rice: *Who next took up the matter with Mr. Windsor?*

East: *Mr. Wightman.*

Rice: *When?*

East: *He called him over the phone.*

Mr. Rowley: *I object unless the witness knows personally.*

East: *And Mr. Wightman called Mr. Windsor over the phone and would like to have another meeting.*

He gave him the address or place where he could find him in Cleveland, and if he would consider another meeting, to wire him there and when and where to meet him.

Mr. Rowley: *I object to the answer and ask that the same be stricken out.*

Rice: *From whom did you learn of this conversation between Wightman and Windsor by phone?*

East: *From Mr. Windsor.*

Rice: *Did Mr. Windsor and Mr. Wightman meet after that time?*

...

East: *Yes sir.*

Rice: *Where?*

East: *At the Forrest City House in Cleveland.*

Rice: *When?*

East: *It was about three days after our Pittsburg meeting.*

Rice: *Who was present at this meeting at the Forrest City House?*

East: *Mr. Windsor and Mr. Wightman and I.*

Rice: *Anybody else?*

East: *No sir.*

Rice: *Mr. Wallace was not there?*

East: *No sir.*

Rice: *Was not expected there?*

East: *No sir.*

— — — — — — — — — — — — — — — —

At this point, with Windsor having been ruled out as the primary conspirator, it became clear that East was pointing at Massillon coach Wightman as the deal's catalyst. The facts that East presented continued to indicate that Wightman had been leading the process all along.

Rice: *You say that you went from the Forrest City House to the office of lawyer Wallace Knight in the Society for Savings Bank at Cleveland?*

East: *Yes sir.*

Rice: *Whose attorney was Mr. Knight?*

East: *Why, Wightman told me that this fellow Knight had been doing some legal business for him and that he was a good friend of his and a fellow we could depend on and all that.*

Rice: *Wightman told you that?*

East: *Yes sir.*

Rice: *And you said there was an agreement drawn by Mr. Knight, which was signed by you, Wightman and Windsor?*

East: *Yes sir.*

Rice: *Was it signed by anybody else?*

East: *No sir.*

Rice: *Have you a copy of that agreement with you?*

East: *Not with me, no sir.*

Rice: *Have you a copy in your possession or control?*

East: *Yes sir.*

Rice: *Where is it?*

East: *In Akron, Ohio.*

Rice: *Can you furnish it to the Notary to have attached to your deposition or a copy of it?*

East: *I have a copy of it—yes, I can furnish it if needs be.*

Rice: *Will you do so?*

East: *Will I do so?*

Rice: *Yes.*

East: *I don't care to let that contract out of my possession.*

Rice: *Will you furnish a copy?*

East: *Yes.*

...

Rice: *Before leaving Cleveland, I will ask you whether Mr. Wightman did not direct you to go back to Massillon by way of the Cleveland-Pittsburg Railroad to Alliance and from Alliance by the Pittsburg, Fort Wayne & Chicago Railroad?*

East: *He advised me not to take the same train that he would.*

Rice's questioning then turned toward demonstrating that Wallace's nonresponsiveness to East's multiple attempts at contact confirmed Wallace's refusal to participate in any deal:

Rice: *You say before leaving Cleveland you telegraphed Mr. Wallace.*

East: *Yes sir.*

Rice: *Did Mr. Wallace ever make any reply to that telegram?*

East: *I never received an answer.*

Rice: *You testified in chief that you wrote Mr. Wallace a letter.*

East: *Yes sir.*

Rice: *From Massillon, Ohio?*

East: *Yes sir.*

Rice: *Did you keep a copy of that letter?*

East: *No sir.*

Rice: *Did you ever receive any letter or reply of any kind to your letter from Mr. Wallace?*

East: *No sir.*

Rice: *You say you telegraphed Mr. Wallace from Pittsburg?*

East: *Yes sir.*

...

Rice: *Did you get any reply to that?*

East: *No sir.*

Rice: *You say that in your telegram to Mr. Wallace in Cleveland you told him to come on—where?*

East: *I wired him to meet me in Akron at the Empire Hotel.*

Rice: *And you say you got no reply to that?*

East: *No.*

Rice: *And Mr. Wallace didn't meet you in Akron.*

East: *No sir.*

Finally, East testified about his dramatic confrontation with Wightman that ended the duplicity:

Rice: *When, before coming to make this deposition, did you last talk to Mr. Wightman?*

East: *The last talk I had with Mr. Wightman was when he released me. We had an argument about this contract that we entered into and he wanted me to send him our two copies down to him.*

Rice: *And you refused to do it?*

East: *Yes sir.*

Rice: *Let me ask you, Mr. East, whether or not* *you had thought of or considered a frame up or arrangement of any kind for the playing of the games between the Canton and Massillon teams dishonestly or otherwise than on the square, before Mr. Wightman suggested the subject to you?*

Question objected to by counsel for the Defendants as immaterial or irrelevant.

East: *No sir, I did not.*

As Wallace's attorney, Rice had masterfully guided East, under oath, through a behind-the-scenes recounting of the scandal to the point at which East pointed his finger at Coach Wightman as the engineer of the deal. If he could prove Wallace innocent of conspiracy, Wallace's libel claim would be justified.

Before East's testimony concluded, Rice brought forth a key afterthought regarding East's mindset after the scandal had broken in the media.

Rice: *This article [*"East Blames Wightman," *Akron Times*, December 6, 1906] *and all that* *you said therein were true at the time you prepared the same for publication, were they not?*

Question objected to by counsel for the Defendants as incompetent and irrelevant and also as to form.

East: *All I said therein was not true.*

Rice: *What part was not true?*

East: *Why part of that statement I said that Mr. Wallace, to the best of my knowledge, was not connected with the deal in any way that I knew of. I also believe I said in there that I believed he had been injured and made the victim of a false report made by the papers to the effect that he was connected with me in framing up the games.*

...

Rice: *And you made this statement without any solicitation or request on the part of Mr. Wallace or anybody on his behalf, didn't you?*

East: *Yes sir.*

Rice: *And so far as you know you made and had this statement published without the knowledge of Mr. Wallace?*

East: *Yes sir.*

Rice: *Or anybody acting on his behalf?*

East: *Yes sir.*

Rice: *Is that all you said in that statement that was not true?*

East: *That is all, yes.*

Endeavoring to salvage what he could from East's damaging testimony, Rowley followed up with a redirect examination on the defendants' behalf:

Rowley: *You may state, Mr. East, why in the statement under date of December sixth, you said that Mr. Wallace had no connection to the affair.*

East: *For the reason that during the entire matter I believed Mr. Wallace to be acting in good faith, with me; that he was going to do what he said and did not have in mind any idea to give me the double cross; that I thought by making that statement, it would take the—would go some ways in removing* the mud from his name. That was my reason, and that though I did not feel there was any reason for drawing him in, there was no question but that I was in the deal. They had my name signed to the agreement down there and contract and all, and as far as I know they did not have knowledge that Mr. Wallace was connected with the deal and I thought I would do him a good turn by saying he was not connected to the deal as far as I know.*

The final phase of East's revelatory deposition was Rowley's reference to a statement signed by East in Rowley's presence. East had been in St. Louis on February 23, 1907, for his father's funeral. The last paragraph of East's handwritten statement provided new information regarding a witness on the Canton team: "Ed Murphy knew of the plan through Blondy. He told me so the day of the first game." Thus, Rowley's next step was to schedule Murphy's deposition, which took place in front of attorneys for both parties in Allegheny County, Pennsylvania, on April 20, 1907:

Rowley: *Who got you to come to Canton for the football season of 1906?*

Murphy: *Blondy Wallace.*

Rowley: *How long have you known Blondy Wallace, Mr. Murphy?*

Murphy: *Personally, two years.*

Rowley: *And how long professionally?*

Murphy: *Four or five years, I should judge.*

...

Rowley: *Do you know Ed J. Stewart personally?*

Murphy: *Yes.*

Rowley: *Do you know H.A. Croxton of Massillon?*

Murphy: *No.*

…

Rowley: *Now Mr. Murphy, I will ask you if you had a conversation with Blondy Wallace with reference to Walter East and the Canton-Massillon football games last fall?*

Murphy: *No direct conversation with him, only with three or four in a crowd talking.*

Rowley: *Did you hear conversation between Blondy Wallace and others including yourself with reference to Walter East and the Canton-Massillon football games last fall?*

Murphy: *Yes.*

…

Rowley: *How many conversations did you hear between Blondy Wallace and others including yourself with reference to the Canton-Massillon football games and Walter East?*

Murphy: *Two or three.*

Rowley: *Where did the first conversation take place?*

Murphy: *At the Courtland Hotel, Canton, Ohio.*

Rowley: *And when to your best knowledge?*

Murphy: *Two or three days before we started for State College; before the first Canton-Massillon game.*

Rowley: *Was anyone else present beside Mr. Wallace and yourself?*

Murphy: *Yes.*

Rowley: *Do you remember who was present?*

Murphy: *No.*

…

Rowley: *Just tell what Blondy said.*

Murphy: *Why he was talking that they wanted him to frame up the games.*

…

Rowley: *What did he say as to who wanted him to frame up the games?*

Murphy: *Why he mentioned the Massillon people and Walter East.*

Rowley: *Now, Mr. Murphy, you say he mentioned Massillon people. Now what Massillon people did he mention?*

Murphy: *Why he just mentioned Massillon bunch, Massillon people, he didn't mention any names.*

Rowley: *And did he say anything else at that time?*

Murphy: *Why he said they wanted him to sign papers.*

Rowley: *Yes, go on. Anything else?*

Murphy: *And he said he would not sign.*

Rowley: *Did he say anything else at that time?*

Murphy: *Not that I know of.*

…

Rowley: *By way of refreshing your memory, Mr. Murphy, was there anything said as to who should win the Canton and Massillon games, that is said by Mr. Wallace?*

Murphy: *Yes.*

Rowley: *Now just tell us what that was.*

Murphy: *He said, "If we win the first, we will make them fight for the second."*

Rowley: *Now Ed, so that you will understand my question—Just tell us what Wallace said as to which team was to win the Canton-Massillon games.*

Murphy: *I answered that once, didn't I?*

Rowley: *Then tell us again what Wallace said as to which team was to win the Canton-Massillon games.*

Murphy: *Canton first and Massillon second.*

Rowley: *Did Wallace say that?*

Murphy: *Yes.*

…

Rowley: *Now, Mr. Murphy, did you hear another conversation by Mr. Wallace in your presence with reference to the Canton-Massillon football games or Walter East?*

Murphy: *Yes.*

Rowley: *Now where was that conversation?*

Murphy: *State College, Pa.*

Rowley: *About when?*

Murphy: *About a day or so after our first trip there.*

Rowley: *Was anybody else there?*

Murphy: *Yes.*

Rowley: *Do you know who was present besides you and Mr. Wallace?*

Murphy: *No.*

Rowley: *Just tell us, Mr. Murphy, what was said at that time?*

Murphy: *Why he just said that East was still writing.*

…

Rowley: *By way of refreshing your recollection, Mr. Murphy, what if anything was said by Mr. Wallace about receiving a telegram from Walter East?*

Murphy: *Why he got one telegram.*

Rowley: *Well, just say what he said.*

…

Murphy: *Just said he could not meet him, that is all, in Pittsburg.*

…

Rowley: *How did this come to your notice, Mr. Murphy?*

Murphy: *Lefty McElveen had it and showed it to me.*

Rowley: *Who is Lefty McElveen?*

Murphy: *He is assistant coach of the baseball and football teams at State College.*

Rowley: *Who if anyone else was there when you read this telegram?*

Murphy: *There was quite a few there but I can't remember who they were.*

Rowley: *To whom was the telegram addressed?*

Murphy: *Blondy Wallace.*

…

Rowley: *What did you observe as to how the telegram was signed?*

Murphy: *It was signed with an "E".*

Rowley: *What did you observe that the telegram said?*

Murphy: *I could not exactly word it right; but it was something like "Do not come to Akron, things are off."*

Once again, if Rowley's questioning had been intended to discredit Wallace's case in any way, it did not seem to succeed. Rice's cross-examination of Murphy continued to be masterful in demonstrating how dismissive and open with his team Wallace had been about East's futile attempt to draw Wallace into the scheme:

Rice: *Did you play on the Canton team against the Latrobe Athletic Club team at Canton on Thanksgiving Day?*

Murphy: *Yes.*

Rice: *Have you received from Mr. Wallace full payment of your salary for playing on the Canton football team in 1906?*

Murphy: *No.*

Rice: *How much of your salary is still owing to you from Mr. Wallace?*

Murphy: *About $120.00.*

Rice: *In your testimony in chief you have referred to talks had at the Courtland Hotel in Canton between Mr. Wallace and a number of men whom you said you cannot name. Will you state how many persons were present on the occasion of these talks you refer to?*

Murphy: *Four or five or more.*

Rice: *How many of these talks in which Wallace took part concerning the Canton-Massillon games did you hear?*

Murphy: *Two or three.*

Rice: *Is it not a fact that these talks occurred in the open lobby of the hotel and without any special attempt at secrecy among the men who took part in them?*

Murphy: *There was no secrecy about them at all, they were mostly players and there might have been outsiders.*

Rice: *In your testimony in chief you have testified as to the number of telegrams. Were any of those shown to you by Mr. Wallace?*

Murphy: *Most all of them but one or two.*

…

Rice: *Was there any attempt at secrecy on the part of Mr. Wallace or any of the other men who showed you telegrams, when they showed you telegrams and with regard to the telegrams.*

Murphy: *No secrecy at all.*

The final statements in the case file, provided by Croxton, Stewart, and the Gleaner Publishing Company, were identical answers to Wallace's petition. One of the Massillon parties' points of divergence with East's testimony was the group's position that East had approached Shiring and Maxwell before he had approached Wightman. Each of the defendants stated under oath that Shiring and Maxwell had reported East's attempted bribe to Wightman even before East approached Wightman directly.

In their joint statement, the essential fact that triggered the fateful reaction from the Massillon group to entrap East was that, in communicating with Wightman, East identified Wallace as a coconspirator:

> That after the said verbal agreement has been entered into between the plaintiff, Charles E. Wallace, and the said Walter R. East, the said East reported to the said S.H. Wightman that the plaintiff, Wallace, had become a party to the plan and conspiracy to play dishonestly and unfairly each of the two foot ball games, as aforesaid that the said Wightman informed one E.J. Stewart, manager of the Massillon Tiger Foot Ball Team and one H.A. Croxton of the attempts of said Walter R. East to corrupt the management and players of the Massillon Tiger Foot Ball Team, as above set forth, and that the plaintiff, Wallace had become party to a conspiracy; ...

As the Massillon parties believed that a conspiracy was at hand, they determined to implement a contractual plan that exonerated Wightman in the entire matter:

> ... that thereupon an agreement was drawn up and signed by the said Croxton, Stewart and Wightman which in substance provided that the Massillon Tiger Foot Ball Team would not be a party to any plan or conspiracy to play either of the two games of foot ball scheduled between the Canton and Massillon teams unfairly and dishonestly, but that they said S.H. Wightman, coach of the Massillon Foot Ball Team should pretend to be a party to such a plan and conspiracy for the purpose of obtaining evidence against the said East of his treachery to the Massillon Tiger Foot Ball Team and against his accomplices in said plan and conspiracy, and that said S.H. Wightman should pretend to accept the money offered by the said East and his accomplices to him and it was further agreed that after evidence of the treachery of the said East had been obtained, he, the said East, should immediately be discharged from the Massillon Tiger Foot Ball Team.

The agreement to which the Massillon parties referred does not appear in the case file. But in the final analysis, the leeway they extended to

Wightman to accomplish their goal of snaring East and Wallace was apparently boundless and excessive. While the group succeeded in documenting East's attempted fraud, the preponderance of the evidence indicates that East victimized Wallace in misrepresenting Wallace's collusion in the deal to Wightman.

It is a matter of conjecture what happened after East's deposition was taken and affidavits were submitted before the case was closed for Wallace's nonpayment of court costs. Had the case gone to trial, the event would have attracted significant media attention in Ohio and nationally. Given East's sworn testimony, it is possible that the defendants' attorneys recommended paying Wallace to settle the case quietly and outside the public eye, with a nondisclosure clause being part of the bargain. The court clerk's office packed the public record into a box, where it sat for more than 100 years before being recently rediscovered in the twenty-first century. Unfortunately for Wallace, the only details available to historians in contemporary press accounts and Dr. March's book 26 years later did not reveal his truth.

Wallace's mistake was playing along with East's pitch long enough to try to discern his intentions. East's deposition proved Wallace's earlier statement in the press to be true that he sensed a trap and never pursued the deal beyond an initial conversation with East. Thus, for the record, Wallace committed no crime other than, perhaps, guilt by association. For that, Wallace has paid an extremely steep price in terms of his infamous legacy in professional football. Instead of being remembered for his innovations in building the Canton Bulldogs, the team that would eventually form the nucleus of the National Football League, he was defamed by accusations of game-fixing that have finally been revealed to be false.

Blondy Wallace has now been redeemed by the revelation of the details of his legal case presented here that never had its day in court. So, too, have his fellow bold pro football pioneers. Their collective legacy has been restored and should be honored. The wheels of justice may turn incredibly slowly, but they do turn, in one way or another. History had it wrong. Or, as journalist Heywood Broun wrote in his 1924 book *Sitting on the World*, "Posterity is as likely to be wrong as anybody else."

⇝ The Good Guys ⇜

The character demonstrated by the Tigers' honorable field leaders who refused Walter East's attempt to bribe them continued to manifest as they grew into other leadership roles throughout their lives. Tiny Maxwell's later success in football as a collegiate referee, including officiating Army-Navy and Harvard-Yale games, and as a sportswriter in Chicago and Philadelphia was well documented, as was his untimely death. While driving with a colleague,

the colleague's wife, and another woman in Norristown, Pennsylvania, early on a Sunday morning, June 25, 1922, he attempted to pass a stalled car on a one-lane road. An oncoming six-ton truck carrying a group of 25 campers from a scout organization struck Maxwell's vehicle in a violent accident. He initially suffered several broken ribs and a broken thigh. When rescue personnel arrived, he instructed them to tend to the children first.

Maxwell was eventually treated and spent three days at a nearby hospital, where he was able to enjoy a visit from a close friend. He told his friend that he felt he would be well enough to leave the hospital with him the next day. Maxwell passed away in his sleep that night at the age of 37.

The *Philadelphia Inquirer* issued a sentimental tribute to Maxwell on July 1, 1922:

> Nature cast Bob in a big mold. He needed a giant body to carry the heart of him; he required a big frame to house the spirit of him. Courageous as a lion, simple as a child, he was a nobleman of nature and the noblest work of God-an honest man.

Bob Shiring and Doc McChesney paired up again to win amateur championships from 1907 through 1909 with the Pittsburg Lyceum.

:: LYCEUM'S BIG COACH ::

In 1937, the Maxwell Award for College Player of the Year was named in his honor. After the Heisman Trophy, many consider it college football's next highest annual accolade.

Bob Shiring and the Tigers' other pros continued to be revered as icons in Massillon. Several were offered jobs to stay and live in their strong and loyal community, and some did. But Shiring's family roots in Pittsburgh were too deep, and he chose to return there to grow his family and business career.

Through 1909, Shiring also served as player-coach for the strong Pittsburg Lyceum amateur team that played out of a facility in downtown Pittsburg on the grounds now occupied by PPG Paints Arena. With his old friend Doc McChesney also starring for the Lyceum, the team was unbeaten for nearly three years. In one of Shiring's last games, Pop Sweet reappeared opposite him for Latrobe. Sweet was again ejected from the game after punching Shiring on separate incidents. The Latrobe team was disqualified after its captain refused to allow Sweet to leave the game.

In 1910, Georgetown University's football captain, Vincent Dailey, sent Shiring a letter inquiring whether he would be interested in coaching the Hoyas. As Georgetown required a college degree for the job, he had a decision to make. Family lore has it that, when asked about his educational background, Shiring had jokingly told some people that he was a "Marquette" alumnus. This was technically true, as Marquette was the name of an amateur club in Pittsburgh for which he played early in his career. However, Shiring chose not to misrepresent his credentials for employment purposes and admitted to Georgetown that he did not qualify.

After his playing career, Shiring briefly stayed involved in sports as a baseball umpire, like teammate Charley Moran. Instead of making a living behind the plate as Moran did, Shiring continued to build his business career at the Westinghouse Air Brake Company. Eventually, he was able to leverage his reputation to serve his community as a business leader. In 1927, he founded the Shiring Agency, the financial services hub of his home in Wilmerding, Pennsylvania, providing tax, insurance, and real estate services. Upon his retirement in 1948, he turned the business over to his youngest daughter, Irene Keyser, the author's maternal grandmother. The agency continues to operate, though outside of the family's control.

Shiring was also elected tax collector in Wilmerding from 1930 to 1949, borough secretary for 18 years, and justice of the peace for 6 years, thereby adjudicating hundreds of cases to maintain community harmony. Few people were likely to take issue with him or challenge his authority. In this role, he

Bob Shiring as president of the Shiring Agency in Wilmerding, Pennsylvania, circa 1930

was affectionately known as "the Squire." There were nine Shiring children, and the family prospered and was well regarded in the community. Shiring's daughter Irene, with tongue in cheek, called the family "the Kennedys of Wilmerding."

Shiring passed away on July 23, 1957, at the age of 81, having left a legacy of excellence, integrity, and service. In 1983, he was inducted posthumously into the Pennsylvania Sports Hall of Fame, East Boros Chapter. According to his obituary in the *Pittsburgh Press*, Shiring was selected by legendary sportswriter Grantland Rice as the "all-time center." *Press* sportswriter Chester Smith wrote in a separate tribute titled "A Real Player Passes On" that Shiring "was one of the last of our early football greats to go." Smith also referred to a vignette that the author's grandmother often mentioned, in which Shiring said that he refused to wear shoulder pads "because they hindered me going through the line." Shiring was survived by 31 grandchildren and 18 great-grandchildren at the time of his death.

⪤ Honoring the Heroes ⪥

While pro football at its highest level did end for a period in Ohio after the 1906 season, it is essential to understand the root cause of its collapse, especially in light of the fallout on the legacy of pro football's pioneers. Whereas testimonies clearly show that the Chicago Black Sox scandal involved several of the team's players having accepted money to lose at least some of its World Series games in 1919, that was not the case in pro football's attempted gambling scheme 13 years earlier. Nor was there involvement of the mob on the football side. Although Massillon's management made a mess in dealing with the situation, the reputational damage to several individuals, the Canton and Massillon organizations, and the game itself was far worse than any alleged player fraud that never took place related to the games.

It must be considered that gambling, whether on sports, "the numbers," or other activities, was as prevalent in American society in 1906 as it was in 1919, with little regulation or enforcement in place to control it. Hall

The 1919 Chicago Black Sox scandal differed from the 1906 pro football scandal in that none of the football players agreed to participate in the fraud.

of Fame pitcher Cy Young of the Boston Americans also confirmed the attempted influence of gamblers on the first World Series between his team and the Pittsburg Pirates in 1903. Although the group's efforts to shield pro football's legacy from scandal were ineffective, and perhaps misguided or even harebrained, the integrity of the sport on the field was not tarnished. Indeed, it was protected and preserved by the captains of both teams: Massillon's Bob Shiring and Canton's Blondy Wallace.

In that sense, the Tigers and Bulldogs were heroes. Dark forces had attempted to penetrate the teams early in the season, but the players acted individually and collectively to defend their honor. While Stewart was blind to Wallace's actions, this was precisely the point he made in the *Gleaner*'s headline: "Their Honor Inviolate." As complicated as the episode became, the Massillon Tigers' honor was upheld by captain Bob Shiring and leader Tiny Maxwell, coach Sherburn Wightman, and manager E.J. Stewart, as well as the team's owners. The Tigers' management also proactively informed the Bulldogs' administration of the brewing crisis to keep them informed in case they needed to get involved to protect pro football's reputation.

That said, the Tigers' leadership had an attorney prepare the contract to entrap East, though it was technically illegal in that it required Wightman to act unlawfully. However, that move did weed East out and squash the plot. It is also remarkable, especially as East was a law student, that he put himself at risk by agreeing to sign such a document. Rumors of prearranged outcomes persisted, though. Unfortunately, the split result of the two games reinforced cynics' belief in the conspiracy theory.

⇌ Motivations ⇌

The people directly connected with Wallace during the 1906 season were those who came to his defense. East's testimony and several Bulldogs' affidavits supported his innocence, leaving Dr. March's vague account from the 1930s as the only one, aside from the *Gleaner*'s, to accuse him of collusion in the plot.

In assessing Wallace's character, his shrewdness was unquestionable, though he never appeared to clearly step out of bounds ethically during his football career. The media also reported many examples of his good nature and charitable acts. The *Independent* commended Wallace for being a good sport for joining the celebration in Massillon after the Bulldogs' loss in the 1906 rematch. Newspapers also cited his generosity in 1918 for helping Big Bill Edwards collect football uniforms for American soldiers in France during World War I, and again in 1919 for joining a Boy Scouts event in New York City.

Blondy Wallace (second from left) earned the respect of legendary player and referee Big Bill Edwards (right), as referenced in Edwards's book *Football Days*. They are pictured together here at a 1919 game at the Polo Grounds in New York City.

Perhaps more indicative, no example can be found that Wallace ever demonstrated a lack of sportsmanship or respect for the game he loved. To the contrary, Big Bill Edwards, who refereed the first game of the 1906 Canton-Massillon series, tells a story in his 1916 book, *Football Days*, about Wallace's advice to an opposing player during a game:

Lueder, a Cornell tackle, one of the best in his day, mentions a personal affair that occurred in the Penn game in 1900, between Blondy Wallace and himself.

Blondy's friends when they read this will think he had an off day in his general football courtesy. Lueder states:

"When I was trying to take advantage of my opponent, I was outwitted and told to play on the square. I took Wallace's advice and never played a nicer game of football in my life. Just this little reprimand, from an older player, taught me a lot of football."

Contrary to how history has generally portrayed the story, Wallace was not complicit in Walter East's scandal. Instead, it is clear that a series of unfortunate events conspired against him, sending his life into a downward spiral. The question of whether Wallace's fate resulted from nature, nurture, or a combination of both is impossible to discern and, ultimately, a matter of opinion.

In Wallace's case, history should also consider the role of his nemesis in his demise. E.J. Stewart clearly suffered from an obvious conflict of interest between his roles with the Tigers as their founder, initial quarterback, and eventual manager against his concurrent role as the supposedly impartial sports editor of the *Gleaner* reporting on the Tigers. Building the Tigers into a juggernaut for the glory of Massillon was his magnum opus. It was Stewart's idea alone to professionalize the team. He must have felt a strong personal attachment to the Tigers because he sold the idea to Massillon's leaders and, by his own account, recruited every player.

As a player, Stewart even led the Tigers to their 1903 and 1904 Ohio state championships. After he was injured, he brought in a top-notch quarterback, Jack Hayden from Penn, to replace him for the '05 season. Nonetheless, Stewart was the architect of four consecutive championships at pro football's highest level from 1903 through 1906. During those four years, the Tigers lost only two games, including their meaningless 1903 opener. Building the champion Tigers was visionary, ambitious, and a tremendous accomplishment on his part.

As a sportswriter, Stewart was also an adept marketer of his team. He effectively manufactured the rivalry between Massillon and Canton in his columns by creating dramatic prose about the games, unlike the tone in the Canton press. In his dual roles as team manager and journalist, one hand washed the other as he inflamed local passions while simultaneously selling more newspapers and more game tickets.

As one of the Tigers' representatives during negotiations with Canton's leadership regarding the scheduling and financial terms of the '06 championship series, Stewart dueled with Wallace beyond the field. Wallace became the face of Stewart's rival and his personal enemy as a threat to the empire that Stewart had created.

The fact that Wallace had many assets Stewart lacked likely fed Stewart's fire. Wallace had the playing skill and accomplishments that Stewart could not achieve, including All-America accolades and a national championship at a big-name national college program. He also had charisma, bravado, physical stature, and good looks, none of which fell to Stewart. Wallace's persona kept Stewart in his place in more ways than one.

Stewart clearly would have had the motivation to bring not just the Canton Bulldogs but also Blondy Wallace down, by hook or by crook. As his pen was undoubtedly mightier than his sword, Stewart's decision to publish his front-page story in the *Gleaner* on November 26, 1906, after Game 2 of the teams' series, takes on a new dimension in retrospect. The night after Game 2, when public outcry at the Courtland Hotel that the series must have been fixed became too loud to ignore, Stewart was boxed in. He had chosen to delay the story, hoping that the games would go on without further drama jeopardizing fan support. But after the split outcomes of the two games supported the public's conspiracy theory, the people demanded answers. Stewart's calculus fell on the side of narcissism.

Given that the Tigers had already cut East early in the season for his role in the plot, both teams seemingly could have survived if Stewart had left the story at that, with no suggestion that any other player, on either team, had been cooperating in East's proposed deal. Instead, by claiming the white hat for the Tigers and casting Wallace to the shadows by accusing him of complicity in the scheme, Stewart must have known that he was torching any possibility of a win-win outcome. Instead, he sought to ruin Wallace while also claiming the world title after Game 2, maintaining his legacy as the last man standing. If there had been any proof of his claim about Wallace's corruption, Stewart's move could have been considered damage control. Without specific evidence, which he did not have, Stewart should have realized that his firestorm risked making the championship secondary, jeopardizing pro football itself. It was Machiavellian.

While the 1906 world championship could have been the event that made pro football respectable in the public's eyes and taken its popularity to new heights, the taint of the scandal and its subsequent lawsuit set the game back for years. The debacle could have been avoided entirely had it not been complicated by the personal animosity between Stewart and Wallace.

Stewart's initial explanation in the *Gleaner*, that the Tigers lost Game 1 to the Bulldogs due to East's spy tactics, may have satisfied the public. Then, a dramatic, decisive, and lucrative Game 3 could possibly have been arranged to compete for bragging rights that the towns desired and help both teams meet their financial obligations. If only Stewart had not decided to throw Wallace to the wolves in the process. With the facts from Wallace's legal case now known, Stewart's move was irrational and almost inexplicable as anything other than a personal vendetta.

The only logical conclusion for Stewart's decision to publish speculative accusations against Wallace is that his agenda became more important to him than his team or his sport. From the day Wallace arrived in Canton in the middle of the '05 season, his profile had already given him more celebrity in Stark County than Stewart could ever attain. Wallace was embarrassed by not fulfilling his guarantee of a championship, losing to the Tigers in the final game of the '05 season. He did not have time to solve all of the team's problems in a few weeks. But he would not be outdone by Stewart, someone he likely considered his inferior. Wallace outwitted Stewart while making up the rules as he went along, luring some of the Tigers' best players away, financially or otherwise, heading into the '06 season. Stewart was likely deeply wounded by his players' breach of loyalty. Hayden's switch was understandable since he and Wallace were former Penn Quakers, but Kerkhoff had been one of Stewart's foundational stars in the '04 season. There were not yet rules of engagement off the football field, which suited Wallace's style perfectly. For Stewart, however, Wallace's actions showed neither honor nor respect.

Wallace went mano a mano with Stewart in protracted negotiations over arranging their series, and he made sure that he and his team at least did not come out on the short end of the deal. However, he did not take advantage of Stewart, either. If anything, Wallace felt that Stewart was unscrupulous in demanding a home game for his team on Thanksgiving Day, as well as gaming the rules by using the smaller Victor ball in Game 2. That Wallace added Stevenson, who had a violent reputation, to his roster for the '06 season must have just convinced Stewart further that things were going to get ugly on the field. Countering Wallace by signing Tiny Maxwell for the Tigers was a rich counterstrike.

When Canton handed Massillon its first defeat in four years in their first game, it could have pushed Stewart over the edge, and he may have simply snapped. Wallace was already more famous, younger, stronger, and better looking than Stewart. On the field, in a bar fight, or in competing for ladies' affections, Stewart would not have stood a chance against his nemesis. But those were his personal demons. Now that Wallace's Bulldogs had beaten his famous Tigers in Game 1, his lone claim to superiority over Wallace had been shattered.

True, the Tigers came back to take care of business in Massillon in Game 2 to retain their world championship from 1905, but the reality was that it was a split decision. As he had already refused to have the Tigers participate in a tie-breaking Game 3, Stewart's public reputation was tarnished. The stress to his ego and community standing was all probably more than he could manage. The Tigers-Bulldogs showdown was a fight between cats and dogs in more ways than one. It was a contest he was not willing to lose.

Stewart had one thing that Wallace did not have: his platform in the press. But he leveraged it to tear Wallace down. Beyond a border war in a sporting rivalry, beyond personal jealousy, it was pure, selfish hatred. But, consciously or subconsciously, by destroying Wallace, he destroyed pro football, at least for a time. If Stewart was not assured of winning, he made sure that nobody else could.

There was no going back after Stewart's allegations against Wallace were printed. Everything else took a backseat to the ensuing drama, including the game's future. The public lost trust and interest in the pro game, and it was unclear if it would recover. Nobody was interested in playing with Stewart anymore. So, he did the logical thing and found somewhere else to play. Without any aspersions cast upon him in the press throughout the ordeal, his notoriety was still able to land him coaching work elsewhere. So, he vacated his roles at the Massillon Athletic Club and the *Gleaner*, and he embarked on a full-time collegiate coaching career while Wallace was unfairly left a broken man.

Wallace and Stewart were flawed men, perhaps striving for greatness to fill psychological needs for themselves and their communities. In that regard, they were not unique in trying to scratch out a living in the chaos of early pro football, nor the first to try, as the Pittsburgh period showed. These men were exceptionally talented and hungry to succeed, and the Industrial Revolution brought with it new opportunities at every turn. Without Walter East's unseemly introduction of fraud and greed to a new business model already struggling to find its way, the pro game may have continued to muddle through toward profitability and stability. However, the weight of the scandal was more than the young sport could bear and led to its fall from grace. Pro football had been born, lost its innocence, and died. But its story was not over.

Football's rules continued to evolve to accommodate the forward pass. In 1912, end zones were added to fields to create defined space for receivers to catch passes beyond the goal line for touchdowns.

OVERTIME: 1907-1920

PROFESSIONAL FOOTBALL'S RESURRECTION

All these people came to watch old Jim run.
—Jim Thorpe, Canton Bulldogs, 1915

The arc of the rise and fall of Ohio's great pro football teams spanned less than four years, from 1903 to 1906. Yet, the fallout from the gambling scandal lasted even longer. From 1907 through 1911, pro football was still played in the United States, but only sparingly, and nothing like the magnitude of its former glory in Ohio.

Former Canton Bulldogs running back Paul "Twister" Steinberg returned to upstate New York in 1907, hoping to play professionally for the Watertown Athletic Association, which had participated in the 1903 indoor championship at Madison Square Garden. He also began a career as a sportswriter. On October 23, 1907, the *Buffalo Commercial* ran Steinberg's story titled "Syracuse 'Pros' Are Discouraged," describing the challenges of continuing the pro game at that time:

> The "good old days" of thriving professional football are gone, at least for the time
>
> being. The All-Collegiates, which promised to be the most brilliant team of players
>
> ever organized in this city, have practically thrown up the sponge.

"You can't arouse the public interest for some reason," said a prominent team member. "We played a game the other day with the All-Oswego team and barely 300 rooters turned out. It will not pay to continue with no better patronage than that, when we used to draw them by the thousands, and the men are discouraged and not getting out for practice.... After all, it's college spirit that keeps the game alive and makes it a permanent fixture, and to rely upon general public support of professional football furnishes a fickle basis."

Professional football is in a similar slump all over the country. The days of the Philadelphia Athletics, Sayre, and Franklin are no more. Even Massillon and Canton, those Ohio cities which long maintained fierce rivalry, engaging the best veteran players to be found in the country, are no longer in the game. If they were, I, Paul Steinberg of Watertown would be in his old place as a back with the Canton team.

This latter defection, however, is not due to any ebb of public interest in those cities. "Blondy" Wallace, the old Penn lineman and manager of the Canton team, and Millionaire Croxton who financed the Massillon team, are engaged in legal differences which render continued meetings between the teams out of the question.

⇐ The *Gleaner* Goes Bust ⇒

As a symbolic exclamation point at the end of this controversial era, the Gleaner Publishing Company ceased operations on June 30, 1908. A controlling interest in the publication was previously purchased by H.E. Moffett, former editor of Iowa's *Grundy Republican*, in October 1907. Insufficient community advertising support and increasing labor costs were the initial reasons provided for the end of the paper's six-year run. However, Moffett soon announced the real reason. The former management had concealed the company's heavy debt so well that he did not discover the extent of its liabilities until months after his purchase.

⇐ The Parratt Period ⇒

With the game's embers still smoldering in Ohio, it was left to Akron to carry the ball forward. When Massillon stopped fielding competitive semi-pro teams after 1907, the Akron Indians won the Ohio state championship in 1908 and 1909. They were then dethroned in 1910 by the Shelby Blues, a team organized and promoted by former Massillon quarterback Peggy Parratt.

Slowly and cautiously, Ohio teams grew the professional model again. A new Canton team nicknamed the Pros reentered the picture in 1911 and became fast rivals of Parratt's Blues. Before the season, Parratt merged his team with the Shelby Tigers, organized by another former Massillon

The Lost Period

Peggy Parratt (far right) began his coaching career with the 1908 Shelby Blues (above). The 1909 Massillon Indians (below) were one of several amateur Massillon teams before the pro Tigers returned in 1915.

MASSILLON INDIANS.

quarterback, Homer Davidson, to make the Blues even more formidable competitors. As he had been in Massillon, Parratt was wise enough to defer to Davidson as the team's quarterback. While increasing the talent on his team, Parratt also managed player compensation effectively, as well as the Blues' profitability, by employing only the best players

Heading into the highly anticipated Canton-Shelby matchup in Canton on November 26, 1911, venom flowed between the teams in the local media in ways reminiscent of the previous Canton-Massillon rivalry. The contest took a turn for the worse when a Canton player punched the Blues' Dan "Bullet" Riley, a Canton resident and former Massillon Tiger. Further fisticuffs followed in the scoreless first half. Late in the third quarter, Shelby was driving toward the goal line when Davidson fumbled. Canton's Harry Turner recovered the ball, but an offsides penalty negated the turnover, and the ball was placed on Canton's 2-yard line. As captain, Turner led his team off the field in protest, and the officials awarded the victory to Shelby. Despite dramatically announcing his retirement from football after the game, Turner returned to play for Canton the following season. The Blues went on to defeat Akron in consecutive games on Thanksgiving and the following Sunday for their second straight state championship.

Parratt left Shelby to take over the Akron Indians for 1912 and leveraged his prominence to rename them Parratt's Indians. By then, time had healed old wounds in Canton, and its fans were again ready to join the professional fray. Jack Cusack, who had witnessed the fracas at Canton's Courtland Hotel after Game 2 in 1906, had matured to become a 21-year-old young business professional in 1912. He was working an office job at the East Ohio Gas Company when he started moonlighting as the Canton Pros' secretary-treasurer on a voluntary basis.

Cusack fondly remembered the excitement of the games and the brawl that broke out at the hotel over whether the 1906 Canton-Massillon games had been fixed. He longed to be part of the action. "At that time I was already an avid football fan, but after that brawl at the Courtland—which was to set back professional organizations for several years—I was convinced that this sport was for me. It offered such exciting possibilities, both on and off the playing fields," wrote Cusack in his autobiographical memoir, *Pioneer in Pro Football*.

Canton manager H.H. Halter was at loggerheads negotiating with Parratt for a game in 1912. "Parratt was a hard man to do business with, when it came to dividing gate receipts. He liked to divide the money half horse and half rabbit, his preference being the horse end," Cusack said in his book. Parratt agreed to work things out with Cusack instead, which they did in a matter of a few hours. This irritated Halter, who called a team meeting to take a vote on firing Cusack. Meanwhile, Cusack outwitted Halter, revealing that he had secured a five-year contract on Canton's League Park, with an option for five more years, providing him with leverage to force Halter's resignation and succeed him as manager.

After losing out in 1912 to the Elyria Athletics, which included several of Parratt's former Shelby players, Parratt's Indians won the Ohio Independent Championship again in 1913. They expected nothing less for 1914 after Parratt recruited Knute Rockne and several of Rockne's Notre Dame teammates to join the Indians. But Canton's Harry Turner had other ideas. After failing to avenge his 1911 loss to Parratt in the two years after his "retirement," Turner finally had his day on November 15, 1914. Canton defeated Parratt's Indians 6–0, but Turner was fatally injured during the triumph, breaking his spine while tackling Akron fullback Joe Collins. According to Cusack, who was at his bedside when he died, Turner's last words were, "I know I must go, but I'm satisfied, for we beat Peggy Parratt." These words left an indelible impression on him. Turner's death was the first for professional football in Ohio. The grieving Canton squad lost the championship in its rematch with Akron two weeks later, 21–0.

Parratt's run of success ended in 1915. The Massillon Tigers restarted by raiding much of his roster. Canton's Cusack also nabbed a few Akron

LINE UP
PARRATT'S INDIANS

Criss, Horn and Jenkins	L. E.
Costigan and Muff Portman	L. T.
Elzholz and Hartman	L. G.
Olson	C.
Hess	R. G.
Pendleton	R. T.
Burrell and Parratt	R. E.
Woozley and Maranville	Q.
Kagy	L. H.
Wertz	R. H.
Collins and Nesser	F. B.

LINE UP
ELYRIA

Wells	L. E.
Deutsch	L. T
Kahler	L. G.
Esch	C.
Cass	R. G.
Dumont	R. T.
Hanley	R. E.
Davidson and Blythe	Q.
Schriener	L. H
Goss and McKenney	R. H.
Carolin	F. B.

Parratt's Indians lost to Elyria, 16–4, in this program's game on October 5, 1913, but defeated them later in the season and won the Ohio state title. Elyria's quarterback was 1906 Massillon QB Homer Davidson.

players, leaving Parratt's Indians decimated. Just before the season-ending two-game series between Canton and Massillon, Cusack made a seminal move in pro football history by signing the great Jim Thorpe to play for Canton. In his book, Cusack explained what led to Thorpe's recruitment:

> The year 1915 brought the beginning of the big-time era in professional football, and happily it brought Massillon back into play.... Their decision to field a team brought back the old rivalry that all of us needed so badly and furnished the drawing power that meant good gates. With the return of Massillon, another pleasant thing occurred—the sports writers, having all but forgotten the 1906 scandal, began referring to the old rivals again as the Canton Bulldogs and the Massillon Tigers. We were back in business once more at the old stand.
>
> I knew that in order to compete properly with Massillon that we had to recruit the best available talent, so I contacted every All-American I could locate … but found the response somewhat reluctant. The colleges and most sports writers around the country were opposed to professional football, as were the coaches and graduate players, and many of those I contacted refused to play.
>
> Then, just in time for Canton's first game with the Massillon Tigers, I hit the jackpot by signing the famous Jim Thorpe, the Sac and Fox Indian from Oklahoma who was rated then (and still is today) as the greatest footballer and all-around athlete the world has ever seen!

⇐ Jim Thorpe: The Savior of Professional Football ⇒

Jim Thorpe had become commonly known as the world's greatest athlete after dominating the 1912 Olympics in Stockholm by winning gold medals in the decathlon and classic pentathlon. After the Olympics, he returned to the Carlisle Indian Industrial School. In college football, the 1912 Indians led the nation in scoring with 454 points in 14 games, with Thorpe accounting for a record 198 of those. The team posted a 12–1–1 record, including its only loss to Penn and a win over future president Dwight D. Eisenhower's Army team. Eisenhower later reminisced, "On the football field there was no one like him in the world. Against us he dominated all of the action.... I personally feel no other athlete possessed his all-around abilities in games and sports."

In 1913, the AAU stripped Thorpe of his Olympic medals for violating his amateur status. He admitted that he had accepted $60 per month to play minor league baseball in the Eastern Carolina League during the summers

of 1910 and 1911 between school years at Carlisle. In a letter to the AAU president, Thorpe wrote, "I did not play for money. I was not very wise in the ways of the world and did not realize this was wrong. I hope I will be partly excused by the fact that I was simply an Indian School Boy and did not know what I was doing wrong because I was doing what many other college men had done, except they did not use their own names." The AAU was unyielding, though fans continued to support Thorpe, inspiring him to continue his athletic career.

Having lost his amateur status, Thorpe embarked on a professional baseball career with the New York Giants in 1913. Legendary Giants manager John McGraw took a chance on signing the highly marketable Thorpe, despite his lack of baseball experience. He signed Thorpe for three years at $6,000 per year when most players made less than $2,000. Thorpe played sparingly for the talented Giants, a team that included another player with a pro football connection. Christy Mathewson, who had played for the 1902 Pittsburg Stars, was on the mound. The Giants won the pennant to reach the World Series but lost to the Philadelphia Athletics. The A's were still managed by Connie Mack, who had held the same role with the 1902 Philadelphia pro football organization of the same name on which Blondy Wallace had played.

After the Series, the Giants capitalized on Thorpe's celebrity by partnering with another baseball entrepreneur, White Sox owner Charles Comiskey, on a 46-game national and world tour that lasted from October 1913 until spring training in 1914. With no major league teams west of St. Louis at the time, fans poured into ballparks in western states, including Kansas, Iowa, Oklahoma, Texas, Arizona, and California, to enjoy the first of the exhibitions. The teams then journeyed westward across the globe to introduce baseball and Thorpe to Japan, China, the Philippines, Australia, Sri Lanka, Egypt, Italy, France, and England. Their stop in Cairo was highlighted by Giants catcher Ivy Wingo throwing a ball over the Great Sphinx to White Sox outfielder Steve Evans. Thorpe also put on a discus and shotput throwing exhibition in Nice. The tour concluded in London, where over 20,000 people, including King George V, enjoyed the contest. The teams returned home on February 28, 1914, on the British luxury ocean liner *Lusitania*, which would be sunk by a German submarine the following year in World War I.

Late in the 1915 season, Cusack and his Canton Bulldogs were contending with the new iteration of the Massillon Tigers for the state championship. Having recognized what Thorpe had done for baseball, Cusack correctly surmised that bringing this global icon to Canton to play pro football would be transformational. Thorpe's return to football could simultaneously carry Canton to a title and generate exponentially greater profits for the Bulldogs and their opponents. In the bigger picture, it would also provide legitimacy to help the public move past its resistance and embrace pro football. In his memoir, Cusack later recounted how he recruited Thorpe and the difference that Thorpe made:

> In 1915, when I conceived the idea of hiring this already living legend of sportdom, Jim had already lost his amateur standing … and at the moment was doing backfield coaching at the University of Indiana. I sent Bill Gardner, his old Carlisle teammate, over to Indiana to see him, and shortly thereafter I had Thorpe under contract to play for the Canton Bulldogs for $250 a game. The signing also marked the start of a warm friendship between us that lasted until Jim died of a heart attack, in 1953.

Jim Thorpe was a feature attraction on baseball's 1913–14 World Tour with the Giants and White Sox.

HISTORY of WORLD'S TOUR
CHICAGO WHITE SOX AND NEW YORK GIANTS
BY
TED SULLIVAN

Price 25 Cents

Some of my business "advisers" frankly predicted that I was leading the Bulldogs into bankruptcy by paying Jim the enormous sum of $250 a game [when the best players typically made about $100], but the deal paid off even beyond my greatest expectations. Jim was an attraction as well as a player, and whereas our attendance averaged around 1,200 before we took him on, we filled the Canton and Massillon parks for the next two games—6,000 for the first and 8,000 for the second. All the fans wanted to see the big Indian in action.

As in 1906, the two-game series with Massillon at the end of the season would determine the state title. The first game was played on November 14 at Massillon's Driving Park. Canton coach Harry Hazlett did not let Thorpe start the game, either due to lack of practice time with the team or resentment over his salary, and gave him only limited playing time thereafter. Thorpe's modest rushing output was outdone by Massillon's passing attack in a 16–0 Tigers win. In its game summary, the *Canton Repository* stated, "After a lapse of nine years barren of the intense rivalry that has always been the outstanding feature of the athletic relations between the two cities, the same old Massillon Jinx still holds its power over Canton." Cusack summarily relieved Hazlett of his duties and installed Thorpe as his replacement.

Two weeks later, in Game 2 in Canton, a Thorpe dropkick and a placekick had the Bulldogs leading 6–0. (The value of field goals dropped from four points to three in 1909.) With three minutes remaining in the game, Massillon's Maurice "Windy" Briggs broke free after a pass reception and sprinted across the goal line for what appeared to be the tying score. (The value of a touchdown increased from five points to six in 1912.) However, Briggs ran into a wall of "standing room only" spectators behind the goal line. Due to the overflow crowd, both teams had agreed to ground rules before the game such that any player crossing the goal line into the crowd must have possession of the ball when he emerged. With Briggs buried on the ground within the masses, the ball shot loose and was recovered by Canton, preserving the Bulldogs' victory. Briggs protested to the referee that a uniformed Canton policeman had kicked the ball from his hands. Fearing for his safety from thousands of fans who had broken down the fences and stormed the field, the referee ended the game and announced that he would issue his sealed decision that night at 30 minutes past midnight. His verdict sided with the Bulldogs after he learned that the city of Canton did not employ uniformed officers. However, Cusack related in his book that he solved the "Mystery of the Phantom Policeman" nearly 10 years later. While on a streetcar in Canton, he ran into an old friend, also the conductor, who admitted to doing the dirty deed to Briggs because he had wagered $30 on the Bulldogs. The conductor's uniform matched

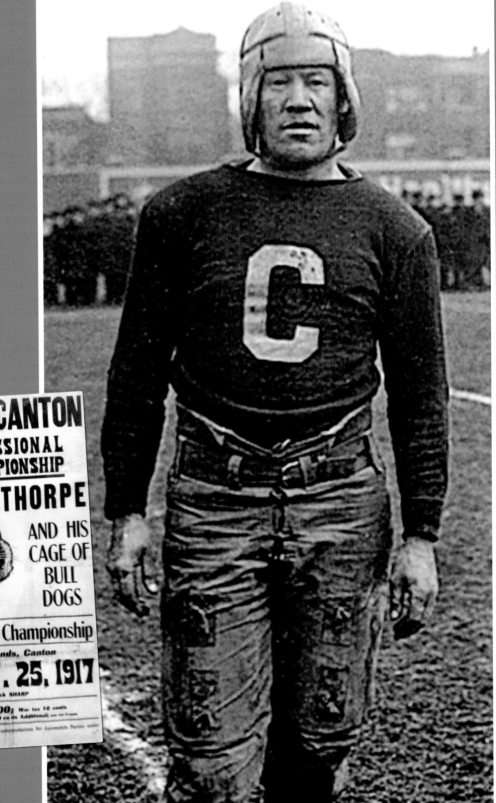

**Jim Thorpe,
Canton Bulldogs,
circa 1915–1920**

MASSILLON VS. CANTON
WORLD'S PROFESSIONAL FOOTBALL CHAMPIONSHIP
BRICKLEY ✠ THORPE

AND HIS DEN OF TIGERS	AND HIS CAGE OF BULL DOGS

First Game for World's Championship
Myer's Lake Park Grounds, Canton
SUNDAY, NOV. 25, 1917
GAME CALLED AT 2:00 O'clock SHARP

General Admission $1.00; War tax 10 cents
North End Grand Stand and Bleacher Seats 50 cents Additionally war tax 5 cents.

*Special Cars on all lines of Northern Ohio Traction Co.   Ample accommodations for Automobile Parties, under police protection.
Buy tickets early.   Avoid the crowd at the game.*

Briggs's description of the policeman's uniform down to the shiny buttons. Several teams had similar records that year, and no consensus existed on a champion. However, the explosion in attendance for the two Canton-Massillon games confirmed that pro football was on the rise again.

Thorpe led Canton to consecutive Ohio state championships in 1916 and 1917, with the only loss in those years to Massillon at the end of a 9–1 campaign in 1917. World War I and the Spanish flu pandemic washed out the 1918 season, and Cusack turned the Bulldogs' ownership over to a friend, Canton automobile dealer Ralph Hay, during the break when he entered the oil business in Oklahoma. The Bulldogs returned with an undefeated 9–0–1 championship run in 1919, with Thorpe still at the helm.

At this point in pro football's developing business model, it became clear to team owners that a few problems needed to be addressed for the teams' viability: rising salaries, players freely jumping teams, and the employment of current college players. Thus, on August 20, 1920, the owners of the Canton Bulldogs, Akron Pros, Cleveland Tigers, and Dayton Triangles met in Ralph Hay's Jordan Hupmobile auto showroom in Canton to form the American Professional Football Conference. It was the first step to create the structure for a professional league to standardize teams' business practices.

A few weeks later, on September 17, representatives from 11 teams met at Hay's dealership and changed the league's name to the American Professional Football Association (APFA), with Thorpe as its first president while he was still a player-coach for the Bulldogs. The original 14 teams were the Akron Pros, Buffalo All-Americans, Canton Bulldogs, Chicago Cardinals, Chicago Tigers, Cleveland Tigers, Columbus Panhandles, Dayton Triangles, Decatur Staleys, Detroit Heralds, Hammond Pros, Muncie Flyers, Rochester Jeffersons, and Rock Island Independents.

Many team owners were interested in having a Massillon Tigers team as part of the new APFA since the team's name provided an excellent draw on their home fields. Hay and Jim Thorpe tried to find backers for the team to no avail. Vernon Maginnis, manager of the unsuccessful 1919 Akron Indians, proposed a traveling squad called the Massillon Tigers, but Hay blocked this effort out of respect for the Tigers' tradition. Instead, for the 1920 APFA meeting's official purposes, Hay installed himself as the Tigers' team spokesman and announced that Massillon would not participate in the league.

Thorpe's presidency was essentially a public relations gesture for 1920 and lasted only one year. He went on to play for eight different teams over the next eight years. The league, its teams, and its rules would continue to evolve, but pro football's roots had finally taken hold. In 1922, the league changed its name to the National Football League.

Team owners gathered at Ralph Hay's Hupmobile dealership in Canton on September 17, 1920, to form the American Professional Football Association that became the National Football League in 1922.

DIRK ROZICH

⇌ The Pro Football Hall of Fame ⇋

For many, Latrobe was still considered pro football's birthplace due to the ongoing belief that its team's John Brallier had been the first to play professionally. Thus, the town had the opportunity to land the Pro Football Hall of Fame when organizers discussed plans for its location before its 1963 opening. However, the small Western Pennsylvania town could not raise public support or financing in its community to accomplish the project. The location for the Hall was then proposed to Canton, not as pro football's birthplace, but as the birthplace of the first professional league, the APFA, which became the NFL. Not long after the opening ceremony, the Hall's discovery of the 1892 Allegheny Athletic Association accounting ledger that documented payment to Pudge Heffelfinger proved that Brallier had not been the first to play pro ball and that Latrobe had not been "pro football's birthplace" after all. Ultimately, the choice of Canton turned out to be for the best.

⇌ The Human Condition ⇋

Imperfectly and awkwardly, in fits and starts, as is human nature, American football's pioneers persevered and moved the game forward. There were brief moments of creation and extended periods of evolution. As with the human

journey, there were also eras, starting with the initial formation of collegiate football, amateurism, the first professional era in Pittsburgh, the lofty heights and crash of the Ohio pro era, and ultimately the formation of the NFL.

Professional football hit a near-extinction event in 1906. Or, perhaps its story is more like Jesus's in the Bible, in which there was a birth, death, and resurrection. It was born in Pittsburgh when Pudge Heffelfinger was first paid in 1892, experienced adolescence there, transitioned to adulthood in Ohio, suffered from its sins, and died. After a period, it was resurrected and transformed into glory in the form of a new league destined for greatness. Like Christ, its savior was not what some people may have expected: a humble Native American. He performed incredible feats unlike anyone else, but he was still persecuted and stripped of his glory for his perceived transgressions.

On the journey of pro football to the NFL, there were numerous heroes who felt visceral passion for the sport, intuitively felt its potential, took chances, innovated, and refined its methods of play so that generations to come could enjoy the essence and experience of this uniquely American sport. There were peaks, valleys, and obstacles on the road. Mistakes were made, and there was scandal. It was a glimpse of the future, as only the names and circumstances have changed in many of the issues associated with the game's current form. It is not perfect, but it is beautiful.

In tribute, given the prominence of the few outstanding first professional teams in the pre-NFL era and a group of its most significant players, it would be reasonable to hope that the Pro Football Hall of Fame may find a better way to recognize these pioneers or even officially include them in the ranks of its inductees. It was intentionally not named the NFL Hall of Fame, which suggests the possibility of their future consideration. As of this writing, the HOF does not include anyone who played only before the founding of the NFL.

In a conversation with the author at the Hall's induction ceremony in 2015, one of its voting board members said this is because "it was a different game then." This comment cannot refer only to the era before the forward pass since 13 years of football had been played between the pass's legalization and the APFA's founding. The style of play in the pro game did not change when the league was formed. Thus, it is not reasonable to claim that the players who played in the pre-NFL era were not worthy. Regardless, as an analogy, should the Wright brothers and their peers not be included in the National Air and Space Museum because their concepts were still rudimentary before others built and flew more advanced aircraft? Hopefully, the HOF will reconsider this policy soon, as it has an excellent opportunity to expand its presentation of the early game and its heroes' journey to the NFL.

The Canton Bulldogs in action, circa 1920

In his presentation at the 2021 Pro Football Researchers Association conference held at the Hall, former HOF executive director Joe Horrigan offered hope on this subject in responding to a question posed by the author:

> The bylaws of the Pro Football Hall of Fame don't preclude pre-NFL players. As long as it was professional, they can be considered for their contributions. I think the challenge has always been apples to apples, oranges to oranges, and who can really tell us who they were and what their contributions were.... It is imperative, imperative that the story of the pioneers of the game be told.... Collectively, there is a way of saying that these are the men who gave their blood, sweat, and tears to the organization of this empire.

Hopefully, by sharing the contributions to pro football history of several worthy men, *Gridiron Legacy* provides support for their future recognition by the Hall.

THE HEROES' JOURNEY

Furthermore, we have not even to risk the adventure alone; for the heroes of all time have gone before us; the labyrinth is thoroughly known; we have only to follow the thread of the hero path.... And where we had thought to be alone, we shall be with all the world.

—Joseph Campbell, *The Hero with a Thousand Faces*, 1949

Winston Churchill is often attributed as having said, "History is written by the victors." If so, then understanding who the first victors were in pro football, in hindsight, would have been the logical place for a researcher to begin this journey of discovery. For me, learning about these early championship teams was part of a legacy left to me from a forefather. An interesting genealogy project in the early 2000s grew, over the course of nearly 15 years, into a calling to enter an unresolved historical drama and forensically search Ohio law firms and courthouses to solve the mystery that had remained for over a century. Similar to the story of Indiana Jones, the adventure led to the discovery of what some have called the Holy Grail of professional football.

My introduction to this story started when I was a young boy in the 1970s, growing up in the Pittsburgh suburb of Churchill, approximately 10 miles east of the city. Churchill was a new, up-and-coming community developed adjacent to older industrial towns in the Monongahela Valley, including Wilmerding and Turtle Creek. My grandparents on both sides of the family lived in "the Valley."

Bob Shiring, 1902 Pittsburg Stars. Sketch by Bob Weaver, Shiring's grandson-in-law.

Former Westinghouse Air Brake Company plant on Airbrake Avenue in Turtle Creek, Pennsylvania

Though it was a 10-minute drive from Churchill to my grandparents' homes, it felt like traveling decades back in time.

On my family's drives to visit my grandparents, we traveled Airbrake Avenue, an old street decimated with potholes and grit, while passing the abandoned Westinghouse Air Brake Company (WABCO) plant and its blown-out windows. The dim structure seemed haunted by the ghosts of a powerful industry and the forgotten workers who once labored there. Most of the homes and businesses in the area were in blatant disrepair, having suffered both the physical and financial elements of the 75 or so years since the town of Wilmerding had been established to accommodate the development of George Westinghouse's commercial enterprise.

The Valley's contrast to Churchill was striking and somewhat frightening. However, the visible progress in suburban development somehow reassured me that the conditions of my life, and life in general, were improving and more comfortable than in days gone by. I had a distinct sense that time was passing Wilmerding by and that my life would be moving forward in a more vibrant and growing city and era in our country.

My mother's parents seemed to have a higher standard of living than the rest of Wilmerding. Their home was more expansive, with a large yard and fine furnishings. Best of all, for me, was its finished basement with a billiard room, where I could play for hours and hide from conversations about business and family drama.

While I was honing my billiard skills in the '70s, it was often with the background sound of Steelers and Pirates games, whether on the radio or television. Both teams were winning: the Pirates for the first time since before I was born and the Steelers for the first time ever. If you lived in Pittsburgh then, the excitement and joy surrounding the city's sports teams were palpable. Their multiple championships provided Pittsburgh's people with a sense of pride that this predominantly blue-collar city was as good as any other.

My earliest memories include images of my great-grandfather Bob Shiring's football teams in old photos on my grandparents' billiard room wall. There were three large sepia-toned photographs that pictured different adult teams on which he played. One was unidentified. The only clue to what team it might have been was a capital H on a few of the players' heavy white turtleneck sweaters. The other two teams were partially identified. "Tigers 1906" was stenciled in white on one image below the players. My great-grandfather was seated in the middle of the front row, holding the ball in his lap, which I assumed was an honor. "Tigers '05" was also stenciled vertically in white on the top right corner of the third photograph. It seemed that this was the same team from the previous year.

My grandmother, Irene Keyser, was the second youngest of Shiring's nine children. She occasionally mentioned that Shiring played professional

The initial on the sweaters worn by Joe Steen and Frank Maxson were the author's clue to identifying the 1901 Homestead Library & Athletic Club team.

Bob Shiring's gaze in the photo labeled "Tigers 1906" in the author's grandmother's home created a connection that inspired *Gridiron Legacy*.

football for the Massillon Tigers in Ohio. She spun a few related tales, but she never had a cohesive narrative to share. One story was about a game in which Shiring was lauded in the papers for playing the wind when he kicked a game-winning field goal, but only he knew this "strategy" was purely accidental. Another was that baseball Hall of Fame pitcher Christy Mathewson said he agreed to play pro football only if Shiring was on the team to block for him, so that he would preserve his baseball career. Equally as impressive was her statement that legendary sportswriter Grantland Rice named Shiring to his All-Pro team for the first quarter of the twentieth century.

My grandmother's most poignant story was an account of her father's strong character during a scandalous episode in which he would not accept a bribe to fix a championship. These photographs and stories stuck with me forever. Unfortunately, but not surprisingly, she had no documentation of any of these stories. They were family lore. But those three images on the billiard room wall were burned into my mind, including Shiring's imposing glare on that 1906 team picture. I wanted to know more. The digging would come later when I could think more critically and appreciate history more deeply.

"Gram" passed away at the age of 94 in 2007. She was a woman ahead of her time, having served as an elected tax collector for Wilmerding for 40 years. She also simultaneously ran the family insurance and real estate business, the Shiring Agency, which Shiring established in 1927 after both his football playing days and his many years working at Westinghouse. George Westinghouse himself asked Shiring to move his family from Pittsburgh's North Side to Wilmerding to work at WABCO. Shiring had become well known in the town for his character amid his football exploits. He then parlayed his reputation into a second career as the de facto provider of financial services in his community, as well as justice of the peace, from which he garnered the nickname "the Squire."

Shortly after Gram passed away, I discovered a box of original vintage photographs in her basement under the billiard table while cleaning out her house. I was not sure how they ended up there, certain I had never seen them before. After over one hundred years in hiding, they had suddenly appeared, with nobody else living with her in the house for many years after my grandfather passed.

Most of the images were matted on thick cardboard and included individual and small groups of football players in vintage uniforms. They were apparently from the same era as the three pictures on the room's wall. Some were unidentified, but others were identifiable by signatures on the back that looked original.

The most interesting piece in the box was a small personal photo album bound in dark brown canvas. It held 18 three-by-five-inch black-

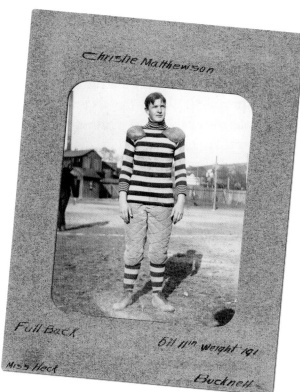

Bob Shiring's 1902 Pittsburg team photo album, including Christy Mathewson, was a highlight in Shiring's collection discovered by the author in his grandmother's home.

(Shiring collection)

and-white photographs of individual early-era football players in uniform, an informal team picture, and an action shot of the team practicing in an open rural field. Each image was inserted into a charcoal-gray paper mat with information about the players written in black ink. The descriptions included each player's name, height, weight, position, college, and nickname. Other than Shiring's, only one name was familiar and not in the context of football: "Christie Matthewson" [*sic*], one of the greatest baseball pitchers of all time. Written on the first page of the album was "Pittsburg Proffessionals [*sic*], David J Berry, Mngr, 1902."

Given the basic but limited knowledge I had of Shiring's pro football background, I started to sense his career had been more significant than I initially understood. This collection was likely historically significant. I recall going through the photographs with a sense of awe and saying to my mother, "I am going to do something with these one day." It was a momentary statement of a dream with no clear sense of purpose. I knew right then, though, that I had discovered something special and felt that those photos were meant for me to find.

⇋ Answering the Call to Adventure ⇌

In the early Internet age, I became inspired to research the background of Shiring's professional football career online, which logically included trying to identify the teams for which he played and his teammates. Soon, I found the Professional Football Researchers Association website and reached out by email to the organization's head, Bob Carroll, to ask for assistance.

Carroll was one of very few historians who focused on documenting the story of the pre-NFL professional era. A native of Wheeling, West Virginia, Carroll was the executive director of the PFRA, which he founded in 1979, and he served in this role until he died in 2009. As an author of many books on various aspects of football history, Carroll became known as one of the subject's leading historians. His collaboration with Joe Horrigan of the Pro Football Hall of Fame in the PFRA's early days led to their authoring some of the most comprehensive content available on the subject.

Despite his advanced age and declining health, my story and the opportunity to view Shiring's photo collection resonated with Carroll, given his previous work and the proximity of Wilmerding to his home in North Huntingdon, Pennsylvania. He was eager to see the images and assist in my research.

What initially seemed like an impossible task—to identify obscure football players associated with my great-grandfather from over a century before—now seemed possible with Carroll's help as my mentor. The connection to such an expert was exciting. I mailed him photocopies of the images and followed up with an email describing what little I knew about each. He responded, identifying nearly every person in the pictures and providing background on many.

In our first phone conversation shortly afterward, Carroll explained that the mounted photos were called cabinet cards, commonly produced in the late 1800s and early 1900s. The initial step in the identification process was easy for Carroll, as some of the photos included original signatures on the reverse sides. He recognized the names and indicated that these men were some of the greatest players from the best pro teams of that era, from Pittsburgh and Eastern Ohio. I was unfamiliar with their names, such as stars George "Peggy" Parratt and Robert "Tiny" Maxwell. Their prominence in the game's history was startling.

Carroll explained that Parratt was Massillon's quarterback, whom historians believed had thrown the first forward pass in a professional football game. This milestone took place in 1906, the first season after revolutionary rule changes initiated by President Teddy Roosevelt. Thus, as the team's center, Shiring had snapped the same ball for the first pro forward pass, which is a fun historical footnote.

Maxwell and Shiring were pictured together on one cabinet card as teammates on the 1906 Massillon Tigers. Their signatures appeared on the reverse side. This was the only photo in the group that included two people, so I assumed that Shiring must have had a closer relationship with Maxwell than with many of his teammates. Their connection became apparent when

Bob Carroll sketched all of the art for the PFRA's *Coffin Corner* newsletter. He drew this piece of Bob Shiring as a gift to the author.

I learned from Carroll's article on the PFRA website that, as the team's leaders, they were approached by teammate Walter East to fix the Tigers' championship games with Canton.

The scheme sounded like something out of a more recent era of professional boxing, in which one contestant would agree to win the first fight, with the other winning the second. Gambling profits could then be made on both with a massive payday from the turnout at the ultimate third bout, which would be contested fairly.

However, Shiring and Maxwell reported the attempted bribe to their coach, Sherburn Wightman, ultimately spoiling the scheme. They turned out to be the "good guys" in the story, which was excellent news for my family's legacy. Yet, subsequent events and a lack of closure still soured fans on professional football's development for nearly a decade.

Some of the unidentified pictures included small groups of players, "buddy pictures," if you will. Others appeared to be of teams, but the hodge-podge of jerseys made them appear to be loosely assembled teams at best. Given Massillon's rivalry with Canton, it was interesting that Carroll identified the lone photo in the collection of a team without Shiring as the 1905 Canton Bulldogs.

Another image portrayed an African-American man dressed nicely in solid black street clothes and a Kangol cap, which seemed out of place among the football photos. Carroll told me that this man was Charles Follis (aka "the Black Cyclone"), the first professional African-American football player—the Jackie Robinson of a different sport in an earlier era. I later learned that Follis played against Shiring's Massillon Tigers for the Shelby

The names of baseball's 1909 world champion Pittsburg Pirates on the rear ends of this group (likely from Bob Shiring's Pittsburg Lyceum) suggest name-calling amid a friendly rivalry between the top local football and baseball teams.

Blues in 1904. Follis and Shiring likely also played together at some point, given that Shiring occasionally played for Shelby when Massillon did not have a game. I could only guess that Shiring came to know Follis and his life story well enough to understand the significance of his achievement and had asked him for his photograph as a souvenir and sign of their friendship.

Other photos included the original local Massillon Tigers with whom Shiring started playing when he joined the team in 1903. One was Julius "Baldy" Wittman, a Massillon native who was the team's captain in 1905, after nationally known players had replaced many of the originals. Baldy was aptly nicknamed because of his hairless head, which he covered with a hat in nearly every photograph. Others were Frank Botoner, a full-time Massillon policeman, as well as Bob Featheringham and Herman Vogt, whose family names are still well known in Massillon.

My grandmother also told me that Shiring was offered a job in Massillon after his playing career to continue living in the community where he was much admired. So, it is no surprise that he saved photos of his first friends and teammates.

The most mysterious photo, which Carroll could not identify, was of a team before the Massillon era. For years, my mother had an oversized black-and-white photograph in her office, a team picture in which a player held a ball on which "Champions 99" was printed. The players all wore white and dark striped sweaters. The man in the center of the middle row sported a bushy mustache common in that era, a blazer, and a white sweater with some combination of the letters A, C, and L overlaid in no apparent order.

Fortuitously, in 2012, my research led me to the University of Pittsburgh's Hillman Library, where I found a Pittsburgh Athletic Club team picture in bound editions of the 1894 *Pittsburgh Commercial Gazette*. The image's caption identified the player with the same mustache as James Lalus.

By the mid-1890s, the contingent of Pittsburgh's professional teams consisted of the Pittsburgh Athletic Club (PAC), Allegheny Athletic Association (AAA), Duquesne Country & Athletic Club (DC&AC), Latrobe Athletic Association, and Greensburg Athletic Club. Lalus, a full-time local policeman, was a former PAC player who played in the now-famous game against the AAA in which Pudge Heffelfinger was the first to be paid to play. In 1895, Lalus started his own athletic club with a football team, located in Allegheny City, now Pittsburgh's North Side. With the pro teams still needing to round out their schedules with local club and college teams, the Lalus Athletic Club (LAC) became the training ground for several professional players of the next era, including Shiring.

After observing this photo over many years, identifying Lalus in the library's photo triggered my connection between Shiring and the LAC team. The manager and coach of the team wearing the sweater was clearly James

Identifying James Lalus and the 1899 Lalus Athletic Club team added key pieces to the author's historical puzzle.

Lalus. Shiring was in the center of the third row, directly behind Lalus, and looked every bit the fresh-faced amateur in this image compared with the hardened veteran in the Massillon images from six and seven years later. Interestingly, through Lalus, there was only one degree of separation between Heffelfinger and Shiring.

A few collectors of historic football images also helped on my journey. I met them initially through reaching out to auction houses specializing in vintage sports memorabilia. After initial reservations, I decided to reveal my relationship to Shiring to deepen our conversations. One mentioned that he owned a team photograph on which "P.J. Lawless 1900" was written. Lawless sounded like Lalus to me, but the "P.J." did not make sense in connection to the name James F. Lalus. However, I had seen an image of P.J. Lawlor in Shiring's 1902 album. The collector sent me an image scan. Shiring, Lalus, and Lawlor were identifiable, as were the uniforms matching those in the 1899 Lalus team image. As I had guessed, an earlier photograph owner had confused the players' names when writing the team's name on the image.

Acquiring photographs and memorabilia from passionate collectors is never easy. I had to make a deal for the 1900 Lalus team photograph. However, I realized that the owner would drive a tough bargain now that he knew my relationship to Shiring. Sure enough, a lengthy negotiation resulted: a three-way trade with another collector from Dallas, which included copies of some of my images and cash. Nonetheless, I was excited to have completed the timeline of Shiring's career with a rare, perhaps unique, photograph from the last missing year between 1899 and 1906.

From time to time, I also searched eBay for anything to do with the Massillon Tigers of that era. I found a few books and articles about the pro Tigers' legacy that the team had left for Massillon's Washington High School, which continues to carry the Tigers nickname. Massillon Washington is one of the most storied high school programs in the country, winning the Ohio Associated Press state championship 24 times and producing players such as Chris Spielman of Ohio State and Detroit Lions fame, as well as coaches Paul Brown and Earle Bruce. Vintage postcards of the 1905 and 1906 pro teams, which I could acquire for a reasonable amount, also surfaced occasionally. Some even had the same images on my grandmother's billiard room wall.

Massillon's Chris Spielman is the only high school football player to appear on a Wheaties box.

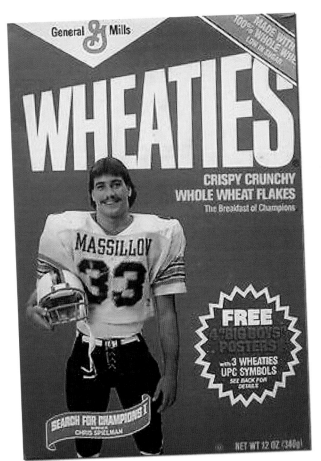

Eventually, I decided to have copies made of the 1906 Massillon team postcard on high-quality photographic paper and listed them for sale on eBay. My plan was not to profit, as the item header listed that they were copies. The opening bid was $0.99, and the item description indicated my intention to connect with anyone who had interest or knowledge about the team or its players.

Within a day, I received an email from a great-granddaughter of Baldy Wittman. She had started doing some genealogical research and had little information to share other than knowing that "Baldy" had also been a Massillon policeman. It was still an exciting connection, suggesting greater possibilities. Over time, connecting and building relationships with descendants of Shiring's teammates and rivals (Perry Hale, Herman Vogt, Herman Kerkhoff, and Blondy Wallace) led me to invite them to contribute their thoughts on the legacies of their families' football heroes to this book.

In 2011, a rare program from Game 1 of the 1906 Canton-Massillon championship series surfaced on eBay. It had a spectacular artistic cover larger than the narrow 1905 Canton-Massillon program I had acquired from a Massillon resident the previous year. I could not believe it existed. Only one other person placed a bid on it, a hefty one at the last second, but I won it. While the Hall of Fame and the Massillon Museum have copies of the 1905 program, I knew neither owned this one. With this piece in place, I had assembled a collection of images and memorabilia to accompany a narrative worthy of creating an interesting memoir for my family.

⇶ Crossing the Threshold ⇶

Pro football's missing origin story then found a spark to bring it to life. In November 2010, I received a call from veteran *Sports Illustrated* writer Richard Hoffer, who said he was working on a story for the magazine on the 1906 Canton-Massillon championship and the controversial events that surrounded it. The article would be titled "The First Super Bowl." He had received my contact information from the Pro Football Hall of Fame's vice president of museum and exhibit services, Saleem Choudhry. I had the foresight to suggest to Choudhry after our first conversation in 2007 that anyone interested in researching the subject could call me. Hearing from a *Sports Illustrated* writer for a feature story was beyond my imagination.

Hoffer already understood how little information was available on the subject, and I was thrilled to contribute to his effort. I first offered the list of books I had identified that included limited accounts of the rivalry and the scandal's consequences. Then I realized he might want to include some of my photographs.

THE FIRST SUPER BOWL

A century ago two Ohio powers, Canton and Massillon, battled for supremacy of professional football. Back then the game was a cross between a three-ring circus and trench warfare, and the players were team-switching mercenaries. The championship series might even have been fixed

BY RICHARD HOFFER

On Thursday, Nov. 15, 1906, operatives of the Central Union Telephone Company began stringing wire around Mahaffey Park in Canton, Ohio, preparing a little trial in turn-of-the-century technology. The idea was, a Central Union agent would stride up and down the stadium's sideline the next day, telegraphing accounts of the action between the Canton Bulldogs and the Massillon Tigers to newspaper offices throughout the country. This experiment took into account two national preoccupations: the fascination with anything modern—especially electrical—and professional football.

This would be the first of two games (with a third if required) to decide the championship of the world. Pro football had been slow to gain favor, being alternately deadly and dull, but by 1906 it had grown into a fairly important pastime, especially in the hinterlands of Ohio and Pennsylvania. The bigger cities, with grander ideas of themselves, clung to the more refined entertainments, such as opera and baseball, leaving football to the blue-collar towns, where few felt the need to apologize for their tastes in recreation.

Still, even city sophisticates were beginning to take notice of this new phenomenon. Grantland Rice, sporting editor of the *Cleveland News*, had been obliged to divert his attention from second baseman Nap Lajoie's comparatively balletic Cleveland Naps to account for the popularity of football skirmishes, a kind of choreographed mayhem. Rice was particularly attuned to the heated rivalry to the south, in Stark County, where football had been fully professionalized and was being played with eye-opening zeal.

Had Rice understood that the 1906 championship series had been developed as a civic centerpiece, a way to indulge a municipal grudge, he might have been more careful with his mythologizing. For that matter, he might have guessed how this would

"You have photographs of this stuff?" he said. "*Nobody* has photographs of this stuff!" I confirmed that, indeed, I did. He then referred me to *SI*'s photo department, and we coordinated their ability to use some of the images.

The article was initially supposed to run on Super Bowl week of 2011, which would have been especially nice from my perspective, as the game turned out to include my hometown Steelers against the Packers. However, when the issue hit the newsstands, the article was not included. Hoffer said it had been left, figuratively speaking, on the editing room floor, bumped by some other current stories that had come up that week, but that it could run the following year since it was an "evergreen" piece that would not become out of date. It seemed unlikely to me that the story would ever run, but Hoffer was right. The story did run in the February 5, 2012, issue, *SI*'s preview of Super Bowl XLVI.

"The First Super Bowl" article was compelling for readers in 2012 for the same reasons as this project is now. It was an "Aha!" moment for sports fans to learn pro football's interesting backstory, predating the NFL era and deemed worthy of a major national publication. The eight-page feature was more substantial than most by *SI* standards, both entertaining and well researched. It also included a photo of my original postcard of the 1906 Canton Bulldogs, for which I received a photo credit.

Hoffer had only limited time to research and limited space in the magazine to present his version of the narrative. However, he rightly concluded the piece by stating that there were still unanswered questions about the scandal's details. Ultimately, *SI* laid the perfect foundation for this project, as it opened the door for the story to be developed on a larger scale, as it so rightly deserved. My research had largely been done. All that remained was the execution. For the sole proprietor of a company, with a working wife and two active children, this was much easier said than done. I would need help, guidance, and catalysts.

⤛ Approaching the Throne ⤜

Inspired by *Sports Illustrated*'s article, I arranged a meeting with executives at the Pro Football Hall of Fame in April 2012 to share my findings. It initially seemed to me as though it might be the logical end of my journey. My mother joined me in Atlanta, and we drove to Canton together, the car loaded with framed and boxed photographs. I had no expectation of how the Hall's group would react. Perhaps my hope, deep down, was that my great-grandfather Bob Shiring would be considered for induction as a senior nominee one day.

Saleem Choudhry, the HOF research expert who gave *SI* my name as a contact, met us in the parking lot with a cart so that we could push the collection to the conference room in the Hall's archives. After I finished organizing a presentation on the conference table, now-retired executive director Joe Horrigan and chief of staff and vice president of communications Pete Fierle joined us. They enjoyed the display and asked many questions to ascertain the extent of my knowledge of everything they were viewing.

When they realized that I was closer to an expert than an apprentice, Horrigan said, "Okay, we've got to put our cards on the table. We don't have any of these things. To us, this is like finding an original Constitution. We've got a $25 million renovation going on around us, part of which is to better tell the story of the pre-NFL era, and we'd like to display some of these."

I was ecstatic but concerned that I would have to decide whether to part with some of the photos for the greater good, something I had not considered. Probably reading my expression, Horrigan then said, "The good news for you is that we don't want to keep the originals. We'd just like you to leave them with us to scan and resize them for exhibit."

I was relieved, then more than surprised when he followed that up with, "What do you want?" I had no idea how to answer because I did not want anything in return. I responded, "I don't want anything. I just came here to share the photos with you all to see what you thought of them and what you might want to do with them to share them with the public." Then it was Horrigan's turn to be relieved.

"I do have two simple requests, though," I said, thinking on my feet. "First, that the Hall doesn't use them in a book because I plan on doing one.

I'd also like to go through the archive here to request digital copies of any photos that include Shiring that I don't have."

Horrigan agreed. Done deal.

Everything was coming up roses, so the time was right to ask the big question.

"Joe, since you've acknowledged that Shiring was the greatest center of his era, is it possible that he could be inducted into the Hall one day?"

The answer was not what I had hoped. Horrigan explained that the Hall's policy was not to induct players from the pre-NFL era because there was not enough information available by which to make such decisions. Also, since as many as 20 players from that period could be considered worthy of the honor, it would be impossible to induct them all.

It was an anticlimactic moment. I sensed that perhaps the ultimate purpose of my undertaking was to facilitate Shiring's induction into the Hall of Fame, along with some of his peers. But it was made unambiguously clear this was not in the cards, at least given the philosophy of the Hall's selection committee in 2012.

Nonetheless, it was fulfilling and joyful on several levels for both my mother and me to visit the Hall of Fame together, meet the executive team, and receive a personalized, private tour of its archive, including many pieces not on public display. Primarily, the place of Bob Shiring (her grandfather and my great-grandfather) in the game's history was confirmed, and so was the uniqueness of his photo collection.

Pro Football Hall of Fame executive Joe Horrigan provided ongoing insight and encouragement for *Gridiron Legacy*.

⇋ The Holy Grail of Pro Football ⇌

I am not sure exactly when, but I had a dream sometime in the late '90s that I was visiting some sort of sports museum in Pittsburgh. It was futuristic, with holograms of famous Pittsburgh sports stars like Franco Harris and Mario Lemieux in action, moving through the air. The only other thing I remember from the dream was looking down a hallway at myself meeting a staff person and giving him something. Pittsburgh had museums in the '90s, of course, but not a sports museum. Then, the Senator John Heinz History Center's Western Pennsylvania Sports Museum opened in November 2004.

In January 2000, a few years before the sports museum's opening, our family's first child was born on the day after the Super Bowl. The excitement of Super Bowl XXXIV between the Rams and Titans during a massive ice storm in our home city of Atlanta must have been too much for my wife and our unborn child to take. It became clear at halftime that we needed to rush to the hospital to start the delivery. As a new parent, and with our second child born in 2002, I did not learn about Pittsburgh's sports museum for several years.

When I finally made my first visit to the museum in 2010, I brought an 8-by-10 photograph of Shiring's Homestead team, hoping to meet a staff member who knew something about the group. I set the photo down on a bench to explore the recently installed "Immaculate Reception" exhibit, which included the turf from the spot in Three Rivers Stadium where Franco Harris caught Terry Bradshaw's deflected pass and ran for the winning touchdown with seconds left to defeat the Oakland Raiders in the 1972 playoffs. When I came back to retrieve the photo, it was gone. I searched in a panic and found who I thought was a security guard holding the picture. "Is this yours?" he asked. When I said yes, he added, "Why did you bring this here?" I explained my intentions, and he introduced himself as a museum associate. Then he said, "Come with me." I was not sure of *his* intentions.

The staff member took me up an elevator to another floor, where he showed me large images of both my great-grandfather's 1901 Homestead team and 1902 Pittsburgh Professionals, displayed in an exhibit on professional football's birth in Pittsburgh. We had a lot to talk about, and our connection led me to join him to work on several of the museum's projects.

My favorite of these projects is what I like to call "the Great Wall of Pittsburgh." Its goal was to display all of the Pirates and Steelers trading cards from the beginning of their production in the 1880s and 1930s, respectively. It became my passion project to add as many missing cards as possible, most of which were pre–World War II. Fast-forward a few years, and we had filled the beginning section with a variety of sepia-toned tobacco cards from the late 1800s and colorful ones from the early 1900s. The exhibit even included all but the famous Honus Wagner card that recently

Art Rooney Jr. was moved by seeing familiar faces in Bob Shiring's 1902 Pittsburg team photo album.

sold for $6.6 million from the popular 1909 T-206 set. The museum's visitors were enthralled by the spectacular colorful presentation.

While visiting Pittsburgh in December 2011, I stopped at the museum to donate a few more cards. At the same time, its annual book fair happened to be taking place. Art Rooney Jr. was in attendance, sitting at a table selling his book *Ruanaidh: The Story of Art Rooney and His Clan*. It was another happy coincidence that I happened to bring Shiring's 1902 Pittsburgh Professionals photo album with me that day. I was going to show it to the sports museum's director, and now I could also share it with Mr. Rooney. Surprisingly, Mr. Rooney said he had heard about the team. As he leafed through the delicate pages, he said, "I knew some of these guys."

Mr. Rooney was the first person I had ever met who had a personal connection to any of my great-grandfather's teammates, and it gave me chills. I told him that I had heard through my father that his father, Steelers founder Art Rooney Sr. (aka "the Chief"), knew Shiring from when they spent time at the horse racing tracks near Pittsburgh. There was deep reflection and emotion in Mr. Rooney's Irish eyes. I stepped away from our encounter feeling that the story was alive and real. He looks so much like his father that it almost felt like I was talking with the Chief himself.

As Mr. Rooney and I parted, the director stopped me on my way out and asked if I would speak with her. She said I had become the museum's top donor through my contributions to their collections. My initial thought was that this did not say much for the other donors since I did not feel like I had given much relative to its extensive displays. Nonetheless, she asked if I would consider participating on the museum's Champions Committee, which essentially serves as an advisory board, chaired by Franco Harris. It took less time than a goal-line plunge for me to gratefully agree.

At my first committee meeting in June 2012, all attendees were asked to introduce themselves at the conference table. It felt odd introducing myself among many luminaries of Pittsburgh sports, and I mentioned my connection to Bob Shiring and his Homestead team as part of my connection to the museum.

I sat next to Harris, who was at the head of the table, while we watched a draft of the museum's new video on the greatest plays in Pittsburgh sports history. When the Immaculate Reception was shown, I turned to him, then back to the images on the screen of the fans pouring onto the field. It was a surreal moment.

After the meeting, a man at the other end of the table introduced himself and asked if I had ever been to Homestead to see the club out of which Shiring's team played. He was from Homestead and well known there as an educator, sportswriter, and past chairman of the Pennsylvania Sports Hall of Fame, to which both Shiring and my father had been inducted. Astounded, I said, "What club?!" He explained to me that the facility formerly called the Homestead Library & Athletic Club in 1901 was still operating as the Carnegie Library of Homestead. He said he would be glad to introduce me to a former board member who would give me a tour at my convenience.

I wasted no time arranging the meeting and returned to Pittsburgh for the tour a few months later. I did not expect the building to be huge, maybe a typical small local public library. Much to my surprise, it was a glorious relic of the Industrial Age. Completed in 1898, it was the sixth library commissioned by Andrew Carnegie of nearly 1,700 Carnegie libraries in the United States and more than 2,500 worldwide.

This Carnegie library is a diamond in the rough in the otherwise struggling hometown of the former Homestead Steel Works. Its interior reminded me of the Biltmore House in Asheville, North Carolina, with a vintage swimming pool in its basement and duckpin bowling alleys that had been replaced by batting cages for current members to train in a more modern sport. There is also a vintage elevated running track suspended by

The Homestead Library & Athletic Club later became known as the Carnegie Library of Homestead.

wires on the walls overlooking a basketball court with century-old hardwoods on which league play still takes place.

An operating community library with an ornately crafted reading room inhabits the center third of the structure as one enters the building. The left third of the building houses a concert hall refurbished to maintain its original appearance. Familiar performers from decades ago still entertain over 1,000 people per event.

My guide met me at the library's entrance, where I showed him the picture of the 1901 Homestead team while describing the nature of my interest in touring the facility. He had not heard about the team.

I pointed out that the building's cornerstone next to us showed 1898 as its year of construction, then explained that the club started an amateur football team the following year before hosting the best professional team in the country the next two years. We entered the building, and my guide asked a few other staff members, but none knew about the team. He was intrigued, though, and offered to help me look through the library's archive.

The archive was small but included a few hundred unorganized photos from the early 1900s, loosely stored in classic gray metal filing drawers. A few pertained to basketball and swimming, but not football. It was surprising, and I felt like I had come to a dead end.

We continued the tour and found a shadow box on a wall displaying vintage baseball equipment with references to the club's original teams and another with a heavy wool swimsuit and a 1936 Olympic medal of a swimmer who had trained at the facility. Still, there was nothing about the renowned Homestead football team.

As we returned to the front of the building to conclude our conversation, we passed a final closed door. I asked my guide if there was another room to explore there. He casually replied that it was only a storage closet filled with files ... and "some old trophies." His trophy comment made me raise an eyebrow. I mentioned that I owned a newspaper clipping from 1901 that included a photo of their football team's championship trophy, won that year by beating a team from Philadelphia. I asked him if I could look in the closet, but he said that the door was locked. Ever persistent, I asked if he could get the key. My expression made him realize I would not be deterred, so he agreed.

Behind the tall, heavy wooden door was a large, well-lit room filled with rows of relatively new tall, cream-colored metal shelves filled with nondescript items. In the middle of the room, however, was an old, narrow, and steep set of black iron stairs with handrails on both sides, leading to a balcony encircling the room above.

I bounded eagerly up the stairs and came face to face with a few pieces of frightening taxidermy in the dim space. Above them, on top of the metal filing shelves holding the dead animals, was a row of old silver trophies of various shapes and sizes. One, an oversized bowl that looked like the top of the Stanley Cup, looked familiar.

"That's it! I've seen it before," I said. "The 1901 trophy!"

"Not possible," my guide replied.

"Let me get it down," I persisted, and he brought over a small stepladder.

I climbed the wobbly ladder cautiously in the dark and musty corner, then slid the remarkable piece toward me. It was covered with a century of dust, which I swiped away, revealing a decorative font that required closer examination to read.

I pulled the trophy off the shelf and handed it gently to my helper below. My heart was racing, and I nearly fell as I descended the ladder. We examined the trophy together and read the inscription: "Athletic Club Football Championship 1901."

We looked at each other in disbelief and then exchanged a high five with our free hands. I was holding the trophy my great-grandfather's team had won and that he had probably held.

1901 Homestead Library & Athletic Club world championship trophy

My senses were on high alert, and I continued to scan the row of trophies. On the far end, another one caught my attention.

"That one looks like a football!" I said.

I climbed the ladder again, handed the much smaller trophy down, then wiped away more dust. It was a beautiful loving cup in the shape of a football, with a handle on each side, and covered with a lid inscribed: "1900 Pittsburgh Commercial Gazette Championship Trophy."

This trophy was won by the club's team the previous year, its first as a professional team. Laces were molded on the front of the ball, with scores from the team's games inscribed below them. On the other side of the ball was a detailed football action scene. It occurred to me that these were possibly the first known professional championship football trophies, preceding the NFL by 20 years.

The Pro Football Hall of Fame agreed, and it has hosted them on display ever since. The 1900 trophy tours the nation with the Hall's Gridiron Glory traveling exhibit, and the 1901 trophy sits on permanent display in Canton in the rotunda marking pro football's timeline.

⇋ Redemption and Reward ⇌

To those interested in psychology and mythology, some have described the spiritual aspect of the journey to discover this story and its lost treasure as another unique iteration of scholar Joseph Campbell's fascinating hero's journey monomyth. Campbell's 1949 book, *The Hero with a Thousand Faces,* expanded on Carl Jung's earlier work on archetypes, theorizing that myths from all over the world are built from common elementary stages, or "archaic remnants," in humanity's collective subconscious. The origins of this theory date back to the fourth and fifth centuries B.C. to Plato, who expressed the idea of a circular human soul.

Heroes' journeys appear in many beloved films. Campbell's work served as inspiration for George Lucas in his process of developing the story of Luke Skywalker's magical journey in *Star Wars*, in which Skywalker learned to "use the force" to follow his calling. Similarly, parallels exist to the popular 1989 film *Field of Dreams,* based on the novel *Shoeless Joe* by W.P. Kinsella. As protagonist Ray Kinsella, Kevin Costner follows an inner voice calling him on an adventure, leading to a spiritual connection and reconciliation with his deceased father. In these and other stories, the heroes join allies on their redemptive paths to heal and grow, while encountering villains attempting to thwart their missions.

Beyond the connection with a descendant, there is also the spot-on similarity between *Field of Dreams* and *Gridiron Legacy* in both ancestors' teammates' need for emotional healing. Whether in baseball or football, the

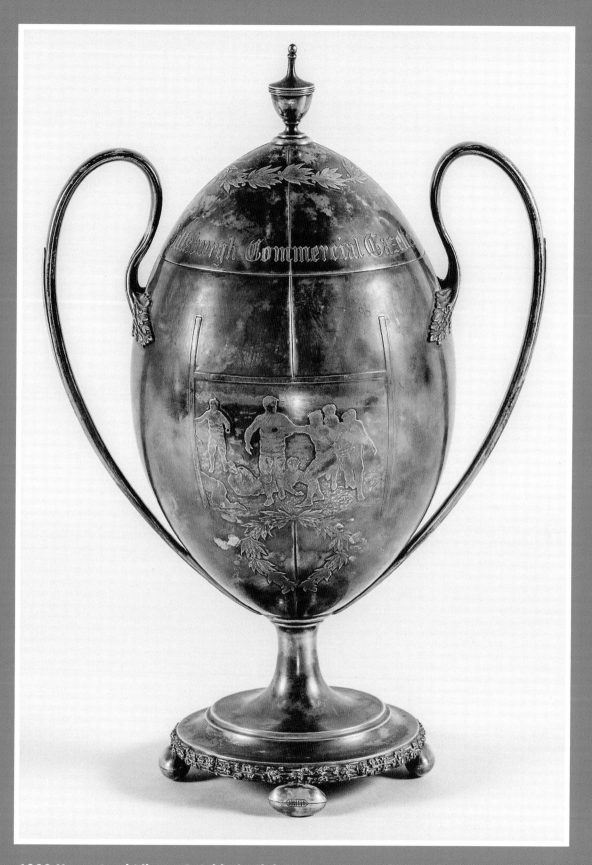

1900 Homestead Library & Athletic Club Western Pennsylvania championship trophy

lives of an infamous group of professional athletes in the early twentieth century were altered forever by a gambling scandal in which they were implicated. Baseball's scandal occurred in the 1919 World Series and, as with Blondy Wallace, the team's leader, "Shoeless" Joe Jackson, claimed to be innocent. Unlike Wallace, though, Jackson and seven other White Sox players had their day in court. A judge declared them innocent despite evidence to the contrary. Nonetheless, the commissioner permanently banned them from playing Major League Baseball, including Jackson, despite his impeccable play in the Series. Ray Kinsella's calling was to "ease his pain," which he first thought referred to Jackson's burden among the team that has since and will forever be known as "the Black Sox."

Wallace also lost a world championship series, was shunned from the sport he loved, lived a hard life thereafter, and died a shamed and broken man. That his ashes were spread over Franklin Field at the University of Pennsylvania seems to reflect his wishes to recapture the innocence of his early playing days and the glory of his team's national championship there.

One can imagine Blondy Wallace echoing the thoughts of Shoeless Joe Jackson, as played by Ray Liotta in *Field of Dreams*:

> Getting thrown out of baseball was like having part of me amputated. I've heard that old men wake up and scratch itchy legs that have been dust for over fifty years. That was me. I'd wake up at night with the smell of the ballpark in my nose, the cool of the grass on my feet … the thrill of the grass.

Imagine Wallace's joy in knowing that the depositions in the case file, discovered in Stark County from a lawsuit that never came to fruition, would exonerate him. Let the permanent record show that he has been redeemed.

Later in *Field of Dreams,* Kinsella's father's appearance from the great beyond revealed to Kinsella that Jackson's pain was not the only wound requiring healing, given their broken father-son relationship. This family connection makes me question how my great-grandfather felt about the scandal that beset the sport in which he invested over a decade of his life. Was it heartbreaking to him despite his efforts to preserve the game's integrity?

Did he wonder whether he or his team's management could have handled the situation differently?

Was I chosen to be the conduit to heal his and Blondy Wallace's pain?

Could my real-life journey be another manifestation of Campbell's hero's journey, varying in detail without losing its basic pattern, as Jung said of archetypes?

The seventh of the 12 stages in Campbell's monomyth is called Reward. After overcoming various challenges and threats in the Ordeal phase to triumph when others may have failed, victory is achieved by realizing one's potential. Often, this phase correlates with the successful completion of the hero's mission. Other scenarios may also involve an outcome or the discovery of something that could not be imagined. Campbell makes the analogy of the Arthurian quest for the Holy Grail, often referred to as the Grail myth.

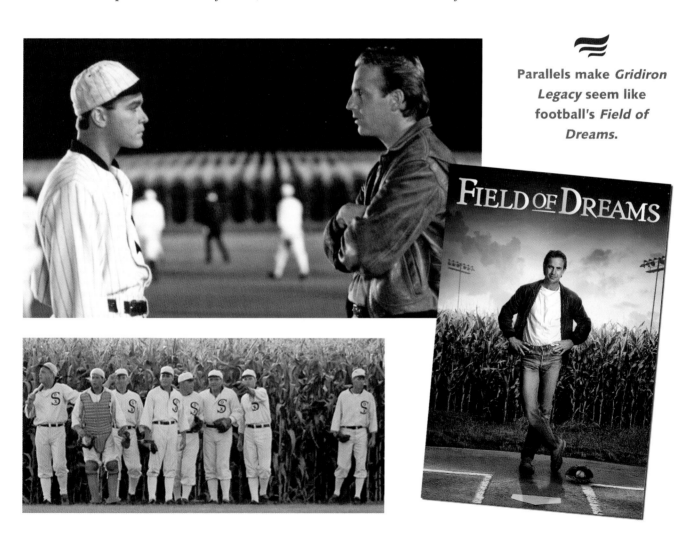

Parallels make *Gridiron Legacy* seem like football's *Field of Dreams.*

The author began sharing the *Gridiron Legacy* story at events at the Pro Football Hall of Fame in Canton and the Massillon Museum in 2021.

The author's quest closely tracked the path of Joseph Campbell's hero's journey.

Finding the Holy Grail would effectively prove that God exists. The Grail is often represented by a chalice or a cup in a tangible form, as in Da Vinci's *The Last Supper* and *Indiana Jones and the Last Crusade*. Along with intangible personal growth, the hero's journey may yield a tangible reward that could take on various forms. In my case, though, the trophies from the Homestead Library & Athletic Club team for which my great-grandfather played are literally cups awarded as prizes. They were prizes to the early pro teams that battled for them on the gridiron, and they were the reward on my journey of discovery. Moreover, in my opinion, they are symbols of glory, not just of historic sporting victory for the public to enjoy at the Pro Football Hall of Fame, but as examples of God's glory in the design in our souls to reveal His plans for us. Thereby, we are fulfilled by discovering Him and realizing that He has always been with us, guiding us throughout the journey.

According to Campbell, when heroes return to the "ordinary world" from the "special world" experience, their responsibility is to share their wisdom with their communities to encourage others to embark on their unique journeys. One version of the cover of Campbell's *The Hero with a Thousand Faces* powerfully depicts a mosaic with hundreds of tiny faces composing one image of the head of a bronze statue, intended to represent an anonymous hero. We are all wired for the journey, but we must answer the call.

As much as has been accomplished through publishing *Gridiron Legacy*, my journey is far from over in some ways. The story seems to be taking on a life of its own, with its original heroes calling for it to be told. There are still hurdles to be crossed to fulfill its potential and complete my journey, some apparent and others yet unknown. One challenge is the development of a related screenplay or miniseries on which I have partnered with sports filmmaker Richard A. Cohen to produce. The script has been written and is ready to be produced by an interested party. Collaborating on the writing process was a terrific experience, yet I had some control. If and when the project lands and what it ultimately becomes is a mystery.

The journey has been long, wonderful, and, at times, very challenging, which is to be expected for anything worthwhile. While many who have learned of the story have expressed that it has the potential to become a film production, realizing this next dream seems even more daunting.

Wherever it leads, bringing *Gridiron Legacy* to publication is a substantial step in the heroes' journey of pro football's pioneers. Hopefully, this project will provide a historically significant contribution to preserve the story and memory of the heroes who blazed the trail for the game of pro football that the world enjoys. It is my great privilege to share it with the world.

That you are here—that life exists and identity,
That the powerful play goes on, and you may contribute a verse.
—Walt Whitman

A CELEBRATION OF MASSILLON TIGERS FOOTBALL TRADITION

In 2016, the author experienced Massillon-Canton rivalry weekend for the first time and became part of the Tigers family.

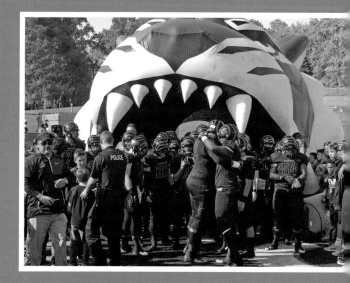

THE START OF A NEW TRADITION

In 2021, the author hosted his cousins, George and Gene Shiring, and their wives to share the family history during Massillon-Canton rivalry weekend. A tour of Massillon included stops at Paul Brown Field at Massillon Washington High School and the newly opened Paul Brown Museum Library in Memory of Bob Shiring at the Massillon Museum.

The Shiring cousins also enjoyed viewing the 1901 Homestead trophy at the Pro Football Hall of Fame in Canton and the Tigers-Bulldogs game, played at Tom Benson Hall of Fame Stadium, which is the Bulldogs' home field. During the trip, the group decided that the annual Shiring family reunion would be revived and held in Massillon during rivalry weekend going forward.

ACKNOWLEDGMENTS

Thank you to the many people who provided invaluable support to this passion project: my wife, Kristy, for her love and encouragement; my mother, Norene Shiring Keyser, for her inspiration; Jim Buckley at Shoreline Publishing; Tom Carling at Carling Design; Edward Starkman at Star Print Brokers; Prof. Eric Koester at Georgetown University; Brian Bies and Sean Doherty at New Degree Press; Joe Horrigan, Saleem Choudhry, Jon Kendle, and Jason Aikens at the Pro Football Hall of Fame; Alexandra Coon, Mandy Stahl, and Bailey Yoder at the Massillon Museum; Massillon historian Margy Vogt; Ron Prunty at the Massillon Booster Club; Bob Carroll (posthumously), Mark Ford, and Ken Crippen at the Pro Football Researchers Association; Craig Britcher and Andrew E. Masich, PhD at the Heinz History Center; Mary Lou Townsend at the Latrobe Area Historical Society; Randal McKenzie at McKenzie Illustrations; Brooke Beach and the Marketwake team; memorabilia dealers Mike McKee and Rod Winzinek; Rhys Yeakley at RMY Auctions; John Adcox at Gramarye Media; Lou Aronica at The Story Plant; editors Laura Street and Michael Bailey; proofreader Patricia MacDonald; Marilyn Hale Brooks, Billy Fusiek, and Bob Ryerson, descendants of Bob Shiring's teammates and rivals; Massillon Tigers head coach Nate Moore; Bob Vogel of the Baltimore Colts; and Franco Harris, Rocky Bleier, John "Frenchy" Fuqua, and Merril Hoge of the Pittsburgh Steelers.

ABOUT THE AUTHOR

Gregg Ficery *is a native of Pittsburgh, Pennsylvania, and lives in Watersound, Florida. He is a graduate of Georgetown University and founder and president of Integgra Valuation & Advisory Services. Due to his love for family, sports, and his hometown, he spent over 10 years researching* Gridiron Legacy. *He is also the executive producer of a related television miniseries in development.*